Roadside History of

WYOMING

Best Wishes,
Candy Moulton

Candy Moulton

Mountain Press Publishing Company
Missoula, Montana
1995

Unless otherwise credited, photos are by the author.

Maps by Jennifer Hamelman.

Library of Congress Cataloging-in-Publication Data

Moulton, Candy Vyvey, 1955-
  Roadside history of Wyoming / Candy Moulton.
    p.   cm.
  Includes bibliographical references (p.   ) and index.
  ISBN 0-87842-315-X (cloth : alk. paper). — ISBN 0-87842-316-8
(paper : alk. paper)
  1. Wyoming—History. 2. Wyoming—Guidebooks. 3. Automobile
travel—Wyoming—Guidebooks. I. Title.
F761.M68   1995   95-22419
978.7—dc20   CIP

PRINTED IN THE U.S.A.

Mountain Press Publishing Company
P.O. Box 2399 • Missoula, MT 59806
(406) 728-1900

For Shawn and Erin Marie

Contents

Acknowledgments

I have spent my entire life gathering information for this book. I started learning Wyoming history on my grandparent's homestead south of Encampment. Before I started school, my dad took me to a place on our land where we stood in the travois tracks on one branch of the Cherokee Trail. A few years later my sister Penny, some neighbor friends, and I found tipi rings close to our home. I spent nearly every Sunday of my childhood listening to my parents and my legion of aunts and uncles tell stories about the "good old days."

I experienced the crowded conditions of a homestead house by standing in the doorway of my grandmother's log cabin. I fell in love with the great wide-open spaces and the beauty of free-ranging wildlife herds on trips to the high country with my family. I learned about coal mining from early-day pioneers like Gertrude Anderson, of Coyote Springs, and from modern-day miners like my brother, Kelly Vyvey.

By far most of my research comes from my more than twenty years as a news reporter for various publications including the *Saratoga Sun*, University of Wyoming *Branding Iron*, Rawlins *Daily Times*, *Wyoming Livestock Roundup*, and most particularly the Casper *Star-Tribune*. That latter publication and its editors—especially Dick High, Anne MacKinnon, Dan Neal, Paul Krza, Angela Pelkey, Debra Thunder, Tom Rea, Wyoma Groenenberg, Dan Whipple, and Emily Quarterman—opened doors that allowed me to experience the front lines of Wyoming's recent history.

For the *Star-Tribune* I have written of water deals, forest management, agricultural upheaval, and politics. I've reported on wind turbines, hostage crises, executions, and court fights. I've traveled by wagon train on both the Bridger and Oregon trails, ridden horseback through the backcountry of Yellowstone, and climbed Elk Mountain to show the importance of access to public lands. I am deeply indebted to my friends and editors at the *Star-Tribune* for giving me those opportunities, and for bearing with me as I prepared this manuscript while writing for them "around the edges," as we say in the newspaper business.

A number of other Wyoming people also lent great support and assistance in the making of this book. I am particularly indebted to Dr. T. A. Larson, of Laramie, Wyoming's premiere historian, and to Rick Ewig, research services manager at the University of Wyoming American Heritage Center, for reading my manuscript. Others who reviewed the manuscript are equally important, including Bud Milliken, Penny Walters, and Rick Young. Any mistakes that remain are mine alone.

For their help and encouragement through the years, I thank Grace Healey, Dick Perue, Gay Alcorn, Franny Fisher, Vera Oldman, Shelly Ritthaler, Mike and Kathy Gear, Fred Heyl, Chuck Coon, Ed Cook, Eric Sorg, Ken Belveal, Bill Romios, Tahna Naylor, Jim Shirran, Elva Evans, Bobbi O'Mara, Bob and Bobbie Herring, Carol Sherrod, Chuck Bowlus, Jim Tiemann, Leon Metz, Dale Walker, Renee Thompson-Heide, Dan Greer, Larry Borowsky, and my parents, Fox and Betty Vyvey.

I am indebted to the Wyoming State Museum's Historical Research Department, particularly Ann Nelson, Jean Brainard, Roger Joyce, Paula West Chavoya, and Lavaughn Breshnahan; to the Wyoming State Historic Preservation Office, specifically Richard Collier, Kathy Martin, and Todd Thibodeau; and to the curators of Wyoming's wonderful collection of big and little museums, state historic sites, and the staffs at Yellowstone National Park, Grand Teton National Park, Fort Laramie National Historic Site, and Devils Tower National Monument. I am especially grateful to my good friend Dan Abernathy for opening his photo files and sending a wonderful collection of Wyoming images to help illustrate this book.

Finally, my biggest thanks and outpouring of love goes to my family—Steve, Shawn and Erin—for putting up with my absences, piles of paper, notes and books, and for joining me in excursions to such places as Burntfork, Medicine Mountain, Spotted Horse, Aladdin, and Sybille. Our roots run deep in Wyoming's arid soil; they go back five generations. We love the endless horizons, the independence of the people, and the freshness of the air. The wind, however, is another matter: We curse it when it blows the snow and makes driving impossible, and we lie awake at night listening to it howl around the logs of our home. But we tolerate the wind because we can't stop it.

My children, Shawn and Erin, learned their fourth-grade Wyoming history lessons as we drove the roads in this state to attend mountain-man rendezvous and Indian powwows, and when we visited forts and forests, museums and mountains. Erin took notes and Shawn took pictures, and their labors are also in the pages of this book. We camped with a moose in our "backyard" in the Big Horns and bounced on the board seat of a wagon on the Bridger Trail.

It's been quite a journey in our native state. We think you'll like the stories we found along the way.

About the Cover Artist

R. M. "Skip" Glomb
18 September 1934—28 May 1988

Skip Glomb was reared in Jackson Hole and took off on his own before the age of sixteen to ride the rodeo circuit from Wyoming to Florida. He topped broncs and painted rodeo scenes on store fronts, but found the rodeo life a tough road to follow. So he returned to Wyoming, where he guided big-game hunters and worked on ranches near Cody. He then headed north to the Yukon as a big-game outfitter before once again settling in Wyoming to work on ranches near Saratoga.

In the 1970s Skip moved to a remote place near Encampment where he painted and sculpted full time. He concentrated on wildlife, cowboys, and historical scenes and often said, "I may not have painted it exactly as it was, but I did paint it exactly as it should have been." Skip eventually settled near Laramie, where he used a horse barn for his studio. He traded artwork for flight time and eventually bought a Beechcraft Staggerwing D17S cabin bi-plane that he loved to fly.

In 1985 Skip marked a milestone in his career when he sculpted a bronze to be given to the All-Around Cowboy at the Las Vegas National Finals Rodeo. He continued painting and sculpting until May 28, 1988, when he and his longtime companion, Ila Whitt, lost their lives in a crash of the yellow airplane he so dearly loved. He is survived by a son, Marty, daughter-in-law, Brenda, and granddaughter, Amanda Jo.

Broken Treaty, on the cover of this book, depicts a meeting of Indian chiefs Gall and Red Cloud with William F. Cody and Col. Fred Steele near the North Platte River and Fort Fred Steele as the Union Pacific Railroad started its run across southern Wyoming Territory in 1869.

Wyoming Chronology

20 M.Y.B.P. (million years before present)	Much of southern Wyoming is covered by an inland sea
2 M.Y.B.P.–600,000 B.P.	Volcanic upheaval climaxes in Yellowstone
8,300 B.P.	Prehistoric people live and hunt in the Big Horn Basin
2,500 B.P.	Ancient hunters and gatherers build pit houses in the region north of Rawlins and in the Hanna Basin
1500s	Modern Indian tribes (Shoshone, Arapaho, Sioux, Crow, Gros Ventre, Bannock, Ute, Comanche, and Cheyenne) live in and roam the Rocky Mountain country that is now Wyoming
1670	Hudson's Bay Company receives its charter from the British government
1743	January—Francois and Louis-Joseph Verendrye reach the Big Horn Mountains near Sheridan, making them the first white people to visit Wyoming
1762	November 3—France cedes all of Louisiana west of the Mississippi River to Spain in the Treaty of Fontainebleau, making Wyoming land a Spanish possession
1783	British North West Company organizes as a competitor to the Hudson's Bay Company
1800	October 1—Spain retrocedes Louisiana to France in the Secret Treaty of San Ildefonso, which is ratified by the Treaty of Madrid on March 21, 1801
1803	April 30—The United States purchases Louisiana under the Treaty of Paris
1804	March 10—Maj. Amos Stoddard takes possession of Upper Louisiana, which includes the land that is Wyoming
	March 26—Congress establishes the District of Louisiana, which includes all of the land east of the Rocky Mountains and therefore most of Wyoming. President Jefferson approves the Act in 1805

1807–8	winter—John Colter visits northwest Wyoming, passing through the areas now known as Cody, Jackson Hole, and Yellowstone
1808	April 6—The American Fur Company is chartered
	August—The Missouri Fur Company organizes at St. Louis to trade with Indians on the Upper Missouri
1811	Wilson Price Hunt's Astorian expedition ascends the Missouri and enters Wyoming, where it meets trappers John Hoback, Edward Robinson, and Jacob Reznor, who act as guides over the Bighorn Mountains, across the Wind River, up the Hoback River, and eventually to the Snake River, which they follow to the Columbia
	September 26—The Astorians camp north of Pinedale
1812	October 22—Robert Stuart and five other Astorians wander through western Wyoming, then cross near South Pass in the Rocky Mountains, the first white men known to cross the continental divide in that area
	November 2—Robert Stuart and his companions build a cabin, the first known to be built by white men in Wyoming, at the mouth of Poison Spider Creek about twelve miles west of Casper
1822	March—Gen. William Ashley and Maj. Andrew Henry organize the Rocky Mountain Fur Company and call for men to trap the western streams
1824	Thomas Fitzpatrick "rediscovers" South Pass
1825–40	Major fur trade era in Wyoming
1825	General Ashley and a few others are the first white men to descend the Green River into Utah
	Jim Bridger discovers the Great Salt Lake Valley
	summer—General Ashley holds the first rendezvous on Henry's Fork of the Green River, at a site near the present town of Burntfork
1829	Jackson Hole gets its name from beaverman David Jackson, a partner in the Rocky Mountain Fur Company
1832	July—Capt. Benjamin L. E. Bonneville takes the first wagons across South Pass and establishes Fort Bonneville, known as Fort Nonsense, just above the confluence of the Green River and Horse Creek near Daniel
1834	Robert Campbell and William Sublette build the trading post Fort William near the confluence of the Laramie and North Platte rivers

1835	Fort William sells to the American Fur Company and is renamed Fort John, for John B. Sarpy, a clerk with the company
	Narcissa Whitman and Eliza Spalding are the first white women to cross the Rocky Mountains, at South Pass
	August 23—The Rev. Samuel Parker delivers the first Protestant service in the Rocky Mountains, at a site north of Pinedale
1840	July 5—Jesuit missionary Pierre De Smet celebrates the first Roman Catholic mass in Wyoming at the traders' rendezvous on the Green River near Horse Creek and the present town of Daniel
1841	Fort Platte is built in the vicinity of Fort John on the North Platte River
1842	John C. Frémont explores and maps the West, with assistance from the mountain men and local Indians
	Mountain man Jim Bridger and partner Louis Vasquez open the trading post Fort Bridger "in the path of the emigrants" on the Black's Fork of the Green River
1843	The "Great Migration" on the Oregon Trail begins two years after the first wagon trains travel the route
1846	Mormons begin emigrating westward
	May 19—President James Polk approves an act of Congress to provide military posts along the Oregon Trail
	June 15—Great Britain relinquishes its claim to Oregon Country, placing all of Wyoming except a small tract in the southwestern corner (claimed by Mexico) in possession of the United States
1847	Mormons establish the first ferry across the North Platte River near the present town of Casper
	June 28—Mormon leader Brigham Young and mountain man Jim Bridger meet near the Little Sandy Crossing, west of Farson, but they have a disagreement and Bridger directs the western-bound Mormons to the Great Salt Lake Valley, which he claims is not much good for anything
1848	February 2—Mexico cedes a large tract of land (including its claim to southwestern Wyoming) to the United States in the Treaty of Guadalupe Hidalgo
1849	The U.S. government purchases Fort Laramie (earlier Fort William and Fort John)
1851	September 17—The Sioux, Cheyenne, and Arapaho agree to a treaty at Fort Laramie establishing boundaries for them and allowing wagon trains to cross their lands in the region

1853	November—Mormons, claiming they purchased the property from Jim Bridger, form a settlement at Fort Bridger and organize Fort Supply, south of Fort Bridger
1854	May 30—President Franklin Pierce signs the Kansas-Nebraska Act, which establishes Nebraska Territory and includes all of the land in Wyoming east of the Rocky Mountains
	August—Lt. William Grattan and twenty-eight men are killed by Sioux, precipitating hostilities along the Mormon Trail
1856	October—More than 200 emigrants die when Mormon handcart companies led by James G. Willie and Edward Martin become stranded between the Sweetwater River and South Pass
1857	July 15—F. W. Lander leaves South Pass to explore what becomes the Lander Road, the first government road in Wyoming
	summer—The Mormon War breaks out when federal troops approach Utah to force the Mormons to accept a new governor; Mormons attack and burn two wagon trains in western Wyoming, then retreat toward Salt Lake, burning Fort Bridger along the way
1858	June 14—F. W. Lander begins construction of the Lander Road, a primary route in use until 1912
1860	April 3—The Pony Express makes its first run from St. Joseph, Missouri, to San Francisco, California
1861	October 24—The Pony Express makes its last run, made obsolete by the Creighton telegraph
1862	The U.S. Army establishes Fort Halleck to protect the Overland Stage Route
	Congress passes the Homestead Act
	Shoshone and Bannock warriors attack telegraph stations along the Oregon Trail, shutting down all movement on the route
1863	Shoshone chief Washakie approves a treaty at Fort Bridger permitting development of towns and a railroad on Indian lands; five treaties in all are negotiated by the Shoshone and Bannock tribes this year
1863	John Bozeman and John Jacobs identify a route through the Powder River country to Montana's goldfields
1864	The Bozeman Trail opens, but Indian resistance to white travelers consigns it to history as "the Bloody Bozeman"
	Jim Bridger pioneers a trail west from Fort Caspar over the Bighorn Mountains and into the Big Horn Basin, as an alternative route to the Bozeman Trail

1864	November 29—Col. John M. Chivington destroys a Cheyenne village at Sand Creek, Colorado; Arapaho and Cheyenne survivors head north into Wyoming
1865	January 7—Indians in Colorado, Wyoming, and Nebraska retaliate for the unprovoked attack at Sand Creek, raiding throughout 1865 along the Overland Trail and in other areas
	July 26—Sioux and Cheyenne kill Lt. Caspar Collins and seven men at Platte Bridge, near Casper, and twenty men with another army wagon train
1866	March 10—Gen. John Pope orders establishment of two new forts along the Bozeman Trail—Fort Phil Kearny, in Wyoming, and Fort C. F. Smith, in Montana
	December 21—Sioux under Crazy Horse and Red Cloud kill Lt. William J. Fetterman and eighty soldiers near Fort Phil Kearny
1867	July—Settlers arrive in Cheyenne, just ahead of construction crews on the Union Pacific Railroad
	August 2—Sioux surround Capt. James Powell and thirty-two men on a hillside near Piney Creek and engage in a desperate battle known as the Wagon Box Fight
	August 16—Fort D. A. Russell is built near Cheyenne to protect the coming railroad
	November 13—The first Union Pacific train arrives in Cheyenne
	December 24—The Dakota legislature incorporates Cheyenne
	December 27—Carter and Laramie are the first two counties formed in what is now Wyoming, by the Dakota legislature
1868	April 29—Sioux under Red Cloud agree to a treaty at Fort Laramie that relinquishes their lands in Wyoming, but reserves hunting grounds
	May 7—Crow cede land to the United States by a treaty concluded at Fort Laramie
	June 20—Fort Fred Steele is built on the North Platte River and remains in use until August 7, 1886
	July 3—Shoshone cede all of their lands in Wyoming, except the Wind River Reservation, to the United States
	July 25—Wyoming becomes a territory
	Carbon becomes the first coal town on the Union Pacific line
1869	May 19—Wyoming establishes a territorial government

1869	May 24—Maj. John Wesley Powell launches an expedition down the Green and Colorado rivers; a second expedition, in 1871, departs near the town of Green River
	September 2—Wyoming holds its first election for members of the legislature and a nonvoting delegate to Congress
	October 12—The first territorial legislature convenes for a sixty-day session in Cheyenne
	December 10—Wyoming grants equal suffrage to women, giving them the right to vote, hold office, and serve on juries
1870	September 6—Louisa "Grandma" Swain is the first American woman to vote, in Laramie City
	Gen. H. D. Washburn heads an exploration party into the Yellowstone region
1872	March 1—Congress forms Yellowstone National Park
	Construction starts in Laramie on the Wyoming Territorial Prison, which operates there until 1903, then moves to Rawlins
1874	August—Lt. Col. George A. Custer leads an expedition that finds gold in the Black Hills of South Dakota
1875	The Cheyenne-Deadwood Stage Route opens
	The U.S. Army builds an iron bridge across the North Platte River near Fort Laramie, making the route the most used during the gold boom in the Black Hills
1876	June 25—Sioux and Cheyenne wipe out Custer and most of the 7th Cavalry in the Battle of the Little Bighorn in southern Montana
	September 26—Arapaho chiefs cede their land in Wyoming to the United States
	November 25—Cheyenne under Dull Knife lose to army troops under Gen. Ranald Mackenzie in a battle that breaks the Cheyenne spirit and avenges the Custer defeat in Montana
1877	August—Nez Perce under Chief Joseph, Looking Glass, and Poker Joe cross Yellowstone National Park while fleeing Col. O. O. Howard in a flight that began in June in Idaho and ends near the Canadian border in October
1878	Otto Franc starts the Pitchfork Ranch in the Big Horn Basin
	August—Outlaws "Dutch Charley" Burris and "Big Nose George" Parrott kill Carbon County deputy sheriffs Tip Vincent and Robert Widdowfield (the first two Wyoming lawmen to die on the job) in an ambush at Rattle Snake Pass

1879	Cattle enter western Wyoming
1880	The Cactus Club, an exclusive gathering spot for wealthy cattlemen and forerunner of the Cheyenne Club, opens in Cheyenne
1881–82	The Oregon Short Line Railroad builds through Kemmerer and Cokeville
1882	The Edmunds Anti-Poligamy Act drives Mormons from Utah to the Star Valley and other areas of Wyoming
1883	Homesteads are claimed in Jackson Hole
1885	June 6—Masked raiders kill sheep at Raid Lake, on the west side of the continental divide near Boulder Creek
	Owen Wister, author of *The Virginian*, visits Wyoming for the first time
	September 2—A riot in Rock Springs leads to the deaths of at least twenty-eight Chinese miners
1886–87	A severe winter kills thousands of cattle on the northern plains, known as the Great Die-Up
1887	The first oil well northwest of Casper is drilled
1889	July 20—Six prominent cattlemen lynch Ellen "Cattle Kate" Watson and James Averell near Independence Rock for allegedly rustling cattle
1890	July 10—Wyoming becomes the forty-fourth state in the Union, one week after Idaho
1892	April 5–12—An anti-rustling cattlemen's group dubbed the Regulators kills two homesteaders in what becomes known as the Johnson County Invasion (or Johnson County War)
1893	Mormon settlers begin developing an irrigation project in the Big Horn Basin
1894	July 15—George Leroy Parker, alias Butch Cassidy, begins serving his only prison term, an eighteen-month stint at the Wyoming Territorial Prison in Laramie
	August 18—Congress passes the Carey Desert Land Act, granting certain states up to one million acres of federal lands if they will irrigate them
1895	June—Bannock chief Race Horse and some Shoshone face off with authorities near Jackson Hole in a dispute over hunting rights that ends with the state supreme court affirming the state's ownership of wild game

1896	Shoshone and Arapaho cede ten acres at the mineral hot springs in Thermopolis to the government under condition that the springs be kept available to the people free of charge
1897	September 23—Cheyenne holds its first Frontier Day celebration
	John and Jesse Bell discover hundreds of fossils in an area later set aside as Fossil Butte National Monument
	Sheepherder Ed Haggarty finds copper in the Sierra Madres, starting a boom at Grand Encampment
1898	April 23—President William McKinley calls for 125,000 volunteers for the war with Spain, leading Col. Jay Torrey of the Embar Ranch in Big Horn Basin to organize a regiment of Rocky Mountain Riders
1900	August 22—The first creamery opens in the Star Valley
1901	July 18—Fourteen-year-old Willie Nickell is killed in a range dispute west of Cheyenne at his family's homestead on Iron Mountain; Tom Horn is later charged with the crime
1902	James Cash Penney opens his first Golden Rule store in Kemmerer, forming the nucleus for the subsequent chain of JC Penney stores
	Owen Wister publishes his classic Western novel *The Virginian*, set in Wyoming
1903	Congress forms the Shoshone National Forest, the first in the United States
	June—An underground explosion kills 171 coal miners at Hanna
	October 30—The last Indian battle in Wyoming takes place at Lightning Creek
	November 20—Stock detective Tom Horn is hanged in the last legal hanging in Laramie County, Wyoming, for killing Willie Nickell in 1901
1906	September 24—President Theodore Roosevelt designates Devils Tower as the first national monument
	The U. S. Bureau of Reclamation builds the Jackson Lake Dam across the Snake River
1909	April 2–3—"Ten Sleep Raiders" kill three sheepmen near Ten Sleep in the last major confrontation between sheepmen and cattlemen in Wyoming
1912	Congress creates the Jackson Hole Elk Refuge to protect the elk herds of the region

1913	America's first transcontinental automobile road, the Lincoln Highway, opens across southern Wyoming
1915	Congress forms the National Park Service to protect Yellowstone and other parks
1917	January 31—The state legislature adopts a design for a Wyoming state flag and designates Indian paint brush as the state flower
1920	The first all-woman town council in Wyoming, and perhaps in the United States, takes office in Jackson
1921	The University of Wyoming adopts the cowboy on a bucking horse as its mascot, with the silhouette taken from a photo of Guy Holt on Steamboat
1922	The Colorado River Compact designates water for use in Wyoming, Colorado, Utah, New Mexico, California, Arizona, and Nevada
	The Teapot Dome scandal emerges over leasing the oil reserve without a competitive bid; the leases are invalidated in 1923 by the U.S. Supreme Court
1929	Congress establishes Grand Teton National Park, excluding the broad valley of Jackson Hole
1930	January 1—Fort D. A. Russell is renamed Fort Francis E. Warren
	The Buffalo Bill Memorial Association, forerunner of the multimillion dollar Buffalo Bill Historical Center, organizes to honor William F. Cody
1933	Congress approves the Kendrick water project, allowing development of an irrigation system that serves central Wyoming
1936	The silhouette of a cowboy on a bucking horse first appears on Wyoming license plates
1942	Federal officials develop Heart Mountain Relocation Center, between Powell and Cody, as an internment camp for about 14,000 Japanese-Americans during World War II; it becomes Wyoming's third largest city before it closes in 1945
1943	March 15—President Franklin D. Roosevelt signs an executive order establishing the Jackson Hole National Monument, between Yellowstone National Park and the town of Jackson, and adjoining Grand Teton National Park on the east
1947	Fort Francis E. Warren becomes Francis E. Warren Air Force Base, a training center
1950	September—Public Law 787 creates an expanded Grand Teton National Park, which includes the area set aside in 1929 and the Jackson Hole Monument established in 1943

1958	Francis E. Warren Air Force Base houses the Strategic Air Command
1963–64	The U.S. Bureau of Reclamation builds Fontenelle Dam on the Green River to store water for irrigation projects in the Eden Valley
1980s	A natural resource boom takes hold in western Wyoming, precipitated by the "energy crisis" of the 1970s and leading to employment of 6,500 workers to build the Shute Creek natural gas processing plant
1982	The world's largest wind turbine starts spinning near Medicine Bow
1988	Hundreds of thousands of acres burn in wildfires in Yellowstone National Park
1990	June 2—Wyoming celebrates its centennial of statehood; a large wagon train follows the Bridger Trail between Fort Caspar and Cody
1995	January 12—Wolves are reintroduced to Yellowstone National Park after being killed off earlier in the century

Wyoming Facts

Territory:	July 25, 1868
Statehood:	July 10, 1890
Nicknames:	The Cowboy State; The Equality State
Motto:	Equal Rights
Bird:	Meadowlark, adopted in 1927
Flower:	Indian paintbrush, adopted in 1917
Tree:	Cottonwood, adopted in 1947
Flag:	White buffalo on a blue background with a red border and the state seal (adopted in 1893) as a brand on the buffalo's side, adopted in 1917 from a design by Mrs. A. C. Keyes
Symbol:	Bucking horse, adopted in 1936 and used on the state's license plates ever since
Mammal:	Bison, adopted in 1985
Gem:	Jade (nephrite), adopted in 1967
Fish:	Cutthroat trout (*Salmo clarki*), adopted in 1987
Fossil:	The fossilized fish Knightia, adopted in 1987
Song:	"Wyoming" (written in 1903), words by Charles E. Winter, music by Earle Clemens, arranged by A. W. Coe, adopted as the state song in 1955 with an arrangement by G. E. Knapp.
Population:	453,588 (1990 census)
Area:	97,914 square miles including 2.39 million acres of national park land; 49.5 percent of Wyoming is federally owned

Wyoming Firsts

First permanent white settlement: Fort Laramie, 1830

First wagon train over Oregon Trail: Bidwell-Bartleson, 1841

First ferry over North Platte River: Mormon Ferry, 1847

First bridge over North Platte River: Richard Bridge, 1851

First state to grant women's suffrage: December 10, 1869

First American woman to cast a ballot: Louisa A. Swain, September 6, 1870, in Laramie City

First major national park: Yellowstone, 1872

First national forests in the United States: Shoshone and Teton, which were part of the Yellowstone Timberland Reserve, established by President Benjamin Harrison, March 3, 1891; they became national forests in 1907

First national monument: Devils Tower, September 24, 1906

First Newlands Act irrigation project: Buffalo Bill Dam, 1902

First woman governor in the nation: Nellie Tayloe Ross, 1924

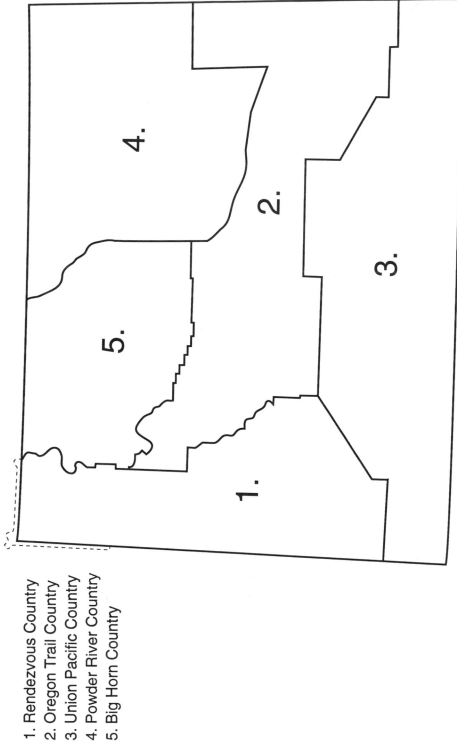

1. Rendezvous Country
2. Oregon Trail Country
3. Union Pacific Country
4. Powder River Country
5. Big Horn Country

Introduction

Wyoming:
Heart of the Rockies

*H*igh atop America is a place so rugged and wild it grabs your heart and spirit and soul: Wyoming, land of the cowboy. The state is a sensation of endless space and unchanged time. Standing atop a granite boulder in the Rocky Mountains, you may feel that you're looking into forever or seeing a country untrammeled and untamed.

Wyoming has lots of elbow room and not much to obstruct the view. Its immensity is matched only by its diversity: rock-strewn mountains, rolling plains, windswept deserts, and pastoral valleys. In every region of the state you can climb to the top of a high peak, spin your gaze like a top, and see nothing but land, rocks, and sagebrush—just as it might have looked when the first people came to this country. In Wyoming your spirit can soar with the eagles and race with the wild horses of the Pryor Mountains or the Red Desert.

In stark contrast to its present semiarid climate, millennia ago Wyoming was lush and tropical, with an inland sea where fish, turtles, and clams lived. Dinosaurs flourished in the region. Over time climatic changes and geologic upheaval changed the face of the land, pushing and gouging, making mountains and rivers where once there had been seas. Prehistoric people came to the region as hunters and gatherers and quarried quartz for stone tools.

Wyoming is a high-altitude place—physically, the second highest state in the nation. Its rivers, called many names by many peoples over the centuries, are now known as the Snake, the Green, the North Platte, the Powder, the Big Horn, the Wind, the Popo Agie, the Shoshone, the Sweetwater, and the Little Snake. The headwaters for the Missouri, the Columbia, and the Colorado lie within Wyoming.

Wyoming entered the union on July 10, 1890, as the forty-fourth state, one of two to join that year. In 1990 Wyoming celebrated its centennial, marked

1

A small herd of wild horses angles for the camera in May 1994 near Adobe Town.

officially as the least populated state in the nation. Over the years Wyoming has had several distinct periods of development and several distinct sets of inhabitants: native Americans, mountain men, overland emigrants, cattlemen, and miners. In most cases the state served as a temporary stopping place and a battleground. Wyoming has always been more a place to pass through in order to get somewhere else than a permanent home. The mountain men wanted only a fortune in furs, emigrants crossed the land simply because it offered the gateway to the West through South Pass, and miners mostly sought the sudden wealth of gold, copper, or coal. But two groups had residency on their minds almost from the start: Indians and cowboys.

Plains Indians did not claim the land: They lived on it and from it. They used territory, but in their cultures the Great Spirit owned the land. Historically, Comanche, Shoshone, Crow, Arapaho, and Cheyenne roved through Wyoming, following game and seasons. Occasionally other tribes passed through, including Ute and Blackfeet. After the 1830s Oglala and Brulé Sioux claimed territory to use as well. The Sioux displaced the Crows by pushing them north, in much the same way that the Arapaho and Cheyenne earlier drove the Comanche south.

In the land that is now Wyoming, the tribes relied on the river basins for their sustenance. They trailed into Jackson Hole to hunt and harvest along the Snake River during summer months, then wintered along the Wind River or the Big Horn. They roamed the North Platte from its upper reaches in the Sierra Madres, and they hunted the rolling grasslands of the Powder and Tongue River basins.

The first white settlements appeared along these waterways as well. Fort Laramie and Fort Bridger became provisioning points for trappers and emi-

Snake River, south of Jackson Hole, on an early morning. —Dan Abernathy

grants. Fort Bonneville had a short life during the mountain-man era and it caused little concern for anyone, but the Powder River forts—Reno and Kearny—inspired a deep hatred on the part of the Indians, particularly the Sioux. The greatest Indian battles in Wyoming's history took place in that basin, as Red Cloud and Crazy Horse's Lakota faced off with the U.S. military under Generals Crook and Carrington in the 1860s. They fought along the foothills of the Big Horn Mountains in battles known as the Wagon Box Fight and the Fetterman Massacre.

In that same Powder River country a quarter of a century later, another turf battle took place. Some early cattlemen took their herds to Montana, but others recognized the value of Wyoming's eastern grasslands and spread their stock on the free range. The big ranchers, used to having the entire range to themselves, took drastic steps in the 1890s to cut down encroaching homesteaders, whom they considered rustlers. They hanged people along the Sweetwater River, hired range detectives such as Tom Horn, and raised an army in the most infamous incident in Wyoming's range history—the Johnson County Invasion of 1892.

Not all of Wyoming's history is about fighting over the land, but it's the land that gives the state its identity.

In the days of the fur trapper and trader there was no Wyoming; it was a place of other countries and other names. Before the explorations by the mountain men, Mexico claimed a portion, as did Britain, France, Spain, and the United States. It was at various times part of Louisiana, Oregon, Utah, Idaho, Nebraska, and Dakota. Not until decades after the fur trappers roamed the great basins and high plains did it become Wyoming, a Delaware Indian word meaning "at the big plains" or "on the great plain."

3

An early view of Fort Laramie when it was part of Dakota Territory. —American Heritage Center, UW

A drawing of Jim Bridger's original trading post by M. D. Houghton. Since Houghton came to Wyoming long after Mormons burned this post, the drawing was based on a verbal description. —Wyoming State Museum

The first explorers in Wyoming may have been Francois and Louis-Joseph Verendrye. The two brothers started their adventure with their father, Pierre Gaultier de Varennes de la Verendrye. Pierre left Montreal in search of a sea and a fur-trade monopoly; seven years later he had a chain of six stockades linking Rainy Lake (near Montreal) to the Assiniboine River, but he hadn't found the sea he sought. His oldest son and his nephew died in the quest. By 1738 Pierre had made it to the Missouri River and the Mandan villages. When he lost his trade goods, Pierre and his remaining sons returned to Canada. That winter trip convinced Pierre he was too old to complete the task he had set for himself, Mark Brown wrote in *The Plainsmen of the Yellowstone*.

In April 1742 Louis-Joseph and Francois again ventured west. They definitely made it as far as Pierre, South Dakota, where they buried a lead plate. There is no direct evidence to show that the Verendryes ventured into Wyoming, but several historians suggest that they camped in the Big Horn Mountains near Sheridan in January 1743.

The dinosaurs, which roamed here ages before the Verendryes, left behind a legacy of oil, gas, and coal that underlies much of the state. From Wyoming's earliest days as a settled territory, mining drove its development. There is coal in southern Wyoming, gold at South Pass City, oil near Casper, and copper at Grand Encampment. Since the 1920s, oil and gas development in southwestern and central Wyoming, uranium production in Fremont County and Shirley Basin, and coal development in the Powder River Basin affected populations, causing great booms followed by equally significant busts.

Scandal and corruption have not been strangers to the mineral industry. During the decades some promoters salted mines, and a furor erupted in the 1920s over the Teapot Dome, a minor oil field near the huge Salt Creek Oil Field in central Wyoming. Secretary of the Interior Albert Fall leased the tract to a close associate's oil company without taking competitive bids. A district judge initially upheld the lease, ruling that its conditions were more favorable to Wyoming than what might be obtained from a competitive process. He appeared to have little concern about the fraud associated with the lease. The U.S. Senate felt otherwise, however, and conducted an investigation leading to fines and jail sentences for the principals.

Although minerals account for a large portion of Wyoming's development, its most stable and long-standing industry has been livestock raising. Much of the land is arid and uninhabitable, but it works well for bands of sheep or cows tended by lonely herders. The earliest ranchers ran thousands of head of cattle on the open range, their herds tended by cowboys who spent long days in the saddle. Those free-spirited figures, with their high-heeled boots, jangling spurs, big-brimmed hats, silk neckerchiefs, and shaggy chaps, knew a thing or two about horses and cows; they recognized ridges, draws, and coulees and gave them names and epithets. As Polly Pry, a columnist for the *Denver Post*, wrote in 1901, "What he doesn't know about life would fill a library, but what he

The Wyoming Hereford Ranch near Cheyenne, once a part of the Swan Land and Cattle Company. —State Historic Preservation Office

knows about this great free, beautiful West would make a story to thrill your soul."

The cowboys came up the Texas and Goodnight-Loving trails, eating the dust of thousands of head of Texas cattle. They worked for huge cattle outfits such as the Swan Land and Cattle Company in southeastern Wyoming, covering most of the land from Torrington to Baggs; the Pitchfork in the Big Horn Basin, encompassing nearly a quarter of a million acres between Meeteetse and Cody; and the Sun Ranch in central Wyoming, marked with the ruts of the Oregon and Mormon trails and the graves of those who died along the way. In their spare time, the men who herded the cattle for those huge ranches tested their skills on the back of a bucking horse or with a rope. In 1897 they went to Cheyenne for the birth of the Cheyenne Frontier Day Rodeo, known as the Daddy of 'em All.

When homesteaders started staking and fencing their land, conflict naturally arose with the huge cattle operations. Cattlemen knew that fences threatened their free-ranging herds, and they feared, abhorred, and in some cases stamped out rustlers and nesters. Then sheep came to the range, and that brewed more trouble. The cattlemen believed the sheep, with their sharply pointed hooves and close grazing habits, ruined the range. The powerful cattlemen drew "deadlines" in the dirt, not to be crossed by sheepherders or homesteaders. If sheep or other unauthorized stock roamed across the deadline, they or their owners often were killed. Ranchers hanged homesteaders Ellen Watson—also known as Cattle Kate—and James Averell from a tree along the Sweetwater River, and federal troops had to quell the violence near Buffalo and Kaycee in 1892 when the Johnson County Invasion—often called a cattle war—erupted. In western Wyoming hundreds of sheep died at Raid Lake and Mosquito Creek as cattlemen made a vain effort to get them off the range.

In another dispute over sheep and cattle range that left its mark on Wyoming, range detective Tom Horn went to the gallows for killing fourteen-year-old Willie Nickell in southern Wyoming near Iron Mountain. Most people believed the bullet was meant for Willie's father, Kels Nickell, and many questioned whether Horn had really pulled the trigger.

During World War I, a Sheridan cowboy serving with the Wyoming National Guard in France drew a picture of a bucking bronco on the company's drum. Patterned after his own horse, the drawing quickly became a symbol of the "Bucking Bronco Regiment." In 1921 the University of Wyoming adopted

Guy Holt on Steamboat at the Albany County Fair, October 1903. The University of Wyoming used this photo to design its Wyoming Cowboy emblem in 1921. The phtoto was taken by UW Professor B. C. Buffum.
—Flossie Moulton Collection

the cowboy as its mascot. In 1936 state officials combined the two logos, stamping the silhouette of a cowboy riding a bucking horse on the Wyoming license plate. Because of its rough reputation as a haven for big-spending, tough-talking, and hard-riding cattlemen, Wyoming is known far and wide as the Cowboy State.

Wyoming is a land of many firsts. It was the first state or territory in the nation to grant women the right to vote—thus the nickname The Equality State. It has the first national monument, Devils Tower; the first national forest, the Shoshone; and the first large national park, Yellowstone. It is a land of abundant contrast, from the splendor of Yellowstone and Grand Teton national parks to the badlands of the Big Horn Basin and the rolling grasslands near Powder River.

Wyoming also boasts a harsh climate. From the hot, dry winds of summer to the brutal blizzards of winter, the weather is unrelenting. Portions of the state are high desert, receiving less than ten inches of rainfall annually. Other areas are more moderate, but the weather can take a toll throughout Wyoming, particularly when the snow swirls and the mercury drops to 30 below zero.

Devils Tower, the country's first national monument, rises 1,280 feet above the Belle Fourche River. An impressive site from all directions, the tower was formed by rising lava more than 60 million years ago. The monument came to widespread fame following the release of the motion picutre Close Encounters of the Third Kind. —Wyoming Division of Tourism

Not every animal makes it to market, as this frost-covered skeleton shows. —Dan Abernathy

Hundreds of thousands of head of cattle died on Wyoming's prairies in the late 1880s, claimed by cold and snow that pounded the land. Despite modern conveniences such as barns, pickups, and snowmobiles, thousands of cattle and sheep fell prey to the elements nearly a hundred years later, in 1984, when late spring snows buried the hills and prairie. Some things can't be controlled, and the weather is one of them. You either learn to live with it, or you leave. Perhaps that's why Wyoming's population is so sparse.

As the least populated state in the union, Wyoming is a place of uninterrupted solitude. There are long stretches of highway with little traffic but with vistas filled with wildlife, sage, rolling hills, and mountain peaks. In 1915 a schoolgirl in Jackson asked God to bless the state and keep it wild.

Rendezvous Country

There are five distinct areas of Wyoming, representing development and geographic differences.

Beaver trappers roamed the area west of the Continental Divide during the first half of the nineteenth century. For our purposes this is Rendezvous Country. It includes all of Lincoln, Teton, and Sublette and portions of Sweetwater, Uinta, and Fremont counties. The section is one of the most scenic in the state; two major river drainages—the Green and the Snake—start their courses

Jackson Hole residents negotiate a narrow road and deep snow. —Teton County Historical Center

to the Pacific Ocean here. It is also perhaps the most spectacular and unusual, encompassing the grandeur of the Tetons and the geysers and mudpots of Yellowstone National Park.

The earliest fur trade in the West largely centered on the rivers, as the voyageurs plied the Missouri, gathering pelts in the western streams and returning them to St. Louis in bull boats, flatboats, and keelboats. The adventure in Wyoming started when John Colter left the returning Lewis and Clark expedition in 1806 at the Mandan villages to return to the mountain country of present-day Montana and Wyoming.

The following year Manuel Lisa established a fur outpost at the mouth of the Big Horn River, and Colter made an exploratory trip to the Crow villages to see if they would trade furs with Lisa. Colter followed a circuitous route that took him up the Stinking Water (Shoshone) River, over the Wind River Mountains, and into the valley now known as Jackson Hole. Colter also passed through part of the area that is now Yellowstone National Park during his solitary journey.

The North West Fur Company, headquartered in Montreal, and the British Hudson's Bay Company dominated the fur trade of the next decade. In 1811 John Jacob Astor, in an attempt to wrest the trade from the British, founded Fort Astoria at the mouth of the Columbia River, but his men abandoned the fort two years later when the War of 1812 forced its transfer to the British. Astoria is important to Wyoming's history because it brought the first white people besides Colter into western Wyoming.

Pierre Dorion and a party of Astorians ventured through in the fall of 1811 headed to the Columbia River. They entered the state east of Sheridan, camped in the vicinity of present-day Buffalo, crossed the Big Horn and Wind River mountains, them camped north of Pinedale before eventually following the Snake River to the Columbia. Robert Stuart crossed Wyoming in 1812, returning from Fort Astoria. He and his party of six men accidentally found South Pass, which became the key to later western migration, and built the earliest known white man's cabin in the present-day state at a site near Casper. Indians crossed the mountains at this location for generations before the first white men used the pass.

After Thomas Fitzpatrick "rediscovered" South Pass in 1824, it became the western gateway. Mountain men used it until the early 1840s. They roamed throughout the land west of the Continental Divide, catching beaver at places like Jackson's Hole and meeting annually at rendezvous along the Green and Wind rivers to sell pelts and obtain supplies for the upcoming year.

Oregon Trail Country

Hundreds of thousands of emigrants walked beside oxen and wagons, rode horses and mules, or pushed handcarts across Wyoming's midsection during the mid-1800s. The Oregon Trail corridor follows the North Platte and

A two-track road marks the Oregon Trail as it crosses South Pass, and the swale of the trail is clearly visible extending to the tall sagebrush.

Sweetwater rivers through eastern and central Wyoming. That section of the state extends from the Nebraska state line to the Continental Divide and includes Goshen, Platte, Converse, Natrona, and Fremont counties. East of Casper the land is flat and fertile, home to farmers dependent upon flows in the rivers for irrigation water. West of Casper it is still primarily flat but not as fertile because water is more scarce and rainfall is sparse.

The great migration west started in 1843, although the first small wagon train made the trip in 1841. During the next thirty years about 350,000 western travelers followed the Oregon Trail corridor across Wyoming to Oregon, California, Washington, and Utah. Travel on the Oregon Trail displaced wildlife and native Americans, who initially acquiesced to the encroachment because the emigrants passed through but did not stay. When it became clear that some emigrants intended to remain in Wyoming, the Indians fought to hold their territory. The Shoshone, Arapaho, Cheyenne, and Sioux lived here when the migration began; only two tribes, the Shoshone and the Arapaho, still claim Wyoming as home. A combined reservation for the traditional enemy tribes lies in Fremont County, at the western edge of Oregon Trail country.

The transcontinental telegraph and the Pony Express roughly followed the Oregon Trail corridor, with stations set approximately twenty miles apart. Perpendicular to the Oregon Trail corridor are the Texas Cattle Trail and the Cheyenne-Deadwood Stage Route. Those pathways extend from Wyoming's southern border to near its northern boundary.

Union Pacific Country

South of the emigrant trails that crossed Wyoming's belly, the transcontinental railroad made its way through the future state in 1867 and 1868, along a line roughly parallel to the Overland and Cherokee trails. Interstate 80 now marks the route of those southern pioneer trails. Union Pacific country is largely Democratic in political persuasion and home to most state governmental institutions, including the capital, university, penitentiary, and state mental hospital. It includes Laramie, Albany, Carbon, Sweetwater, and Uinta

TA Ranch workers with a four-up hitch feed hay as storm clouds gather on Elk Mountain.

counties, which are the state's original five and which once extended from the southern border with Colorado to the northern border with Montana. As development spread from south to north, the counties became a jigsaw puzzle of twenty-three pieces rather than a striped pattern of five.

Brawling, boisterous tent cities preceded the Union Pacific, with communities at Cheyenne, Laramie, Carbon, Benton, Rawlins, Rock Springs, Evanston, and a dozen other places appearing almost overnight. In some cases the "hell on wheels" town disappeared just as quickly.

The railroad brought not only people but also opportunities for development. The government granted land to the Union Pacific in alternating sections twenty miles north and twenty miles south of the tracks. To sweeten the pot, mineral rights went with those sections. When the railroad discovered coal at Carbon just north of Elk Mountain, it quickly began mining operations. Coal miners from Lancashire, England, and Finland did the initial digging, but eventually—in response to a labor strike—Chinese arrived to work the mines there and at Rock Springs.

Conflict and racism lace Wyoming's mining history. In 1885 a riot broke out between the whites and the Chinese at Rock Springs, leading to the deaths of between twenty-eight and fifty-one Chinese miners and a call for federal troops to quell the disturbance.

Powder River Country

Two of the greatest collisions in Wyoming's history center in the Powder River Basin. The area lies in Sheridan, Johnson, Campbell, Weston, and Crook counties and is bordered on the north by Montana, the east by South Dakota, the west by the Big Horn Mountains, and the south by the North Platte River. Some of the final battles of the Plains Indian war took place in this rolling hill country at locations on Crazy Woman Creek and near Big and Little Piney creeks. After whites fought the Indians to gain control of the land, cattlemen fought homesteaders to keep it.

The route pioneered by John Bozeman and John Jacobs from Fort Laramie through the Powder River to Montana became known as the Bloody Bozeman when Sioux and Cheyenne made repeated attacks on wagon trains filled with military troops and gold seekers. The Indians wanted to hold on to that which was theirs by right. An 1868 treaty negotiated at Fort Laramie gave them the Powder River country on paper, but the military started trying to take it back virtually before the chiefs had even made their marks upon the parchment. The tribes succeeded in driving the white men out, but their short-lived victory lasted only until the white hoards rushed to the Black Hills when they heard the cry of "Gold!"

It was also in Powder River country that the cattlemen waged war on homesteaders in Johnson County. It all centered on the issue of free-range use, but the shootout precipitated by the cattlemen's army became a siege when the

A monument for Dull Knife battlefield, Johnson County, near Barnum. —State Historic Preservation Office

local homesteader citizenry outmaneuvered the invaders. The cattlemen stayed, but so did the homesteaders, and the Sioux watched from their South Dakota reservations.

Some of Wyoming's great coal deposits underlie the Powder River Basin, and one of the major mining booms in the state's history germinated there in the 1980s as huge open-pit mines developed.

Big Horn Country

Large cattle ranches, irrigated farms, Mormon settlement, and the Wild West Show characterize the Big Horn Basin country. The area is bounded by the Big Horns to the east, the Big Horn and Owl Creek mountains to the south, Yellowstone National Park on the west, and Montana on the north. It includes Washakie, Hot Springs, Big Horn, and Park counties.

Intrepid mountain man Jim Bridger pioneered the first road through the basin when he located a trail to Montana's goldfields in 1864. Charles Carter drove some of the first cattle into the area, followed by German count Otto Franc, who in 1878 established the Pitchfork Ranch, one of the largest in the state then and still one of the biggest. It took development of water resources to bring stability and prosperity. First a group of Mormons built canals to transfer water from the Greybull and Shoshone Rivers to arid land; they settled at Burlington and Lovell. Then Buffalo Bill Cody and his business partners developed additional canal systems on land farther west, where the town that bears his name was established. Cody achieved fame as a Pony Express rider, government scout, and Wild West showman.

During World War II, Japanese-Americans living on the West Coast found themselves rounded up and herded to "relocation centers" in the nation's interior. Many spent time at Heart Mountain Relocation Center on a barren flat in northwestern Wyoming. More than 11,000 Japanese-Americans lived

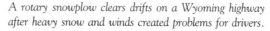

A rotary snowplow clears drifts on a Wyoming highway after heavy snow and winds created problems for drivers.

at Heart Mountain during the war, making it the state's third largest city at the time, with a school, newspaper, hospital, and large agricultural development.

We will begin our roadside journey through Wyoming's heritage in Rendezvous Country and explore the sections generally in the order in which they were developed and settled. In most cases our discovery is from south to north or from east to west.

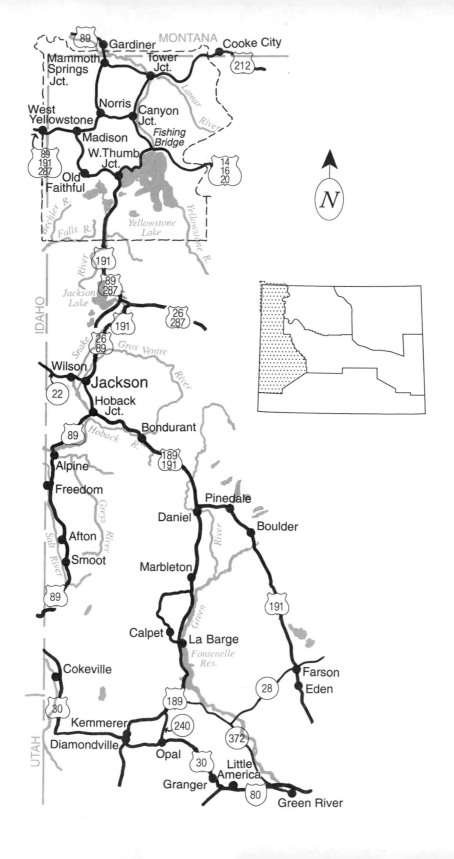

Part 1

Rendezvous Country

The land along Wyoming's western border drew the beavermen after 1807, when John Colter first ventured through Jackson Hole. The cold, clear streams that form the headwaters of the Snake and Green rivers became fur production centers, and the broad valley of the Green a marketplace, from 1825 until 1840.

The earliest fur trade in the West centered largely on the rivers, as the Montreal-based North West Fur Company and the British Hudson's Bay Company sought control of the Pacific Northwest. In 1811 John Jacob Astor, in an attempt to wrest the trade from the British, founded Fort Astoria near the mouth of the Columbia River, but he lost the fort in the War of 1812 and a decade passed before other Americans really became players in the western fur trade.

In 1822 William Ashley and Andrew Henry gathered one hundred young men to start a fur company. Henry built a fort at the mouth of the Yellowstone River and in 1823 attempted to lead an expedition of trappers up the Missouri, but the party met resistance from the Arikaras and the river closed to trader use. So they went overland in 1824 with Jedediah Smith as a guide. The party ascended the Platte or Moonshell River and crossed the Rocky Mountains at South Pass—which became better known during the 1840s as emigrant trains rolled toward Oregon—to begin the mountain trade.

In 1825 Ashley held the first fur traders' rendezvous on Henry's Fork of the Green River, near what eventually became the Utah-Wyoming border and the tiny community of Burntfork. That gathering was nothing like those of later years. It was simply an occasion for the men to replenish their supplies, sell furs, and find out which of their friends had made it through the winter, since they constantly risked attack by hostile Indians. That first rendezvous in the broad valley of the Unita Mountains was not the wild, raucous affair that defined later gatherings.

By 1826 Jedediah Smith, David Jackson, and Bill Sublette bought Ashley's Rocky Mountain Fur Company and operated it for the next four years while making significant contributions to the exploration of the West. Smith journeyed to California while Jackson ventured into the lush mountains and arid plains along the Snake River at the foot of the Tetons. Their efforts, like those of other mountain men, left them with reputations larger than life. In their quest for adventure, they found danger and hardship first and foremost; but they also realized immortality by lending their names to places still prominent in Rendezvous Country, including Sublette County and Jackson Hole.

When the beaver numbers dwindled and pelts saturated the market, the first pioneers started trekking west to settle Oregon. Their route crossed present-day Wyoming, where a broad opening—South Pass—provided passage through the rugged Rocky Mountains.

Although it was the first area of the state in which people lived and prospered, Rendezvous Country didn't settle permanently until much later, at least in part because of its isolation on the western side of the Continental Divide. Indians had passed through, hunted, and harvested in the area for centuries, but not until cattlemen and homesteaders arrived in the 1870s did the region have long-term residents. A few miners, sheepmen, and outlaws spiced the pot.

Today Rendezvous Country—particularly Jackson Hole—is one of the most visited regions in the state. The area struggles with growth in an effort to control the influx of migrants from California, New York, and all places in between.

From the Little Colorado Desert at the southern portion of this region of Wyoming to the rugged Teton mountains and boiling geysers of Yellowstone National Park, this land shows its many colors. The wagon ruts of Oregon-bound emigrants can be clearly seen, as can buckskinners recreating the Green River Rendezvous every summer.

We will begin our trip through Rendezvous Country in the southwest and travel north.

Cokeville—Little America

Cokeville

Long before it became Cokeville, this area on the banks of the Smith's Fork of the Bear River drew trappers, travelers, and Indians. Tilford Kutz built a one-room cabin on the river in 1873 and opened a ferry and trading post. His little business served the diminishing numbers of emigrants on the great overland trails to California and Oregon. Kutz had an Indian wife, and his best customers were her Bannock and Shoshone relatives, who lived in several hundred lodges around the small store.

Eventually others came to the area, including Syl Collett, Robert Gee, and John Bourne and their families. In 1876 Bourne's daughter, Retta, became the first white child born in the remote community, which at that time boasted little more than Collet's store (stocked mostly with whiskey and bacon).

John W. Stoner established a new trading post in 1879 and later built a mercantile store near the Oregon Trail ruts. The settlement started to grow, and two years later it had a post office and a name, Cokeville, which it got from the coke deposits found in the area. When the Oregon Short Line Railroad was built through the valley in 1881–82, Coe and Carter, a huge lumber company that supplied most of the rail ties across Wyoming, opened an office in Cokeville. The railroad brought considerable growth, but it took the sheepmen to bring stability. Eventually the town became a multimillion-dollar sheep-shipping point.

The first sheepman in the Cokeville area could have been Justin Pomeroy of Kansas, who built a cabin at the mouth of Fontenelle Creek on the Green River, likely the first permanent residence in the Green River Valley. Other settlers also raised sheep, and by the late 1870s large operations such as Swift and Company herded sheep from California and Oregon along the Oregon and Sublette trails. They intended to move their sheep all the way to Nebraska, but settlers obtained many of the wooly creatures in western Wyoming territory to start an agricultural enterprise that continues. Through the 1880s sheep raising expanded, but it became a deadly occupation for some, as masked raiders attacked herders and their herds to get them off the range.

A Range Clash

In a land where range was the key to success, the cattlemen and the sheepmen were bound to clash. On the Green, as elsewhere in the state, the sheepmen and the cattlemen traded barbs in the 1880s and 1890s. George W. Rollins wrote, "The thrilling carefree life of the cowboy with his spirited horses,

Sheep shearing, using hand shears. —Wyoming State Museum

fancy saddles and bridles, and his strenuous and adventurous activities cannot be matched by the solitary life of the flock tender who often went on foot, on a mule, or in a covered wagon."

The cattlemen established rules for the range, marking deadlines that sheep and their owners were not supposed to cross. The penalty could be death for animals and people alike, with "justice" carried out by the cattlemen, their cowboys, or the "range detectives" they hired.

The western Wyoming conflict continued to escalate, finally blowing up one fine June day in 1885 at Raid Lake on the west side of the Continental Divide near Boulder Creek. Cattlemen, or their henchmen, bound and blindfolded sheepherders and methodically clubbed their animals to death. Nearly two decades later, in July 1902, about fifteen herds of sheep belonging to Rock Springs ranchers crossed a deadline in the New Fork country of the Green River Valley, and 150 masked men attacked them, according to historian

Nobel and Bragg sheep in camp, 1908. Sheep herding became a risky and often deadly occupation in the late 1800s and early 1900s. Sheepmen and cattlemen warred over the range during that period. Some flocks and at least fifteen men and a boy died at the hands of masked or unknown raiders during the conflict. —Wyoming State Museum

T. A. Larson. The raiders destroyed at least 2,000 sheep, killed one herder, and drove the other herders out of the country after scattering their animals.

Not all sheepmen ended up on the losing side. One year near the turn of the century, Jake Herschler, a prominent western Wyoming sheepman, had several bands of sheep in his care. A blizzard scattered the sheep and drove them across a deadline and onto the desert range of cattle. Herschler went to find them, knowing full well the act could cost him his life.

One factor favoring Herschler was his popularity with the people of the region, including the cattlemen. His daughter, Helen Herschler Beck, wrote in *They Made Wyoming Their Own*, "When Father reached his sheep, he found that the cattlemen of the area, knowing whose sheep the animals were, had been hauling hay on bobsleds in the deep snow to feed the sheep until Father could come to get the flock."

However, avoiding deadly confrontations with cattlemen didn't guarantee a sheep raiser's prosperity. From 1893 to 1896 prices failed to meet expenses; sheep sold for anywhere between five bits and two bucks, and wool brought only five or six cents a pound. The fall in prices came just before establishment of government forest preserves. With the preserves, the forerunners of national forests, came federal regulation, which stockmen resented. Bureaucrats suddenly had a say about when and where livestock operators could graze their animals, and the ranchers didn't like anyone telling them how to manage their stock.

Working cows, Padlock Ranch. —Dan Abernathy

Sheep and cattlemen eventually learned to deal with each other and with government regulation, and they continued to rely on the public lands as pastures for their stock. However, a hundred years later, they got their dander up again when they heard environmental slogans like "Cattle-Free in '93." They argued against substantial grazing-fee increases proposed by various congressmen from nonwestern states and by the head of the U.S. Department of the Interior. In 1994 it appeared the cost of raising livestock on public lands might double, but after a shift in national politics—when Republicans assumed control of both the U.S. Senate and House of Representatives in the November 1994 election—Interior secretary Bruce Babbitt withdrew his proposal to raise grazing fees. However, in an earlier move, Wyoming officials raised fees on state-owned land by 40 percent, from $2.50 to $3.50 per month. Stockmen defended their century-old practice of grazing on public lands and argued they needed the lower costs in order to continue operations.

The Old Lincoln Highway

US 30, also known as the Lincoln Highway, is the oldest transcontinental road in the United States. It crosses southern Wyoming on a route parallel to—and now often covered by—I-80. About four miles south of Cokeville that first automobile route crossed the first pioneer route, intercepting the Sublette Cutoff of the Oregon Trail. The ruts of the wagons are deeply ingrained in the steep Tunp Range, coming straight off Sublette Flat to the Bear River Valley. A modern-day power line, its towers holding their arms to the sky, now marks the route the emigrants took.

Fossils First Noted in 1847

Elizabeth Dixon Smith Geer referred to fossils in southwestern Wyoming as early as August 1847, when she traveled with an Oregon-bound wagon train. She wrote in her diary: "Encamped on Black's Fork, a small river bordered with willows. This large waste of country in my opinion has once been a sea. My husband found on the top of a mountain sea shells petrified to stone. The crevices in the rocks show the different stages of the water."

After following the Bear River, US 30 makes a 90-degree corner at Sage Junction and heads east. At Fossil, midway between Sage and Kemmerer, trappers John and Jesse Bell found hundreds of fossil fish, marine animals, insects, palm leaves, and berries in 1897. E. W. Holland was the first to dig up and market the age-old relics. The fossils—now a part of Fossil Butte National Monument—lay under about thirty-five feet of slate and calcite, but over the last century fossil hunters have taken the protecting layer off parts of the hill. Specimens taken from the site include the remains of a thirteen-foot-long alligator, garfish four to six feet long, other types of fish, a bird resembling a chicken, and small plants.

Diamondville

Prospector Harrison Church located a vein of coal about a mile north of Diamondville in 1868, but it took him nearly thirty years to start production. In 1894 Church finally found enough investors to create the Diamond Coal & Coke Company, formed as a subsidiary of Montana's Anaconda Smelting Company. That year Mine Number One opened with two workable seams ranging from seven to fourteen feet wide. A solid roof of sand and soapstone made safe and easy passage possible for the forty-year life of the mine.

Kemmerer

First a Golden Rule

Named for Kemmerer Coal Company president M. S. Kemmerer, this wide-open town rose in the heart of a rich mining district. It had 900 people, fourteen saloons, two brothels, and a company store in 1902, when a Baptist minister's son scraped together enough cash to open a dry-goods store. In a stone building facing the town's triangular park, adjacent to a barber shop, and catty-corner from the bank, James Cash Penney started one of America's retail icons.

Penney learned retailing in 1898 by working as a temporary clerk for the Golden Rule chain, owned by W. G. Johnson and T. M. Callahan. By age twenty-six Penney had established himself as a tireless worker with a real talent for selling, and in 1901 he was invited to become a partner in the chain. With his life savings of $500 and another $1,500 that he borrowed, Penney went to Kemmerer, selected a twenty-five-foot by forty-five-foot building, and, on April 14, 1902, opened his own Golden Rule store.

Penney's business philosophy revolved around three tenets: work long hours, offer good merchandise, and make employees partners in the company's success. Joining Penney were his wife, Berta, and two sales associates. They opened at sunrise and closed when the street in front of the store was empty at night. Their first day's take totaled $466.59, in an era when a top-quality suit cost less than $10 and overalls and shoes cost 50 cents.

The JC Penney Company started in Kemmerer with a store formerly known as the Golden Rule, which became JC Penney's in 1902.

Kemmerer was a community of coal miners used to trading with the company store on a credit basis. Penney appealed directly to those miners with his personal rule of "one price." Many merchants of the day bargained for whatever they could get. Penney set a price for his goods, allowed for a fair profit, and stuck to that amount. It was a wise policy. Penney got the business of the miners in Kemmerer and lured customers from places as far away as Green River, seventy-five miles—or three days away by wagon—to the east.

The Kemmerer store prospered, as did the others in the Golden Rule chain. In 1907 Penney borrowed $30,000 and bought Johnson and Callahan's shares. Because he got his start when former employers gave him a share of the business, Penney made his own employees partners in the stores they managed. Those early executives trained others, and the chain expanded quickly, making Golden Rule the fastest-growing retail chain in the nation at the time.

The growth created problems, however, and by late 1912 profits could not cover the cost of rapid expansion. Banks balked at loaning funds to such an untraditional company, so Penney organized and incorporated the new JC Penney Company in the state of Utah on January 17, 1913, which gave him more stability and made the company a better credit risk.

The company grew by leaps and bounds. By 1920 there were 312 stores, and by 1929 there were 1,395 outlets. When the company celebrated its fortieth anniversary, in 1942, JC Penney had, on average, opened one store every ten days for forty years, and the chain distributed its large mail-order catalog to customers throughout the country.

Like Sears & Roebuck and Montgomery Ward, JC Penney operated retail stores and sold to rural residents who relied on catalogs for the goods they needed. Yet, despite the enormous size of his enterprise, Penney went out of his way to treat his customers like friends. Kemmerer resident Martin Hangich told the *Casper Star-Tribune* in May 1992, on the occasion of the ninetieth anniversary of JC Penney stores:

> Anytime you wanted to talk to him or have your picture taken with him, he was quite willing. Of course, it was good publicity on his part as well.
>
> When they dedicated the first JC Penney store and later, when he visited back at the old store, he would stand in the doorway and greet people and shake hands with everybody who came in.

Industrial Center

Today southwestern Wyoming is one of the state's industrial centers, with several major plants operating near Kemmerer. The facilities include Pittsburg & Midway Coal Company, Utah Power, FMC Skull Point Mine and Coke Plant, Exxon Shute Creek Gas Plant, and Chevron and Amoco sulfur-loading facilities.

In 1993 Williams Field Services processed 425 million cubic feet of natural gas each day at its plant near Opal. The company distributes the gas to three major interstate transmission pipelines that deliver to consumers throughout the West.

Pittsburg & Midway Coal Company, which produced its first semibituminous coal at the turn of the century in underground operations, has been active in the region longer than any other firm. In 1950 the company shifted to seasonal surface mining, and by 1993 it was producing 3.4 million tons of coal annually in its open-pit operation.

Chevron and Amoco share sulfur-loading facilities. Chevron's molten sulfur travels twenty-two miles from the gas plant in an electrically heated pipeline to the terminal, which handles a thousand tons of sulfur per day. The sulfur must be kept between 240 and 310 degrees Fahrenheit. At higher temperatures it begins to resemble the consistency of molasses, and at lower temperatures it solidifies.

Exxon's Shute Creek Gas Plant separates raw gas into carbon dioxide, methane, helium, and sulfur. Carbon dioxide from the plant is used to enhance oil recovery from oil wells. In addition to leading the world in helium production in 1992, Shute Creek was the largest consumer of electricity in Wyoming. Construction of the facility in the 1980s required 6,500 workers.

FMC opened its Skull Point Mine and Coke Plant in 1976 to work five major coal seams ranging from ten to forty-five feet in depth. Since then, the operation has mined up to a million and a half tons per year. The coke plant is the world's largest commercial facility, providing raw material to the company's phosphorous plant in Pocatello, Idaho. FMC's technologically advanced process in 1993 produced a coke briquette successfully tested by leading domestic and international steel companies.

Construction of the Utah Power Naughton Plant started in 1962, and the plant went into operation the following year. The coal-fired electric-generating facility expanded in 1967 and again in 1972, reaching a capacity of 710 megawatts. Coal mining operations in southwestern Wyoming as early as the 1870s set the stage for industrial development that still continues.

Opal

Opal sits midway between Kemmerer and Granger at the junction of US 30 and Wyoming 240.

In about 1877 Charles F. Robinson moved to Ham's Fork, where he pitched a tent by the river and parlayed a squatter's claim into a sheep ranch. One day in 1881, an official of the Oregon Short Line Railroad and an Omaha newspaperman were walking along the Ham's Fork when one of the men picked up a stone. Robinson immediately identified it as an opal, and when the road went through a year later, the station took its name from the precious stone, although the town's pronunciation draws equal emphasis on the second syllable: "oh-pal."

The Oregon Short Line connected with the Union Pacific main line, making Opal the new commercial and shipping center. Residents appreciated the closer rail terminal. Before its construction, they had to go about sixty-five miles to either Green River or Evanston every three months or so for supplies. Although sixty-five miles might not seem particularly far to travel for supplies in the 1990s, a century ago a sixty-five-mile trip via horse and wagon took two or three days one way. With the distance cut in half, it must have seemed as if the railroad was just around the proverbial corner.

Granger

Fur trappers held the 1834 rendezvous near the future site of Granger, which started as the adobe-covered South Bend Stage Station and Pony Express stop in 1860. The Union Pacific Railroad founded the town, initially called Grange, in 1868 as a rail's-end camp and stock-shipping point.

Granger got a new lease on life in 1880 when the Union Pacific built a branch line northwest toward the Utah Northern and the Oregon Short Line.

The remains of the Granger Stage and Pony Express Station. —Dan Abernathy

Four years later, when the Oregon Short Line reached the Pacific Coast, Granger became an important railroad division point.

Three boxcars on the siding served as a station. The center car became the ticket and baggage office, and the other two were a freight depot and waiting room. In those days of segregation, a chalk line divided the waiting room into men's and women's halves, with men allowed to smoke only on their side.

In time Granger had a hotel, several stores and cafes, a railroad shop, and a saloon. The town's growth continued until 1899, when the Union Pacific bought the Oregon Short Line and moved the division point to Green River. Then Granger became a sleepy little place dependent for its survival on the major highway running through its center. In the 1930s the route of US 30 shifted, leaving the town—which had been on a main highway since the days of Elijah White's wagon train across the Oregon Trail in 1842—a quarter-mile off the side.

US 189
Kemmerer—Daniel
89 miles

Opal Wagon Road

Opal's wagon road opened in 1882, although there was a mail route on the southern portion of the trail as early as 1878. Wyoming 240, which runs due north from Opal to US 189, closely follows the historic wagon route.

The road ran along the west bank of the Green River roughly parallel to present-day US 189. It followed the route of the Sublette Cutoff on the Oregon Trail north to the vicinity of Names Hill, where westbound emigrants carved their names in the soft sandstone. The wagon road continued through LaBarge and along the Green River to the Charles Bird Stage Stop, known as Midway.

Clarence Holden had received the first mail contract on the Opal wagon road, carrying mail, express, and passengers for a $5 fee from Big Piney to Opal and for $3 from LaBarge to Opal. Then, in about 1898, Bird built a two-story, twelve-room house. Bird, a blacksmith by trade, freighted and delivered mail from Opal to Pinedale and Cora. Bird's stage house at Midway burned in 1934.

General William Ashley, a leader in the fur trade, named many streams in western Wyoming, including the creek downriver from LaBarge. That stream gets its name from Ashley's friend Capt. Joseph LaBarge, pilot of the steamboat Omega that plied the upper Missouri.

Names Hill, located just south of LaBarge, offers a natural register of the western migration of the mid-1800s. Among the names carved in the soft

Among the names carved in the rock at Names Hill is this famous inscription, though it's unlikely Jim Bridger did the carving, since he was illiterate.

sandstone is that of "James Bridger—Trapper—1844," but it's doubtful Old Gabe, as Bridger became known, did the carving himself—he was illiterate. Most of the names are of much more recent vintage—the 1970s and 1980s.

Emigrant Crossing

Early westbound travelers had to ford the Green River at the mouth of Steed Canyon, south of LaBarge Creek. The crossing was a little more than a mile northeast of Names Hill. In late June 1847 Mormons built a ferry across the Green, roughly midway between Names Hill and the crossing. In July 1850 John B. Hill wrote in his diary of crossing the Green on the Mormon Ferry:

> The ferryman allowed too many passengers to get into the boat, and the water came within two inches of the gunwale. He ordered every man to stand steady, and we stood, as the boat was liable to swamp. . . . A rope with pulleys on it was stretched across the River, and the current carried the boat across. When we were nearly across, the upper edge of the boat

dipped a sheet of water an inch deep, from end to end, and I thought the boat would be swamped instantly, turn over upstream, cover all of us under water and drown the last one of us. . . . [A] few of us jumped to the lower side of the boat, and it was righted at once. . . . At that time Green River was booming.

Fontenelle Reservoir

Since 1964 Fontenelle Dam has controlled the waters of the Green River. Twenty-four miles southeast of LaBarge and fifty miles northwest of the town of Green River, the earth- and gravel-fill structure sits 139 feet high and 5,421 feet long at the site of a natural ford in the river and an old suspension bridge.

The dam and reservoir get their names from Lucien Fontenelle, an outfitter with the American Fur Company. Constructed in 1963–64, the dam restrains 345,000 acre-feet of water for irrigation, recreation, and operation of a 10,000-kilowatt power plant.

Water from the reservoir irrigates 43,000 acres of hay and grain in the Eden Valley of northwestern Sweetwater County. That desert land is productive when it gets watered, but farmers found in the 1980s they had to switch from flood irrigation, where they let water run freely from ditches onto fields, to the use of large pivoting or rolling sprinkler systems. The change came in an effort to reduce salinity in the Colorado River system, of which the Green is the genesis. By putting less water on the land, farmers reduced the amount of salt that leached back into the river runoff. That, in turn, improved the quality of water for downstream users.

A Horse Tale

Marvin H. Mahaffey moved to the LaBarge area in 1914 to work for a woman he remembered as Mrs. Wisdom. This rancher, assisted by her daughter, Twirl, ran horses out on the Little Colorado Desert. The girl could hold her own when roping and riding, often making a day-long, fifty- or sixty-mile race after wild horses.

Once Mrs. Wisdom complained that a coyote was trying to catch one of her turkey hens. Twirl saddled a long-legged roan gelding, coiled a whip in her hand, and headed out after the predator. The coyote loped across the flat until he realized that Twirl and the horse were gaining fast; then he got down to the urgent business of getting out of there. Twirl snapped the whip like a .22 rifle shot. When the dust cleared, the coyote was running for his life, and Twirl was crowding him hard.

Running horses out on the desert was hard work. Riders kept lariats tied to the hackamore of their mounts; if the horse fell, the rider could jerk the saddle string and release the rope. That way, if horse and rider parted company, the cowboy could hang on to his cayuse via the rope and not be on foot in the desert. According to Mahaffey, "Every rider carried a gun. We never expected anything as dramatic as outlaws, but we always faced the possibility of having

Pam Ready putting out salt in Snyder Basin near Big Piney. —Dan Abernathy

to kill the horse if he fell and broke a leg. We also used the gun as a signal to get help."

Perils of Livestock Raising

Raising livestock in western Wyoming's harsh climate can try the spirits of the best men and women. In summer, the sun sears the landscape, sucking the moisture from the ground. In winter, winds rip and howl as relentless storms sweep across the land in blinding blizzards and icy blasts.

On December 16, 1921, Harold A. Dodge knew from experience that a storm was imminent. The next day he watched as the snow started to pile up, with seventeen inches on the ground before night engulfed the prairie near Big Piney. The flakes continued falling until twenty-two inches covered the land. Two days later Dodge realized that the sheep flocks would be in real trouble, so he hooked his best workhorse on a piece of cottonwood log and struck out across the desert to meet the herds.

The log plowed a path for the sheep. On December 21, Dodge left for Kemmerer. He continued the story: "At that time there was a single file string of sheep, broken by a camp every so often, from Granite Spring northeast of Big Piney to Granger about 125 miles long. The first sheep arrived in Granger the same day that the last sheep left the Granite Spring Area."

It must have been quite a sight to see such a long, wavy line of sheep struggling through deep snow. Driving the route today takes a couple of hours; riding it on a horse then, while dragging a log to clear the way, would have taken several days.

An Oil Find

LaBarge owes most of its development to the dinosaurs that walked this terrain eons ago, when the region was lush and featured an inland sea. When the huge beasts died, their bodies turned to underground rivers of oil and pockets of natural gas. The original oil seep in the LaBarge field was three miles northwest of LaBarge; in 1913 state geologist L. W. Trumball noted that oil there was "gathered for local use or for sale to the ranches along the Green River for lubrication of mowing machines and other farm tools."

The first boom occurred in the 1920s. In 1924 the town of Tulsa—named for Tulsa, Oklahoma—developed at the location of present-day LaBarge. It grew quickly and had a Piggly-Wiggly store, grocery store, garage, the Eagle Bar, Valley Service Station, a dance hall, and many other businesses. Three years later developer W. D. Newlon sold town lots in a nearby place, which he called LaBarge. It soon became a tough little boomtown filled with oil workers, loggers, and tie hacks.

In the 1980s another tremendous boom took hold in the area. During construction of the Shute Creek natural gas processing plant, some 6,500 workers earned wages in the area. LaBarge became a boomtown once again, as did other communities in Sublette, Lincoln, and Uinta counties.

The boom faded, as all booms do, when major construction finished, but LaBarge still had a stable work force and thriving business community in the mid-1990s. It was far from becoming a ghost town, as so many boomtowns do.

Calpet

The opposite happened at Calpet. During the summer of 1907 an oil discovery took place near the town's future location, and W. D. Newlon's company, Beneficial Oil, began drilling. In 1926 California Petroleum Corporation bought Newlon's interest for $2.75 million and built Calpet Camp three miles west of LaBarge. The settlement quickly boasted a population of 300 men, and in 1927 the company built a small refinery, which provided electricity for Calpet and gas for local use. In 1928 the company built a thirty-eight-mile pipeline to the Oregon Short Line railhead at Opal. Calpet thrived until the refinery closed in 1956. Unlike "booming" LaBarge, Calpet is now a ghost.

The First Budd

In November 1879, Pennsylvanian Daniel Budd and his partner, Hugh McKay, trailed nearly a thousand head of cattle from Nevada, intending to ship from Point of Rocks on the Union Pacific Railroad main line in southern Wyoming. But winter caught the men in the lower Green River Valley. After searching for a place where they could hold their cows, the two eventually settled on the mountain country west of Big Piney. They and their animals made it through the cold and snow, and the pair decided to stay along the Green's tributaries, forming the 67 Ranch.

The trail to Wyoming had been a long one. Budd left Atchison, Kansas, February 15, 1879, and headed to Nevada, where he met McKay. By June the men had put a herd together, and in August they started east. At Point of Rocks, a major shipping point, they could load the cattle onto rail cars and ship them to eastern markets. It was a good plan at the time.

Hereford cattle string over the hills in a roundup. The first cattle brought into the state came from Texas, Oregon, and Nevada, but later cattlemen imported "blooded stock" such as Herefords from England. —Wyoming State Museum

Budd's diary tells the story of their movement from Nevada and their decision to stay in the Green River Valley.

> Sunday 10, Aug 1879—Started for Nebraska with 777 head of Cattle Branded 13 Calves Camped on Davies Creek
>
> 16, Aug 1879—Damned poor feed

As the herd moved across Nevada, Budd made constant references to the short feed. In late September the herd finally neared Wyoming. Budd never said how much help he and McKay had to move the cattle, but it's reasonable to assume several cowboys were involved.

> 27 Sept 1879—Moved camp 13 miles to Bear River good Road good feed. no water on road.
>
> Sunday 28—Passed through Soda Springs 5 miles Drive good feed & Water Rained Most all night Lander Road 20 miles of timber
>
> Monday 29—Snowing like Hell Laid in camp at Soda Springs Snow all gone at 11 o'clock A.M.

By October 16 the herd had moved down the Thomas Fork and left Fort Bridger to graze along Smith's Fork. But the partners realized they weren't going to get their cattle to the railroad shipping point farther east. Their good plan went bad as winter approached.

> Friday [October] 17, 1879—Laying over on twin creek nice day overhead but muddy under foot has the appearance of more snow cannot say where we will Winter yet Cattle are doing pretty well considering the Storm on herd.
>
> Tues 21, 1879—McKay Started to Fontnell to look for winter range Splendid weather.
>
> Sunday October 26, 1879—McKay came back concluded to winter on Blacks Fork.
>
> Monday 27—On the move down Hams fork 6 miles and crossed over has the appearance of a storm on guard at night
>
> Tuesday 28—Down Hams fork 5 miles
>
> Wednesday 29—Left Hams for the little Muddy 18 miles no water Mired 60 head 10 head Died in Mud Hell of a Muddy Worked all night
>
> Nov. 1—Moved camp to Granger station
>
> Nov. 6—drove up Green River 8 miles No feed. Windy hard Driving Sand Blew like forty
>
> Nov. 7—Up Green River to Stade Creek crossed river twice no feed cold but pleasant
>
> Sat. 8—Up Green River 8 miles to Fontnell Creek little feed left 2 calves 4 head of cows gave out on guard Snowed.
>
> Sunday 9—Snowing but Warm up Green River 10 miles to the LaBarge Creek.

Wed. 12—Moved to Big Piney up Green River 15 miles hard Days work
cold but pleasant good feed & Water Winter quarters.

Budd spent part of that first winter in Wyoming before heading back to
Nevada, where he spent Christmas in Eureka. The following year he returned
to the Big Piney country to stay, sending to Kansas for his wife and four young
children. They arrived on the Union Pacific Railroad in Green River City.
Budd sold his share of the 67 Ranch to McKay in 1885, but he remained in
the area, claiming homestead land that became the townsite of Big Piney.

The original Big Piney post office was located at the Nicholas Swan Ranch
in 1878, but by 1887 Daniel Budd had become postmaster. In 1892 Budd erected
a store with a second-floor dance hall. The first school was a log cabin with a
dirt roof, but in 1902 the community built a new school on land Budd donated.

Before long Budd constructed another building, which would serve as a
community landmark until the 1950s. The eight-sided Budd Hall was a dance
hall, but it also housed the school, bank, and newspaper. Budd was a big man
in town who contributed much to its early success. His family continues to
play an active role in Sublette County and Wyoming.

Budd's grandson and namesake, a state senator, represented his area's interests by arguing against proposals to sell unused Colorado River tributary water

*Herding cows into the corral as the stock trucks roll in
to load at the Padlock Ranch, Dayton.* —Dan Abernathy

37

to downstream interests in Nevada, California, and Arizona. Knowing water is the lifeblood of the arid West, Dan Budd and his fellow ranchers vociferously oppose Nevada's recurrent offer to buy Colorado River water.

The Colorado River Puzzle

The Colorado River, with its headwaters in Wyoming, provides water for municipal, domestic, and agricultural use in seven western states and Mexico. There are two huge reservoirs on the main stem of the river—Lake Powell, behind the Glen Canyon Dam at Lee's Ferry, Arizona; and Lake Mead, behind the Hoover Dam on the Arizona-Nevada border. Both are operated by the U.S. Bureau of Reclamation.

The "Law of the River," a complex set of guidelines developed between 1922 and 1992, includes several key elements that affect Wyoming water use. The 1922 Colorado River Compact apportions 7.5 million acre-feet annually to the Lower Basin states of California, Arizona, and Nevada and an equal amount to the Upper Basin states of Wyoming, Colorado, Utah, and New Mexico. The Boulder Canyon Project Act of 1928 provided for construction of Hoover Dam and divided the water to be used by Lower Basin states, and the Mexican Treaty of 1944 stipulated that 1.5 million acre-feet be delivered to Mexico annually.

Other rulings, including a U.S. Supreme Court decree, provide further details for the way Colorado River water is apportioned. The U.S. Bureau of Reclamation said the Lower Basin states must not use more than the 7.5 million acre-feet allowed by law. However, in 1991 those three states neared their limit, consuming 7.1 million acre-feet of water. California and Nevada both used more water than they were entitled to, but Arizona allowed the excess use because it didn't need its entire portion.

Meanwhile, Wyoming and other Upper Basin states took a dim view of proposals by California to increase its use of water from the river.

In the early 1990s, Wyoming found itself embroiled in numerous court battles over management of the North Platte, Wind, and Big Horn rivers, but the Colorado has been the cause of even bigger lawsuits. Wyoming's top state water officials agree that resolving the issues surrounding the Colorado River promises to become their next big challenge.

One concern is that Wyoming generally uses only half of the Colorado River water to which it is entitled. That water originates in the state on the Green, Sandy, Little Sandy, Bear, and Little Snake rivers. The state wants to protect its legally recognized share, because other states seem constantly to eye Wyoming's excess supply.

In November 1992 Nevada water officials told the Wyoming Water Development Association that Nevada would buy all the water Wyoming would sell. With Nevada looking for more water, California already using more than its allotment, and Arizona soon to begin taking its entire share, Wyoming had rising concerns.

California promised to cut consumption, but its water officials said such a change would take up to eighteen years; in the meantime, the state needed a supply. To get the water it needed, California proposed that a water bank be established to help the seven Colorado Compact states meet supply needs during critical periods. Water in the bank would be transferred on a "willing seller/willing buyer" basis. Gordon W. Fassett, Wyoming's state engineer, warned that "if we can be bought, we will" and that Wyoming could lose its water rights.

California also wanted an escrow account. The big water consumers in California would put money into the account for each acre-foot of water used in excess of regular appropriation. The money in the escrow account would be apportioned to each state along the river system for any impact associated with the extra water use. The money would fund water conservation and environmental protection measures, help create recreational opportunities, and ensure firm water supplies for the interstate water bank, among other purposes.

In years when Lake Powell and Lake Mead hold enough water to meet Lower Basin needs (as is usually the case), Wyoming would gain the escrow payment and would not really lose anything. If Lake Mead's water level should fall, however, the Upper Basin states would have to release water. In such a scenario, farmers in the Eden Valley, who get part of their supply from Fontenelle Reservoir, and industrial users in southwestern Wyoming could have their supply shut off.

Wyoming and California officials agree that California can meet its needs with its current water appropriation. They disagree on when that can happen. California claims it needs until 2010 to implement conservation measures and become more efficient in the use of water. Wyoming says such reforms could occur much more quickly if California better regulated its river water.

Wyoming is in control only because the Colorado River's headwaters are in the state. Population, and therefore power, rests with the Californians. But by the mid-1990s the power appeared to be shifting; the federal government seemed ready to ignore the long-standing "law of the river" and to take control of the water through the use of such federal regulations as the Endangered Species Act and the Clean Water Act.

Wyoming water officials and residents feared federal officials would force upstream states—Colorado, Utah, New Mexico, and Wyoming—to let water flow down the river, ostensibly for endangered species protection; once in the lower portion of the system, the water could be used for municipal and agricultural needs in Arizona, Nevada, and California.

As Dan Budd told the *Casper Star-Tribune* in November 1993, "Whoever controls the water, controls the growth of the West."

National Cold Spot

Government meteorologists chose Big Piney as the site for an official weather station in the 1930s because it had the coldest year-round average temperature of any spot in the nation. For example, in January 1937 Big Piney had twenty-seven days when the mercury never rose above zero. On New Year's Eve in 1978, Big Piney's termperature plunged to 65 degrees below zero, the coldest day on record for the state. The next day it warmed only slightly, to 63 degrees below zero. The summer of 1993 may have been a record-setter as well—only a few days were frost-free.

Long a stock-raising town, Big Piney got a real shot in the arm in the 1950s when energy companies expanded operations. The *Big Piney Examiner* reported on August 15, 1956, that citizens "literally danced in the streets" when the eighteen-year-old field finally produced gas. Governor Milward L. Simpson turned the valve to release the first cubic foot of gas on its way to an Oregon consumer.

Lontime ranchers Ira and Edna McWilliams, in Snyder Basin near Big Piney. —Dan Abernathy

Marbleton

Ethel Mills Black spent her childhood in Marbleton, just north of Big Piney on Middle Piney Creek. In 1894, at age nine, she left with her family to move back east. Black returned to the Piney country in 1911 to find that much had changed. By then, she wrote in *They Made Wyoming Their Own*, ranches were larger than ever, with more land and more cattle. Ranchers knew they had to feed their stock during the winter, and they fenced as much land as possible, removed the sagebrush, and scattered timothy and redtop seeds to make more hay and increase grasses for feed.

Daniel

Daniel, situated just above the confluence of the Green River and Horse Creek, takes its name from Thomas P. Daniel, who became the community's first postmaster in 1900. The town sprang up near the site of Fort Bonneville, two blockhouses and a stockade built in late summer 1832 by Capt. Benjamin L. E. Bonneville. The fort remained in place until 1839 and stood near the meeting point of several mountain-man rendezvous.

Capt. Benjamin L. E. Bonneville, who built Fort Bonneville near Daniel in 1832.
—Wyoming State Museum

Horse Creek meanders through the valley near the town of Daniel,
where several mountain-man rendezvous took place in the 1830s.

The U.S. Army gave Bonneville a two-year leave to explore the West.
Bonneville said his purpose was to

> Establish prominent points of that country, ascertain the general courses
> . . . of the principal rivers, the location of the Indian tribes and their
> habits, visit the American and British establishments, make myself ac-
> quainted with their manner of trade and intercourse with the Indians,
> finally, endeavor to develop every advantage the country affords and by
> what means they may most readily be opened to the enterprise of our
> citizens.

Bonneville left Independence, Missouri, on May 1, 1832, headed for Pierre's
Hole in northeast Idaho. With a party of 110 men, Bonneville's expedition
was the first to take wagons across South Pass. He used oxen to haul supplies
to the Green River. Bonneville reached the valley of the Green on July 13,
1832, finding it "strewed in every direction with the carcasses of buffaloes,"
Washington Irving wrote in *The Adventures of Captain Bonneville*. From the
Green, Bonneville used a pack string to reach Pierre's Hole.

Bonneville recorded his insight into the commercial activities of the West,
which he termed a "smoke screen." Of course, nobody admitted it at the time,
but the true aim and purpose of the beaver trade was to gain control and
possession of the Northwest Territory. The players were Russia, Great Britain,
and the United States, which had already acquired a huge chunk of the West
with the 1804 Louisiana Purchase.

The captain established Fort Bonneville in an area that had a good view in
all directions and that could expect to be heavily trafficked. However, the

harsh winter weather forced Bonneville to abandon the post soon after its completion. Those not thinking of its strategic location dubbed it Bonneville's Folly or Fort Nonsense.

Rocky Mountain Fur Company Clerk W. A. Ferris gave a description of the fort in *The Adventures of Captain Bonneville*. Intended for a permanent trading post, it sat on an open plain some three hundred yards from the Green River. According to Ferris, the square edifice had "posts or pickets firmly set in the ground, of a foot or more in diameter, planted close to each other, and about fifteen feet in length." Blockhouses sat at two of the corners. "The whole together seems well calculated for the security both of men and horses," Ferris said. Bonneville, according to Irving, competed with the Rocky Mountain Fur Company to get the best territory. At rendezvous in 1833 all trappers gathered amicably. Irving wrote:

> The three rival companies, which for a year past, had been endeavoring to out-trade, out-trap, and out-wit each other, were here encamped in close proximity, awaiting their annual supplies. About four miles from the rendezvous of Captain Bonneville was that of the American Fur Company, hard by which was that also of the Rocky Mountain Fur Company.

Fort Bonneville didn't last, but the site became a small town when the Merna post office opened in 1900.

La Prairie de la Messe

The first Roman Catholic mass celebrated in Wyoming took place July 5, 1840, at the trapper's rendezvous on the upper Green River, about three miles east of present US 189 and two miles south of the Daniel town cemetery. The celebrant was Jesuit missionary Father Pierre De Smet.

De Smet, born in Termonde, Belgium, on January 31, 1801, came to the United States in his youth as a missionary for the Society of Jesus. He went west in response to Flathead Indian appeals for instruction, arriving at rendezvous with a supply train on June 30, 1840.

Before an altar of green boughs and flowers overlooking the junction of the Green River and Horse Creek, Father De Smet addressed his listeners in French and English. He also communicated with the native Americans. During mass the Canadian voyageur-trappers sang in French and Latin while the Indians chanted in their languages.

On July 5, 1925, religious leaders dedicated a cross to commemorate "La Prairie de la Messe" in memory of Father De Smet. The monument sits upon the rocky benchland above Horse Creek, where the rendezvous occurred, and provides a wide vista of the creek (or "crick," as it's usually pronounced in Wyoming) as it snakes through the valley toward Pinedale.

Father Pierre De Smet, the first "Black Robe" to arrive in Wyoming in 1840. A lake near Sheridan is named for the Jesuit missionary. —Wyoming State Museum

This monument at the Daniel Cemetery marks the location where Father Pierre De Smet conducted mass on July 5, 1840, at the trapper rendezvous on Horse Creek. Horse Creek lies in the valley below the hillside location of the service.

Rock Springs—Hoback Junction

Three roads scoot up the west side of Wyoming's Lincoln and Sublette counties. The central route, US 189, runs through LaBarge, Big Piney, Marbleton, and Daniel. It parallels the Green River and may be accessed via Wyoming 372, which heads northwest from the town of Green River, to the historic Oregon Trail sites of Names Hill, the Mormon Ferry, Emigrant Springs, the Sublette Crossing, and the Lombard Ferry. To the west US 89, which enters Wyoming from Utah west of Kemmerer, bisects the Star Valley. And to the east US 191 connects Rock Springs with Jackson Hole, passing through Eden, Farson, Boulder, and Pinedale. The central and eastern routes join just north of Daniel, and the western route joins them at Hoback Junction.

Traveling US 191 is an adventure in open spaces. From Rock Springs north, the desert is home to wild horses, antelope, and thousands of head of sheep. The distances are vast and the vistas sharp in this alkali and sagebrush country. At Eden the land is lush with alfalfa, its growth made possible by the 28,000-acre Seedskadee Irrigation Project connected to Fontenelle Reservoir. Huge pivot sprinklers nourish the land, and western Wyoming officials closely guard the water for these crops from downstream users, who constantly eye the supply.

Eden and Farson

Oregon Trail Greenwood Cutoff

In July 1844 the California-bound Stevens-Townsend-Murphy wagon train, guided by Isaac Hitchcock and eighty-one-year-old Caleb Greenwood, headed southwest from South Pass, traveling parallel to today's Wyoming 28. Greenwood, who knew the country from his days as a trapper in the 1920s, took the emigrants across roughly fifty miles of semiarid desert, passing close to the town of Farson. Their route differed from that taken by most westbound emigrants; by continuing west instead of heading south to Fort Bridger, the party saved about five or six days' traveling time.

Of the estimated 30,000 Forty-niners traveling overland in the California gold rush, nearly two-thirds followed the route, first known as the Greenwood Cutoff. Because of an error in Joseph E. Ware's 1849 guidebook, Greenwood's path ultimately became known as the Sublette Cutoff. It split from the main trail at a location northwest of Farson called the "Parting of the Ways." However, the various branching points in western Wyoming were not true "part-

Highway road signs, Wyoming 28 west of Farson.

ings," as all the shortcuts eventually rejoined the main westbound route. In reality the Oregon and California trails didn't divide until a point in Idaho. The Mormon Trail forked near Fort Bridger.

The Greenwood-Sublette Cutoff roughly parallels Wyoming 28 from Farson west to its junction with Wyoming 372. It then generally follows Wyoming 372 to US 189 near Frontier, where it runs north of the present highway. The route heads into the Tunp Range, crossing the Ham's Fork of the Green south of Commissary Ridge and leaving Wyoming near Cokeville. A marker on US 191 about ten miles north of Farson denotes the Sublette Cutoff; the Oregon Trail swale is clearly visible on the ridge to the east, with the Wind River Range to the north.

Several other shortcuts pioneered during the western migration include the Kinney, Slate Creek, and Dempsey-Hockaday cutoffs. All headed roughly west from Farson to Cokeville, following any number of drainages over Oyster Ridge and Rock Creek Ridge. Emigrants taking one of the cutoffs faced a fifty-mile dry stretch between the Little Sandy River and the Green. They camped by day and started their journey in the evening, driving through the night and all the next day. By the second evening they would be at the Green, having maintained a walking pace beside their oxen or mules of about two miles per hour.

A Tough River Crossing

Ferries operated at many points to carry Oregon Trail travelers across the Green River. The Green itself was never bridged, as was the North Platte near Casper. Crossing the mighty river was treacherous, even deadly, during the period of the great migration. It remained daunting in 1993, as members of the Historic Trails wagon train found when they followed the Oregon Trail from Independence, Missouri, to Independence, Oregon. At the Green, the only major river they attempted or intended to ford, they found firsthand how difficult wagon travel was.

Ben Kern, driving his Percheron team, headed into the swift water, following wagon captain Morris Carter of Casper. As Carter picked a route, Kern followed, whipping, cajoling, talking to, and remonstrating with his team. The big horses made it across, but at one point they had to swim, the Conestoga wagon floating behind them.

Carter's other wagon drivers, who happened to be his teenage daughters, didn't fare so well. Ivy Carter's wagon got hung up on rocks not far out into the river. Her passengers, tourists along for the adventure, were rescued by horseback riders, who helped them out of the wagon and gave them a ride to the bank. Airian Carter and her passenger, her sister Oneta, also had to be rescued when their wagon came apart after getting stuck in a deep, rocky hole. The wagon itself got a tug from a Wyoming Army National Guard truck, though horses could have pulled it free if the Guard hadn't been present.

Katrena Carter, the youngest driver in the party at age fourteen, borrowed Ben Kern's whip and had her path picked. She was determined to make it across the river with her team and wagon. Both her dad and Kern said they think she would have done just that, but Morris Carter decided two wagons stuck in the Green were enough for one day, and he made Katrena cross on the highway bridge.

Jim Bridger and Brigham Young Meet

The Little Sandy crossing just west of Farson is the site of an historic meeting on June 28, 1847, between Mormon prophet Brigham Young and mountain man Jim Bridger. Bridger, who ran a trading post on Black's Fork, invited Young and his flock of Latter-day Saints to settle in the Bridger Valley so the fort would have a population base with which to trade. Young declined because, in order to escape the persecution that dogged the Mormons, he needed land no one else would seek. Bridger told Young about the Salt Lake Valley, a largely useless alkali basin the mountain man had discovered in 1825.

Jim Bridger, mountain man.
—Wyoming State Museum

A granite monument with a bronze plaque at Farson marks the overnight camp spot where the Bridger-Young conference took place. According to legend, a skeptical Bridger offered $1,000 for the first bushel of corn grown in the Salt Lake Valley. The legend doesn't say whether he paid off on his bet when Young delivered the corn.

Directly south of the Bridger-Young monument is the site of the Big Sandy Pony Express Station, burned by Indians in 1862.

A Fight at Simpson's Hollow

When the Mormons under Brigham Young settled in the Salt Lake Valley in 1847 it was Mexican territory, which was fine as far as Young's followers were concerned. The end of the Mexican War and ensuing peace treaty of 1848 put that land—and therefore the Mormons—back in the fold of the hated United States. Young's followers responded by forming the State of Deseret in 1849, an action Congress ignored when it created Utah Territory in September 1850, with portions of present-day Wyoming in it. Brigham Young became governor in February 1851, and Mormons held most other territorial offices, too. However, two of the three district judges didn't follow the Mormon faith, and they charged the Saints with various murders and other treasonable acts.

Soon after President James Buchanan took office in 1857, he appointed new territorial leaders not connected with the Mormon Church. Buchanan sent an army of 2,500 men to accompany the new governor, Alfred Cumming, and other officials to ensure their installation at Salt Lake City. As Cumming started toward Utah in July 1857, Brigham Young celebrated the first decade of settlement in Utah with several thousand of his followers. The festivities went awry when Young heard an army was on its way with the new leaders. The Mormons made plans to defend their settlements.

Col. E. B. Alexander, in charge of the first military detachment, headed toward Utah on July 18 and reached Ham's Fork on the Green, about thirty-five miles east of Fort Bridger, on September 28. There he established Camp Winfield and awaited further orders. Almost immediately the Mormons sent out a squadron to annoy and harass the military.

Meanwhile, changes in leadership delayed the rest of the U.S. troops. Col. Albert Sidney Johnston took command in late August, but the squad halted to obtain horses and provisions for a winter campaign, as Young said the army would not be allowed to set foot in the Great Salt Lake Valley.

While Alexander awaited Johnston's arrival, one confrontation with the Mormons took place at Simpson's Hollow, a depression in the nearly flat landscape along Wyoming 28 west of Farson. On October 5, 1857, Mormon raiders captured a wagon train headed for Johnston's army. The attackers burned the wagons and freight, then burned Fort Bridger and retreated toward Salt Lake. Johnston's army continued to the fort site and survived a harsh winter with limited provisions. Eventually, and without further major conflict, the new leaders took their positions in Utah.

The Lander Road

F. W. Lander supervised construction of the Lander Cutoff, the first government-engineered and -financed road in Wyoming. It went from Rocky Ridge, east of South Pass, to Fort Hall, Idaho, and provided a shorter emigrant route. Officially the route was known as the Fort Kearny, South Pass, and Honey Lake Road.

A monument on US 191, just north of its junction with Wyoming 351, marks the Lander Cutoff as it crosses the highway. Lander's road roughly parallels Wyoming 351, crosses it near Marbleton, then runs north of Wyoming 350 over the Salt Range and into the Star Valley, exiting Wyoming near Afton.

Lander and fourteen men, including six engineers, left South Pass on July 15, 1857, and began exploring the wagon route. By the end of summer the group had investigated sixteen mountain passes, surveyed the Wasatch Mountains, and discovered several possible wagon routes. The one Lander preferred went from South Pass along the Sandy and Green rivers to Thompson Pass. It entered Idaho, crossed the headwaters of the Blackfoot and Portneuf rivers, and continued to Ross Fork. Lander liked this corridor because of the avail-

Brig. Gen. Frederick W. Lander, who led the development of Wyoming's first government-built road. The route started at South Pass and provided a northern pathway through the Star Valley to Idaho.
—Wyoming State Museum

50

ability of grass, timber, and pure water. He found plenty of fish and game and believed the route could also possibly accommodate a railroad line.

On June 14, 1858, eleven months after he first stood at South Pass, Lander and his men started constructing the wagon road. His crew of Mormon laborers, lumbermen, and bridge builders from Maine dug, chopped, and blasted their way into Idaho, building fifteen miles of road a day. The rapid progress was possible, at least in part, because much of the country they crossed just west of South Pass sloped gently. Sagebrush and greasewood covered the land.

In 1859, the first year it was open, the Lander Road had 13,000 Oregon-bound travelers. It remained in use as late as 1912.

New Fork and Boulder

Just north of the junction of US 191 and Wyoming 351 near the New Fork River are the remnants of the community of New Fork and the old Valhalla Dance Hall. The ghost town's false-fronted buildings are reminders of livelier days.

John Vible and Louis Broderson settled in 1888 near the confluence of the New Fork and East Fork rivers. Vible built the Valhalla Dance Hall, which he named after the Norse heaven populated by heroes slain in battle. For years

Valhalla Dance Hall, New Fork. —State Historic Preservation Office

the huge building hosted dances and political rallies. Tragedy reared its ugly head when diphtheria broke out among the Vibles before Christmas 1915. Before the disease ran its course, three of Vible's children had died, and John Vible succumbed soon after to Bright's disease. The store closed, and the New Fork post office moved north to the small town of Boulder, which already boasted a mercantile store, big hotel, dance hall, and blacksmith shop. The land around New Fork remains in use for ranching operations.

For decades, the Valhalla sat empty or stored equipment, but in 1977 the dances resumed. Ranchers moved their machinery out of the hall, and the old building's cast-metal ceiling, wood paneling, and balustraded balcony reverberated again with the beat of music.

Pinedale

Mountain men and Indians are the first people known to have spent time in the Pinedale area. They gathered for rendezvous on Horse Creek and likely camped and grazed their horses near the future townsite. Mountain men and Indians were wanderers by nature, so no permanent homes were established in the neighborhood until the arrival of the cattlemen.

Like most other towns of western Wyoming, Pinedale started as a ranch that happened to double as a post office. In Pinedale's case, that was the Bob Graham ranch, where the post office opened May 5, 1899. The town organized in 1904 and officially incorporated in 1912. In Pinedale's infancy, each person who promised to erect a building received two lots. Nicknamed the "City Beautiful," Pinedale became the county seat when Sublette County organized in 1921. It edged Big Piney for the honor, even though that community existed long before Pinedale came along.

Taking the cows home through Pinedale, 1991. —Dan Abernathy

The First White Men

Sixty-one Astorians of the American Fur Company, accompanied by Pierre Dorion, his Indian wife, and their two young sons, are believed to have been the first white men to enter Sublette County. The Astorians crossed the Rocky Mountains and on September 26, 1811, camped twenty-eight miles north of Pinedale, just where the valley narrows. There they met and traded with Snake Indians and killed some buffalo, curing the meat for their journey.

After this hiatus, three legendary trappers—John Hoback, Jacob Reznor, and Edward Robinson—guided the party down the stream and through the canyon that now bear Hoback's name. The travelers followed the Hoback for two days, watching as it swelled to a river. The stream meandered among rocks and precipices, and the trappers had to ford often, usually at great peril to themselves.

The steep sides of the canyon made travel difficult, as horses sometimes lost their footing and plunged down the slope. Eventually the Astorians reached another river, "which from its rapidity and turbulence, had received the name of the Mad River," Washington Irving wrote in *Astoria*. The party greeted the Mad—or Snake—River with delight. "The Canadian voyageurs rejoiced at the idea of once more launching themselves upon their favorite element, of exchanging their horses for canoes, and of gliding down the bosoms of rivers, instead of scrambling over the backs of mountains," Irving wrote.

The tortuous route taken by the Astorians in 1811 roughly follows US 189 between Bondurant and Jackson.

A year later, on October 10, 1812, Robert Stuart of the Astor firm and six companions camped at a site near Pinedale. They were on their way back to St. Louis from Fort Astoria with news of the fort's failure. By chance, on October 22, 1812, Stuart and his party ambled through the Rocky Mountains near the broad swale later known as South Pass. But Stuart didn't really know where he was, and more than a decade passed before that key to western migration became clearly identified, although Indians undoubtedly used it.

The First Protestant Sermon

North of Pinedale, just where the valley narrows to cross the pass before the highway drops into Bondurant, the Rev. Samuel Parker delivered the first Protestant service in the Rocky Mountains. The date: Sunday, August 23, 1835.

Jim Bridger, Kit Carson, and their brigade of trappers listened to Parker's preaching with the proper respect—until they saw a herd of buffalo. The mangy beasts moved across the sage, and before Parker could give the benediction, the men were on their horses chasing the bison down into the basin known as Jackson's Little Hole, which is now the site of Bondurant. No preacher could hold the attention of mountain men when they had an opportunity to "make some meat." Bridger, Carson, and their comrades had climbed into their robes with no food in their bellies enough times that they weren't about to spend time at a church service if the meat walked right past them. The more pious among them, such as Jedediah Smith, might have quickly given thanks for the bounty as they rushed to make a kill.

Bondurant

Located in a lush valley in the heart of the Bridger-Teton National Forest, Bondurant is named for a prominent early resident. B. F. Bondurant moved to the area in about 1900, established a store and post office, and ran a dude operation in a twelve-room, two-story log house with an organ in the living room.

Sarah Bondurant made fine soda biscuits, light bread, and cottage cheese with cream and nutmeg. Four tame antelope and four little black bears entertained the guests. The dude ranch—a place where Easterners could ride horses, live in log cabins, and pretend they were Westerners—was in business perhaps by 1904, making it one of the earliest operations of its kind in Wyoming.

Steve Sikes, Upper Green River. —Dan Abernathy

Mailboxes, Merna Junction. —Dan Abernathy

White civilization came to the upper reaches of North Beaver Creek near Bondurant in 1861, when Charles Davis and his partner built a cabin and began prospecting for gold. William K. Roy obtained the property in 1891 and established an Indian trading post in 1893. Native Americans had long favored the valley north of Beaver Creek for camping and used it as a racetrack.

Sagebrush Communications

Living in some of Wyoming's isolated areas can be both a blessing and a curse. People who like wide-open spaces and solitude appreciate Wyoming's expanses, but having to drive seventy or more miles to visit a doctor or to attend a movie can be aggravating. Often miles away from their nearest neighbors, rural residents cheered the arrival of telephone communication. Their first, crude system evolved from the use of barbed-wire fences. The owners attached wires from the fences to their houses and rigged "speakers" for the homes in much the same way children connect two tin cans with a string.

Whenever someone placed a call, the phone rang in every house on the line. That, combined with people's innate curiosity, meant that the intended receiver, plus as many as half a dozen other people, answered to see what was up. Those who listened in (or "rubbered") on other people's calls became known as "rubbernecks."

The telephone connections, even under the best circumstances, left much to be desired. With only two people on the line the sound was fairly clear, but as more people picked up the line it became harder and harder to hear.

According to one story, Sublette County doctor John W. Montrose received a call, which people all along the line knew was for him by the series of short and long rings. Agnes West George continued the tale:

> They all picked up to listen, making it difficult for the doctor to hear where he was needed. Finally, exasperated, he shouted in the mouthpiece, "If you damn rubbernecks will hang up so I can hear, I'll phone each one of you individually when I get back from this call and tell you all about it!"

One constant thing about Wyoming, from its early history into the 1990s, is the security many rural folks feel about their homes. William G. Stepp of Sublette County wrote in *Wyoming's Own*, "We didn't have a key to our house, and I don't think most people ever locked their doors. Once I saw this sign on a bachelor's cabin door: 'Go in and eat all you want, but dam (sic) you wash the dishes.'"

Fish Creek Cow Camp, Upper Green River, with the cowdog in charge of security.
—Dan Abernathy

Hoback Junction

Hoback Canyon and the Hoback River get their name from John Hoback, the Astorians' guide through the region in 1811. Towering cliffs wall the canyon along US 189/191. The highway clings to narrow ledges, sometimes at the very edge of the Hoback River, twisting and turning down the canyon, crossing back and forth over the swirling waters.

A Fight over Wildlife

Managing Wyoming's free-ranging game herds is the task of the Wyoming Game and Fish Department. It's a big job; Wyoming has the largest free-ranging elk herd in the country (it winters in Jackson Hole), the largest herd of pronghorn antelope in the world, and a host of other animals, including rare black-footed ferrets and even rarer Wyoming toads, Rocky Mountain bighorn sheep, moose, mule and white-tailed deer, wild turkeys, ducks, and fish. One past state deputy game warden, Bryan Archer, recalled his first years as a warden:

> I remember asking one of the supervising wardens what were the best hours to work. He told me . . . get out early in the morning. Early morning patrolling is a good time; take your frying pan and a few biscuits and stay out all day, also most of the night, and you will find you haven't covered enough territory when you finally decide to return home in the small hours of the morning.

Game management has never been easy. A century ago near Granite Hot Springs, midway between Bondurant and Hoback Junction on US 189, Jackson Hole residents and Bannock Indians skirmished over hunting rights. The confrontation gave Battle Mountain, northwest of Granite Creek, its name. Prior to 1885 game, especially elk, ranged to lower elevations, wintering in the Big Horn Basin, Red Desert, and Green River country. From 1886 to 1893 excessive hunting, settlement, and grazing drove the herds back to high elevations. In the 1890s Wyoming established game laws that restricted the number of animals people could kill each year.

Shoshone and Bannock Indians immediately protested that the Fort Bridger treaty of July 3, 1868, guaranteed them the right "to hunt upon the unoccupied public lands of the United States so long as game may be found thereon." In early 1895 Bannock Indians from Idaho entered Wyoming to kill animals and gather hides. In Jackson Hole the Bannocks and Shoshone, threatened with arrest for game-law violations, faced officers. Both sides had Winchesters. The Indians left, but Sheriff William F. Manning telegrammed the U.S. secretary of war that if the government wouldn't keep Indians from hunting out of season, he would.

True to his word, Manning, without warrants, arrested several small bands of Shoshone and Bannock. The Indians appeared before Jackson Justice of the Peace Frank A. Rhodes and were convicted of illegal hunting. Jackson

Judge Percy W. Metz killed this animal, known as the Bridger Lake Moose, using special moose license No. 1. It was the first moose killed during the 1921 hunting season. —Wyoming State Museum

authorities held four Shoshone Indians but sent the Bannocks to Evanston, where the arrests were voided because they had taken place without benefit of a warrant.

The situation was far from settled. On July 25, 1895, Justice Rhodes issued an arrest warrant for four Indians, including Bannock chief Race Horse. Manning immediately formed a posse of between sixteen and forty residents. The vigilantes followed the Indians into the Hoback Basin, surprised them at sunup, and destroyed hundreds of deer, elk, and antelope hides. One circle of the sun later, the posse started back toward Jackson with the Indians in custody. Everyone rode, and as the caravan passed along a winding path through the timber at Granite Creek, a yell signaled the Indians.

Shots flew in all directions as horses and riders flashed among the trees. All the Indians but two escaped—one was killed, and another, a small child, was left behind in the melee. The child was taken to Jackson and eventually returned to the tribe. The skirmish sent fear racing through the hearts of whites living in Jackson Hole and gave Battle Mountain its name.

When news of the affair reached the East Coast, a New York paper solemnly reported: ALL RESIDENTS IN JACKSON HOLE, WYOMING, MASSACRED. Of course, that report was nowhere near the truth.

Chief Race Horse, later arrested by the posse, gained his freedom in state district court, which ruled that his Indian treaty rights allowed hunting. The

State of Wyoming appealed the case to the Wyoming Supreme Court. There justices reversed the lower court decision, and the case set the precedent establishing state ownership of wildlife.

Smoot—Hoback Junction

The "Star of All Valleys"

Star Valley, an isolated glen on Wyoming's western border, is some five to seven miles wide, fifty miles long, and watered by the Salt River. Its first white inhabitants were some of Wilson Price Hunt's Astorians, who worked the area looking for beaver as early as 1812. Streams in the area are named for explorers and trappers John Day, John Hoback, and Jedediah Smith.

From the late 1850s until the late 1860s, emigrants bound for Oregon passed through Star Valley over the Lander Road, but only when Brigham Young included the region in his colonization project did actual settlement begin. The population here is still predominantly Mormon.

As the Utah Eden became crowded, Young, to enforce his decree that church members till the soil, sent emissaries to adjoining regions to look for suitable lands. In 1877 Apostle Moses Thatcher and Bishop William B. Preston visited the upper Salt River. They "found neither trappers nor settlers in the valley, but a large number of Shoshone Indian wickiups, built of willows; no Indians, however, were in sight," according to a 1937 article by Mary Geer.

Before 1870 the Shoshone spent summers in Star Valley. Wyoming historian Velma Linford wrote, "They spoke of it as a land where grass was plentiful for their horses and there was a 'heap' of game, fish and fine water to drink. Legend has it that one Shoshone, known as Indian John, led the first white man [Thatcher] to the spot."

On August 29, 1878, Thatcher, Preston, and Brigham Young Jr. stopped teams on the west bank of the Salt River about five miles west of present-day Afton. Young dedicated the valley as a gathering place for the saints.

On May 7, 1879, Thatcher and Charles C. Rich, both apostles of the Latter-day Saints (LDS) church, received appointments to supervise founding of the settlements in the upper Salt River Valley. They began that summer, building three small cabins. Thatcher, standing on a rocky point overlooking the Mormons' new home, is remembered by some to have said, "I hereby name this valley Star Valley . . . because it is the star of all valleys." Another version of Thatcher's comments comes from Linford, who wrote: "When God made the world, He reserved the finest part and hid it among these mountains. It shall be called Star Valley, for it is truly the star of all valleys."

Smoot, Wyoming, 1916. The tall man by the burro is Slim Oakley, who later became sheriff. —Wyoming State Museum

A contradictory tale says the area was originally dubbed "*Starved* Valley" because the earliest settlers had insufficient food during their first winter there. Still other stories suggest that some cowboys, lying under the stars one night, named the valley for the glittering canopy and that the five peaks at the east end of the valley resemble a star.

Afton comprised thirty sections of ten acres each at the time of its earliest survey in 1880. That same year mail service started in Star Valley, with a regular route to Afton from Montpelier, Idaho. But it was not until Congress passed the Edmunds Anti-Polygamy Act of 1882 that migration to the area began in earnest.

There was no effective enforcement of laws against polygamy in Wyoming territory. Quite the contrary, the region wanted settlers, and men with several families were effective colonizers and stable citizens in a frontier community. The more who came, the better the chance that Wyoming could soon become a state. Federal authorities attempting to prohibit polygamy received little cooperation in Wyoming. The Star Valley thus became known as a safe haven for Mormons seeking to avoid harassment.

The tenuous settlement at Afton was joined in 1885 by several newly formed communities, including Fairview, Freedom, Glenco (now Thayne), Cotton-wood (now Smoot), and Grover. In 1886 C. D. Cazier, A. Lu Hale, Harvey

Dixon, and others conducted a new survey of Afton under the direction of Henry Harmon. According to a Works Progress Administration (WPA) report issued half a century later, "A rope was measured by a square and bearings were taken from noonday sun and north star, guided by reference to the almanac." The WPA officials, who conducted their own survey, found the original version to be only four or five feet off despite the primitive methods used.

The Cheese Industry

On August 22, 1900, a creamery opened in Afton. It was the beginning of what would become a major industry in the isolated valley. Dairy cattle herds increased, and residents made butter and cheese from their excess milk and cream. They used barrel churns to make the butter, which they formed in wooden molds. Cheese making generally took place in galvanized laundry tubs, with a smaller vat placed inside a larger one. The small vat held milk, and the larger one held water. A fire under the vats heated the milk double-boiler style.

The cheese makers watched the curds to know when their product was done. Then they molded it in hoops and cheesecloths, squeezed it in a wooden press to separate the whey from the cheese, spread butter on the cheese (because they didn't have wax), and placed it on the shelf. At first, cheese was made solely for the family's own use, but as milk yields increased the settlers started selling their excess cheese. Freighters took the cheese to Evanston, Almy, and Montpelier, Idaho, where it was sold in stores and door-to-door.

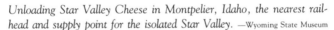

Unloading Star Valley Cheese in Montpelier, Idaho, the nearest railhead and supply point for the isolated Star Valley. —Wyoming State Museum

Some dairymen built equipment for cheese and butter making and supplemented their own supplies with milk and cream they purchased from neighbors.

In 1900, the first officially incorporated creamery in Star Valley—the Burton Creamery—opened in Afton. By 1913 the Jensen Creamery Corporation was in business in Thayne. That firm sold stock and changed its name to the Mutual Creamery Association. The association built three additional plants and distributed products under the "Maid O'Clover" brand name for about fifteen years.

By 1920 nine cheese factories were operating in the valley, and in 1924 the Star Valley Dairymen Association formed with the intention of making Swiss cheese. This type of cheese brought more profit because it could be made only in certain localities—those that, like the Star Valley, had an absence of certain minerals in the grass and water.

In March 1926, Kraft-Phenix Cheese Corporation bought the Burton cheese factories. At that time thirty farmers from the Freedom area joined efforts to establish a Swiss cheese factory. Dairymen bought stock and signed contracts to sell milk to the factory for a five-year period. That October work commenced on the building, but when costs exceeded projections some of the original backers dropped their support. Mary Geer wrote in 1937, "Wagers ranged from a Stetson hat to half a farm that there would never be a can of milk received in the creamery."

Nevertheless, work continued, and on August 22, 1927, the factory was completed and ready to receive milk. Skeptics insisted the operation wouldn't run for six months. Processing Swiss cheese is a slow affair, as the cheese has to cure for two to four months before going to market. During that time producers got no money.

Finally, at Christmas 1927, the first sleigh load of Star Valley Swiss cheese made its way over the Salt Range headed for Soda Springs, Idaho, for eventual shipment to Portland, Oregon. The cheese went for 54 cents a pound. Geer reported:

> Debts were paid, and the New Year began auspiciously as prosperity beamed on the shareholders. Stock rose in value from $50 to $144 a share. Only shareholders could sell their milk to the factory, and some of the people who had given their stock away to be relieved of the responsibility, when it was valued at $50 a share, now bought stock again at $144 a share.

Two other Star Valley Swiss cheese factories opened, one in Osmond and the other in Thayne. The number of dairy producers selling milk to the three units soon grew from two dozen to 433. Three Swiss brothers—Ernest, Fred, and Paul Brog—ran the operation. In 1931 Kraft-Phenix Company sold its plant at Freedom to Star Valley Swiss Cheese Company. Between 1932 and 1937 Star Valley produced about one million pounds of Swiss cheese annually. In later years the Thayne cheese plant processed Italian cheeses such as

mozzarella, provolone, and ricotta, all of which could be marketed more quickly than Swiss cheese. Several cheese operations rose and fell through the years until 1993, when the plant produced about 1.5 million pounds of cheese per month for markets across the United States. Then the company announced its closing because local dairymen could not supply the milk needed to keep the factory operating. Star Valley farmers supplied about 100,000 gallons of milk daily, but the plant needed 600,000 gallons to operate efficiently.

Grey's River

Grey's River originally took its name from John Day, the Virginian trapper who accompanied Wilson Price Hunt to Astoria in 1811 and who set out with Robert Stuart on the return trip the next year. Before the Stuart party progressed far up the Columbia, Day went insane and was taken back to Astoria. Later, some historians say, he trapped for Astor on the headwaters of the Snake and spent about eight years in the Star Valley region. Although the river there first went by the name Day, it soon became Grey's River.

Coe and Carter, a major tie-cutting company of the 1800s, established a camp near the mouth of the Grey's on the Snake River about 1881 and built a commissary a mile and a half up the Salt River from its mouth. Lumberjacks hacked trees into ties, then floated them down the rivers for use in construction and maintenance of the West's railroads.

Floating ties down a river is a risky proposition, however. More than one tie hack lost his life by slipping beneath the logs and drowning. Once Coe and Carter lost a million ties when the boom holding them near Idaho Falls broke, allowing the ties to escape into the Snake River.

In the 1920s, Star Valley residents got riled over a proposal to build a dam in the narrows of the Grey's. The *Star Valley Independent* reported December 17, 1920:

> The important feature of the proposition is that if the dam were built it is sure that immediately every water user in the [upper and lower] valleys would have his water measured to him at the head of the ditch the year round and would get only as much water as is appropriated to him by the state. It is the opinion of every man talked to that he could not farm on that amount. In fact some have gone so far as to say that they could not get the water to their land if they only had the amount appropriated.

A Place of Freedom

Freedom lies on the state line, with the west side in Idaho and the east side in Wyoming. In the summer of 1879, when Mormon Apostles Thatcher and Rich entered the Star Valley over the Crow Creek route from Bear Lake Valley, Idaho, they built the first wagon road connecting this area with settlements farther south. As other Mormons arrived, one who surveyed his new domain declared enthusiastically, "Here we shall find freedom"—and so the

settlement got its name. Later, when federal authorities in Idaho prosecuted polygamists, the town proved that its freedom was more than a title: During a raid, residents on the Idaho side could step across the street into Wyoming and avoid arrest.

A century later the Freedom Arms gun-manufacturing plant opened, providing a lucrative business for the community.

Alpine

In the fall of 1812, Robert Stuart and his companions, on their way back to Missouri from Astoria, passed through the Alpine area as they attempted to shake off a party of Indians who harassed them for several hundred miles. On the Snake River, near its junction with the Salt, they lost their horses to the Indians. There they burned their heavy baggage, ascended the Snake on improvised rafts, made their way north to Hunt's (Teton) Pass, and eventually turned eastward on foot into Jackson Hole. They were damn glad to see the familiar "Pilot Knobs," as they called the Tetons.

Homesteaders claimed land around Alpine in 1912, and the town soon developed in the area where a ferry provided a crossing on the Snake River as it had since 1889. The ferry lasted until 1914, when the first steel bridge spanned the river. The builders had planned to errect the bridge in Wyoming, but the particulars of the river channel dictated that one end be in Wyoming and the other end in Idaho. Each state paid $10,500 for the work.

Alpine's original layout placed part of its main street in Wyoming and the rest in Idaho. Then, in 1941 Congress authorized construction of the Palisades Dam by the U.S. Bureau of Reclamation, and water in the reservoir would flood the area. The 1914 bridge and the entire communtiy had to move east into Wyoming.

Wyoming 22 and US 26/89/191
Jackson—Yellowstone National Park
43 miles

In the Footsteps of Fur Trappers

Traveling homeward on the Missouri River with Lewis and Clark in 1806, John Colter made it as far east as the Mandan villages before the lure of the West caught him again and he began to retrace his steps. The following year Colter, at the urging of Manuel Lisa, made a solitary journey hundreds of miles long that took him through much of northwest Wyoming. His are the first

With a dog on the wide-plank floor and their guns hanging on the log walls of this cabin, a group of early trappers relaxes by the fire. —Teton County Historical Center

white feet known to have walked through this the country, zigging and zagging over mountain passes and along wild rivers. Colter crossed the Wind River Mountains and passed through Jackson Hole twenty years before David Jackson's name became associated with the deep valley. Eventually Colter went through portions of Yellowstone National Park.

It wasn't until William Henry Ashley's fur brigades scoured the West's streams starting in the 1820s that the hole became a popular place. In 1829 William Sublette and David E. Jackson, owners (with Jedediah Smith) of the Rocky Mountain Fur Company, met at the large natural lake near the Tetons, and most agree that's when Jackson's Hole and Jackson's Lake got their names. Trappers called the upper Snake River country Jackson's Big Hole and the area along the Hoback, Jackson's Little Hole. Eventually the possessive dropped from the names.

An Outlaw Here and There

Isolated by mountain passes and having a short summer season, Jackson Hole rarely received visitors after the decline of the fur trade in the 1840s. For nearly thirty years, few men ranged into the region. There were some who refused to quit trapping, and others came to the valley to do a little mining, but it wasn't until the late 1870s that Jackson Hole saw much activity. Then a loose-knit gang of horse thieves moved into the territory.

The leader was Harvey Gleason, who went by William C. "Teton" Jackson, a name taken from the country into which he moved stolen animals. He spent his early life in the East. He was born in Rhode Island in 1855, had a scrape with the law in Joplin, Missouri, and may have run pack trains and scouted with Gen. George Crook in the 1876 campaign against Sioux Indians.

The *Chicago Herald* called Jackson "the premier horse-thief of the mountains." Jackson and his gang stole horses in Nevada, Utah, and Idaho, then took them to Jackson Hole or Teton Basin for rebranding. When the fresh brands healed, the men drove the horses east onto the plains of Wyoming or South Dakota to sell. Once there, the gang reversed its operation. It was a slick action that involved a number of outlaws. Some reports say as many as three hundred men took part in the business.

In 1883 one of Jackson's cohorts, Ed Trafton, concocted a plan to kidnap President Chester Arthur and hold him for ransom when the president visited Yellowstone National Park. Whether Jackson supported Trafton's suggestion isn't known, but Arthur's contingent to western Wyoming included a large delegation of heavily armed military and civilian guides.

Jackson and Harry Thompson crossed snow-covered Teton Pass in February 1884 to report the death of Robert Cooper to authorities in Eagle Rock (now Idaho Falls), Idaho. Jackson and Thompson said they quarreled with Cooper, whom they killed in self-defense. Deputy Sheriff Ed Winn and a colleague, Bob Tartar, climbed on horses and made the wintery ride over Teton Pass to Jackson Hole, where they found Cooper's frozen corpse. They couldn't take the body back with them, so they used an axe to chop off the head, which they took as evidence. Although indicted for the murder, Jackson and Thompson won acquittal because of a lack of evidence—the victim's head notwithstanding.

The following year Johnson County sheriff Ed Canton nabbed Jackson as he moved stolen horses through the Big Horn Basin. Canton said Jackson had killed numerous deputy U.S. marshals from Utah and Idaho. By November 5, 1885, Jackson found himself a prisoner at the United States penitentiary in Boise City. But less than a year later, on August 27, 1886, Jackson escaped his prison cell. He dodged the law for a couple of years before Montana authorities collared him near Billings in April 1888 with a herd of fifty-eight horses bearing brands from thirteen different Nevada ranches. He spent four years in prison before getting a pardon. In part because of Teton Jackson's activities, Jackson Hole became known as a hideout for outlaws and horse thieves.

Settlers Claim the Land

The first permanent settlers in Jackson Hole, John Holland and Johnny Carnes, moved in from southern Wyoming in 1883. The two built cabins on the Little Gros Ventre River (known today as Flat Creek, which cuts through the National Elk Refuge).

Johnny Carnes left Ohio after the Civil War and claimed homestead land on Fontenelle Creek near LaBarge, working as a mail carrier. Holland also lived in the LaBarge area, where he made his living trapping in the summer and timbering in the winter. Holland knew of Jackson Hole because he had trapped there in the 1870s.

In the summer of 1883, Holland and Carnes walked up the Green River, crossed Bacon Ridge, and followed the Gros Ventre River to Jackson Hole. That summer they built a cabin for the Carnes family, and the next year they raised one for Holland.

Johnny Carnes, center, was one of the first homesteaders in Jackson Hole, shown here with two unidentified men, although one is believed to be his brother. —Teton County Historical Center

John Holland claimed his homestead in Jackson Hole in 1884, one of the first to do so. —Teton County Historical Center

Carnes and Holland played hosts to the bachelors who constantly surged to Jackson Hole as the area settled. At one such gathering, the men corralled a bunch of elk and made bets as to who could ride them. About forty men assembled to celebrate Thanksgiving in 1888; each brought something for the feast, and all stayed until the food was gone. Stephen Leek, who later made a name for himself as a conservationist, brought a trumpeter swan, which he described as "Swell for size, but Hell for tough."

A Trapper's Trail

The route into Jackson Hole over Teton Pass was part of a well-used trappers' trail. It is now Wyoming 22. Early men in the region called the mountain crossing Hunt's Pass for Wilson Price Hunt, who traversed it in 1811 with the Astorians. The first wagons crossed the pass in the late 1880s.

In 1889 Mormon Bishop Sylvester Wilson of Wilsonville, Utah, joined by several relatives, left his home in search of a better place to raise stock and families. The Wilsons first stopped in Salem, Idaho, where Sylvester's brothers, Nick and Henry, had homes. Nick was in Jackson Hole harvesting hay, so the Wilsons' covered wagons headed north to St. Anthony, Idaho, where the men cut logs for a house. They had it partially built when Nick Wilson returned from Jackson with stories of a grand valley and plenty of hay for cattle.

The families discussed sending the young men with the cattle but ultimately decided that the entire party would move to Jackson Hole for the winter. Some went ahead to put up hay, borrowing a hay-mowing machine and storing the harvest on "Slough Grass" Nelson's ranch, according to a 1949 account by Melvina Wilson Robertson in the *Jackson's Hole Courier*.

It was November before the entire Wilson clan crossed the pass. Moving the six covered wagons from St. Anthony to Jackson Hole took two weeks. In making the crossing, the Wilsons chopped trees to widen the road. They also took the two large wheels from the back of the wagons and put them both on the downhill side to better balance loads on the steep terrain. It took a twelve-horse-hitch to pull one wagon to the top, and on the downward trip they rough-locked the wheels and dragged trees to slow the wagon speed. For many years both grades to the summit could be descended only with the aid of rough locks—large untrimmed trees chained to the wheels to prevent their turning.

The Wilsons reached Jackson too late in the season to build cabins, so those already living in the valley opened their doors. John Carnes, who had just built a new cabin, gave the use of his old one to Sylvester Wilson and his family. Will Crawford shared his cabin with Nick Wilson and family, John Holland took in Selar Cheney and family, and John Cherry opened his home to Sylvester's son, Ervin Wilson, and his family.

The first road over Teton Pass was a one-lane track and difficult for wagons to cross. —Teton County Historical Center

As new families arrived—even until near the turn of the century—they often spent their first Jackson Hole winter in one of the Carnes or Holland homes. Jackson writer Fern Nelson remarked on that tendency in 1976:

> Millie Carnes must have been the most accommodating and agreeable woman in the West. In reading the stories of the early comers to the valley we see time after time, We stayed the first winter in the Johnny Carnes cabin, or, We used John Holland's cabin. Or sometimes we hear they used both. We wonder where the owners stayed?

Holland often went horseback or on snowshoes over Teton Pass to Victor, Idaho, to get mail for Jackson Hole. On one such trip he met Maude Carpenter, whom he married in the 1890s. Not long after their wedding, they sold their homestead and moved to Scio, Oregon. Johnny and Millie Carnes got the patent to their homestead in 1897, but they were no longer in Jackson Hole—in 1895 they moved to the Fort Hall Reservation in Idaho to live on an eighty-acre tract Millie owned. Both the Carnes and Holland homesteads are now a part of the National Elk Refuge lands, just north of Jackson.

Movement over Teton Pass remained a challenge for people wanting to get to Jackson Hole. Troops sent to Jackson during the Bannock scare of 1895 found that their horses could not pull the wagons up the pass, so they hauled them up by hand. In 1901 Uinta County, which at that time included Jackson Hole, appropriated $500 to build a wagon road over the pass. That same year engineers did a road survey, but construction didn't occur until 1905.

Wilson

Wilson, at the foot of Teton Pass on Wyoming 22, is named for Elijah "Uncle Nick" Wilson. Nick spent several childhood years among the Shoshone and later rode for the Pony Express before settling with his family in Jackson Hole. He became the hero of H. R. Driggs's *The White Indian Boy or Uncle Nick Among the Shoshones*.

Wilson's first post office, established in 1898, was managed by Matilda Wilson, Nick's wife. She died a year later, so Nick became postmaster for three years. He also operated the town's hotel and first general store, which the "Gasoline Alley" comic strip once characterized.

Jackson

Jackson, the major town in Jackson Hole, was originally called Marysvale after the settlement's first postmistress, Mary White. The town incorporated in 1901, and by 1909 Jackson had about two hundred people while the Jackson Hole population neared fifteen hundred, according to the first issue of the *Jackson's Hole Courier*, January 28, 1909.

That issue of the newspaper further noted that Jackson Hole had nine post offices, located at Jackson, Cheney, Elk, Moran, Grovont, Zenith, Brooks, Wilson, and Teton. Six-day-a-week mail service came from St. Anthony, Idaho. The schools were "at least up to standard," and Jackson Hole boasted three sawmills on the west side of the valley, the *Courier* reported. Jackson businesses included two general stores, a drugstore, hotel, restaurant, feed and livery barn, blacksmith shop, and saloon. The community had a schoolhouse, a Mormon church, and a clubhouse. The Episcopal mission announced plans to build a church during the summer.

By comparison, in 1990 Jackson had a permanent population of 4,472 but played host to several hundred thousand tourists annually. More than a hundred retail businesses and restaurants, two newspapers, a hospital, and numerous churches served residents and visitors alike. Although the pace and lifestyle had totally changed since the community's early days, some businesses operated out of Jackson's historic homes, and the flock still gathered at the small, dark brown log St. John's Episcopal Church.

A Women's Government

Jackson residents believe theirs was the first town in the nation to have a woman mayor and an all-woman council. In 1920 Grace Miller was a two-to-one winner over Fred Lovejoy in the mayor's race, Rose Crabtree and Mae Deloney were elected two-year councilwomen, and Genevieve Van Vleck and Faustina Haight became one-year councilwomen. Mrs. Crabtree defeated her husband, Henry, but he didn't begrudge her the position; she had done a good job in running the Crabtree Hotel, he told reporters, so he considered her competent to run the town.

Newspapers across the nation reported the election results. The *New York Sun* said the "sole issue was that of sex and the two gun man didn't stand a chance with his wife and her rolling pins." A Boston paper reported, "Governor Calvin Coolidge in an address yesterday referred to the action of the citizens of Jackson, Wyo., in electing women to all town offices and paid a high tribute to the good sense of the people of the town."

Mayor Miller later told reporters, "We were not campaigning for the office because we felt the need of pressing reforms. The voters of Jackson believe that women are not only entitled to equal suffrage, but they are also entitled to equality in the management of government affairs."

Jackson's new elected officials quickly named other women to appointed positions. Pearl Williams Hupp took over as marshal, Marta Winger became town clerk, and Edna Huff served as the town's health officer.

The women didn't let any time slip by after their election. They met to discuss plans for their administration, focusing first on city finances. Learning there was only $200 in the treasury, the leaders checked the books and discovered uncollected taxes and fines. The first evening of their administration,

In 1920 Jackson elected an all-woman town council, believed to be the first town in the nation to do so. The council included, from left, Mae Deloney, Rose Crabtree, Mayor Grace Miller, Faustina Haight, and Genevieve VanVleck. —Teton County Historical Center

notices went out to the delinquents. Impatient for the money to begin flowing, the women personally contacted those who owed. Within two weeks the town had about $2,000 in its treasury.

With funds in hand, the women then set to work on other concerns: The town water supply ran in ditches that often created stagnant pools, posing a health problem; narrow culverts across the ditches in town were inadequate; no garbage disposal system existed; the cemetery was a slatternly operation; and streets needed grading and a few lights for dark nights.

The women took charge of those concerns with the same gusto they displayed in handling the financial crisis, according to Genevieve Parkhurst in *The Delineator*'s September 1922 issue. With the $2,000 they had collected, the women ordered new culverts put into the ditches, had the streets graded, and commissioned board sidewalks to replace pioneer trails through the lush grass. They also organized a clean-up week, during which crews gathered up the refuse and hauled it out of town; established a permanent dumping spot; and passed health laws banning the leaving of garbage in the streets or on vacant lots.

Finally, attention went to the cemetery. Although it was a gorgeous spot for a final resting place, high on the mountain among the aspens, the cemetery had no road connecting it to town. Winter found pallbearers struggling up the steep, icy grade, and in the summertime mourners made the same tough walk under a hot sun. The old site got a face-lift, gaining a new fence, stones to mark the graves, and a road up the hillside. Funding for the road came partially from the Women's Pure Food Club, which devoted its Liberty Bonds at the request of Mayor Miller.

"We simply tried to work together," Miller said of the council's accomplishments. "We put into practice the same thrifty principles we exercise in our own homes. We wanted a clean, well-kept, progressive town in which to raise our families. What is good government but a breathing-place [sic] for good citizenship?"

Tusk Hunting and the World's Largest Elk Herd

Every elk has two ivory teeth called tusks. By 1900 the wasteful practice of tusk hunting was firmly entrenched in Jackson Hole. A loosely knit band of six or seven men killed large numbers of bull elk for their tusks, leaving the meat to rot. The Wyoming game department couldn't stop the tusk hunters, so a group of local residents, concerned with the wanton slaughter of the valley's big bulls, took matters into their own hands. Three men apprehended some "tuskers" and gave them forty-eight hours to get out of Jackson Hole. Those men left, but it wasn't until the Benevolent Protective Order of Elks decreed that the elk tusk should no longer be the symbol of their lodge that tusking really came to a halt.

Concern about the elk herds in Jackson Hole was hardly new. Stephen Leek—the man who served trumpeter swan at Carnes and Holland's 1888 Thanksgiving gathering—made a mark on Jackson Hole through his interest in the scenery and game of the area. A photographer, Leek had many pictures published in national publications. He also went on the lecture circuit to describe the plight of wild animals, particularly elk that starved because of a lack of feed.

Elk feeding along Flat Creek started during the severe winter of 1908–9, when about 20,000 of the animals were starving in Jackson Hole. Valley residents raised $1,000 to buy hay, and the Wyoming State Legislature appropriated $5,000 to purchase additional feed. Heavy snow fell throughout the winter of 1909–10, with avalanches running on Teton Pass as early as January. The snow pushed elk to lower country, where they starved. Ranchers became alarmed and called upon the state to investigate.

Finally Governor Bryant B. Brooks came to Jackson Hole to look over the situation. When he got there the weather had changed and there was a big thaw. Elk that survived the winter were foraging on the south hillsides. Anne McDonald Kent, who was twenty-one that year and making her first trip into Jackson Hole, wrote in Wild Life Magazine, "The dead animals were polluting the air with the odor of decay. It was too late to be of any use."

In answer to an appeal from the Wyoming state game warden, the U.S. Bureau of Biological Survey helped feed the big herds through the next year.

Through Leek's efforts and because of his heart-wrenching photos, the U.S. Biological Survey Elk Refuge—later the National Elk Refuge—received congressional approval in 1912, with an initial allotment of a thousand acres. With increased governmental appropriations and donations from national sportsmen's organizations, the refuge expanded to its present size, 24,000 acres of meadow and foothills. Between 7,000 and 12,000 elk migrate from Yellowstone National Park, the Bridger-Teton National Forest, and Grand Teton National Park annually to winter on the refuge, located adjacent to Jackson east of US 26/89/191.

In the early years of the elk-feeding operation, workers harvested hay from the meadow in summer and gave the animals additional, concentrated foods, including cottonseed cake. In 1943 the refuge accommodated 10,000 elk. By the early 1990s that figured had dropped to about 8,000 head per year. Crews no longer harvest hay from the meadows; instead they let the grasses cure in the fall, to provide forage for the elk until actual feeding operations start, usually in January.

In 1921 the area also became a haven for birds of any species. The National Elk Refuge is one of the spectacular tourist attractions in Jackson Hole. Horse-drawn sleighs haul visitors around and through the huge herd during

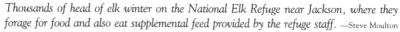

Thousands of head of elk winter on the National Elk Refuge near Jackson, where they forage for food and also eat supplemental feed provided by the refuge staff. —Steve Moulton

the winter. It is one of the best places in Wyoming to observe the natural winter habits of wildlife. Rocky Mountain bighorn sheep, many species of birds (including trumpeter swans), and predators such as coyote and fox are protected from hunters on the refuge as well. To control herd numbers, a limited elk hunting season is now allowed on the refuge each fall.

In winter hundreds of bull elk feed along the highway north of Jackson. Most cows and calves segregate themselves in the center of the range. Some leave the refuge grounds and wander into town; one cow in the winter of 1993 spent a few days on the porch of the Wildlife of the American West Art Museum, then located within the town of Jackson. Some tourists didn't realize the elk was real until they approached too closely and she shook her head or stamped a foot.

Grand Teton National Park

In August 1915 Stephen Mather, head of the National Park Service for the Department of the Interior, and Horace Albright, superintendent of Yellowstone National Park, toured the West. At Moran the two made a spur-of-the-moment decision to head down into Jackson Hole. After seeing the massive Teton Range, Mather asked why they weren't already in the national park.

The following summer Albright returned to the foot of the Tetons with a small party of Washingtonians. They stayed at the hunting lodge of Ben Sheffield, and the view of the Tetons astounded them. Jackson historian Lorraine Bonney wrote, "They were simply left gasping as they realized what they were looking at—a wild, beautiful country with nobody living there except a few ranchers and several dude ranches."

From that day on, Mather and Albright felt the Tetons should be preserved as a national park. It took thirty-five years for the entire area to be set aside, and during that period Jackson Hole residents became sharply divided about the prospect of having another national park in their neighborhood. Like others who enjoyed the natural beauty of Jackson Hole, novelist Owen Wister supported the creation of Grand Teton National Park. He wrote Jackson resident Fritiof Fryxell in 1929: "Many a time I told [President Theodore] Roosevelt that whole place should be a Park, and he quite agreed."

At first Mather and Albright, with support from Wyoming congressman Frank W. Mondell, attempted to extend the boundaries of Yellowstone National Park so that it included the Teton Range. On July 8, 1918, President Woodrow Wilson issued an executive order withdrawing more than 600,000 acres of the Teton National Forest from development. The U.S. Forest Service screamed.

There was little other opposition, however, until 1919, when ranchers raised objections. Senator John Nugent of Idaho, flooded with complaints from Idaho sheepmen who thought (erroneously) that the new park boundary would extend to the Idaho state line, torpedoed legislation that would have added the Tetons to Yellowstone.

In July 1919 Albright conferred with Wyoming governor Robert D. Carey, and the two hit upon a plan to improve roads into Jackson Hole to boost tourism and provide better service for valley residents. Albright and Carey visited Jackson to promote their plans, but local residents were used to and relished their isolation. They opposed new roads and wanted no invasion of commercialism. To his surprise, Albright found a whole community against development and his view of progress. Struthers Burt told Albright, "We just don't want the public and the park in here."

Over the next four years ranchers and the U.S. Bureau of Reclamation engaged in a flurry of activity to develop water for irrigation projects in Jackson Hole and Idaho. It became clear that the area at the base of the Tetons could be widely developed before long. Concern over Idaho's efforts to get control of Jackson Hole water caused some to change their stand on park expansion. Others worried about the building going on along the valley of the Snake River.

By 1923 some of the opposition to park expansion had eased. Struthers Burt now said a national recreation area might be just the thing to protect the land and keep it pristine. A year later sentiment for restricting further growth took a leap forward when Albright learned that John D. Rockefeller would visit Yellowstone. With teenage sons John, Nelson, and Laurance, Rockefeller arrived by Pullman in Gardiner, Montana, where he met Albright. Though under strict orders from his Washington superiors not to present park problems or proposals to Rockefeller, Albright nevertheless let the family catch a glimpse of the Teton Range.

After Rockefeller returned to New York, he wrote Albright about the unsightly roadsides he saw in Yellowstone. The park official replied that workers had left the debris along the roads during construction and that Congress hadn't appropriated adequate funds to clean the mess. Rockefeller said he would provide the money. Over the next four years he anonymously funded the cleanup.

Rockefeller then turned to preserving the land along the Teton Range, launching the Jackson Hole purchasing plan in 1927. Over the next dozen years the Snake River Land Company bought up the land along the base of the Tetons. Rockefeller provided the money, but most people didn't know that until years later. One park historian wrote, "Mr. Rockefeller's sole purpose was to insure the preservation for future public enjoyment of the Jackson Hole region, with its unsurpassed views of the Grand Teton Mountains and its unusual opportunities for the conservation and study of game."

In 1929, fourteen years after Mather and Albright launched their effort, Congress established Grand Teton National Park. It encompassed the mountain range but did not extend to the broad valley west of the Snake River. To

Mount Moran, Grand Teton National Park, with Jackson Lake in the foreground.

protect that basin, which many considered essential wildlife habitat, preservationists began pushing for the creation of Jackson Hole National Monument.

Once again the people of Jackson Hole became bitterly divided. The *Jackson's Hole Courier*, which supported designation of the national monument, was prophetic in its prediction of August 21, 1930: "From our experience have [come] the firm belief that this region will find its highest use as a playground, and in this way will eventually become the greatest wealth-producing region of the state."

By 1933 the Snake River Land Company, the major proponent of the national monument, controlled more than 35,000 acres on both sides of the Snake River, which it bought for an average price of $39 per acre. During congressional debate over the national monument issue, Jackson Hole's history became paramount. As Newton B. Drury, director of the National Park Service, said:

> Jackson Hole was favored by the early trappers because of its wealth of wilderness resources. . . . Jackson Hole has an important relation to the early history of this country. It is recognized by historians as one of the important scenes of two significant movements—the fur trade era and the era of frontier settlement. It remains, relatively unchanged, largely as it was when those important historic events took place.

In July 1938 Secretary of State Lester C. Hunt, supported by local and state organizations, wrote the president opposing the creation of a national monument. Many residents fought the government's and Rockefeller's plans. Cattlemen made the headlines when they defied a Park Service ban on cattle grazing in the area. The *Jackson's Hole Courier* reported in 1943:

> In their unanimous decision to graze their stock despite any letters from the Park Service to the contrary, the Jackson Hole cattlemen threw down the gauntlet with a clang that will be heard from coast to coast.
>
> Five thousand head of cattle are now on the monument and the Park Service be damned!

The wrangling continued until March 15, 1943, when President Franklin D. Roosevelt signed an executive order establishing Jackson Hole National Monument, located between Yellowstone National Park and the town of Jackson and adjoining Grand Teton National Park on the east. The preserve included 99,354 acres of National Forest lands, 39,640 acres of land already withdrawn from the public domain—so it could not be claimed by homesteaders—31,640 acres of lakes, 1,406 acres of state school land, 33,795 acres of land owned by Rockefeller, and 16,101 additional acres of private land. The total size was 221,936 acres. By 1995, expansion projects had increased the park size to 310,521 acres.

Wyoming officials were furious. On May 13, 1943, the state filed suit challenging the validity of the executive order. Almost two years later, on February 10, 1945, U.S. District Judge T. Blake Kennedy dismissed the suit. In his order, Kennedy wrote, "This seems to be a controversy between the legislative and executive branches of government in which the court cannot interfere."

However, Congress rescinded the president's order, and the squabble continued through the decade. In December 1949 Rockefeller gave the government his 35,000 acres in Jackson Hole, clearing the way for settlement of the controversy. Finally, in September 1950, Congress created the expanded Grand Teton National Park.

For our trip through Teton National Park, we'll start at Jackson and head north. The main highway from Jackson to Moran provides access to park headquarters at Moose, the Chapel of the Transfiguration, Menor's Ferry, and the Cunningham Cabin, where a shootout with two alleged horse thieves took place in 1892. Side roads provide access to Kelly, Grovont, Signal Mountain, Slide, Leigh, and Jenny lakes, as well as the Jackson Lake Dam.

Menor's Ferry

Before the Snake River had any dam across it, the current ran wide, fast, and turbulent through Jackson Hole. Crossing the Snake—the "accursed mad river," as early French trappers called it—required skill and bravado. At least, that was the case before Bill Menor happened on the scene and built a ferry in 1894. It crossed the Snake near Moose, just north of the current Grand Teton National Park Visitor Center.

Tall and thin, Menor spent his early life in Ohio and came to Wyoming in 1892, squatting on the west bank of the Snake River. He built a low log house among the cottonwoods along the bank of the river and had a cow or two, some chickens, and a horse. The hard-talking Menor set up a blacksmith shop, planted a garden, and plowed a field. Eventually he opened a store on the shore of the Snake, where he sold fishhooks, tin pans, groceries, and Bull Durham tobacco. Ever the entrepreneur, he built his ferry to provide an additional source of income and to attract more customers to his store. Constructed as a railed platform on pontoons, it was guided by ropes attached to an overhead cable. On either side of the river a massive log, called a "dead man," secured the cable.

When the Snake ran bank-full and raging, Menor's ferry was the only crossing place in a forty-mile stretch—practically the length of Jackson Hole. But if the river ran too fast and furious, Bill wouldn't put his ferry at risk. Travelers would then have to go all the way to Moran, where they could cross a toll bridge.

Bill knew the Snake's foibles and the power of the water firsthand. Once a huge uprooted tree swept against the ferry with such force that the ropes broke, carrying the pontoon craft—and the madder-than-hell Bill, who was on board—downstream several hundred yards before it grounded on a submerged sandbar. Neighbors rushed to the rescue as Bill cursed them and the river for his predicament.

Bill Menor built the first ferry across the Snake River, charging passengers up to a dollar to ride across. —Teton County Historical Center

Bill Menor's younger brother, Holiday, also eventually settled on the banks of the Snake River in Jackson Hole. Upon his arrival in 1905, Holiday lived with Bill, but the two, being brothers, fought and argued. Eventually Holiday moved out of Bill's house and claimed land on the east shore of the Snake. The two brothers' houses sat directly opposite each other, and the mad river, running between them, became a buffer zone. The Menors needed it. Both believed strong hatred was a mark of character; accordingly, they hated each other strongly. Although they didn't speak *to* each other, they spoke *of* each other to friends, often letting their pride in the family show.

The brothers' personalities contrasted markedly. Bill seldom read the newspaper; Holiday subscribed to a number of magazines. Holiday liked the summer visitors in Jackson Hole; Bill put up with them. During the wild berry season in late summer, when the fruit along the ridges and around the lakes under the Tetons dripped with juice, Bill charged "huckleberry rates" to local people wanting to cross on his ferry. Holiday liked berry season, too. He canned up to sixty quarts of huckleberries every year, using them—and prunes, beets, raisins, and anything else that was handy—to make a little home brew. He called it wine but seldom gave it time to mature.

When fall turned to winter in Jackson Hole, Bill took his ferry from the river. From that time until he resumed operation in the spring, people wanting to cross with either horses or wagons had to ford the Snake on their own. Those traveling on foot could cross on a little platform car. They boarded and sat down, and Bill released the car. With a quick movement, it ran down the slack cable to within feet of the current. The passengers then hauled themselves up the cable to the opposite bank.

Eventually Menor and people living nearby built a winter bridge across the river. Neighbors up and down the river, who might want to cross the river before the ferry was back up and running in springtime, readily gathered to put the log structure in place in the fall. The story was different in the spring, when it came time to remove the logs from the river. By then the ferry was zipping back and forth between the banks. Men had planting to do but no the time to tear down an old bridge. One spring only Bill Menor, Holiday Menor, and one other man showed up to remove the bridge pole by pole, nail by nail, and curse by curse. Logs too heavy for the small crew to remove got pushed into the river. There wasn't a winter bridge after that.

Until Bill Menor built a ferry across the Snake River at Moose, the river crossing was treacherous during high water. The ferry, shown here in use to transport a vehicle, three horses, and several people, is now restored as an attraction in Grand Teton National Park. —Teton County Historical Center

In 1918 Bill Menor sold his ranch and his ferry to Maude Noble and associates. He said he had had enough of high water and low water, of fog, wind, rain, and snow. But he didn't seem able to drag himself from the banks of the Snake. He paced a floor no longer his and cursed when a meal wasn't ready. Finally he packed his bags and left for California. Holiday followed him there.

By 1926 a huge bridge spanned the Snake near Moose, not far from the Menor houses. The ferry sat beached until April 1965, when reconstruction took place at the original site. The old whitewashed cabin is preserved as a memorial to Menor, with an interpretive trail connecting his cabin and ferry to Maude Noble's place.

A Scenic Church

Not far from Menor's Ferry is the log Chapel of the Transfiguration, built in 1914. The grounds, set off from the surrounding flat by a buck fence, are entered through a peak-roofed gate. The window behind the altar frames the Tetons. Maude Noble donated land for the Episcopal chapel after she heard that "dudes" visiting the area wanted to attend church services but didn't like to ride all the way in to Jackson.

The Episcopal church holds regular services in the Chapel of the Transfiguration. —Teton County Historical Center

82

A fan-shaped section of the Gros Ventre Range gave way in 1925 during the Gros Ventre slide.

Mother Nature Rages on the Gros Ventre

A large hog-shaped butte hunches in the center of Jackson Hole, east of Moose on the east side of US 26/89/191. Blacktail Butte is a marker for Jackson residents, and roads completely encircle it. The highway runs between the butte and the Snake River. At the bridge spanning the Gros Ventre River between Jackson and Moose, a dirt road takes off to the east and follows the stream to the small community of Kelly and the ghost town of Grovont.

Indians didn't like the region named for the Gros Ventre in spite of that tribe's traditional lands lying farther to the north. In the stillness of the night they could hear the earth rumbling, which they believed to be the sounds of an underground buffalo hunt. As a result the Indians spent little time in Gros Ventre Canyon.

In 1895 Billy Bierers claimed a homestead near Sheep Mountain. He worked his land, listened to its strange murmurings, and watched the peak. He predicted that some day, after heavy rains, when the mountain was woozy, it would come down "like a beaver's slickery slide." Bierers said: "Anywhere on that slope, if I lay my ear to the ground, I can heard water tricklin' and runnin' underneath. It's running between strata and some day, if we have a wet enough spring, that whole mountain is gonna let loose and slide."

On a day in late June 1925, his forecast came true. That was a wet winter and spring, with heavy rains falling almost constantly. Rancher Guil Huff, who by then owned Bierers's homestead, worked outside that morning along the Gros Ventre and noticed the rumbling of the mountain. Finally, he put his work team away and headed toward the hillside to see what was causing the noise.

Not long after he started up the canyon, the whole side of the mountain broke off and, with the force of a waterfall, rushed down. Huff turned and raced for his life up the canyon and toward higher ground.

Cowboys Forney Cole, Leonard Peterson, and Boyd Charter were across the river, high up on a canyon slope. They watched in horror as the mountain gave way, chasing Huff up the incline. Charter spurred his horse toward the Horsetail ranger station, up the river a few miles. The others raced toward the Huff ranch.

Huff's wife watched the slide and remarked to her daughter that it was coming awfully close. She didn't know that her husband was desperately trying to outrun the mountain. When the rocks and debris settled, they covered the riverbed and pushed up on the canyon walls. The waters soon started to rise, and it became evident the Huff ranch and others lay in the path of the rapidly building flood. That night the Huffs, assisted by ranger C. E. Dibble and the cowboys, packed their belongings and left their homestead. The following morning the house floated away on the newly forming lake.

A few days later, Dibble and his family got ready to leave their ranger station home because the waters were now lapping near their front door. They packed and decided to spend one more evening, but during the black night they heard a sound that put terror in their hearts. The mountain roared and rumbled. As they raced out the back door in their nightclothes, the water surged at the front entryway. At dawn the Dibbles returned to their home, grabbed the rest of their belongings, and left the station forever. Three days later it floated onto the lake, logically christened Slide Lake.

Several years earlier, in 1911 and 1912, a slow slide had run on the mountain upstream from Slide Lake. That avalanche partially dammed the Gros Ventre, forming a small reservoir. After the birth of the second lake, the first became known as Upper Slide Lake.

Trees still lace Slide Lake Dam. They are crisscross, horizontal, vertical, and leaning at every conceivable angle. The rocks intermingle with trees and other vegetation. Soon after the slide, Wyoming state engineer Frank C. Emerson estimated that decomposed material made up 25 to 30 percent of the dam's mass.

One of the first to write about the great landslide was William O. Owen, who became familiar with the area when he surveyed it for the government in 1892–93. At that time, he noticed that the soil was "naturally disposed to slides and is generally treacherous where the slopes become at all steep." In September 1925 he wrote:

> Some of the great spruces and firs are still standing erect and virile, as vigorous and as firmly planted as before the slide occurred, although many of them are a mile and a half from the spot on Sheep Mountain where their tiny sprouts first shot through the soil to kiss the sun, some hundreds of years ago!
>
> It is interesting to note that most of the springs south of the river in the near vicinity of the slide instantly ceased flowing and have shown no sign of life since.

W. O. Owen climb of Grand Teton, 1989. —Teton County Historical Center

As the scientists who came to study the landslide left Slide Lake, its tranquil waters surrounded by a tangle of overturned trees and a tumble of huge boulders, they pronounced the naturally constructed earthen dam safe. But Kelly residents weren't sure they trusted the eminent scientists. Some packed their belongings every night and slept out on the higher hillsides. Eventually their fear that Slide Lake Dam might break subsided, and life in Kelly resumed a normal pace.

Kelly's Daylight Nightmare

Two years later the canyon had another wet spring. The morning of May 18, 1927, ranger Dibble and a group of Kelly men worked to remove debris from the bridge across the Gros Ventre. As they labored, Dibble saw a sight that froze him: A hayrack came floating down the river—not just any old hayrack, but one Dibble recognized. It had been floating on Slide Lake for two years.

Fearing the worst, Dibble and another man jumped into his car and raced up the river toward Slide Lake. But they didn't get to the lake because they met a wall of water. Dibble turned the car, floored the gas pedal, and headed for Kelly to give warning. He stopped at one ranch long enough to warn the residents and have them call others. Then, spurring the seat of his car the way he would the flanks of his horse, Dibble raced toward Kelly.

Schoolchildren ran for home as their parents loaded belongings into wagons and cars. Neighbors who lived on higher ground watched in horror as a fifteen-foot-high wall of churning water swept over Kelly, taking trees, livestock, wagons, and people with it. Some of those captured by the racing waters managed to break free and cling to trees until rescuers arrived. Six weren't so lucky. Sisters Maud Smith and May Lovejoy grabbed some belongings and loaded them into their wagon; then, with one sister lashing the whip and the other whipping the reins, they urged their horses away from the water. They turned at a right angle to the onslaught, which hit them before they got to high ground. Searchers found Smith's body a few miles downstream. Lovejoy was never found.

When the water subsided, just two buildings remained standing. Although the town was rebuilt, its heart has not fully recovered from the Kelly Flood of 1927.

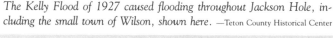

The Kelly Flood of 1927 caused flooding throughout Jackson Hole, including the small town of Wilson, shown here. —Teton County Historical Center

Grovont: Home of Mormon Row

Mormons claimed the first homesteads in the area that is now Grand Teton National Park. James May rode into Jackson Hole in 1894 in search of land on which to raise crops, cattle, and a family. Under the ramparts of the Tetons, May found what he was looking for, a broad, flat valley with sagebrush up to his stirrups. He rode across the land, chose a spot he liked in the lee of Blacktail Butte, and then headed out of the hole for his home in Idaho. The tract he selected is about a mile west of Kelly.

It took May two years to gather the wherewithal to return to Jackson Hole with his wife, Ann, and son, Henrie. Several other families accompanied the Mays. On the trying trip over Teton Pass, the men had to double-team the wagons going up and rough-lock them on the downhill stretch. The mosquitoes chewed hungrily. May and those traveling with him claimed their homesteads near Blacktail Butte and started improvements the following spring. They grubbed sagebrush from the land, dug irrigation ditches, and planted grain and hay. Henrie May spent nights burrowed like a rabbit into haystacks, firing his old rifle at intervals to chase elk away.

More Mormon families came and eked out a living on their 160-acre homesteads. When efforts to create Grand Teton National Park and the national monument began, some settlers on Mormon Row, tired of their hard lifestyle

John Moulton homestead, Mormon Row in Jackson Hole, 1993.

and ready to take it a bit easier, sought to sell their acreage. Some sold fairly quickly; then several deals fell through, and those acquiring the land—backed by John Rockefeller's millions—said they wanted a package deal: They would either buy *all* of Mormon Row or none of it.

A few families held out until the 1950s and 1960s before selling to the National Park Service. Only one, Clark Moulton, held on to his ground. In 1995 he still owned one acre on Mormon Row and had no intention to sell. The barn that he and his father, Thomas Alma Moulton, and brother, Harley, built became a symbol of Jackson Hole. It was used as a location for scenes in the film classic *Spencer's Mountain*, as well as various country music videos, and it shows up on postcards, jigsaw puzzles, and the Jackson State Bank credit card.

Incident at Cunningham's

In the fall of 1892, cowboys Ed Spencer and Mike Burnett brought a fine herd of horses to winter in the north end of the valley. They bought hay from J. Pierce Cunningham, who let them use his cabin on Spread Creek—today, midway between Moose and Moran on US 191 in Grand Teton National Park.

During the winter a rumor—which may or may not have had any basis in truth—spread that Spencer and Burnett were horse thieves. The wheels of justice started turning, and in April a group of men from Montana and Idaho snowshoed over Teton Pass. Claiming to be a United States marshal and deputies, they "deputized" seven reputable citizens to form a posse of a dozen and

Snow covers the J. Pierce Cunningham cabin, where cowboys Ed Spencer and Mike Burnett died in a shootout in 1892. —Teton County Historical Center

headed for Spread Creek. Even though the posse had no jurisdiction in Idaho or Montana and certainly had no legal standing in Wyoming, it was at the Cunningham Ranch at daylight.

Spencer, known as one of the best cowboys in Montana and a dead shot, came out of the cabin wearing his six-shooter. At the order to "throw 'em up," Spencer started shooting instead and fell to the ground riddled with bullets. Burnett came out of the cabin with a rifle and revolver. When commanded to give himself up, he taunted his adversaries instead and was immediately shot. The posse wrapped Spencer and Burnett in blankets and buried them on the south side of a draw southwest of the cabin in a common grave. It has never been clearly shown that the horses they had were illegally obtained.

Beaver Dick, A Late-day Mountain Man

Richard Leigh spent his childhood in England, but he ran away as a boy and went to sea, eventually making it to America. He wandered west to Idaho, where he started trapping in about 1840, just as the fur era climaxed in the West. His two abnormally large front teeth, combined with his ability as a trapper, gave Leigh the nickname "Beaver Dick." Indians called him The Beaver.

Beaver Dick Leigh and family, including his first wife Jenny, seated at right of tipi.—Teton County Historical Center

89

Beaver Dick married an Indian woman known as Jenny. In the fall of 1876, Beaver Dick and Jenny assisted an ailing Indian woman. The woman died of smallpox, and before long Jenny, who was pregnant, and the couple's four children became ill. In a streak of horrible luck, that Christmas Beaver Dick lost his entire family. Jenny bore her fifth child just before Christmas, but the baby, the other four children, and Jenny all died within a week's time. Leigh buried his family in Jackson Hole.

Later he went to Fort Hall, where he married another Indian woman, Susan Tadpole. He brought her back to Jackson Hole and built a new cabin on present-day Leigh Creek near the mouth of the canyon. Leigh never returned to his old home. He felt the area was jinxed, especially after some of his cows, seeking refuge in the cabin, were locked inside when the door blew shut; all starved to death.

In 1872, Leigh guided the U.S. Geological Survey, led by Dr. F. V. Hayden, into Yellowstone country. The lovely Jenny Lake is named for his first Indian wife, and Leigh Lake is named for Beaver Dick himself.

Bring on the Dudes

As early as 1900, John Sargent and Roy Hamilton envisioned a deluxe dude ranch on the shores of Jackson Lake at the north end of Jackson Hole. They built a ten-room log house, which they called Mary Mere. At about the same time, Herb Whiteman and his partner built a cabin north of the lake with a similar purpose in mind; however, they found the transportation of supplies prohibitively difficult and abandoned their plans. And Hamilton and Sargent's operation didn't last because of a tragic accident that claimed Hamilton's life.

Signal Mountain, at the southeast edge of Jackson Lake, got its name when Hamilton lost his way while stalking game. A rescue effort started, and the searchers agreed to light a fire on the mountain when they found him. Nine days later the flames flickered from the summit: Searchers had discovered Hamilton's body in the Snake River. It has never been clearly determined whether his death was entirely accidental. Many in Jackson Hole believed Sargent intentionally told his partner to cross the Snake in a dangerous spot.

Before 1910 Ben Sheffield ran a camp for hunters and fishermen near Moran, but real dude operations in Jackson Hole began with the JY Ranch, started in 1908 by Henry Steward, and the Bar BC, started by Struthers Burt and Dr. Horace Carncross in 1910. The "dudes" came from outside Jackson Hole, most often the East. They wore new high-heeled cowboy boots, blue jeans, and western hats and pretended to be Westerners. By day they mounted horses saddled by wranglers and rode single-file through the high country surrounding Jackson Hole, but at night they retired to snug lodges or small log cabins and soft beds.

*The view east from Signal Mountain, toward the Gros Ventre
Mountain range and the fan-shaped scar of the Gros Ventre Slide.*

Dude ranches quickly became big business in Wyoming's spectacular mountain valleys. For the dudes, it was a chance to live the cowboy life, and for the cowboys and ranch owners it was a way to make a living. Dude ranching started in the early 1900s and peaked during the 1920s. Although some fads wither and die, dude ranching has never completely lost its grip in Wyoming. Many ranches still cater to people who don't know which side of the horse to mount, let alone how to saddle and bridle one.

In those days, according to historian Elizabeth Hayden, visitors to Jackson found the town square boxed in by log and false-front stores, with a few stretches of boardwalk lining the street. Hayden wrote, "They bought their necessities at the mercantile store of Roy and Frank Van Vleck or at 'Pap' Deloney's general merchandise, their drugs at 'Doc' Steele's, ate their lunch at 'Ma' Reed's hotel, and stopped for a quick one at Rube Tuttle's saloon."

Tourists of the 1990s find trendy shops, art galleries, and specialty restaurants mixed with the old-West atmosphere created by board sidewalks and cowboy bars.

Owen Wister, who first visited Wyoming and Jackson Hole in 1885, later wrote of the state in his classic book, The Virginian. —Teton County Historical Center

Western novelist Owen Wister, who became famous for *The Virginian,* was one of the "dudes" in Jackson Hole prior to 1900, although he didn't stay at a dude ranch. Many stories circulate about his writing. Old-timers claim to have been the character upon which he based the Virginian, Trampas, and the others in his novel. One thing is certain: Much of the book's action took place in Wyoming spots such as Medicine Bow, the Goose Egg Ranch near Casper, and the Occidental Hotel in Buffalo.

Wister did spend a considerable amount of time in Wyoming after 1885, when his health broke down and his doctor, S. Weir Mitchell, advised him to head west. Wister first visited Jackson Hole in 1887 on a big-game hunting trip. His daughter, Frances Stokes, wrote in a letter dated January 29, 1958, of visiting Jackson Hole with her family during the summers of 1911 and 1912. Not far from the JY Ranch they built a log cabin, where, some people claim, Wister wrote *The Virginian.* The book first appeared in *Harper's Magazine* and the *Saturday Evening Post* as a series of short stories. Wister spent the winter of 1901–2 living in Charleston, South Carolina, where he turned the tales into his now-famous novel.

In later years, Wister often visited Jackson Hole. In a November 26, 1929, letter to Jackson resident Fritiof Fryxell, he wrote:

That region is the country I have loved best in the world. Were there any part of my life I would live again, it would be the time spent there.

In 1888, from camp between String and Jenny Lake, at the edge of the pines where the creek enters them for its final descent into Jenny Lake, I climbed to that rocky stoop where the real steepness of the Grand Teton begins—and came down again ingloriously.

Jackson Lake Dam

Indians frequented the land around Jackson Lake, as archaeologists found in the 1980s. When workers started to enlarge a Bureau of Reclamation dam, they uncovered rich sites littered with artifacts.

The first dam on the Snake, a temporary log-crib structure at Jackson Lake, was built in 1906 and 1907 to store water for use in Idaho. It cost $30,203 to build, but was washed out in July 1910 and replaced with a $453,300 earthen dam. Moran served as headquarters for the 400-man construction crew, which was twice the population of Jackson. At that time Moran boasted a hospital, four barns, an office building, and other facilities for the workers, who kept at the job year around. Huge fires burned in stoves to prevent the cement from freezing, and a freighting crew hauled six boilers for the facility over Teton Pass through snow up to fifteen feet deep.

From 1914 to 1916 workers increased the reservoir capacity by raising the dam's height. In 1988 the *Jackson Hole Guide* reported on a three-year project

The outlet at Jackson Lake Dam, 1993.

to reinforce and reconstruct Jackson Lake Dam using, for the first time in the United States, a new technology to increase the strength of the earthen dam's foundation. The improvements were sought because of concern that the foundation could collapse during an earthquake, but they didn't come cheap. The cost for the upgrade was $82 million, a far cry from the original log-crib barrier.

YELLOWSTONE NATIONAL PARK

No place in Wyoming captures the imagination quite like Yellowstone National Park, with its towering waterfalls, abundant wildlife, steaming geysers, and bubbling mud pots. During the summertime, Yellowstone is filled to the brim with tourists from every state in the nation and nearly every country in the world. Nearly eight times as many people visit Yellowstone every year as live in the entire state of Wyoming. Its wildlife grazes and roams, preens by the side of the roads, and seems tame. But watch out: Yellowstone is a wild place. Buffalo often raise their shaggy heads from the grass they crop and charge without warning; bears occasionally injure, and even more rarely kill, folks who threaten their territory.

Although most people visit Yellowstone during the spring, summer, and fall seasons, an increasing number of people choose winter to explore the park. Yellowstone is a completely different place during the period of deep snow. Although some animals hibernate and aren't visible, others can be seen more often in winter than in summer. Elk, coyotes, buffalo, swans, otters, foxes, and eagles are among those most visible during the winter months.

Winter visitation at Yellowstone increased during the 1980s and 1990s as people took to the groomed trails—which are the highways in summertime—on snowmobiles, snow coaches, and cross-country skis.

The park concessionaire closes most of the tourist facilities during winter, but the Park Service grooms the trails, and enough places remain open to provide food, gasoline, and lodging. Whereas millions of people visit Yellowstone in the summer, only a few hundred thousand come in the winter. Even so, the Park Service in the early 1990s expressed some concerns about winter visitation. The groomed trails provided a travel corridor for animals, particularly buffalo, to move around; some suggested that those same trails made it easy for the animals to leave the park altogether. Buffalo occasionally roamed north, heading out of the park near Mammoth. When they entered Montana, the problems started. Concerned that the buffalo might spread disease to cattle, Montana authorities allowed hunters to kill the wayward park animals. In those cases, authorities usually gave the buffalo carcass to Indian tribes.

Yellowstone Lake ferry. —Wyoming State Museum

Summer or winter, the majesty of Yellowstone touches and moves visitors. The yellowish canyon walls of the Yellowstone River gave the region its name; Lewis and Clark referred to the "Yellow Stone," though they never saw it. French trappers used names of the same theme, calling the area Roche Jaune (Yellow Rock) and Pierre Jaune (Yellow Stone). Indian tribes referred to the area as Yellow Rock. In Minnetaree (a Siouan language) it was Mi tsi a da zi— Rock Yellow River—and the Crow sometimes called it Elk River.

Yellowstone seems a timeless place, but it has a history. John Colter was the first white man known to have seen the Yellowstone country; he traveled through the area in the winter of 1807–8. Other trappers followed Colter's footsteps, but the country remained largely unexplored because of its inaccessibility. By 1825 or possibly even earlier, mountain men were venturing through Yellowstone. Artist George Catlin visited the West in 1829 and soon thereafter suggested to the government that it set apart "a large reservation of public land to be a Nation's Park, contain[ing] man and beast in all the wildness and freshness of their natural beauty." It's not clear whether Catlin meant Yellowstone or if he envisioned another wilderness area for a national park.

The David E. Folsom party explored the region in 1869, but members hesitated to describe the area. Folsom said, "I doubted if any magazine editor would look upon a truthful description in any other light than the production of the too-vivid imagination of a typical Rocky Mountain liar." In 1870, Gen. H. D. Washburn headed an exploration to the area, during which many important features received official names. At that time the move to create a national park carved of Yellowstone country may have started. The following year a government expedition led by Dr. Ferdinand V. Hayden and guided by Beaver Dick Leigh explored Yellowstone. On that journey painter Thomas Moran and photographer William Henry Jackson captured on canvas and film some of the splendor of Yellowstone. Their strong images became proof that the tall tales of the mountain men weren't so tall after all.

Acting on the information provided by the expeditions of 1870 and 1871, Congress in 1872 created Yellowstone National Park. The largest unit in the National Park System, Yellowstone is often recognized as the first national park. That's partly true; it is the first park of any size, but Congress in 1832 designated a one-acre federal reservation in Hot Springs, Arkansas.

In 1886 construction started on Grand Loop Road, the same year the U.S. Army took over administration of the park to preserve it from vandals and poachers. Travelers visited the park in increasing numbers, arriving by horse and wagon or stagecoach until 1915, when the first automobiles traveled the roads. A year later the newly organized National Park Service took over park administration.

By 1970 the park served hundreds of thousands of visitors annually, and the last of the garbage dumps closed in an effort to recondition Yellowstone's famous bear population to live off food from nature rather than the trash of man. In 1988, what some viewed as the greatest tragedy of Yellowstone's history occurred when hundreds of thousands of acres burned in horrendous wildfires throughout Yellowstone's ecosystem.

Where to Enter

A journey through Yellowstone can begin from any point on the compass. The north entrance provides access from Montana through the Gallatin Range to Gardiner and then to park headquarters at Mammoth. A northeastern entrance provides admittance to the park west of the Montana town of Cooke City. The western approach to Yellowstone also comes in from Montana (although Idaho, via US 20, is only a few miles away), while both the southern and eastern access points come from Wyoming, via Jackson and Cody, respectively.

The road system within the park is shaped like a figure eight. The entire circuit, called Grand Loop Road, connects Mammoth with the geyser basins, Yellowstone Lake, the Grand Canyon of the Yellowstone, and Tower Fall. Harry W. Frantz, who in 1923 suggested the name Grand Loop Road, wrote: "Gravel and bridges and engineering skill alone do not make a great road. The footprints and the hooftracks and if you will, the tire prints of countless travelers are required." The Eaton Trail for horseback riders roughly parallels the Grand Loop Road, and an extensive backcountry trail system invites hikers and horseback riders.

For our roadside tour of the park we'll begin in the north, at Mammoth, then circle clockwise, catching the exit roads from the park as we come to them but each time returning to the figure-eight pattern.

US 89 at Gardiner
North Entrance—Mammoth
5 miles

Travel in Yellowstone came by various forms over the years. Early visitors traveled on foot and eventually by horse, and later they used wagons and stagecoaches. The great tourist industry in Yellowstone started just after the area became a national park in 1872 and the Northern Pacific Railroad promoted visits. The trains provided transportation to the park's northern area, where visitors switched to horse-drawn stages to reach the rest of Yellowstone. Guests stayed first in remote camps, later in tent villages, and finally in the sumptuous luxury of the huge hotels at Mammoth, Old Faithful, and Lake.

As the route enters the park, it follows the Yellowstone River through a canyon where James George, better known as Yankee Jim, built a toll road twenty-seven miles long. The tollgate stood at the narrowest point of the canyon, so everyone entering or leaving Yellowstone Park had to pay Yankee Jim an access fee. When the Northern Pacific Railroad started building its line to Yellowstone, it laid track through the canyon only after constructing a new road for Yankee Jim.

The first settlement of Mammoth Hot Springs began in 1871, when James C. McCartney built a crude log cabin in Clematis Gulch west of Liberty Cap. Matthew McGuirk built another near Hot River on the old wagon road connecting the area with what is now Cooke City. In July 1884 park officials opened the original $60,000 Mammoth Hot Springs Hotel, a four-story building that accommodated 800 guests.

An Early Winter Visit

One of the earliest documented wintertime explorations of Yellowstone occurred in 1886–87, when Arctic explorer Lt. Frederick Schwatka attempted to lead a large expedition through the park. Equipped with Arctic sleeping bags, Canadian "web" snowshoes, and Norwegian skis, Schwatka's party carried astronomical instruments and photographic equipment on toboggans. They

Upper Geyser Basin, Yellowstone National Park. F. J. Haynes at left after eruption of Old Faithful Geyser, January 1887. —Wyoming State Museum

convened at Mammoth Hot Springs but soon found conditions very different from those encountered in the Arctic. The elaborate equipment quickly became a burden.

The twenty-mile trip to Norris took three days. Soon after that, Lieutenant Schwatka became very ill and the expedition stopped. Park photographer Frank Jay Haynes, scout Ed Wilson, and two others decided to continue the journey. The four men abandoned their toboggans, strapped their baggage on their backs, and set out, taking winter photographs of Yellowstone as they went. They webbed about 200 miles in twenty-nine days with temperatures ranging from 10 degrees above zero to 50 below. Fierce blizzards swirled around them as they neared Upper Geyser Basin and again when they reached Mt. Washburn. The trip nearly cost all four men their lives, but they returned alive with the first photographs of Yellowstone in winter.

In 1894 park rangers made two winter expeditions to feeding ranges to conduct wildlife counts and take photographs of the animals. They traveled on skis and carried their equipment and food in backpacks. One party traveled more than 300 miles in thirty days, gathering evidence along the way that led to the arrest of a notorious poacher, whom we'll meet on down the road.

Mammoth—Tower Junction
18 miles

In early April 1903, President Theodore Roosevelt visited the park, twenty years after President Chester Arthur had done so. Arthur's had been a high-security trip, perhaps because horse thieves in Jackson Hole threatened to kidnap the president on his journey. By contrast, Roosevelt had few companions during his visit. He knew the Yellowstone country from his visit there in the 1880s, and some historians suggest it was because of his deep interest in this region that Roosevelt became an active conservationist. Although he hunted, Roosevelt hated waste. He once said: "True sportsmen, worthy of the name, men who shoot only in season and in moderation, do no harm what-

President Chester Arthur, center, visited Yellowstone National Park in 1883 with heavy security because of apparent threats from horse thieves in Jackson Hole that they intended to kidnap him. —Teton County Historical Center

99

ever to game. The most objectionable of all game destroyers is, of course, the kind of game butcher who simply kills for the sake of the record of slaughter, who leaves deer and ducks and prairie chickens to rot after he has slain them."

On his 1903 trip, Roosevelt entered the park at Mammoth Hot Springs. The president visited a big field to the east, where a man named Buffalo Jones carefully tended some Texas and Flathead Lake bison he had imported to the park. Hunters and poachers had killed most of the original herd in Yellowstone. Jones's bison eventually roamed freely in the valleys and upon the mountains of Yellowstone.

Roosevelt Lodge at Tower Junction gets its name from the president, who loved the West and appreciated the opportunity to escape into its places of solitude. Of Roosevelt's 1903 excursion, naturalist-writer John Burroughs wrote that the president left behind strangers, newspaper reporters, the Secret Service, his physician, and private secretaries. "He craved once more to be alone with nature; he was evidently hungry for the wild and the aboriginal—a hunger that seems to come upon him regularly at least once a year, and drives him forth on his hunting trips for big game in the West," Burroughs wrote in *Old Yellowstone Days*.

One Indian Route

A great Bannock Indian trail went from Henrys Lake across the Gallatin Range to Mammoth Hot Springs. There it joined another trail coming up the valley of the Gardner River before heading across a plateau to a ford above Tower Falls, then following the Lamar Valley to a fork at Soda Butte. The trail roughly followed the present highway, particularly on the route of Blacktail Plateau Drive. From Soda Butte the trail headed east to intercept the Clarks Fork and Shoshone rivers, which it followed to the Big Horn Basin. It was an ancient, well-traveled road.

Tower Junction—Northeast Entrance (Cooke City, US 212)
29 miles

"It's a Hell Roarer"

Physical landmarks in the West often got their names from whoever discovered them or first mapped the site. Three places north of Tower Junction got their monikers from a prospecting party. The men found gold in a crevice, so they called the first point Crevice Gulch. The following day one of the prospectors hunted in the area to the north. Upon his return his companions asked him what the next stream looked like. "It's a hell roarer," he is said to have replied, so the stream became Hell Roaring Creek. Another day later he again explored ahead of his companions, heading east from Hell Roaring Creek. Upon his return to camp his companions once again inquired about the next stream. "'Twas but a slough," he replied. That wasn't quite so, however; when his companions reached the slough they found a rushing torrent, and in attempting to cross, a pack horse and its load were swept away. The name Slough Creek stuck anyway.

Baronett's Bridge

Just northeast of Tower Junction, the first bridge over the Yellowstone River went in under the watchful eye of Collins Jack Baronett in 1871, a year before Yellowstone became a national park. The bridge provided a river crossing for gold miners from Montana headed to Cooke City. The Scottish Baronett had an adventurous life, mining gold in California, Australia, and Africa, sailing to China, and whaling in the Arctic.

Beginning in the 1860s, Baronett prospected in the Yellowstone area. His bridge served travelers and miners from 1871 until 1877, when Nez Perce Indians destroyed part of it as they fled toward Canada. Baronett, better known as Yellowstone Jack, rebuilt the structure, which was located downstream from the present highway bridge across the Yellowstone near Tower Junction.

A Great Fossil Forest

The wildfires of 1988 created the greatest natural upheaval in Yellowstone's ecosystem in the twentieth century, but hundreds of centuries ago even greater changes affected this region. One of the best places to see the evidence of that metamorphosis is Specimen Ridge, a multilayered fossil forest where some 50 million years ago repeated volcanic mud flows buried both tropical and subtropical forests filled with magnolia, breadfruit, avocado, redwood, sycamore, walnut, oak, and other species. Many areas of the United States contain petrified wood, including upright stumps. However, as William J. Fritz puts it in *Roadside Geology of the Yellowstone Country*, "none has so many upright trees, such well preserved wood, and such good exposures as the petrified forests in Yellowstone."

The petrified forest of Specimen Ridge became grist for Jim Bridger's storytelling mill. As usual, this tall tale has at least one hard grain of truth in it. Park historian Hiram Chittenden tells the yarn this way:

> There exists in the Park country a mountain which was once cursed by a great medicine man of the Crow nation. Everything upon the mountain at the time of this dire event became instantly petrified and has remained so ever since. All forms of life are standing about in stone where they were suddenly caught by the petrifying influences, even as the inhabitants of ancient Pompeii were surprised by the ashes of Vesuvius. Sage

brush, grass, prairie fowl, antelope, elk, and bears may there be seen as perfect as in actual life. Dashing torrents and the spray of mist from them stand forth in arrested motion as if carved from rock by a sculptor's chisel. Even flowers are blooming in colors of crystal, and birds soar with wings spread in motionless flight, while the air floats with music and perfumes siliceous, and the sun and the moon shine with petrified light!

Return of the Wolves

Historically, gray wolves ranged through Yellowstone and all of its surrounding areas, but bounty hunters, ranchers, and others killed all of the native animals. By mid-century the howl of wolves had ceased in Yellowstone's ecosystem. Conservationists wanted to reintroduce wolves to Yellowstone, and in the 1980s the U.S. Fish and Wildlife Service started the environmental studies necessary for that goal. Following years of meetings, studies, and reports, wildlife biologists got approval to trap wolves in Canada and relocate

Jackson Hole resident Roy McBride is one of the bounty hunters who helped exterminate wolves from the Yellowstone region in the early twentiety century. In January 1995 federal wildlife managers reintroduced wolves to Yellowstone National Park and a wilderness area in Idaho as part of a controversial program to restore the animals to their native habitat. —Teton County Historical Center

them in Yellowstone. Some ranchers protested returning wolves to the region and the Wyoming Farm Bureau filed a lawsuit to stop the project. However, in early January 1995 the legal challenge was denied in court and the first wolves arrived in the park.

On January 12, 1995, wildlife biologists, park officials, and Interior secretary Bruce Babbitt carried the cages holding the first wolves to a release area in the Lamar Valley. The recovery plan called for keeping the animals within a fenced area for several weeks before releasing them to run totally free.

Tower Junction—Canyon
19 miles

At a site just north of Tower Junction is Pleasant Valley, once the location of John F. Yancey's hotel, the Wayside Inn, established in 1884. Yancey, whom everyone called Uncle John, operated his hotel as a hunting and fishing retreat. One story goes that Uncle John kept two historic glasses, into which he poured the welcoming libation of "Kentucky Tea." He boasted that the whiskey glasses "had never been polluted by contact with so alien a liquid as water."

Yellowstone gets it name from the coloring of the rocks on the canyon walls, although likely the French trappers gave the river its name at the point where it met the Missouri in Montana. The same yellowish tint exists in both locales. At the Grand Canyon of the Yellowstone, which visitors can view from several access points, the colors result from the reaction of hot water hitting volcanic rock. The canyon walls resemble an artist's watercolor, with yellow rising to orange and red with occasional splashes of blue, purple, or green.

For views of the 308-foot lower falls, go to Grand View Point. A steep trail gives a closer vantage spot to the lower falls. To see the greatest splendor of the 109-foot upper falls and the Yellowstone Canyon, cross the Chittenden Bridge and drive to Artist Point, where a short walk on a mostly wheelchair-accessible path puts you amid the pine trees for a magnificent vista of the raging Yellowstone River and its canyon setting.

Canyon—Fishing Bridge
16 miles

An Early-Day Poacher

In 1894 Emerson Hough went to Yellowstone on assignment for *Forest and Stream* magazine to document the capture of notorious poacher Ed Howell. The winter expeditions to survey wildlife numbers in Yellowstone turned up evidence that Howell had poached a dozen bison.

Prior to Howell's arrest, the park had only feeble regulations protecting park animals. Authorities removed poachers from the park but could not levy fines or put them in jail. Everyone (except the poachers, no doubt) called for federal legislation to back up regulations. The Howell poaching incident and its report by Hough in *Forest and Stream* became a catalyst, and within a month of the report Congress approved the Lacey Act, which provides penalties for wildlife violations.

Howell's undoing came about this way. A park scout named Burgess crossed Howell's trail as it led into the park toward Pelican Valley from Cooke City. Burgess followed the trail and found a cache of six buffalo heads, then came upon Howell's tipi on Astringent Creek in the Pelican Valley. While at the campsite, Burgess heard a shot. He followed the sound and got the drop on Howell as the poacher skinned one of five buffalo he had just killed.

Hough's story about poaching not only led to the Lacey Act of May 7, 1894, to protect the birds and the animals of the park but also gave the author a powerful glimpse into Yellowstone's backcountry. He wrote: "I learned how utterly small, lonely and insignificant a man looks and feels in the midst of solitude so vast, so boundless, so tremendous and so appalling."

Modern-Day Poaching

In the fall of 1993 wildlife poachers stalked and killed game throughout Yellowstone, and park rangers found themselves unable to stop the killing because they spent so much time dealing with Yellowstone's more than three million visitors.

Among the poachers caught in the 1990s was Donald E. Lewis, a professional bow hunter who stalked Yellowstone elk for nine years in his goal to become the world's greatest archer, according to a report in the *Billings Gazette*. Lewis tripped himself up by videotaping a 1991 hunt that showed him and a partner shooting thirteen elk; wildlife officials recognized the setting as Yellowstone. Lewis pled guilty to shooting three elk and was fined $5,000 for each offense.

In 1991 Yellowstone rangers charged thirty-three people with wildlife crimes, including poaching and "horn hunting"—the illegal collection of antlers shed by elk. (There is a market for the antlers in the Far East, where they are ground and sold as aphrodisiacs.) The next year rangers caught thirteen poachers but told the *Billings Gazette* many such crimes go unnoticed. The nabbed poachers explained that it is cheaper and easier to take Yellowstone wildlife illegally and risk getting caught than to pay an outfitter thousands of dollars for guided hunting elsewhere. In the fall of 1993 poachers killed two trophy elk in separate incidents. Park rangers said poachers sometimes use helicopters to enter Yellowstone, where they kill trophy animals and then fly them out of the region.

The penalty for poaching in Yellowstone in 1993 included a $5,000 fine, up to six months in jail, and seizure of weapons used in the crime. From 1988 through 1993, no convicted poachers in Yellowstone went to jail. By 1995 park rangers had begun photographing and videotaping Yellowstone's trophy-sized animals to use that documentation against suspected poachers. To many people the animals, and particularly the elk, may all look similar, but game managers can quickly identify individual animals by the size and shape of their antlers. Some of the animals are so unique that they have been given nicknames.

Fishing Bridge—East Entrance
(US 20/16/14)
27 miles

One prime grizzly habitat area lies between Fishing Bridge and the east entrance gate in the huge Pelican Valley north of the highway. This area is also heavily used by bison and sometimes elk or moose. During winter much of the ground along the lakeshore remains clear of heavy snow because of an underground furnace, in the form of a slightly active geyser basin, that sends steam trails toward the sun on cold days.

Not everyone likes Yellowstone, with its bubbling mud, crusty ground, and sulfurous stench. In 1889, Rudyard Kipling wrote: "The Park is just a howling wilderness of three thousand square miles, full of all imaginable freaks of a fiery nature." But most take the view of artist Frederick Remington, who said Americans should jealously guard the national treasure of Yellowstone because it is a place where nature made wild patterns, brought boiling water from deep underground to rise above snowcapped peaks, and then scattered lakes like jewels. Remington advocated respect for the natural landscape and no mercy for vandals. He suggested they spend "six months where the scenery is circumscribed and entirely artificial."

Vandals wreaked havoc in Yellowstone's early years. They chipped petrified fragments from trees near Specimen Ridge, put soap into geysers to see their reaction, and killed game with no regard to law or regulation. Initially,

Congress didn't provide adequate funding to provide protection from such atrocities. Finally, in 1886, the U.S. Cavalry arrived in Yellowstone to administer and care for the park. It remained until formation of the National Park Service in 1915.

Fishing Bridge—West Thumb
21 miles

A Hotel on the Lake

Seattle architect Robert C. Reamer had a hand in the design of Lake Hotel, originally built in 1889 at the upper end of Yellowstone Lake to serve visitors who reached the area by train. Reamer added soaring Grecian columns to the lakeside facade.

In spite of its splendor, which remains in the 1990s, Lake Hotel had another problem: bears in the garbage. Early in the park's history, managers made no effort to restrict bear feeding. At the various hotels and facilities, bears routinely waited for scraps; traffic jams resulted when they begged by the highway. They'd eat whatever the tourists would feed them: apples, cookies, and peanut butter or bologna sandwiches.

Of the unnatural bear behavior in Yellowstone, President Theodore Roosevelt wrote: "It is curious to think that the descendants of the great grizzlies which were the dread of the early day explorers and hunters should now be semi-domesticated creatures, boldly hanging around crowded hotels for the sake of what they can pick up, and quite harmless so long as any reasonable precaution is exercised."

As early as July 1903, James Barton Key, then manager of the Lake Hotel, had trouble with the bears. He sent a telegraph to Maj. John Pitcher, who commanded army troops in the park, telling him that as many as seventeen bears appeared in the evening at the Lake Hotel garbage dump. Key said campers and "people not of my hotel" threw items at the bears to scare them away.

Concerned, Key asked for a trooper to patrol the area and "make people remain behind [the] danger line." He suggested that if the army arrested some of the campers for harassing the bears, the practice might stop. Major Pitcher issued the order as requested, but not until the 1970 ban on garbage dumps within the park did the problem begin to abate. Closing the garbage dumps set off a storm of controversy, as all management decisions in Yellowstone seem to do.

Bear researchers Frank and John Craighead advocated closing the dumps and forcing the bears to return to natural food sources. However, they thought the dumps should be eliminated in phases to allow bears to reacclimate themselves to the wild. Park managers, according to the Craigheads, believed there were two bear populations in Yellowstone—one living in the backcountry and another relying on the garbage dumps. By eliminating the garbage dumps, the Park Service would prevent bears from relying on a human source for food. But the change had to be gradual.

The Craigheads argued that all bears within the park visited the garbage dumps on occasion and that eliminating that food source quickly would adversely affect the entire bear population. The two researchers correctly argued that such action would force bears to look for food in other locations, such as park campgrounds, and would therefore increase human-bear conflicts, which nobody wanted. After closing the garbage dumps, the Park Service tried to minimize human-bear conflicts by closing some facilities, such as campgrounds, then capturing and relocating some problem bears while killing others.

In the summer of 1993, sightings of grizzly bears came from all points in the Yellowstone ecosystem, a huge area including the park and surrounding lands. Ranchers on Togwotee Pass, south of the park between Moran and Dubois, reported numerous head of cattle apparently killed by grizzlies. Residents living on the South Fork of the Shoshone River, southwest of Cody, sighted grizzly bears near their homes. One bear was spotted within five miles of the town. Some wildlife managers and area residents believe the bear population is burgeoning and that the animals need to expand their territory to find food. In 1994 U.S. Fish and Wildlife Service officials considered taking the grizzly bear off the federal endangered species list.

West Thumb—South Entrance
(US 89/287/191)
21 miles

Facilities at West Thumb are among the newest in Yellowstone, as the architecture clearly shows. While the hotels at Lake and Mammoth are reminiscent of an elegant, bygone era, the style at West Thumb is modern and more severe.

The route between West Thumb and Grand Teton National Park follows the Lewis River, which is named for Meriwether Lewis even though he never saw the Yellowstone country. The 1988 fires in Yellowstone charred many acres, including those along this route. Connecting Yellowstone National Park and Grand Teton National Park is the John D. Rockefeller Jr. Memorial Parkway. When Rockefeller visited Yellowstone in the 1920s he found new roads and a lot of debris left behind. Park officials showed Rockefeller much of Yellowstone, and even provided him with a glimpse of the Teton mountain range. After this son of the famous oil magnate returned to New York, he inquired about the trash along the roads he'd traveled and learned the government had no funds for a cleanup project, so, in the charitable tradition established by his father, Rockefeller donated money to beautify the roadside. (See page 76)

West Thumb—Madison
34 miles

In May 1834, Warren Angus Ferris, a clerk for the American Fur Company, visited Yellowstone accompanied by two Pend d'Oreilles. He entered the region from the south and traveled to the geyser basin north of Old Faithful. The first white man known to see that basin, he later wrote:

> I ventured near enough to put my hand into the waters of its basin, but withdrew it instantly, for the heat of the water in this immense caldron was altogether too great for my comfort; and the agitation of the water, the disagreeable effluvium continually exuding, and the hollow, unearthly rumbling under the rock on which I stood, so ill accorded with my notions of personal safety, that I retreated back precipitously to a respectful distance. The Indians, who were with me, were quite appalled and could not by any means be induced to approach them. They seemed astonished at my presumption in advancing up to the large one, and when I safely returned congratulated me upon my "narrow escape."

An Early Excursion by Bicycle

W. O. Owen made a mark for himself in several locations in Wyoming. He surveyed much of the state, climbed the Grand Teton, and made the first trip by bicycle into Yellowstone National Park. Owen and some companions pedaled furiously up hills, then threw their legs over the handlebars at the crest and "flew down the mountain with the speed of the wind." While descending one hill at breakneck speed they noted a large moving body in the road and headed toward it. Before long it became clear that the object in the road was a party of Indians headed west. Owen wrote in *Old Yellowstone Days* that he and his companions didn't know whether "these Americans were peaceable or on the warpath, and, fearing it might be the latter, it was deemed best to make a rush and frighten them before they could realize what was in the wind."

Owen and his companions released their brakes and raced down the hill, quickly closing the quarter-mile gap separating them from the Indians. The bicyclists burst through the middle of the Indian party, which scattered in all directions. Owen said: "It was a desperate charge, but entirely successful, and, passing the Indians, we reached the foot of the hill in safety."

Surveyor W. O. Owen made an early-day bicycle trip through Yellowstone Park. —Teton County Historical Center

Old Faithful Inn

One great treasure in Yellowstone is man-made: Old Faithful Inn, built under the direction of Seattle architect Robert C. Reamer and opened in the spring of 1904. "I built it in keeping with the place where it stands. Nobody could improve upon that. To be at discord with the landscape would be almost a crime. To try to improve upon it would be an impertinence," Reamer said.

The best way to appreciate Old Faithful Inn is to spend time there, for to simply walk through the vast building is, as Reamer might put it, an impertinence. However, if you stay at Old Faithful, it is possible to soak in the ambience. Climb to the third floor of the lobby. There you can sink into the seat of a leather-covered chair, listen to the tinkle of a piano and the hum of words spoken in myriad languages, and, most of all, look at the construction of this huge log lodge, believed to be the largest of its kind in the world.

The knotted burl wood that forms the staircase bannister and the balcony railing, the huge logs that tower all the way to the high ceiling, the rich leather

109

chairs, and the wood rubbed to a polished sheen by the millions of hands that have trailed over its edges tell a story of Yellowstone much different from the elegance of the Lake or Mammoth Hot Springs hotels. This place, as Reamer wanted it, fits with the landscape. It is a wilderness lodge in America's premiere wilderness park, even if there are millions of people teeming down the boardwalks through geyser basins or bumping along over the highways.

During the summer fires of 1988 that scorched thousands of acres in and around Yellowstone, Old Faithful served as a command center, and only heroic efforts kept the historic lodge from burning. Huge sprinkler systems squirted water on the building and the grounds to keep it wet and safe from the raging flames.

Hamilton's Stores

Charles Ashworth Hamilton of St. Paul, Minnesota, started spending summers in Yellowstone as early as 1905. In 1915 he became a park concessionaire when he bought the Klamer store at Old Faithful. The store became Hamilton's office, headquarters, warehouse, and home whenever he visited Yellowstone. He soon expanded the business, and in 1927 Hamilton opened soda fountains in his various stores, starting a tradition that continues.

As part of his operation, Hamilton built a swimming pool and bathhouse at Old Faithful, but a new lease agreement in 1946 forced him to demolish those buildings because park officials wanted no artificial recreational facilities in the park. Gwen Peterson wrote in *Yellowstone Pioneers: The Story of the Hamilton Stores and Yellowstone National Park*, "By the end of the summer 1951 the 'artificial' swimming pool was no more; it has since been covered with 'natural' asphalt."

Hamilton operated facilities at Old Faithful, Fishing Bridge, West Thumb, and Lake. His success came at least in part because the owner catered to the needs of people in automobiles. He located his stores conveniently so motorists could buy gifts and souvenirs and, more important, gasoline for their cars.

Flight of the Nez Perce

Yellowstone in 1877 became a scene of flight involving the U.S. Army and Nez Perce Indians as Chief Joseph, Looking Glass, and Lean Elk (also known as Poker Joe) led their people on a desperate run for freedom that began near the Idaho-Oregon-Washington border.

In June the Nez Perce were being forced to move onto the reservation in Idaho when some young warriors killed several white people. An army of soldiers and volunteers under the command of Gen. Oliver O. Howard went after them, but at every encounter the Nez Perce defeated or eluded their pursuers. During the chase the Indians first decided to seek refuge with their allies, the Crows, in Montana, and later decided to leave the country by crossing into Canada. Eventually, on October 5, 1877, the army caught the Indians just forty miles south of the Canadian border.

Late in August the Nez Perce entered Yellowstone just north of the Madison River near West Yellowstone and trailed toward the east, though not always as a unified group. After crossing Grand Loop Road south of the Firehole Canyon at a stream now called Nez Perce Creek, the main body forded the Yellowstone River near Mud Volcano, then moved up the Pelican Valley to Mist Creek and its confluence with the Lamar River, where they turned north and followed the Lamar Valley to Miller Creek. Outside the park, they followed the Clarks Fork River and continued fleeing north toward Canada.

At about the same time the Nez Perce entered Yellowstone, a tourist party from Montana also made its way through the park. Included were Emma Cowan, her husband, George, and her sister, brother, and some other men. Early in the trip the Cowan party met with Gen. William Tecumseh Sherman, who told them the Nez Perce might be near. Emma Cowan later wrote, "The scout who was with the General's party assured us we would be perfectly safe if we would remain in the Basin, as the Indians would never come into the Park." But the Nez Perce did enter the park, and as luck would have it the tourists and the Indians met.

Yellow Wolf, one of Chief Joseph's men, wanted to kill the white visitors, but other members of the tribe argued for leniency, and when one of the tourists boldly stood up and shook hands with the warriors, Yellow Hand supposedly said, "that put me in a mind not to kill him." Instead the Indians took the tourist party with them on their flight from the army. As they reached the area of Nez Perce Creek, George Cowan protested, not wanting to go any farther with his captors, although he had little choice. About ten miles to the east, near Mary Mountain, the Nez Perce finally stopped to rest. There Poker Joe, in fairly good English, told the Cowan party he wanted to trade for their horses; then they would be free to leave.

After the trade, Poker Joe told the Cowan party to "go quick" with several worn-out horses, a mule that had been shot in the shoulder, and only one saddle. Two of the party escaped into the forest, and the remainder headed back down the path now called the Mary Mountain Trail. Before long, however, twenty to thirty Nez Perce warriors recaptured them. In the melee that followed, George Cowan fell with a bullet in his leg. Then, as his wife watched, another Indian shot Cowan in the head. Emma later wrote, "My husband's head fell back, and a red stream trickled down his face from beneath his hat."

Indians grabbed Emma, Ida, and their brother Frank Carpenter. Before long, Poker Joe came down the trail and took charge. He ordered the three whites placed on horses. The party turned east to camp that night in the Hayden Valley and this time they found themselves in the company of Chief Joseph. Emma later wrote that the chief was "sombre and silent . . . grave and dignified . . . he looked a chief."

The following day the party crossed the Yellowstone River about six miles north of Yellowstone Lake, and soon after that Poker Joe informed Emma and Ida they would be released, along with a soldier who had been captured that morning. Emma refused to leave without her brother, and the Indians agreed; they held the soldier instead. The siblings made their way north out of the park to Bozeman, where Emma grieved the death of her husband.

But the bullet that hit George Cowan in the forehead didn't kill him. Some time after his wife and other friends and relatives disappeared, Cowan regained consciousness. He later said, "I then thought the ball had passed entirely through my head in some way. Feeling my leg, I found it completely benumbed, but there were no bones broken."

Cowan crawled nearly ten miles to the lower geyser basin, taking five days to reach his party's old camp, where he found a dozen or so matches, a handful of coffee, and an old can in which he boiled water and made coffee. The following day he dragged himself through East Fork Creek to the bank of the Firehole River. But he could go no farther. His strength deserted him, and Cowan gave himself up for dead. Just a couple of hours later army scouts found him beside the trail. It took a month for Cowan and his wife, who believed herself to be a widow, to be reunited.

In 1881, at the forks of Nez Perce Creek and the Firehole River, park superintendant Philetus W. Norris built a two-room, sod-roofed bathhouse, which he allowed the public to use free of charge.

Madison—West Yellowstone
14 miles

Mountain men followed the Madison River along a route that now is the road between Madison and West Yellowstone. One of three rivers that give rise to the Missouri River at Three Forks, Montana, the Madison begins at the confluence of the Firehole and Gibbon rivers and lies in an area the Indians called Summit of the World.

The North Fork Fire of 1988 burned hot in this area. More than 385,000 acres went up in smoke after July 22 because of a woodcutter's cigarette. Although park officials immediately tried to suppress the fire, it blew out of control and eventually threatened West Yellowstone, Madison Junction, Norris, and Old Faithful before sweeping north toward Mammoth and Tower. Fire fighters didn't stop the blaze until snow fell in October.

Madison—Norris
14 miles

Elk and buffalo almost always graze along the Gibbon River between Madison and Norris. The Gibbon is named for Col. John Gibbon, who explored the region in 1872. He tried to ascend the river's north fork, but didn't complete the journey. Besides the river, his name is attached to many other Yellowstone sites: Gibbon Canyon, Gibbon Falls, Gibbon Meadows, and Gibbon Paint Pots.

Philetus W. Norris was the second superintendent of Yellowstone National Park, a position he held between 1877 and 1882. Like Gibbon, his name is on many park features, including a pass, a geyser basin, and a road junction. A rather flamboyant character who often wore a fringed buckskin hunting shirt and a broad-brimmed white hat decorated with an eagle feather, Norris built the first roads in the park, traveled all of its trails, and wrote and published a great many articles about the park.

He named many of the features in the park, including some for himself, which led a Bozeman newspaper reporter to write:

> Take the Norris wagon road and follow down the Norris fork of the Firehole River to the Norris Canyon of the Norris Obsidian Mountain; then go on to Mount Norris, on the summit of which you will find Monu-

Norris Lunch Station, Yellowstone National Park, 1907. —Wyoming State Museum

113

ment Park of the Norris Blowout; and at its northerly base the Norris Basin and Park. Further on you will come to the Norris Geyser plateau and must not fail to see Geyser Norris. The Norris Falls of the Gibbon are worth a visit. The next point of interest is the Gibbon, half a day's ride from the Norris Hot Springs.

Norris—Canyon
12 miles

The road between Norris and Canyon is an excellent place to see bald eagles during winter snowmobile trips in Yellowstone. The route follows the Gibbon River through Virginia Meadows and past Cascade Meadows. Fires burned much of the area north of the highway in 1988, leaving a mosaic of charred timber and living trees.

Norris—Mammoth
21 miles

Only One Tribe Lived Here

Yellowstone's earliest trails came from the footsteps of the Indians, including Crow, Blackfeet, Bannock, Eastern Shoshone, and Takuarika or Sheepeaters, the only tribe known to have lived year-round within the Yellowstone area. "The larger tribes never enter the basin, restrained by superstitious ideas in connection with the thermal springs," said an 1870 Yellowstone Expedition report. Obsidian Cliff became a quarry for ancient and Indian weapons and tools. Some authorities suggest Indians may have avoided the area not because of superstition but because snow made it inaccessible during most of the year.

Jim Bridger left his footsteps all over Wyoming, and Yellowstone is no exception. At rendezvous he regaled listeners with tall tales, including one about an obsidian cliff located south of Mammoth. Bridger's story went something like this:

One day he came upon a magnificent elk and took careful aim before firing, but he watched in amazement when the elk didn't drop, and in fact it appeared the animal hadn't heard the report of the rifle. Bridger shot a couple more times with the same result. He then grabbed his rifle by the barrel and decided to use it as a club, as it had failed as a firearm. He rushed toward the elk, but an immovable vertical wall of perfectly transparent glass stopped him.

Sheepeater Indians such as this family group are the only tribe known to have lived year-round in the Yellowstone region. —Teton County Historical Center

Through the glass mountain he watched the elk contentedly grazing. As he watched, Bridger saw that the mountain not only was made of pure glass but also acted as a telescopic lens; although the elk seemed to be grazing only a few hundred yards off, it was in reality twenty-five miles away.

Flames Race across Yellowstone

The firestorm that swept Yellowstone's ecosystem during the summer and early fall of 1988 blackened thousands of acres of trees and claimed one human life, a firefighter near Cody who died when a tree fell on him. A separate, but equally fiery, inferno erupted at the national policy level, as accusations flew fast and furious about how Yellowstone's managers allowed the fires to rage so out of control.

Starting in 1972, Yellowstone allowed naturally caused fires to burn unchecked, as they would in the wild. Under normal conditions, natural fires, like those started by lightning, clear out dead and dying timber so an area can regenerate. During the summer of 1988, however, drought conditions throughout the West, and particularly in northwest Wyoming, left Yellowstone a tinderbox. Yellowstone's managers allowed early natural fires to burn, but the unusually dry conditions caused fires of epic proportions throughout the park and in surrounding forests or wilderness areas.

Hot, fast winds blew the flames out of control for weeks. In *Roadside History of Yellowstone National Park*, Winfred Blevins quotes Denny Bungarz, incident commander on the North Fork Fire: "We threw everything at that fire from Day One. We tried everything we knew of or could think of, and that fire kicked our ass from one end of the park to the other." Thousands of men and women, including U.S. military troops and highly trained firefighters, battled the flames, but it took winter snows to finally quench them. By the time the fire advance halted, about 900,000 acres—nearly half the park—had burned.

A campground outhouse stands alone in a forest charred by fire in 1988. The new shoots of pine trees start their journey toward the sun in 1993, five years after the massive fires that tore through the region.

During the fiercest fire inferno, many park roads could be used only by emergency traffic and the firefighting crews that simply couldn't stop the flames. Those working the fire lines said they'd never seen blazes like those in Yellowstone. One park publication said, "the raw, unbridled power of these fires cannot be overemphasized."

Driving the roads in Yellowstone today offers a mere glimpse of the impact of the 1988 fires. Although stands and falls of blackened trees clearly show the fire's aftermath, much of the burning took place in Yellowstone's backcountry and cannot be seen from the roads. Hiking or riding a horse through the backcountry is an entirely different experience. Such a trip in the summer of 1992 from Pahaska Teepee at the park's eastern gate, up the North Fork of the Shoshone River to the Little Lamar River, and then down Mist Creek and through the Pelican Valley revealed many acres of charred forest. The dead and dying trees crashed and fell in high winds and after soaking rains. Low-growing plants sprouted luxuriantly in most places, and wildflowers provided splashes of color. In some areas the regrowth hadn't started, or had barely begun; the forest floor remained as black as the day after it burned.

Gardners Hole and Golden Gate

Grand Loop Road follows Obsidian Creek from Norris to Mammoth and crosses an area heavily used by bison. Near Swan Lake the highway crosses Gardners Hole, named for Johnson Gardner, a free trapper for the American Fur Company in 1832. In *Yellowstone National Park*, Hiram Chittenden calls the river the Gardiner and says "the discrepancy in the spelling has no significance." Chittenden uses a letter written by Jesuit missionary Pierre De Smet dated January 20, 1852, as the basis for spelling Gardiner with an *i*. But Chittenden clearly says the river is named for Gardner, and more recent maps and references always call the landmarks by the name Gardner, even though the town in Montana spells its name as De Smet did.

Just north of Gardner's Hole and the Gardner River is Golden Gate, a site once called Kingman Pass for Lt. Daniel C. Kingman, the first road engineer in the park. Construction of the 200-foot-long Golden Gate Viaduct in the late 1880s required eleven piers to support the highway along the cliff. High winds blow constantly through the area and created some problems for workers building the original wooden viaduct. One man suffered more than most when the wind blew him from the concrete form on which he worked to the rocks below.

Artist Frederick Remington visited Yellowstone in 1893 and made the following comments about Golden Gate:

> It is one of those marvellous vistas of mountain scenery utterly beyond the pen or brush of any man. Paint cannot touch it, and words are wasted. . . . But as the stages of the Park Company run over this road, every tourist sees its grandeur, and bangs away with his kodak.

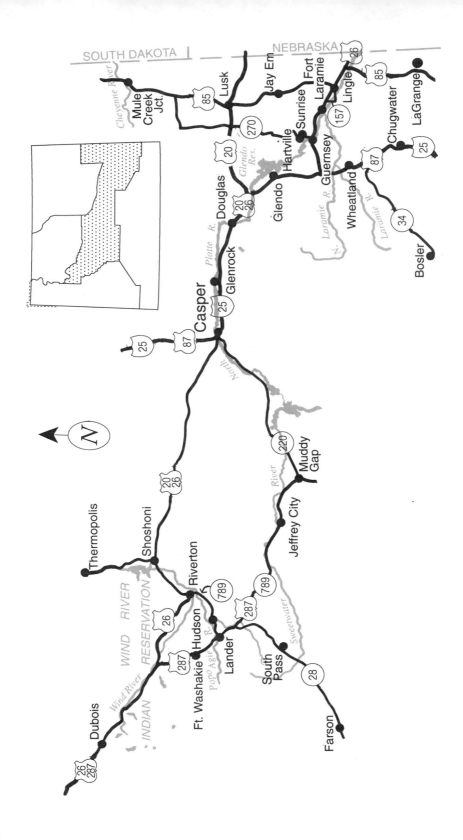

Part 2

Oregon Trail Country

*T*he North Platte and Sweetwater rivers provided useful corridors for Indians, fur trappers, and emigrants traveling overland. The native Americans followed the waterways for generations, so it was only natural that the mountain men should do the same. Near the rivers they could find food and water for themselves and their animals. The route along the streams had clear markings by the time pioneers began moving west on the Oregon, California, and Mormon trails in the 1840s.

Emigrants seeking land, gold, and religious freedom followed trails along the rivers and across the mountains. They struck out for Oregon, a country the United States and Great Britain shared since 1818 under the Joint Occupancy Treaty. "Manifest Destiny" became the cry of Americans, and by 1846 they had claimed Oregon for the United States. Few of the thousands of travelers crossing Wyoming's broad expanse between 1843 and 1865—a period characterized by the term "Great Migration"—remained as permanent residents. For most, Wyoming was part of the journey, not the destination.

Then, as now, a trip across Oregon Trail country follows the North Platte and Sweetwater rivers much of the way. But the region has a history much more diverse than that solely of western-bound emigrants and gold seekers. It served as a corridor for the Pony Express during that operation's short life in 1860–61 and then became the route of the Creighton telegraph.

When miners sought gold in the Black Hills of South Dakota after 1874, they followed a route from Cheyenne to Deadwood across the eastern grasslands and Hat Creek breaks. The dust of the miners' horses and the first Cheyenne-Deadwood stagecoaches had barely settled when cattle herds from Texas trailed north, crossing the rolling country on the Texas Trail, which that ran parallel to the stage route.

The earliest major Indian-army conflict in what we now know as Wyoming took place in the middle of Oregon Trail country in July 1865, when a party of Sioux and Cheyenne attacked Platte Bridge Station and a nearby military wagon train, killing several soldiers. Meanwhile, Wyoming's most infamous incident in the conflict between homesteaders and ranchers took place along the Sweetwater River in 1889 when six prominent cattlemen hanged two homesteaders, one of whom was a woman—the legendary Cattle Kate.

Although today the lands along the North Platte River feature lush, irrigated acres, much of this region is little changed from the way it appeared in the 1840s when the earliest emigrants trekked across it. There is a lot of sagebrush, few trees, and more dirt roads than paved highways.

We begin our trip through Oregon Trail country the way emigrants saw it—starting in the east and heading west.

US 26
Nebraska Line—Fort Laramie
28 miles

Several roads enter Wyoming from Nebraska in the Torrington area, but the most heavily used is US 26. It follows the north bank of the North Platte River to Guernsey, then cuts west to connect with I-25 a few miles north of Wheatland. It parallels the Oregon-Mormon-California-Pony Express trails and bisects both the Texas Cattle Trail and the Cheyenne-Deadwood Stage Route, crossing through one of the most productive agricultural valleys in Wyoming. Sugar beets, corn, and beans fill almost every acre. The crops get their water from the North Platte Water Project, a massive irrigation system managed by the U.S. Bureau of Reclamation. Much of Wyoming gets battered by wind and snow, but this area has milder winters than the rest of the state. The summers can be intense, however, with severe thunderstorms and tornadoes sweeping across the plains.

The First Treaty

Two years after Fort Laramie opened as an army outpost in 1849, the federal government realized that something needed to be done to ensure that people could continue to pass through Indian lands en route to fertile farmland in Oregon and Washington or goldfields in California. In response to an invitation from the United States, an estimated 10,000 Sioux, Cheyenne, and Arapaho gathered at Fort Laramie in 1851. They spread their tipis on the lush bottomlands along the North Platte and Laramie rivers and prepared to discuss an agreement to let emigrants cross their territory.

However, the large number of people and livestock quickly took a toll on the land, and it became necessary to move the encampment downstream, where there was more grass for the animals. The final negotiations took place about thirty-six miles east of the fort on Horse Creek, just at the present-day Wyoming-Nebraska state line along US 26.

After eighteen days of feasting, smoking, visiting, and parleying, the assembled tribes agreed "to abstain in future from all hostilities whatever against each other, to maintain good faith and friendship in all their mutual intercourse, and to make an effective and lasting peace." The chiefs also agreed to divide the country into separate areas for the various tribes and to "make restitution or satisfaction for any wrongs committed . . . by any band or individual of their people, on the people of the United States, whilst lawfully residing in or passing through their respective territories."

Father Pierre De Smet called the treaty "the commencement of a new era for the Indians—an era of peace." But in fact the "era of peace" ended with the conference, according to James C. Olson in *Red Cloud and the Sioux Problem*.

The chiefs had agreed to let wagon trains cross their lands in return for annual payments of goods valued at $50,000. However, the ink had barely dried on the paper before the white treaty makers and the powers-that-be in Washington started changing the conditions—in particular, by shortening the term of payments from fifty years to only fifteen. As a result, the 1851 treaty is often considered a cause of hostilities that terrorized the northern Plains in subsequent years.

Also, the chiefs who made their marks upon the treaty had no real authority within their own tribes. The government treaty makers designated the Indians who signed "chiefs" and held them responsible for bringing their "followers" into line when necessary. In reality, the chiefs didn't speak for anyone besides their own factions, and even then they often had trouble keeping a tight rein on the young men.

The Grattan Massacre

Under the 1851 treaty, once a year the government would provide goods—annuities—for the Indians. The tribes gathered for their "gifts" near Fort Laramie in the fall of 1854. Officials stored the supplies at a nearby post called the Gratiot Houses and waited for the proper authorities to arrive and make the distributions.

In mid-August, while the tribes waited, one of the first incidents that strained relations between the military and the Indians happened just west of present-day Lingle in a place that is now a cornfield. (To get to the site, take Wyoming 157 between Lingle and Fort Laramie.) The milestone event involved a cow, an Indian, an army lieutenant, a drunk interpreter, and a big misunderstanding.

It all started when a Mormon's cow strayed from camp, or perhaps was left behind when it became footsore, and a Miniconjou Sioux named High Forehead killed it for meat. The Mormon reported the incident to authorities at Fort Laramie. Sioux leaders, knowing the cow should not have been killed, also reported the incident at Fort Laramie. Man-Afraid-of-His-Horses met with the soldiers and tried to make payment to the Mormon by giving horses in exchange. Government officials rejected his offer.

The military ultimately decided to take action. Second Lt. John L. Grattan convinced superiors to let him visit the Sioux camp with a company of soldiers. Accompanied by twenty-five privates, two musicians, and interpreter Lucien Auguste, Grattan took two mounted cannon and headed to the Brulé camp of Conquering Bear, where High Forehead was staying. Auguste spent his time on the ride to the Indian camp drinking whiskey, and some of the soldiers may have been imbibing as well.

When the detail arrived at the camp, Auguste, his courage bolstered with plenty of whiskey, taunted the Indians. Grattan met with Conquering Bear (often called simply The Bear). Speaking through his drunken interpreter, Grattan explained that the killing of the cow wasn't allowed and that the Indian perpetrator needed to go with him to the fort. Not unexpectedly, the Indian refused. Harsh words filled the air, and soon the incident blew all out of proportion as the soldiers opened fire, wounding Conquering Bear. A second volley took down more Indians, and the fight was on. In the ensuing melee, many soldiers escaped the camp and fled toward Fort Laramie but fell when Sioux arrows found their marks. Grattan died in the Indian village, and Conquering Bear died later of his wounds. One enlisted man escaped and hid near the North Platte River. He eventually reached Fort Laramie but soon died of his wounds.

Many Indians and white traders witnessed the incident, including Man-Afraid-of-His-Horses and James Bordeaux, both of whom tried to dissuade Grattan from his mission. All agreed the fatal encounter was caused by misunderstanding on the part of the Indians and rashness by the officer. Unfortunately, it escalated hostilities along the Oregon Trail for the next several years.

One year later, soldiers took their revenge upon the Sioux. Brig. Gen. S. William Harney left Fort Leavenworth with 1,200 men and orders to restore peace on the trail. On September 3, 1855, at Blue Water Creek, just west of Ash Hollow in Nebraska and a hundred or so miles east of the spot where Grattan and his command died, Harney encountered Little Thunder's band of Brulés. In a confrontation known as the Bloody Blue Fight (sometimes called the Harney Massacre), at least 90 and as many as 136 people died, most of whom were Brulé. It didn't seem to matter to Harney and his men that the Indians they attacked weren't necessarily those who had been at the Grattan Massacre a year earlier.

Harney then went to Fort Pierre, where he forced the Sioux to agree to a treaty restating their willingness to permit white travel along the Oregon Trail and agreeing to the establishment of a military road from Fort Laramie to Fort Pierre. Those two events—the Grattan Massacre of 1854 near Fort Laramie and the Harney Massacre of 1855 near Ash Hollow—set the stage for years of conflict between the encroaching whites and the Plains tribes.

The Tribes Watch the Trail

The Oregon Trail passed through or near the territories of almost sixty Indian tribes. Early emigrants were a source of great curiosity, and some concern, for all of the tribes. Native Americans' reactions to the migration ranged from feelings of helplessness to outright aggression. But there were few problems prior to the 1851 treaty and the Grattan and Harney incidents. After that, though, the tribes knew that displacement, relocation, and disease threatened their very existence.

Already they saw that the buffalo and other animals upon which they depended for food and shelter no longer flocked to the Platte—or Shell River, as the Lakota called the waterway. The animals moved away from the nearly constant stream of white-topped wagons following the Platte River Road. Even knowing the threat to their own way of life, the western tribes didn't react with full-scale hostility toward the whites until a decade later, after yet another massacre by the military upon Indians at Sand Creek in Colorado.

Most tribes did not refer to the Oregon Trail by that name. Prior to 1851 the Lakota called it Wasichu Canku (White Man Road); after the treaty was signed they called it Holy Road. That name resulted from one treaty provision allowing the emigrants to pass through Indian country unmolested as long as they remained on the trail. Some Lakota believed that the treaty had apparently "sanctified" the trail, as if it were holy. The name had nothing to do with any real spiritual or religious aspect of the trail or its travelers, according to Lakota writer Joe Marshall.

The Shoshone didn't participate in the 1851 treaty negotiations, but under Chief Washakie they nevertheless adopted a policy of peace with the emigrants. However, they saw reduced numbers of game animals and a loss of their free way of life. The Shoshone called the Oregon Trail "River of Destruction."

Bordeaux

James Bordeaux, who was in charge of the trading post on the Laramie when Francis Parkman visited in 1846, built a road ranch on Chugwater Creek in 1867 when officials laid out a road and telegraph line between Fort Laramie and the newly created Fort D. A. Russell at Cheyenne. Bordeaux's road ranch was at a strategic location and enjoyed protection from nearby Fort Laramie. The site eventually became the settlement of Bordeaux, although now it is just a ghost town.

Fort Laramie

Natural gathering places have always featured plentiful food and water. In Wyoming it's not unusual to find remains of historic and even prehistoric campsites along creeks and rivers. By the 1820s, the spot where the Laramie River dumps into the North Platte had become a popular trapper rendezvous and trading ground. One early trapper, Jacques La Ramee, lent his name to the fort and the river in this area, as well as other landmarks in southeastern Wyoming.

In 1834 Robert Campbell and William Sublette built a trading post on the banks of the Laramie called Fort William. The following year they sold it to the American Fur Company, and the post became Fort John, for John B. Sarpy. The name changed again a few years later when a clerk wrote "Fort Laramie," rather than "Fort John on the Laramie." Rival trappers built Fort Platte in 1841, about a mile and a half from Fort John and nearer the confluence of the Laramie and Platte rivers.

In his diary in 1846, Heinrich Lienhard described Fort Laramie—which was not yet a military post—as a rectangle with sixteen- to twenty-foot-high walls of dried brick. The interior was divided into various rooms. That same year Francis Parkman wrote, "Found ourselves before the gateway of Fort

Fort Laramie, sutler's store, August 1993.

124

*Some of the buildings at Fort Laramie have been restored,
while others remain as deteriorating walls and foundations.*

Laramie, under the impending blockhouse erected above it to guard the entrance. . . . The little fort is built of bricks dried in the sun, and externally is of an oblong form, with bastions of clay, in the form of ordinary blockhouses, at two of the corners."

In 1842, John C. Frémont explored the West and recommended that Fort John become a military post to protect emigrants heading west. Seven years later, after about 50,000 travelers already had passed Fort Laramie en route to Oregon country, the U.S. government purchased it for $4,000 from the American Fur Company. Its location enabled the new military post to protect the increasing numbers of people headed to Oregon or California.

In addition to guarding the emigrant route, the fort became a major supply post for westbound pioneers. It also served mountain men and Indians and hosted historic peace conferences between the tribes and the federal government in 1851 and 1868. Indians had often gathered at the fort from its earliest days as a fur-trading post to exchange buckskin goods for trinkets. Sometimes more than 100 lodges of various tribes stood nearby, and at least a few tipis usually cast their shadows on the land.

Fort Laramie was the first permanent white settlement in Wyoming. Trappers may have established earlier, temporary settlements in western areas of the present-day state, but only Fort Laramie survived the test of time. Twenty of Fort Laramie's original buildings remain. Among them is the officers' quarters, known as Old Bedlam and believed to be the oldest standing structure in the state. Construction of the two-story block building took place by the winter of 1849. Through that doorway passed people now legendary in Wyoming's history: Jim Bridger, Father Pierre De Smet, Red Cloud, Man-Afraid-of-His-Horses, John C. Frémont, Lt. John Grattan, Col. Henry B. Carrington, and John "Portugee" Phillips.

The adobe-built sutler's store went up in subsequent years and is perhaps the second-oldest building in Wyoming. More than a general supply house, the store served as the chief banking institution for outlying posts. The sutler and his clerks processed promissory notes, checks, and deposits of credit from places as far away as Utah and Ireland, according to the Wyoming Writers' Program guide, published under the auspices of the WPA in 1941.

Buildings and grounds at Fort Laramie were sold to homesteaders in 1890, when the military abandoned the post. In 1937 the State of Wyoming bought 214 acres and the then-remaining structures and began a move for restoration. Federal officials designated Fort Laramie a National Historic Site in 1938, and the state transferred ownership to the National Park Service.

The heavy adobe blocks insulated against cold in the winter and against heat in the summer. In 1993 the sutler's store remained in use as a poolroom-bar; however, it dispensed no pool cues or beer but instead had a fresh-faced "bartender" passing out bottles of sarsaparilla or paper cups of apple cider. Either was a welcome relief to tourists sweltering in 90-degree heat as they visited the remains of old Fort Laramie.

The First White Women

Marcus Whitman and the Rev. Henry Harmon Spalding brought their white brides to Fort Laramie in 1836, en route to rendezvous and eventually to Oregon. Those two pale-faced women, the first ever seen in these parts, caused quite a stir as they crossed the Indian country. They graced the halls of Old Bedlam in Fort Laramie, stood with their dresses blowing in the wind at South Pass, and camped with the mountain men at rendezvous on Horse Creek in the Green River country. For many of the mountain men, they were a reminder of mothers, sisters, wives, or sweethearts left back at home.

River Ferries

After resting and restocking at Fort Laramie, emigrants crossed the North Platte River before continuing their westward journey. On June 11, 1859, Joseph Price wrote in his diary: "When we crossed the Platt down at Fort Cearny [sic] we under Stood that we was clear of the Platt but the further we

A monument to Narcissa Prentiss Whitman and Eliza Hart Spalding at South Pass credits them as being the first white women to cross the pass, July 4, 1836.

came up the more we became convinced that we was under a great mistake it is said that a mountain goat cant go up this side of the river and consequently we had to cross at this point."

Most travelers ferried the river. By 1849 a privately operated ferry was serving emigrants; later the army provided a barge for the same purpose. The craft remained in place until 1875, when the army built an iron truss bridge. That structure, which still stands today, is believed to be the oldest existing military bridge west of the Mississippi River.

The bridge became a significant factor in development of the stagecoach route from Cheyenne to Deadwood, South Dakota, in the late 1870s. Approval for the bridge predated news of gold in the Black Hills and the opening

The U.S. Army built this iron bridge across the North Platte River near Fort Laramie in 1875. It made the route from Cheyenne to Deadwood, South Dakota, the trail of choice after the discovery of gold and opening of mining operations in the Black Hills. The bridge remains in place, but is open only to foot traffic.

of that area to white intrusion. A route from Sidney, Nebraska, directly north to Deadwood was more practical, but because the bridge was in place at Fort Laramie much of the traffic into the Black Hills went via Cheyenne.

That bridge, with its three iron arches, spans the Platte near Fort Laramie National Historic Site, just west of the present town of Fort Laramie on Wyoming 160. Only foot traffic can cross. The bridge clearly shows that the river was once much stronger, deeper, and wider than it is today; more than half of its length spans a grassy slope (now a picnic area) that obviously used to wash free every spring during flood stage on the North Platte.

The Pony Express

When William Russell, Alexander Majors, and William Waddell started the Pony Express in 1860 along the Oregon Trail, Fort Laramie became the first station in Wyoming.

Wyoming's "pony boys," those daredevil riders of the short-lived enterprise, resided at stations spaced roughly twenty miles apart from Fort Laramie to Fort Bridger. From April 3, 1860, until October 24, 1861, they maintained a postal link between East and the West during a critical period in American history, racing the mail across the country in record time. In its eighteen-month life, the Pony Express had only one rider killed while on duty. The station tenders, who waited and watched for the next rider to gallop over the ridge, were in much greater danger than the horsemen. They became sitting targets for the various Indian tribes, which became more aggressive toward white men as each year passed.

The Pony Express never would have existed if William Russell hadn't acted upon his own initiative in obtaining John Hockaday's stage line, which ran on the Oregon Trail. Russell's partners had no real desire to begin running mail or passengers on that central route; they thought it too expensive and risky. But Russell had already given his word to federal officials that the company would establish a mail service, and Majors and Waddell, with their reputations on the line, fell in behind Russell.

To his credit, Russell showed a nose for opportunity and a willingness to take necessary risks. He believed in himself and in the potential of the Central Overland California & Pikes Peak Express Company, which operated separately from the Pony Express. In a letter to Waddell in mid-summer 1860, he wrote of the company, "I was compelled . . . to build a world-wide reputation, even at considerable expense and also to incur large expenses in many ways, the details of which I cannot commit to paper," according to Raymond and Mary Settle in *Saddles and Spurs: The Pony Express Saga*.

Despite Waddell's financial commitment and that of his partners, the company never met its expenses, leaving it with the unflattering nickname "Clean Out of Cash & Poor Pay." Nonetheless, the Pony Express did successfully deliver the mail and did it in record time. The key to the achievement was the hard riding of some eighty young men averaging nineteen years of age, mostly orphans, who raced across the plains and mountains.

Ironically, the Pony Express didn't use ponies. For the most part it relied on well-bred horses, often with thoroughbred blood; sometimes it employed the endurance-tested mustangs of the West. Riders changed mounts every twenty miles—if all went well. Once in a while fresh horses disappeared to marauding Indians or renegade whites, and the riders raced on, urging the same tired steed another twenty miles to the next station. That overuse, unfortunately—but, in the eyes of the company, necessarily—killed an animal from time to time. The riders may have been young, but they did everything they could to get across the continent with the mail, often breaking their own speed records and risking their lives in the quest.

On one ride Jim Moore, who later became a prominent rancher in Wyoming and Nebraska, galloped 280 miles in less than fifteen hours, an average speed of eighteen miles per hour (see page 136). Several factors enabled the riders to cover such vast distances in such good time. They had top-quality horses, which they switched at regular intervals, and they carried the mail in specially designed pouches called *mochilas*, which were actually leather cover-

An artist's rendition of placing the mochila *on the horse at a Pony Express station.* —Wyoming State Museum

ings that fit over the saddle frame. At each station the incoming rider simply jumped off his horse, pulled the *mochila* over the horn and cantle, and repositioned it on a new saddle atop a fresh horse. Then he swung into place and took off in a cloud of dust.

The Pony Express made its first cross-country delivery—from St. Joseph, Missouri, to San Francisco, California—in ten days. The quickest crossing coincided with the inauguration of President Abraham Lincoln in March 1861. Then riders raced 1,966 miles in seven days and seventeen hours, an average speed of just over ten and a half miles per hour, with the paper carrying the text of Lincoln's inaugural address.

Although it was a financial disaster, Russell, Majors, and Waddell's Pony Express served a vital function, keeping people on the West Coast informed about the status of the Union during that tense period prior to the outbreak of the Civil War. When the Southern states seceded from the Union, some rebel leaders attempted to force California out of the Union, according to Waddell F. Smith in *The Story of the Pony Express.* A vocal minority of California's population traced its roots to the South and sympathized with the rebel cause.

As Southern eyes turned westward for support, the Pony Express brought word that California must be defended if it were to remain in the Union. Petitioners pointed out California's importance to the Union and noted that it was much easier to retain a state in allegiance than to overcome disloyalty disguised as state authority, Smith wrote.

Loyalists won a state election in September 1861, putting to rest the fears that California would side with the South. Throughout the crisis, news regularly passed between East and West, carried in the heavy leather *mochila* of the Pony Express.

The Pony Express died not from financial losses but from competition. The day William Creighton's transcontinental telegraph went on line, it marked the end for the Pony Express. Yet during its short life span the service made history, and the riders became recognized as brave young men. Many of their exploits happened on Wyoming's plains, and we'll return to them later.

The Story of an Indian Girl

The Brulé chief Spotted Tail had a long-standing, mostly peaceful association with the whites of Wyoming. His tribe spent much time at Fort Laramie, and his daughter Ah-ho-appa, or Falling Leaf, often sat on a bench by the sutler's store watching the fort's activities. Many believed Ah-ho-appa loved one of the soldiers.

In 1865 and 1866 the Plains Indians fought gold seekers and the military as those intruders forged a road and built forts in the Powder River country, a land set aside by treaty for the native Americans. Spotted Tail and his band of Brulés lived in the Powder River Basin and engaged in some of the conflicts. When Ah-ho-appa died of tuberculosis in the fall of 1866, he acceded to her dying request that she be buried at Fort Laramie.

The chief sent word to Col. H. E. Maynadier asking permission to place a burial platform for her near the premises. The military leader, seeing an opportunity to bring Spotted Tail to Fort Laramie and thus render him neutral in the ongoing Powder River war, agreed. When Spotted Tail arrived with his daughter's body, Maynadier personally escorted the chief to his headquarters and told him preparations would be made for the burial at sunset. In *Red Cloud and the Sioux Problem*, Olson said Colonel Maynadier told Spotted Tail that particular time was chosen for the burial because "as the sun went down it might remind him of the darkness left in his lodge when his beloved daughter was taken away; but as the sun would surely rise again, so she would rise, and some day we would all meet in the land of the Great Spirit."

Ah-ho-appa had her own burial platform, and Maynadier's troops accorded her honors as well in the fort's cemetery. (Some years later, according to the Wyoming Writers' Program guide, Spotted Tail removed the burial platform to the cemetery at the Rosebud Agency in South Dakota.) Although Spotted Tail was preoccupied with the loss of his daughter, Colonel Maynadier encouraged him to participate in peace talks. Spotted Tail told the officer he couldn't talk business with grief weighing heavily upon his mind, but he pledged that later he would "see the counsellors the Great Father will send."

Sioux chief Spotted Tail. —Wyoming State Museum

It wasn't unusual for Ah-ho-appa's burial to take place at Fort Laramie. In the early days, the Sioux maintained a "tree-burial" ground just beyond the Laramie River east of the fort. Some sources say the "papoose tree," a big box elder, contained the bodies of at least forty children, wrapped in buffalo skins and lashed to the branches.

End of the Ride

One of Wyoming's historic horseback rides ended at Fort Laramie on Christmas night 1866 when John "Portugee" Phillips summoned aid for Fort Phil Kearny following the Fetterman Massacre (see page 314). Phillips had ridden 236 miles from the Powder River to Fort Laramie. He disrupted a holiday dance going on in Old Bedlam with an account of the disturbing incident. Lt. William J. Fetterman's entire unit had been killed in a fight with the Sioux under Red Cloud. The soldiers already knew of the disaster, having received a telegram Phillips had sent from Horseshoe Station earlier.

Legend has it that the fine horse that carried Phillips to the fort dropped dead. The story that he rode Col. H. B. Carrington's thoroughbred, Grey Eagle, all the way from Fort Phil Kearny, is doubtful. Although it's possible Phillips rode the same horse the entire journey, it's more likely he switched mounts when he stopped to rest at Fort Reno or to send the telegram from Horseshoe Station, near present-day Glendo. Some historians suggest Phillips didn't use Carrington's horse at all, but that the colonel himself rode the thoroughbred at Fort Phil Kearny the day after the fight.

Regardless of fact, Wyoming recognizes both the thoroughbred horse and Phillips's ride with a monument near Fort Laramie. Whatever the particulars of his ride, Phillips did cross hostile Indian country, and most of the journey took place during a brutal Wyoming blizzard.

Phillips was not the only man who sought help after the Fetterman battle. At 7 P.M. on December 21, 1866, Colonel Carrington hired Phillips and another "citizen courier"—Daniel Dixon—to take messages of the disaster to the telegraph operator at Horseshoe Station. Each man completed the trip and earned $300 for his efforts. Although Phillips and Dixon might have ridden from Fort Phil Kearny separately, they joined forces before reaching Horseshoe Station, by which time other men also accompanied them. The couriers

This rendition of Portugee Phillips's Christmas 1866 arrival at Horseshoe Station near Glendo is by Merritt Dana Houghton. —Wyoming State Museum

delivered their message, which was duly sent to Fort Laramie, Omaha, and Washington.

Lt. Col. Henry W. Wessells, commanding officer at Fort Reno, had given Phillips a separate message to deliver to Col. I. N. Palmer at Fort Laramie. It is not clear if Dixon or anyone else accompanied Phillips on the forty-mile ride from Horseshoe Station to Fort Laramie to deliver that message. At any rate, after a short rest at Horseshoe, Phillips climbed into the saddle again and struck out for the fort, riding through ten or fifteen inches of fresh snow on a bitterly cold night. The thermometer at Fort Laramie read 25 degrees below zero when Phillips stomped in on the Christmas night dance at Old Bedlam.

Phillips's message from Wessells effectively ended the party. The army ordered reinforcements for Fort Phil Kearny, and on January 3, 1867, those troops left Fort Laramie and headed north. They reached Fort Reno on January 11 and Fort Phil Kearny five days later. Phillips also returned to Fort Phil Kearny (we'll catch up with him there again).

Phillips's ride, though remarkable, was not the longest ever made by a single rider in times of adversity in Wyoming. That honor goes to a young Pony Express rider by the name of Bill Cody. We'll get to that tale a bit farther west.

A Second Indian Treaty

The Wyoming plains north of the Platte River, in the vicinity of the Tongue and Powder rivers, became a hotbed of hostilities in the mid-1860s. Congress created a peace commission in 1867. A year later the new body negotiated a treaty with Red Cloud and other chiefs by which the country north of the North Platte River and east of the summit of the Big Horn Range—the Powder River Basin—was held to be Indian territory. Once again, the ink on the document had no time to dry before white treaty makers began to ignore provisions for and promises to the Indians. That set the stage for the last great Indian battles.

US 85
LaGrange—Mule Creek Junction
135 miles

The Texas Cattle Trail

The first cattle to winter in Wyoming were starving, footsore animals left behind by emigrants. That they survived at all on Wyoming's range during the long cold months surprised many, but the evidence was clear, and it walked on four legs. Cattle turned loose in the fall as gangly, nearly starved scarecrows

Mexican longhorn steers owned by J. W. Hammond near Cheyenne in the early 1880s. The light colored steer in the center went by the name Geronimo. —Wyoming State Museum

not only made it through the period of cold and snow but actually appeared in pretty good condition in the spring.

Though several other locales make the claim, the country from Goshen Hole to Chugwater probably harbored the first wintering herds in Wyoming when first Seth Ward and then Pony Express owners Russell, Majors, and Waddell turned loose their freighting oxen. In the Laramie Valley, others turned cattle loose in the fall and found them healthy the next spring, and in western Wyoming Daniel Budd released his Nevada herd in November 1878 and found the majority alive and well when winter snows melted some six months later.

Cattle came into Wyoming in large numbers during the 1870s and 1880s from a variety of directions. Some cattle, like Budd's and those of a German baron, Otto Franc, moved into western Wyoming and the Big Horn Basin from Nevada or Oregon. By far the majority came from Texas. Texans rounded up the wild longhorns south of Red River and pushed them north on a network of trails that became highways of beef. Oliver Loving, Charles Goodnight, and Jesse Chisholm made their marks upon the land as they forged the earliest trails across Texas, Oklahoma, Kansas, Nebraska, and Colorado.

The first large herds of cattle entered Wyoming Territory by following the Goodnight-Loving Trail across Colorado via Fremont's Orchard on Crow

Creek, some fifty miles east of Denver (about where Greeley, Colorado, now sits), and then arrived in Cheyenne in 1860. John Wesley Iliff, a cattle buyer in Colorado since 1859, received the herd. Over a period of years he bought between 25,000 to 30,000 head of Texas longhorns from Goodnight. In *The Great Range Wars* by Harry Sinclair Drago, Goodnight told about his first meeting with Iliff: "He came to the Apishapa where I was holding a trail herd. After looking the cattle over, he said he would buy them if I would deliver them at Cheyenne, which I agreed to do."

Goodnight's partner, Oliver Loving, had earlier trailed cattle as far north as Denver, but the deal with Iliff effectively lengthened the Goodnight-Loving Trail into Wyoming. The next year Goodnight took cattle as far north as Chugwater, about fifty miles beyond Cheyenne.

Texas cattle came north on the Goodnight-Loving Trail and other routes across Oklahoma, Kansas, and Nebraska. One early path, known as the Jones and Plummer Trail, ended at Ogallala, Nebraska, until the late 1870s, when cowboys started driving the herds beyond Nebraska's railheads and on through Wyoming to Montana. The Jones and Plummer Trail thus became the Texas Trail, and from then on most stock entering Wyoming from the southeast came on that route.

The Texas Trail entered Wyoming where the town of Pine Bluffs now sits. It coursed up the east side of the territory on a line parallel to today's US 85 until it reached the Cheyenne River, about where Mule Creek Junction divides US 18 from US 85. Continuing north, the trail turned slightly west, passing over the lush Wyoming grasslands and crossing the future I-90 corridor at Moorcroft. There it angled further to the west toward Sheridan and, eventually, Montana. Much of the trail paralleled the Cheyenne-Deadwood Stage Route. It was up in the Cheyenne River country along the Texas Trail that cowboy Badger Clark wrote that famous old poem, "The Cowboy's Prayer."

Most of the early herds passed right on through Wyoming and were used to establish Montana's ranching industry, but it didn't take long for cattlemen to recognize the value of Wyoming's grassland. Large ranches started between 1875 and 1885, including the Swan Land and Cattle Company, the CY, the Sun, and the Pitchfork. The entire eastern section of Wyoming and all of the Powder River Basin filled with beef from Texas. Cattle from Oregon, Nevada, and Montana moved into the Big Horn Basin and western Wyoming during that same era.

Jay Em

Jim Moore followed the Texas Trail north in the 1860s and watered a herd on Rawhide Creek, near the future location of the town of Jay Em. Moore realized the importance of water in the dry climate and bought eighty acres on the creek. Although he rode for the Pony Express during its short life, he is best known for operating one of the largest cattle ranches in Wyoming Territory, which he had started by 1869. His cattle, wearing the J Rolling M brand, roamed from Running Water Creek and Rawhide Creek to Lodgepole Creek, near present-day Sidney, Nebraska.

In 1875 Moore died when a runaway team threw him from a wagon. His brand changed several times, and the ranch split into smaller parts. The J Rolling M brand remained in use, and his initials became the name of a creek and a new town.

A post office started on Jay Em Creek in 1899, but when postmaster William "Uncle Jack" Hargraves had a dispute with a visiting postal inspector, the outsider picked up the large wooden box containing supplies and closed the place down. For the next decade, local residents got their mail at Rawhide Buttes Station, ten miles north, or at Fort Laramie, twenty miles south.

In 1905 Silas Harris of Waupon, Wisconsin, and his three sons moved to the area, where Silas assumed control of the Jay Em Cattle Company. One of the sons, Lake Harris, saw the need for better mail service and agreed to ride horseback from Jay Em Creek to Rawhide Buttes Station to get the mail every

Most of the businesses in the town of Jay Em are abandoned like these two once owned by Lake Harris. They still remain the property of his family. The general store, to the right, is fully stocked with items of a generation ago.

other day for three months. Harris got no pay for his trouble, but at the end of the three-month period the U.S. Postal Service opened a post office in the bunkhouse at the Jay Em Ranch.

In 1912 Lake Harris made a homestead claim on Rawhide Creek. He soon planned and built the town of Jay Em. Eventually it included his home, a feed store, the post office, a general store, and Farmers State Bank. From 1917 to 1921, Harris edited the *Jay Em Sentinel and Fort Laramie News*, a weekly newspaper with a circulation of 300. Jay Em served ranchers and homesteaders through the 1920s and 1930s. In 1935 Harris and other men built the Jay Em Stone Company, which made tombstones, fireplaces, tabletops, and other products from material quarried near Rawhide Buttes.

Highway improvements and increased use of automobiles spelled doom for Jay Em. As it became easier for homesteaders and ranchers to travel elsewhere for supplies, Jay Em grew smaller and smaller until, eventually, all of the businesses closed. The community still has a small number of permanent residents, but most of the buildings owned by Lake Harris's family sit idle. However, maintenance continues, and each of the businesses looks as if it could open tomorrow.

The Legend of Rawhide

During the great western migration, travelers often felt threatened by native Americans. In a few instances, jumpy emigrants may have killed Indians just because they were Indians. Legend has it that the names of Rawhide Buttes and Rawhide Creek come from just such a situation. This particular tale has no basis in fact, but that hasn't stopped people in the area from perpetuating the myth in an attempt to promote tourism.

The story is this: A wagon train got to the vicinity of Rawhide Buttes when one of the men, who had earlier said he would kill the first Indian he saw, did just that. The Indian was a young girl, and the tribe became furious, demanding that the killer be turned over to them and threatening to massacre the entire wagon train if he wasn't. The train leaders initially refused but eventually acquiesced and turned over the killer. The Indians promptly skinned the man alive—thus the name "rawhide."

Of course, the entire story is a fabrication, as is an identical one associated with Rawhide Creek in eastern Nebraska, and similar tales crop up as far east as Tennessee. Even so, the citizens of Lusk reenact the tale every summer in the city's "Legend of Rawhide" pageant.

Another story about the naming of the Rawhide landmarks is that a trapper station once located in the vicinity, bringing in a lot of raw hides. Whatever their etymology, the buttes stand out as you travel US 85 along the old Texas Trail and the Cheyenne-Deadwood Stage Route.

Cheyenne-Deadwood Stage Route

Scout Charley Reynolds had big news when he rode in to Fort Laramie in August 1874: The Black Hills had gold! Horatio Nelson Ross and William McKay, miners with a military expedition led by Lt. Col. George A. Custer, had found nuggets and flakes in French Creek. Although Indians had known it for years and miners had suspected it, too, this was the first official confirmation of gold in the region.

Indians often swapped nuggets at Fort Laramie for supplies. Though some suggested the Indians took the gold from prospectors returning from California's diggings, others speculated it came from the Black Hills. Old Jim Bridger told of gold in the hills, but most disregarded his information because he was a well-known storyteller. It's hard to believe someone who talks about "putrefied [sic] forests," mountains of glass, and streams that run two different direc-

Ruts of the Cheyenne-Deadwood Stage Route north of Lusk, August 1993.

tions. Though many dismissed Bridger's tall tales, most of them contained more than a few grains of truth. That certainly was the case regarding gold in the Black Hills.

Belgian missionary Pierre De Smet knew the gold was there, too. He told the Indians not to let the white people know of its existence, because once word got out fortune seekers would demand an opportunity to mine the riches. They would take the land from the tribes, De Smet warned.

Other western mines played out, and the Panic of 1873 and ensuing economic downturn caused people to look carefully at every possible new source of wealth. Attention focused on the Black Hills, which, rumor had it, contained the next great lode. By the spring of 1874, companies in all parts of the country geared up for an assault on the hills whether the government would permit it or not. The military had to enforce the Treaty of 1868 and maintain peace in the region. The situation was a powder keg ready to blow.

Lt. Col. George A. Custer left Fort Abraham Lincoln in the Dakota Territory with about 1,000 troops on July 2, 1874, and headed for the Black Hills, ostensibly to determine whether a military post could be built. Another likely goal of the mission was to determine if the area had gold and, if so, in what quantity.

Sioux scouts kept an eye on Custer's party, not trusting the soldiers' claim that they wanted to build a military post to protect the Indians from white intrusion. The Sioux recalled the warnings of De Smet and remembered how the military and the government had broken earlier promises concerning Indian lands. They and other tribes repeatedly had found themselves pushed from territory supposedly theirs forever when emigrants and miners decided *they* wanted it. The Black Hills country was the Indians' last refuge, reserved for them in the treaties of 1851 and 1868 at Fort Laramie.

After miners Ross and McKay found gold, Custer and some of his party accompanied Reynolds to the Cheyenne River, but from there the scout rode alone through Sioux and Cheyenne territory. Upon reaching Fort Laramie, Reynolds found himself swarmed by listeners, who immediately started devising schemes to elude the military and get to the Black Hills' gold.

Within weeks, prospectors had started sneaking into the region. However, it was late 1875 before the open push began. Several routes led to the hills, but the most popular trail started in Cheyenne. It led from there to Fort Laramie and then turned north, up the eastern side of Wyoming Territory, and entered the Black Hills north of the Cheyenne River. (Today, I-25 roughly parallels the path from Cheyenne to Chugwater, and US 85 follows it north of Fort Laramie.) The route split at Hat Creek Station north of present-day Lusk, with one trace headed east toward Nebraska and the other angling north past modern Newcastle, then east to Deadwood. Much of it paralleled the Texas Trail.

Although townspeople in Sidney, Nebraska, touted their community as the gateway to the Black Hills, Cheyenne became the main jumping-off point because of the iron bridge built in 1875 by the army across the North Platte at Fort Laramie. The road, located and developed by freighters, became known as the Cheyenne-Deadwood Stage Route. Every Monday and Thursday, stages pulled away from the InterOcean Hotel in Cheyenne and headed toward the Black Hills. They returned on Tuesdays and Saturdays. The trip to the mining camp of Custer was 182 miles by way of Cheyenne and 195 miles on the Nebraska route.

Travel to the Black Hills gold diggings started and continued despite the fact the land belonged to the Sioux. As they had done many times before, governmental leaders, miners, and settlers ignored the tribes. They schemed and maneuvered until they forced Red Cloud, Man-Afraid-of-His-Horses, Spotted Tail, and the other Sioux chiefs to relinquish the Black Hills.

Superintendent of the Line

Luke Voorhees followed the gold rushes in Colorado and discovered gold on the Kootenai River in British Columbia before coming to Wyoming to serve as the superintendent of a new stage line for Gilmer, Salisbury, and Patrick. He eventually became superintendent of the Cheyenne and Black Hills Stage Company, with full authority to establish the necessary stations and to equip the line fully, according to Agnes Wright Spring in *The Cheyenne and Black Hills Stage and Express Routes*.

The rocking, rolling ride took place in red coaches with bright yellow undercarriages built by Abbot and Downing of Concord, New Hampshire. Leather straps supported the coach bodies, enabling them to swing up and down over ruts and rough roads without injuring passengers.

Stage stations, located an average of twelve miles apart, provided services for the line. One station sat at Silver Cliff, where a mining boom in the early 1880s attracted the Great Western Mining and Milling Company. The mine was near the stage barn. Ellis Johnson erected other facilities, including a saloon, stores, and hotels, but when the Wyoming Central Railroad wanted to buy the land, Johnson held out for the best price he could get. Unfortunately for him, he demanded too much, and nearby rancher Frank S. Lusk slid in on the deal, selling a parcel of his property to the railroad. There a new town, named for the opportunistic landowner, quickly grew. Although the railroad helped the community of Lusk achieve stability, it was the Cheyenne-Deadwood Stage Route that really put the place on the map.

J. W. Dear, post trader at the Red Cloud Agency on White River, made several attempts to build a stage station on the route. He had some property at Rawhide Buttes that included a four-room house, a corral, and plenty of grazing land with nearby wood. But just a week after Dear advertised that land for sale in 1876, Indians burned the ranch house and a wagon in the corral.

At Running Water (L'Eau-qui-Court), also called the Niobrara River, Dear built another station in the spring of 1876. Indians immediately burned it. Finally, Dear built a station that fall at Sage Creek near the bluffs and broken country of the Hat Creek Breaks, which become South Dakota's Pine Ridge country. As Dear might have expected from his other experiences, native Americans torched it. The sequence of events makes you wonder just what sort of trader Dear was and what kind of relationship he had in later years with the people at Red Cloud Agency in northwestern Nevada.

Late that same autumn, John (Jack) Bowman built a ranch. He had intended to build it on Hat Creek in present western Nebraska, but he missed the mark, building on Sage Creek in Wyoming Territory. Unperturbed, Bowman called his outfit Hat Creek Ranch anyway.

The site later became Fort Hat Creek, an outpost for cavalry from Fort Laramie, and Hat Creek Station. Today it is located on the east side of US 85 approximately fifteen miles north of Lusk. By exiting onto a county road seven miles north of Lusk, travelers can follow the Cheyenne-Deadwood route over the Hat Creek Breaks. The well-maintained gravel road includes a stretch of the original US 85, complete with weather-beaten, single-board guard rails and rock-work culverts. In places, scars of the freight wagons and stagecoaches are deep and clear, cut into the sandstone by the pounding of hundreds of hooves and iron-rimmed wheels. You can see the Black Hills from the top of the breaks. When miners reached this point they were only about halfway to their destination, but as they gazed on the distant hills they felt they had nearly arrived.

From the breaks, the route drops into the Sage Creek Valley, where the county road crosses an old iron bridge installed when workers constructed the

Hat Creek Stage Station, 1875. —Wyoming State Museum

original US 85. Hat Creek Station is located on that county road, about a mile east of the present highway.

Bowman's Hat Creek Station, located in territory given to the Sioux under terms of the 1876 treaty at Fort Laramie, was in a precarious position. Yet it was also a good location from which to witness the passage of an era. The facility included a telegraph and post office, livery stable, brewery, bakery, butchery, and blacksmith shop. Bowman and his bride, Sallie C. Smith of Denver, operated the ranch until September 1879, when he sold to Charles Hecht, known as "the boss freighter." At the time of the sale, the ranch totaled about 200 fenced acres and had buildings, corrals, and four hundred head of American cattle. It brought $10,000.

John Storrie and Tom Swan obtained Hat Creek Station during the 1880s and raised a two-story building near the original log structure. The new edifice included a general store and roadhouse that became popular with stage drivers and cowboys. It stood sturdy and strong in August 1993 as local residents worked to restore the station to its former appearance.

At Hat Creek Station (which, you will remember, is on Sage Creek), the stage route forked. The road less traveled headed almost due east to the Harding Ranch on Indian Creek; clay bluffs served as walls for one side and the back of the station. The other side and front were made of logs. A passage led into the clay bank, where there was a dug-out fort with a log roof and portholes on every side. A few men could easily defend the post. A separate excavation served as a stable for the horses. The eastern fork continued to the Cheyenne River Ranch, built by J. W. Dear in 1876, which served as a telegraph office and provided accommodations. It gained its reputation as the hangout for "Persimmon Bill" Chambers and his brother, alleged leaders of a gang of horse thieves.

The other, more popular road headed north from Hat Creek Station to Old Woman's Fork, named for the ghost of an Indian woman supposedly seen dancing nearby in the moonlight, according to Spring in *Cheyenne-Black Hills Stage and Express Routes*. Known as the Jenney Stockade Route, it ran somewhat parallel to today's US 85. One of the most well-known stage stations was Robbers' Roost on the Cheyenne River. The highway heads through a cut in the hills and drops into the river bottom. During the era of the Cheyenne-Deadwood line, this location, with its steep embankments, became an ideal place for outlaws to set up an ambush.

Travel on the Cheyenne-Deadwood stage was an adventure in more ways than one. Although leather braces lent some support, the coaches still shook the daylights out of anyone riding inside. Passengers crowded into the coach's interior and sat for hours on hard plank seats covered with canvas pads that were stuffed with horsehair and tied down with leather straps. Dust swirled through the open windows; if the shades were drawn, the air became stifling.

Besides the general hazards of stagecoach travel, such as wheels breaking on rocks and blizzards sweeping down across the prairie, there were difficulties with marauders as well. Native Americans were the first concern. They burned stations—particularly those built by J. W. Dear in 1876—and attacked coaches. But Indians weren't the only moving threat to travelers on the line. Gangs of white highway robbers, drawn by the wealth of miners coming to and from the Black Hills, also preyed upon the coaches.

The Final Sioux Campaign

Heaviest use of the Cheyenne-Deadwood route coincided with the military's final campaign against the Sioux, Cheyenne, and Arapaho Indians in the Powder River country. As men built stage stations in the spring and summer of 1876, the Sioux gathered along the Big Horns for the final confrontations. One of the most important was the fight on the Little Big Horn River in Montana, where Sioux warriors under Crazy Horse and Sitting Bull destroyed most of Custer's command.

The Sioux won the battle, annihilating the soldiers who had marched through the Black Hills in 1874 and sent word of gold deposits to their white brethren, but they lost the war. Crazy Horse finally surrendered to the military in eastern Wyoming, not far from Hat Creek Station. Before long the Sioux and other tribes found themselves confined to reservations far from the sacred hunting grounds, and white men and women started the long process of assimilating the Indians.

It almost worked. Nearly an entire generation of Sioux turned their backs on their culture. Following the massacre at Wounded Knee in 1890, they no longer practiced the Ghost Dance or other aspects of their native religions, and they stopped teaching their children traditional rituals. They couldn't; the white government wouldn't let them. Some became ashamed of being Indian because of bigotry and racism. Not until passage of the American Indian Religious Freedom Act in the late 1970s was it legal again to practice Indian religions.

US 26
Fort Laramie—Guernsey
13 miles

Register Cliff

Two significant remnants of the Oregon Trail lie near Guernsey, west of Fort Laramie: Register Cliff and the Oregon Trail Ruts National Landmark. The meadow at the foot of Register Cliff, originally called Sand Point, was the emigrants' first stopping place west of the fort. Travelers carved their names on the soft sandstone all along the bluffs.

Shawn Moulton, 11, stands in the sandstone ruts of the Oregon Trail west of Guernsey.

The ruts through the sandstone just west of Register Cliff are said to be the most clearly defined on the entire Oregon Trail. Although initially carved during the Oregon migration, the ruts probably were deepened by heavy wagons hauling building material to Fort Laramie. Freighters took limestone from a quarry west of the ruts to the fort during construction of some of that facility's buildings. The wagons went over the rocky outcrop rather than around the base, as Wyoming 160 does, because in earlier days the low area was often wet and boggy, making travel difficult or impossible at some times of the year.

Guernsey

Guernsey, the small town that provides the most direct access to both Register Cliff and the trail ruts, was named for Charles A. Guernsey, an early cowboy and rancher who turned author and penned *Wyoming Cowboy Days*.

Guernsey spent his early years in New York but in 1880 came west, where he became an influential cattleman. He advocated construction of a dam on the North Platte River at a site he selected with Wyoming State Engineer

Guernsey Reservoir, now a state park. —State Historic Preservation Office

Elwood Mead; forty years later the Guernsey Dam stood on the spot. Eventually a state park was created at Guernsey Reservoir.

Construction of Guernsey Dam took place with financial backing from the U.S. government and farmers in the Goshen Valley, and water impounded by the structure made the surrounding land into a productive crop-raising area. The dam is part of the massive North Platte Water Project that provides irrigation for eastern Wyoming and western Nebraska (see page 176).

A lot of silt fills the reservoir, so each July supervisors drain nearly the whole basin in order to wash it out. The silt lines irrigation canals and keeps them from leaking. The Goshen Irrigation District, headquartered in Torrington, endorses the annual silt run. Guernsey officials and some wildlife

Spillway at Guernsey Dam. —State Historic Preservation Office

groups just as strongly condemn it because of its negative effects on the recreation industry.

Guernsey became a supply base for the Sunrise mines and the adjacent limestone quarries and serves as the headquarters for the Wyoming National Guard, which has a cowboy as its insignia.

The First Bucking Bronc

A colt belonging to a member of the Wyoming National Guard was immortalized as Wyoming's first bucking horse symbol. George N. Ostrom of Sheridan was at a rodeo in 1913 when a group of Indians brought horses for the half-mile race. One of their animals was a tall, rangy, high-strung sorrel mare of good breeding. As the race started the horses took off in a whirl of dust, but when they reached the far side of the track a young colt leaped the fence to join the sorrel mare. The race continued with the two horses neck and neck to the finish line. Ostrom eventually obtained the colt and named him Red Wing.

Ostrom served with the Wyoming National Guard and during the First World War found himself in Bordeaux, France, where in 1918 he painted a picture on a bass drum of Red Wing bucking. The logo attracted the attention of Col. Burke Sinclair, who arranged to have a stencil made of the painting so plates could be attached to each vehicle of the 148th Field Artillery. The unit became known as the Bucking Bronco Regiment from Wyoming. They used the logo on vehicles, helmets, drinking steins, lapel buttons, and road signs. "When we got to Germany, the Germans even made jewelry with the bucking bronco on it," Ostrom wrote.

In 1973 Wyoming governor Stanley Hathaway acknowledged Ostrom's drawing: "Now therefore be it known that the Wyoming bucking horse is dedicated to all veterans of the State and that George N. Ostrom is hereby commended for his original idea of this now famous insignia."

Although Red Wing was the model for the original insignia, another bucking horse is recognized as the state's symbol (see page 153).

Slade Canyon's Namesake

Slade Canyon, west of Guernsey, gets its name from Joseph Albert "Jack" Slade, a rough character who for a time served as superintendent of Ben Holladay's Overland Stage Route between Julesburg, Colorado, and Salt Lake City. When Slade took over at the Julesburg Stage Station on the South Platte, he displaced Jules Reni, a French Canadian. The two became bitter enemies. Once Reni attempted to kill Slade, who responded by threatening that he would wear one of Reni's ears as a watch charm. Slade's temperament was about as violent as any man's; indeed, that is probably why Holladay hired him to clean up the ruffians along the Overland Stage Route. Slade hated many men but particularly French Canadians and most specifically Jules Reni.

The story goes that Slade's men captured Reni near Guernsey and tied him securely until Slade arrived. Then, with Reni backed up to the wall of a corral, Slade fired at him repeatedly, announcing before each shot where it was going to hit his victim. Eventually, so the story goes, Slade cut off Reni's ears and put them in his vest pocket. Slade apparently reported the killing to authorities at Fort Laramie, but officials filed no charges against the stage agent.

There is a persistent belief that Slade led a robber gang, stealing stock from emigrant trains and in many instances selling it right back to the owners. Diligent searches have never revealed the caches of stolen gold and jewelry supposedly hidden in Slade Canyon. Men who knew Slade well say he was killed in Montana so soon after his dismissal from the stage line that it is quite unlikely he could have carried on such operations.

Vigilantes in Virginia City, Montana, hanged Slade in 1864, not for any of his more vicious misdeeds but for riding his horse into the general store. Actually, the charge was a little more serious than that. Slade, known for his drunk and disorderly conduct, tended not to pay the fines levied against him, and he did a considerable amount of damage one night, for which Sheriff J. M. Fox swore out an arrest warrant. As the sheriff read the warrant, Slade grabbed the paper, tore it up, and stamped on it. Warned to behave by a member of Montana's Vigilance Committee, Slade instead went to the home of Judge Alexander Davis and threatened him with a pistol. That was the last straw. The vigilantes, who had great power in Montana at that time, became involved in a more direct way.

The vigilantes really had nothing against Slade; he had even been one of them for a time. But when 600 miners marched into town and said something had to be done with Slade because nobody was safe while he remained free, the committee was left with no choice. Slade sent a message to his wife, Virginia, but before she could get to town from their ranch twelve miles out Slade swung from a high gateway.

Slade's death became a black spot on the activities of the Montana vigilantes, who previously had been involved in the execution of road agents, not the hanging of men who didn't know how to conduct themselves in an orderly manner.

Sunrise and Hartville

No matter where a miner might have been, he always thought there might be better pickings somewhere else. Consider what happened at Hartville, five miles north of Guernsey on Wyoming 270. When prospectors found copper nearby in 1881, news of the strike brought hundreds of miners and speculators from the Black Hills into the region. Hartville quickly became a roaring mining camp, with saloons, dance halls, and gambling houses running at full swing. When the mining boom died down—most likely because news arrived of a bigger or newer strike somewhere else—only the saloon and a lodging house remained to serve local ranchers.

In 1899 eastern capitalists started developing the iron deposits at the Sunrise and Chicago mines, and the area experienced its second boom. That boom-to-bust-to-boom cycle happens a lot in mining economies and has constantly recurred throughout Wyoming.

Rancher Charles Guernsey obtained mining claims in the area in 1903 and sold them to a Colorado company, which established the town of Sunrise. Open-pit mining in a "glory hole" uncovered iron ore at the Sunrise mine. By the 1930s, production averaged 500,000 tons annually, though during peak periods it reached 800,000 tons. As many as 200 workers mined the material, which then went to smelters in Pueblo, Colorado. Evidence found during the excavations showed that Indians once quarried the area, probably to obtain pigments.

A Lucky Stiff

In 1902 a gambler known as the White Swede died in Hartville. Local legend has it that three gambling companions agreed to conduct the wake. Tired of staring at one another and at the corpse, they started a poker game. After sampling a bottle of whiskey, they decided to cut the corpse in on the game; by morning, the dead man had won enough to pay for his burial. Some might say his luck held to the very end, but he ended up in a hole in the ground anyway.

I-25
Chugwater—Douglas
79 miles

Legend of the Dreamer

The best-known legend of the Chugwater country involves a mighty chief of the Mandan tribe of the upper Missouri. In a fall hunt on the Wyoming plains, a buffalo bull badly injured the chief. Unable to conduct the next effort to surround the herd and make a kill, he ordered his only son to take charge. Known as the Dreamer because he was a man of thought rather than action, the young man called the braves to council during the interval between surrounds. It was a waste of time, he said, to gallop around the buffalo and throw spears at them. He directed his tribesmen to stampede the herd over the bluff. They did, and as each shaggy creature crashed to the ground below, it made a chuglike sound. The stream was thereafter known as Chugwater Creek, the "water where the buffalo chug."

A Cheyenne-to-Deadwood Stop

In the period of the Cheyenne-Deadwood Stage Route, stages and freighters made regular stops at Chugwater. The Chug Water Ranch opened for business in March 1876. It was operated by John "Portugee" Phillips, who had made history a decade earlier when he rode from Fort Phil Kearny with news of the Fetterman fight (see pages 132 and 313)

Phillips earned his nickname because he was born to Portuguese parents on Pico, one of the islands in the Azores. They named him Manuel Felipe Cardoso. In about 1850 he reached California on a Portuguese whaling ship, which he left to join the gold rush. Cardoso mined in California, Oregon, and Idaho; he was living in the Boise Basin in 1862 when he Americanized his name to John Phillips.

Phillips joined a party of miners in Montana, who in the spring of 1866 moved into the Pryor and Big Horn mountains of southern Montana and northern Wyoming. That enterprise put him at Fort Phil Kearny at the time of the Fetterman battle. Eventually Portugee Phillips became a government contractor, supplying both Fort Laramie and Fort Fetterman from 1869 to 1878, and during that period he ran a Cheyenne-Deadwood stage station. He also served as postmaster in Chugwater, ran a few head of cattle, and operated the Chug Water Hotel. In 1878 Phillips sold his business enterprises at Chugwater to Hambleton & Company of Baltimore for $16,000. He moved to Cheyenne, where he died November 18, 1883.

Wheatland

Farming and cattle raising dominate the land near Wheatland, the Platte County seat. The community played host in early days to cowboys from the Swan Land and Cattle Company holdings. Today a major power plant operates just north of town.

The earliest known Indians in Platte County were the Shoshone, called the Mountain Comanche by the Cheyenne. In the early 1700s the Kiowa displaced the Shoshones in the southeastern part of Wyoming. Later the Arapaho, Cheyenne, and finally the Sioux entered the area. The Crow came to the region about 1800. They once claimed land north of the Platte, but the Sioux pushed them to the northwest, out of the Powder River country. Even later, the Shoshone chased them from the Big Horn Basin to Montana. The Shoshone eventually moved into land west of the Rocky Mountains. Their traditional enemies, the Arapaho, believed the Great Spirit erected the Rockies as a barrier between themselves and both the Shoshone and the Ute.

The Arapaho ranged between the Platte and Arkansas rivers, trailing back and forth between Medicine Bow and Fort Laramie across the Wheatland Flats. In 1976 two of their old trails still marked their former territory. In Halleck Canyon, piles of rock stood like sheepherder's monuments to mark one trail. The other, on upper Cottonwood Creek, remained distinctly visible, having been worn into the ground by many feet and the trailing poles of many travois, according to Virginia Cole Trenholm in *Platte County Heritage*.

Trenholm, author of *The Arapahoes, Our People*, and other books about the various tribes, wrote that the Indians didn't think of the West as wild. She reported that Sioux chief Standing Bear once said:

> We did not think of the great open plains, the beautiful rolling hills, the winding streams with tangled growth as wild. Only to the white man was nature a wilderness, and only to him was the land infested with wild animals and savage people. To us it was tame. Earth was bountiful, and we were surrounded with the blessings of the Great Mystery. Not until the hair man from the east came, and with his brutal frenzy, heaped injustices upon us and the families we loved, was it wild to us. When the very animals of the forest began fleeing from his approach; then it was that for us, the "wild west" began.

151

Goshen Hole, a large depression southeast of Wheatland, is commonly thought to have been named for the Land of Goshen. But in fact its name comes from Goche, the crafty left-handed chief of the Assiniboines, Trenholm said.

Swan Land and Cattle Company

Wyoming was largely unsettled, a huge area of public domain, when members of the Swan family came from Iowa to seek their fortunes. The vast, grass-covered, unfenced ranges were ideal for the type of life brothers Alexander, Henry, and Thomas "Black Tom" Swan sought, a place where cattle could roam at will, getting fat on natural grasses.

The three joined to organize the Swan Brothers Ranch near Cheyenne and brought the first Hereford cattle into Wyoming Territory, receiving two carloads of Hereford bulls at Cheyenne on May 14, 1878. According to the *North Western Live Stock Journal*, the shipment was the "heaviest importation of blooded stock . . . ever made to the territory."

Alexander Swan was over six feet tall and had a magnetic personality. The public-spirited man supported a number of civic, state, cultural, and educational movements. He helped form the powerful Wyoming Stock Growers Association, serving as president from 1876 until 1881. Swan served in the territorial legislature and, although he didn't campaign, was nearly elected to Congress in 1880, losing the election by only twenty-five votes. After becoming a territory in 1869, Wyoming had one nonvoting representative to Congress. Since statehood in 1890, Wyoming has always had two U.S. senators and one representative.

In quick succession, Alexander founded the Swan and Frank Livestock Company, the National Cattle Company, and the Swan, Frank and Anthony Cattle Company, located in Carbon, Albany, and Laramie counties, respectively. In 1883 he traveled to Scotland, where he successfully sold the opportunities of the American West, in the form of shares in his three businesses. He became manager of the newly organized Swan Land and Cattle Company, earning a salary of $10,000 per year plus expenses.

The period from 1883 to 1886 was prosperous for Swan and his Scottish investors. From an initial investment of $15,000 in 1873, the empire grew in value to $15 million. Swan also formed the Horse Creek Land and Cattle Company, the Wyoming Hereford Association, Swan Brothers, Frank and Bernheimer, and the Ogallala Land and Cattle Company, all of which operated alongside the gigantic Swan Land and Cattle Company.

By 1885 Swan was a true cattle baron, controlling more than 200,000 head on a range that extended from Ogallala, Nebraska, to near Saratoga, Wyoming, a distance of well over 200 miles. But his Scottish investors began to accuse him of mismanagement when only 480 of the 11,500 Texas steers bought in 1884 could be accounted for in 1885. On paper, at least, the herd was inventoried at 113,625 head in 1886.

Then came the swirling snows of 1886-87, taking a tremendous toll on the stock. As in past winters, the thousands of head of cattle ran on the open range, fending for themselves during periods of severe weather. That winter started early, with cold and snow that didn't let up. The cattlemen lacked hay to feed their animals, and the herd losses became staggering.

In March 1887 the Alien Land Act went into effect. Its goal was to prevent foreigners, and foreign countries, from acquiring American land. Swan had overextended himself and the Scots could no longer bail him out. In addition, much of the herd died during that winter, so Swan's Scottish backers lost confidence in his management. Like a row of dominoes, Swan's empire began to crumble. In May 1887, Finlay Dun of Edinburgh, Scotland, replaced Swan as manager of the company.

Even without Alex at the helm, the Swan Land and Cattle Company prospered. At one point the company held or used a million acres, including public lands used for grazing. In its glory days the company had so many brands it was necessary to publish a brand book so foremen and ranch hands could identify their own livestock. By 1912 the Swan Land and Cattle Company had thirty-two separate ranches, among them the Diamond, Kelly, M Bar, and Two Bar, all in the Wheatland and Chugwater area, and the Ell Seven near Saratoga, owned by a nephew of Alexander Swan.

On the Two Bar Ranch, located west of Wheatland on Wyoming 34, hands such as Jimmy Danks, Guy Holt, Fred Dodge, Frank Stone, and Hugh Clark first challenged Wyoming's most famous bucking horse, Steamboat. Two Bar cowboys were the first to see the dynamite explosion possible when that gelding decided to unseat a rider.

A Symbol of Wyoming

There is an old and ongoing argument over which bronc, which rider, and which photograph inspired the bucking horse depicted on Wyoming's license plates. This silhouetted figure has become better known as a symbol for Wyoming than any other emblem. The official story is that the silhouette is merely an artist's conception and is not intended to represent any individual. There is little argument about the horse, however: All agree it is Steamboat.

In the 1930s Secretary of State Lester C. Hunt wanted to put a bucking horse and cowboy on Wyoming's license plates to represent the state's nickname—the Cowboy State. Hunt contacted Denver artist Allen True, who had painted the murals in the House and Senate chambers at the Wyoming State Capitol in Cheyenne. Hunt later wrote that he was "pleased that I had Mr. True do the drawing rather than use a photograph of a bucking horse, in that Mr. True, through his knowledge of art, understood what design could be stamped out in steel and retain its identity at some distance. He therefore made the drawing with only one bridle rein, and only one front left foot on the horse and with only one rider's foot."

The 1936 license plates, the first with the bronc, were white with black letters and manufactured by the Gopher Stamp and Die Company of St. Paul, Minnesota. The University of Wyoming celebrated its fiftieth anniversary in 1937, and Hunt chose yellow and brown as the license plate colors in honor of that institution. Ever since the plates traditionally have been yellow and brown, although periodically the colors have varied.

Glendo

Horseshoe Station

The Mormons, who had a contract to deliver mail between Fort Laramie and Salt Lake, established one of their many stations on Horseshoe Creek, located near Glendo. The establishment also served as an emigrant trading post in the 1850s. The Mormons planned a large complex and an agricultural production center, complete with an irrigation system. They claimed 640 acres, on which they maintained about 75 horses and 125 work cattle. A stockade enclosed thirty or forty houses.

Judge W. A. Carter, who became post sutler at Fort Bridger, mentions in his records that the Mormons left the ruins of Horseshoe Station smoldering in

Judge William A. Carter, Fort Bridger.
—Wyoming State Museum

their wake when he entered the valley with Col. Albert Sidney Johnston and the army in 1857 (see pages 49 and 288).

In 1858, Russell, Majors, and Waddell, of Pony Express fame, bought the Hockaday-Liggett stage line and built additional stations at which to exchange horses and let passengers rest. They rebuilt Horseshoe Station in 1861, leaving the infamous Jack Slade in charge. The stage route shifted southward in 1862 because of trouble with the Indians, but the telegraph line remained, and Horseshoe Station continued to operate. Portugee Phillips stopped here to wire ahead news of the 1866 Fetterman battle near Fort Phil Kearny before continuing his famous ride to Fort Laramie.

Platte County witnessed only one battle of consequence between Indians and whites, a three-day encounter at Horseshoe Creek. In mid-March 1868, Lakota chief Crazy Horse led about seventy Oglala and Miniconjou Sioux against the stockade at Horseshoe Creek. The white men fired, and the battle was on. Eventually the white men retreated to Mouseau's Road Ranch at Twin Springs, which they burned to keep it from falling into the Indians' hands. Their valuables, cached beneath the building, lay hidden in the debris. The white men then headed toward Fort Laramie, but they had a running fight with the Sioux. The battleground stretched from Horseshoe Station to Diamond A Hill, which sits beyond the Cassa Flats south of I-25 between Wheatland and Glendo.

John Bozeman and John Jacobs's trail through the Powder River country left the Platte River road at Horseshoe Creek and headed north toward the Montana goldfields.

Wyoming 312/34
Wheatland—Bosler
57 miles

Iron Mountain Mystery

Tom Horn's life ebbed at the end of a rope in the last legal hanging held in Laramie County. Before coming to Wyoming, Horn had played a part in forcing the final surrender of Geronimo. His experience in tracking renegade Apaches served as good training for his subsequent job as a detective, hunting down train robbers for the Pinkerton Agency in Denver. However, the work was "too tame" for Horn, and he landed in Wyoming around 1894. Horn went to work as a stock detective for the Swan Land and Cattle Company and lived at John Coble's Iron Mountain Ranch. Eventually he went to work for Coble himself.

A drawing by M. D. Houghton shows the homestead of Kels P. Nickell at Iron Mountain, sketched prior to the death of Willie Nickell in July 1901. Willie was killed about a mile west of the homestead and in 1903 Tom Horn was hanged for the deed. —Viola Nickell Bixler

The site of the Kels Nickell homestead as it appeared in July 1991. This view is similar to the perspective used by M. D. Houghton when he sketched the homestead more than ninety years earlier.

Horn was believed to have killed a number of men, most of them thought to be cattle rustlers. Two of the men Horn supposedly dispatched in 1895 were William Lewis, a Mill Creek rancher, and Fred Powell, a one-armed man who lived on Horse Creek, north of Cheyenne. Although people quickly linked Horn's name to the two killings, no clear or direct evidence was ever found to prove he was the gunman. In 1898 Horn once again was suspected in a pair of shootings, this time in the Brown's Park area of Colorado, where someone gunned down cowboys Isom Dart and Matt Rash. Once again, no one could prove Horn had committed the murders.

The Wyoming range Horn rode lay between Wheatland, Cheyenne, and Laramie and included the Iron Mountain area. Kels Nickell homesteaded in 1885 on Iron Mountain in the large, rough, isolated country extending down the Laramie Range from present-day Wyoming 34 to Wyoming 210. The ranch is still private property, located on a gravel road that heads south from Wyoming 34 about twenty miles southeast of the I-25 junction. Though he first raised cattle and horses, early in 1901 Nickell imported sheep. Cattlemen claimed that the sheep, with their sharply pointed hoofs, ruined the prairie grassland. Animosity festered between Nickell and John Coble after Nickell brought in his herd. In one altercation, Nickell stabbed Coble in the stomach.

Besides Coble, a number of other people in the area, including the cattle-raising Miller family, held grudges against Nickell. Another knifing took place in February 1901, when Jim Miller stabbed Kels Nickell.

It is here that the story takes a lethal twist—as Tom Horn enters the scene.

It was raining and misty the morning of July 18, 1901, when Nickell's fourteen-year-old son, Willie, started out on an errand in place of his father. As he dismounted from his father's horse to open a gate about a mile from the house, someone fired a shot from an ambush and killed the boy.

Suspicion immediately fell upon the Millers because of the long-running feud between the two families. It was thought Jim Miller, lying in wait for Kels Nickell, accidentally shot Willie with a bullet meant for his dad. There was speculation that Victor Miller, Jim's son, was involved because of past fights between him and Willie Nickell. The evidence, however, wasn't sufficient to warrant an arrest of either of the Millers.

As the months went by without an arrest, attention turned to Horn. Whoever killed young Willie Nickell fired from an ambush and then placed a flat rock under the dead boy's head. The rock was a symbol Horn used to identify his victims so his employers would know he had completed a job and would pay him.

In 1902 Sheriff E. J. Smalley and County and Prosecuting Attorney Walter R. Stoll sought the aid of U.S. Deputy Marshal Joe LeFors to gather evidence against Horn. During a drinking spree in Denver, the range detective supposedly had boasted of killing Nickell. LeFors joined him for another drinking bout in Cheyenne before heading to the U.S. marshal's office. It was there

157

Tom Horn. —Wyoming State Museum

that Horn told the lawman he killed Nickell. "It was the best shot I ever made and the dirtiest trick I ever done," Horn said to LeFors.

Unbeknownst to Horn, U.S. Marshal Les E. Snow and stenographer Charles J. Ohnhaus were listening to the conversation—and recording the confession. Two days later LeFors arrested Horn at the bar of the InterOcean Hotel in Cheyenne. It was on the basis of the unsigned confession that Horn was convicted and eventually hanged November 20, 1903, for the killing of Willie Nickell.

For years Wyoming residents have argued about whether Horn actually shot Nickell or if he took the rap for someone else. Volunteers conducted a crime-scene excavation in 1991, but it yielded no concrete evidence. In September 1993 a volunteer jury heard testimony in a new trial for Horn. Held under the auspices of the Tom Horn Kick & Growl, a promotional group in

Cheyenne, the new trial had a new ending as well: The jury acquitted Tom Horn. However, that verdict came ninety years too late for the defendant, who lies buried in a Boulder, Colorado, cemetery.

A Place for the Wildlife

Wyoming's wildlife is "Worth the Watching," according to a modern slogan for the Wyoming Game and Fish Department. One place to do just that is the Sybille Wildlife Research Center, midway between Wheatland and Bosler in Sybille Canyon. Here researchers and biologists study various species of animals, including elk, deer, and Rocky Mountain bighorn sheep. Smaller species, such as wild turkeys, other game birds, and fish, also have a home at the research center.

The most unique animals at the center are black-footed ferrets that have been raised in captivity at Sybille since their capture in 1981 at a site near Meeteetse. Game managers took them from their native habitat when an outbreak of distemper in prairie dogs, the ferrets' main food source, threatened to kill them. Thought to be almost extinct when rancher Jack Turnell spotted the Meeteetse colony, the ferrets propagated well in captivity, and the careful, controlled breeding operation at Sybille helped revive the species. In September 1992 the first captive-raised animals returned to the wild at a site near Shirley Basin. Others live in zoos throughout the United States.

I-25
Douglas—Casper
45 miles

Home of the Wyoming State Fair since the first gathering on October 3–6, 1905, Douglas is named for Stephen A. Douglas, Abe Lincoln's opponent in the famous 1860 debates. Surveyors platted the town in July 1886, but the Fremont, Elkhorn & Missouri Valley Railroad would not let people drive so much as a tent stake until the tracks reached the new railroad-owned townsite. Early birds never want to wait, so a thousand or so settlers-to-be congregated on Antelope Creek at the "tent town" until the railroad arrived on August 22. Then they put the entire community on wheels and within three days moved it to its present location. The first passenger train arrived a week later, but the town didn't incorporate until 1887.

Douglas is supposedly home to a rare species of wildlife, the jackalope. A cross between a jackrabbit and some type of deer or antelope, the animal is said to sing before thunderstorms. Actually, the jackalope story is an awful lot like the legend of Rawhide, in that it is pretty far removed from the truth.

Nevertheless, just as Lusk promotes the Rawhide Buttes, Douglas uses the jackalope as a public relations gimmick, calling itself the Jackalope Capital of the World.

During World War II, Douglas housed a prisoner-of-war camp for German and Italian captives. Many of them arrived at Douglas for processing by authorities, then went to other Wyoming locations for the duration of the war. The prisoners provided labor, particularly in the lumber industry, during a period when the United States—and Wyoming—had a shortage of manpower.

First Casualty of the Great Migration

Six-year-old Joel Hembree became the first casualty of the Great Migration when he fell under the wheels of a wagon on July 18, 1843. The boy died the following day, and his parents buried him on LaPrele Creek west of Douglas, with an old oak dresser drawer serving as a makeshift casket.

On July 20, 1843, emigrant James W. Nesmith wrote in his diary, "at noon came up to a fresh grave with stones piled over it, and a note tied on a stick, informing us that it was the grave of Joel J. Hembree, aged six years, who was killed by a wagon running over its body. At the head of the grave stood a stone containing the name of the child, the first death on the expedition. The grave is on the left hand side of the trail close to Squaw Butte Creek."

A later traveler, journalist Matthew C. Field, wrote of finding the pile of stones marking the boy's grave: "How he died we cannot of course surmise, but there he sleeps among the rocks of the West, as soundly as though chiseled marble was built above his bones."

Fort Fetterman

Fort Fetterman started in July 1867 under the direction and command of Maj. William McDye. Named for Brevet Lt. Col. W. J. Fetterman, who died with his entire command at Fort Phil Kearny east of the Big Horn Mountains the previous December, the fort sat atop a hill south of the North Platte River, not far from where the Bozeman Trail crossed the Platte.

Old-timers say an "X" marks that spot; the story is that early travelers planted sweet clover in that shape to identify the trail's terminus. Whether or not that's how it got there, in 1993 the clover bloomed brilliantly when the Oregon-bound Historic Trails wagon train passed the beginning of the Bozeman route.

Some people just seem to have been everywhere, and Jim Bridger is one of them. He had a fort in western Wyoming, a trail in the Big Horn Basin, and a ferry across the North Platte River near Fort Fetterman to serve Bozeman road traffic. The Bridger Ferry probably remained in use from 1864 to 1866, when the trail had its heaviest use. Prior to 1864 there was no need to cut through the Powder River Basin, and after 1866 it became too dangerous— the terrain was officially off-limits to all but native Americans.

Ayres Rock, west of Douglas, is a natural bridge that attracted the attention of Oregon Trail emigrants from 1843 to 1873.

Fort Fetterman, though never popular with troops stationed there, became a main supply base during the campaign against the Indians in the Powder River country in 1876–77. Abandoned in the 1880s, the government buildings were soon purchased by civilians, and the fort served early settlers as a hell-roaring frontier town. Barns and warehouses became businesses; barracks and officers' quarters served as residences and a hospital. Life was good until the Fremont, Elkhorn & Missouri Railroad failed to enter the town in 1886. It soon withered.

Officers at Fort Fetterman. From left: 1st Lt. Henry Seaton, Lt. George O. Webester, Lt. Henry E. Robinson, and Capt. Gerhard L. Luhns, all of the 4th Infantry; and Capt. William H. Andrew, 3rd Cavalry.
—Western History Research Center, University of Wyoming and Wyoming State Museum

Fort Fetterman. Dick's Place, a meat market. —Wyoming State Museum

The Hog Ranch

Before Fort Fetterman closed, its troops went for female companionship and entertainment to William Brown's log cabin on Currant Creek (earlier called Piss Creek), about seven miles away. After the government abandoned the post in 1880, a new operation called the Hog Ranch located near the raucous civilian town of Fetterman. Jack Sanders and John Lawrence established the gambling and dance resort and segregated "recreational" district in 1882. The following year Sheriff Malcolm Campbell arrested Alferd Packer at the Hog Ranch. Colorado authorities later convicted Packer for killing and eating five prospectors with whom he had been snowbound in the high Colorado Rockies in the winter of 1874.

In *The Wyoming Lynching of Cattle Kate*, George Hufsmith includes details about the ranches from a letter by Abe Abrahams, an early patron. Abrahams described the first location—Brown's Ranche—seven miles north of Fetterman as consisting of a couple of log buildings. One housed the bar, dance hall, and rooms for the women. The other sat across the road and contained the kitchen and dining room. Both Brown's Ranche and the Sanders-Lawrence business employed four women. The women were commonly called "hogs"; thus the term "hog ranch."

In 1884 one of the prostitutes, "a fair but frail young half-breed of some forty summers" named Ella Wilson, became involved in a gun battle at the Hog Ranch. (Years later Ed Towse, the editor of the *Cheyenne Daily Leader*, would intentionally confuse her with a homesteader on the Sweetwater River named Ellen Watson, who lived farther west; we'll catch up with her later.) The trouble started in mid-August, when cowboys John Fenix, "Pretty Frank" Wallace, and Harry Crosby shot up all the mirrors behind the bar, blew out most of the windows, blasted holes in the bedroom doors, and generally terrorized the Hog Ranch. Sanders and Lawrence evicted the cowboys and told them to stay away.

On August 29 the three cowboys rode back into the area. They tipped a few at Billy Bacon's saloon in Fetterman and planned to ride to the ES Ranch, where they knew they could find a place to stay. As they prepared to leave town, Fenix recommended a detour to the Hog Ranch. Sheriff Campbell heard of their plan and told them not to proceed, but the cowboys ignored his warning and raced to the Hog Ranch, where an immediate shouting match started with the owners. As might be expected, one thing led to another, and pretty soon the guns blazed.

The shootout left Fenix mortally wounded and Pretty Frank injured in the doorway of the dance hall. Ella Wilson also was wounded, though not seriously. When Fenix and Crosby rode into Fetterman seeking medical attention, Campbell immediately deputized Charlie Cobb, and the two rushed toward the scene of the gunfight. Not far out of town they met Sanders and Lawrence. The businessmen knew that Fenix was at the hospital in Fetterman and that Crosby was with him. They intended to finish what they had started. The Hog Ranch owners and the sheriff had a desperate race to town, with Campbell winning by a slim margin. It made little difference that he faced down the businessmen; Fenix soon died of his wounds anyway.

The illiterate strumpet shot in the fracas gave statements to the sheriff, always marking "X" for her name. In all depositions and indictments related to the case, the woman's name is given as Ella Wilson, but the examining physician, Dr. J. N. Bradley, inadvertently wrote her name as Ella *Watson* when he treated her wounds. The error led to later confusion with the real Ellen Watson.

By the time the Hog Ranch closed in 1886, a daily stage from Rock Creek, ten miles south of Rock River on the Union Pacific Railroad, went through Fetterman on its way to Buffalo. A steady mass of ox teams, mule teams, and horse string teams hauled freight through the area. Often tenders hitched as many as sixteen teams to a load, hooking wagons together in such a way that some could be dropped during muddy days, when it was impossible to pull all of them up steep hills at the same time.

Glenrock

Glenrock is the site of an old campground known as the Rock in the Glen, where thousands of emigrants camped on their way west. The area was a Mormon way station by 1850, but the Mormons abandoned it during the Mormon War of 1857. "Major" Thomas Twiss, Indian agent at Fort Laramie, promptly and without asking permission moved his agency 100 miles up the Platte and established himself in the Mormon houses with his Oglala bride and his pet bear.

Twiss, born in Switzerland of a good family, came to the United States and attended West Point. After serving with distinction in the U.S. Army, he joined the Indian Bureau and took a job at Fort Laramie, probably the most important military post in the country. Initially, Twiss executed his duties with efficiency. In 1859 he proposed a reservation system for the various Indian tribes in his region. He recommended that a treaty council be held to determine the needs of the Indians and that they be provided with annuities until they became self-sufficient in agriculture.

On September 18, 1859, a formal treaty was concluded. For the most part it followed Twiss's recommendations. Among other things, the agreement established a reservation for Oglala Sioux along Deer Creek. The tribes would cede all land outside the reserves to the United States for annuity goods worth $100,000, to be divided among the Oglala, Brulé, Arapaho, and Cheyenne.

In its infinite wisdom, however, Congress didn't ratify the treaty. It gave no clear reason, but it may be that the treaty terms were too liberal and gave too much prime land to the Indians. It will never be certain whether the Indian wars of the 1860s could have been avoided if Congress had ratified the Deer Creek treaty, Bill Bryan wrote in *Deer Creek: Frontiers Crossroad in Pre-Territorial Wyoming*.

Perhaps because of the great disappointment that came with Congress's failure to ratify the Deer Creek treaty, Twiss became less reliable as time went on. Some charged that eventually "the major's bear got more sugar than the Indians did." However, before his efficiency lagged Twiss moved to the former Mormon settlement at Rock in the Glen, calling his new station the Upper Platte River Agency. It sat about four miles upstream from Deer Creek's mouth at the North Platte River.

Deer Creek was the site of other historic happenings as well. A team of topographic engineers led by Captain W. F. Raynolds and accompanied by geologist F. V. Hayden wintered there with Twiss in 1859 and 1860. The next spring, guided by Jim Bridger, they went on to the Yellowstone River Basin for the first official government exploration of that country, although they didn't enter the area that is now Yellowstone National Park.

On March 3, 1861, Twiss resigned as director of the Upper Platte River Agency. Officially, he quit so President Abraham Lincoln could name his own appointee to the position. Following his resignation, the Upper Platte River

Deer Creek Station during the 1860s. —American Heritage Center/University of Wyoming

Agency was moved back to Fort Laramie, but Twiss remained on Deer Creek. He eventually moved to Nebraska, where he died in 1871.

Deer Creek Station

After the Indian agency returned to Fort Laramie, the military established Deer Creek Station just south of the Oregon Trail and slightly northwest of Glenrock. Deer Creek became one of the first mail stations in Wyoming. It was operated by numerous contractors, all of them heavily subsidized by the government.

One of those contractors, John M. Hockaday and Company, acquired the Missouri-to-Salt Lake mail route on May 1, 1858. Hockaday established thirty-six stations, but his tenure as a mail runner was short-lived and a financial disaster.

Like others in the postal business, Hockaday offered passenger service in addition to mail delivery. One of his stops was at the fledgling town of Dakota City, started in 1857 by trader Joseph Bissonette. His trading complex on Deer Creek included a store, blacksmith shop, and post office. Although the trader's hopes for prosperity never materialized, a town eventually grew at the site. First a settlement named Mercedes formed at the mouth of Deer Creek. Then William Nuttal discovered coal and opened a mine nearby, so his name marked the town until January 26, 1887, when Ed J. Wells suggested the name of Glenrock in memory of the old emigrant campground.

Crossing the Platte

Overland travelers, from the native Americans to the emigrants bound for Oregon, California, and Utah, had one thing in common: They all crossed the North Platte River in central Wyoming at locations between the present towns of Glenrock and Casper.

Indians typically forded the North Platte at the mouth of Deer Creek, and several ferries operated at or near there during the Great Migration. Travelers constructed boats and rafts from cottonwood trees growing in the area. After completing their river crossing, emigrants usually sold their crafts to another party for $20 to $30. That meant a single boat might serve hundreds of overlanders. About a half mile upstream from Deer Creek, Bissonette established a ferry comprised of six or eight dugout canoes covered with timbers. He ran the operation in 1849 and 1850, mainly serving the California gold rush traffic.

The Richard Bridge, located just upstream from Bissonette's Ferry, was the first that crossed the North Platte. John Baptiste Richard (pronounced "Reshaw") built his bridge in 1851. Joined by other men, he also established a toll bridge across the river at Fort Laramie.

After a spring flood took out Richard's first bridge near Deer Creek, he built another in 1852 at a site now in Evansville. It served periodically until 1865 but wasn't profitable during later years because of another structure—Old Platte Bridge—built by Louis Guinard in 1858. In 1860 Sir Richard Burton wrote:

Reshaw (Richards) Bridge abutment at the Platte River Crossing on the Oregon Trail near Evansville. The trail entry to the river is visible on the far side of the river. —State Historic Preservation Office

Our station lay near the upper crossing or second bridge, a short distance from the town. It was also built of timber at an expense of $40,000, about a year ago, by Louis Guenot, a Quebecquois, who has passed the last twelve years upon the plains. He appeared very downcast about his temporal prospects. . . . The usual toll is $0.50, but from trains, especially Mormons, the owner will claim $5; in fact, as much as he can get without driving them to the opposition lower bridge [Richard's], or to the ferry boat.

Storing the Water

Wyoming is an arid state. Limited moisture falls in most areas, so water use is always a concern and a priority. In the 1970s Wyoming organized a strong water-development program that provided state funding for municipal projects ranging from small, low-cost wells to mammoth storage systems comprising reservoirs and pipelines. Strong backers of the Wyoming Water Development Commission included Democratic governor Ed Herschler, whose family ranched near Kemmerer and whose father once ran sheep out on the Little Colorado Desert.

The strong feeling among Wyoming water interests is: Use it or lose it. The state contains the headwaters, or is near the headwaters, of several major rivers, and water-development proponents want to keep as much of the supply in Wyoming as possible. Downstream states, however, are just as determined to get their share. When Wyoming announced plans in 1986 to build a dam on Deer Creek to store water for municipal use by Casper and other North Platte communities, users in Nebraska filed a lawsuit to halt construction and to resolve a number of other water-use issues, such as wildlife-habitat protection. The lawyers haggled, the bills mounted, and the $50 million dam project remains on hold.

Casper

Mormon Ferry

In 1847, at the site that eventually became Fort Caspar, Mormons constructed and operated the first ferry across the North Platte. It remained in use through 1851. Brigham Young named nine men to operate the ferry, which was made of two large cottonwood canoes fastened together with crosspieces and covered with slabs. The Mormon Ferry served two purposes: It provided safe passage across the North Platte and it generated revenue for new settlements in the Great Salt Lake Valley.

The Richard Bridge in Evansville stood at the future location of Fort Clay and Camp Davis, established in 1855–56. The post became Camp Payne in

1858 but was officially known as the Post at Platte Bridge (not to be confused with Platte Bridge Station, located farther west).

The military erected loose adobe buildings and tent barracks near the Mormon Ferry site and sent troops to Camp Payne in 1858 and 1859 to protect wagons along the Oregon Trail. The military established Fort Caspar—originally Platte Bridge Station—in 1862 to keep communications open and guard emigrants. It remained garrisoned until 1867.

The Bloody Year

At Sand Creek, Colorado, on November 29, 1864, Col. John Chivington attacked Black Kettle's Southern Cheyenne village of 550 men, women, and children, including a few Arapahoes. Initial reports indicated almost complete annihilation of the native Americans, but later tallies put the toll at about a third of the camp's inhabitants. At the time of the attack, Black Kettle's party was under military protection, which outraged many in the East, though most Westerners expressed support. In March 1865 Southern Cheyenne, Arapaho, and Powder River Sioux leaders met and "accepted the war pipe." Thus began "The Bloody Year on the Plains."

The 1865 diary of Sgt. Isaac B. Pennock, who served at Platte Bridge Station, gives a sampling of the times. He wrote:

> May 27—Have news that the Indians attacked Rocky Ridge (St. Mary's)
> [near South Pass] today in strong force.

Old Platte Bridge Stage and Telegraph Station. —Wyoming State Museum

169

May 28—Hear the Indians crossed the Platte River in front of our provision train. [Col. Thomas] Moonlight has sent reinforcements to the train and a dispatch to Colonel Plumb to send a detachment also from this end of the road. No telegraph communication further east than Deer Creek, not west of Sweetwater [Independence Rock].

June 3—At 3 P.M. received dispatch from Colonel Plumb that Indians have attacked station at Upper Bridge; ordered to cross lower bridge with 20 men and attack them in the rear. Capt. James E. Greer and 20 men started, but the Indians were gone when we got there, but plenty of fresh tracks. Col. Plumb is in close pursuit, and was in fighting distance at two hours before sundown. We have heard from the fight; two of our men killed and one Indian and several ponies. One of our men had ten arrows shot into him; scalped and fingers cut off and terrible mangled.

June 28—Fight on Reshaw [Richard] Creek.

July 7—[Major Mackey telegraphed Captain Greer to send 10 men to Sweetwater 55 miles west of Platte Bridge to repair the telegraph line.] Which order was almost equivalent to an order to march that number of men to shoot them down, scalp them, cut off their hands and feet, cut out their hearts, liver, sinews and send them to the savages. The boys refused to go unless 30 men were sent.

Pennock reported that the troops repaired the telegraph line to Sweetwater but found it cut again on the return trip. En route back to Platte Bridge Station they crossed the trail of between 300 and 500 Indians. The constant skirmishing continued through July.

The Indians made some small raids and stole stock, primarily mules. Then the chiefs decided that, rather than continuing to harass the military with small parties, they would stage a large raid. They gathered in the Powder River country at Crazy Woman Creek to plan the action. Their intended target: Platte Bridge Station. As this was the last crossing of the North Platte, its capture would disrupt emigrant movements and cut the soldiers' line in two.

Dull Knife, White Bull, and Roman Nose led the Cheyenne; the Lakota warriors gathered behind Red Cloud, Old-Man-Afraid-of-His-Horses, and Young-Man-Afraid-of-His-Horses. On July 25, 1865, a small scouting band of Indians attempted to lure the soldiers from Platte Bridge Station. The two sides engaged in a small skirmish, but the troops didn't venture far from their post, unknowingly foiling the Indian plan.

That same day, though warned of Indian danger, Sgt. Amos J. Custard, 11th Kansas Cavalry, headed east from Sweetwater Station at Independence Rock toward Platte Bridge Station with three mule-drawn wagons. The party camped for the night to rest the animals at Willow Springs, just over twenty miles southwest of Platte Bridge Station. Unbeknownst to Custard, as well as the troops at Platte Bridge Station, hundreds, perhaps thousands, of Indians separated the two army groups.

That night, the native Americans camped behind the big hill two miles north of Platte Bridge Station. Their battle plan was to make a second attempt to lure the soldiers from the station, but their war drums remained silent as they lay in concealment. Meanwhile, Lt. Henry Clay Bretney left Custard's wagon train for Platte Bridge Station. He no doubt reported on the status of the train and may have requested that a relief party be sent. Reports vary about whether or not the wagon train requested help. At dawn July 26, Custard's men hitched their mule teams and started rolling eastward along the telegraph road.

Back at Platte Bridge Station, the soldiers had breakfast and watched about ninety Indians riding in the hills north of the river. After consultation among themselves, the officers decided a relief party should go to the wagon train. But when it came down to the matter of who should lead the expedition, everyone with any degree of responsibility found one reason or another why he shouldn't go: Maj. Martin Anderson needed to stay and protect the post; Captain Greer had led the troops in the minor skirmish the previous afternoon; Capt. A. Smyth Lybe's infantry troops used old Springfield muskets; and several other officers were on sick call or had some other excuse.

Having rejected other alternatives, Anderson ordered Lt. Caspar Collins, Sgt. Adolph Hankhammer, Sgt. Isaac Pennock, and Cpl. Henry Grimm of the 11th Ohio Volunteer Cavalry to take twenty-five men of Companies I and K, 11th Kansas Volunteer Cavalry, and relieve the train. Collins's men had seven-shot repeating Spencer rifles, making them fairly well equipped for the task. Anderson might have chosen Collins because of an earlier conflict between troops at the post.

Collins borrowed two pistols from Lieutenant Bretney, who urged him not to undertake the rescue mission because of the number of Indians in the hills. According to Casper historian Alfred J. Mokler, Collins replied: "They are orders, and while I do not like them and think you are right, I have to obey them, and I am going, so lend me your pistols."

With those brave words, the young officer rode across Platte Bridge and started up the hill to the west. Before he'd even left sight of the station, however, Indians raced around his troops. Almost immediately Collins got a hip wound and turned back toward the station. But then one of the men under his command called for help. The officer responded, but the Indians killed him before he could give aid. In another version of the story, native Americans and a French-Cheyenne named George Bent said Collins's horse bolted and forced him into the midst of the enemy.

It was a furious, short fight, lasting only about ten minutes. Those who managed to return to the bridge had Bretney to thank for keeping their escape route intact. Without the bridge across the river, most would have died in the battle. As it was, all the men who returned had wounds.

The Indians wanted to eliminate both the bridge and the station. "If they had succeeded in this object of taking the bridge, they would probably have killed all of the balance of Collins' party and about fifteen or twenty others on the bottom land going to their relief and would then very likely have captured the station also," wrote Lt. William Young Drew, one of the five commissioned officers at the post, in a later report. Sergeant Pennock of Company I told the story this way:

> July 26—Terrible day for our command, and no knowing how it will end. . . . We crossed the bridge and got about one mile from camp, when from the Northeast and Southwest and every point of the compass, the savages came. It appeared as though they sprung up out of the ground. They completely surrounded us. There was no alternative. Death was approaching on every side in its most horrible form—that of the tomahawk and scalping knife of the Indians. We turned and charged into the thickest of them, drawing our pistols and doing the best we could. It was a terrible ordeal to go through. It was really running the gauntlet for dear life. After a terrible break-neck race of I of a mile, we arrived at the bridge, where the boys had run out to our support. In the charge we lost about five killed and about twelve wounded. Lieutenant Collins was killed. Everything was in full view of the station.

That same afternoon Lt. George M. Walker took a party to repair the telegraph wire, which had been cut about half a mile south of the river, in the valley two miles east of the post where the earlier fighting had occurred. Indians attacked Walker's party as it repaired the line, forcing the soldiers to retreat to the fort.

During Walker's unsuccessful attempt to repair the telegraph line, Sergeant Custard's little party approached Platte Bridge Station from the west on the telegraph road, unaware of the fighting. Custard took a difficult route over a steep grade, avoiding an easier route where he could have been ambushed. One of the soldiers at the fort spotted the train at about the same time the Indians did.

Advance riders with Custard escaped to the North Platte when the Indians spied them. Three of the men made it to safety at the station; another died beside the river. Meanwhile, Custard corralled his wagons, and his men defended themselves. Wrote Pennock: "All this we could plainly see from the station, but we could do nothing for them. . . . We could see the Indians in swarms charge down on our boys when they would roll volley after volley into them, it seems as though the boys were in a strong position, twenty in all being their number."

George Bent, who rode with the Indians, described the noon attack on the government wagons in a letter written in 1906. After a siege, likely the one described by Pennock, the Indians finally charged the train. They killed the occupants and burned the wagons. "After this fight we all came back to where we all stayed that night as we had left our packs, ponies and saddles as Indians ride bareback in all fights. Next morning [a] good many small war parties started again in different directions [but the] biggest party started for home. I was with this party," Bent wrote.

An hour after smoke began billowing from the wagon train, some of the men, including Lt. Bretney, crossed the bridge to retrieve the bodies of Lieutenant Collins and those who fell with him. The next day soldiers buried those with Custard. On July 29 Pennock described the scene: "Twenty-one bodies were buried on the battle ground, a horrible sight; all scalped but one, who nearly burned up. . . . They were buried in two graves 7 in one and 13 in another. One body was buried on the other side of the river from where the train was taken."

There is no clear count of the Indian numbers involved in the fighting. George Bent estimated 1,000 warriors joined the party, but Gen. P. E. Connor put the number at 3,000.

From the time of the initial attack on Collins's command July 26 until August 1, there was no telegraph service to Platte Bridge Station because the Indians had cut the line. As the new month began, Pennock wrote: "At four o'clock the joyful word came 'The Line is Working.' The joyful tick, tick, tick put a glad smile on every face. Soon heard the Sixth Michigan Cavalry would be here tomorrow."

Troops reinforced Platte Bridge Station—which soon became known as Fort Caspar in honor of Lt. Caspar Collins. The army abandoned the site in 1867 when it relocated to Fort Fetterman, and the military dismantled many Fort Caspar facilities to build the new post. Indians burned the rest of the station. In 1936 a WPA crew rebuilt old Fort Caspar on the original site. It remains in operation as a national historic place managed by the city of Casper.

On July 26, 1931, the Natrona County Historical Society dedicated twenty marble monoliths and a marker in a swale three miles west of the fort in honor of the soldiers in the Custard wagon train. That fight is called Battle of Red Buttes, although the buttes themselves stand some ten miles to the southwest. The monuments and marker are about a mile from the site of the fighting.

Wyoming Centennial Wagon Train

In 1990 the Wyoming Centennial Wagon Train followed the historic Bridger Trail from Fort Caspar to Cody, across central Wyoming and through the Big Horn Basin. The train included wagons, horses, and riders, along with some Mormons pulling handcarts and other people walking over the dirt and cactus. It was one of the biggest single events of Wyoming's centennial celebration, although activities in Cheyenne and elsewhere on Statehood Day, July 10, 1990, drew thousands of people. The wagon train went 260 miles in thirty days.

Natrona County

On March 3, 1890, four months before Wyoming became a state, Natrona County carved itself from a part of Carbon County. The fight for county seat started immediately, with Casper and Bessemer lobbying for the honor. Officials nullified an election to decide the issue when it became clear that Bessemer tallied more votes than it had residents. A Bessemer resident, Mrs. W. A. Blackmore, told researchers for the WPA history of Wyoming that many residents voted, went home, changed their clothes, and returned to the polls, voting again and again. "My husband wouldn't let me," she said.

Casper grew at the terminus of the Fremont, Elkhorn & Missouri Valley Railroad. The first settlers were John Merrill, C. W. Eads, and the latter's children. The group formed a temporary townsite June 8, 1888. Within a week others joined them to cheer arrival of the first passenger train. Some businesses located near the Eads wagon in a place known as Old Town, hauling green lumber from Casper Mountain for the buildings. That fall a pair of brothers sold lots for $200 to $250, and the town of Casper came into existence.

The town is named for Lt. Caspar Collins, but spelled differently. Like other western towns of the era, Casper was a wild and reckless place. The city council adopted an ordinance making it "unlawful for any woman to frequent or remain in the barroom of any saloon in the town of Casper between the hours of 7 A.M. and 10 P.M." The law was intended to keep the prostitutes of David Street's brothels out of sight, at least during the daytime, but it gave them control of the night, Jean Mead wrote in *Casper Country: Wyoming's Heartland*. Enforcing such a law was more than a nightmare, however, and finally town fathers dropped the "lewd woman" ordinance in 1898.

Black Gold Brings Prosperity

From the drilling of Natrona County's first oil well in 1887 a few miles northwest of Casper, the county fortunes have always been tied to the underground liquid. Drilling began northwest of Casper, but other development took place near Poison Spider Creek, at Bessemer Bend, Big Muddy, Ervay, and in the Shannon Field, just north of Salt Creek.

Railroads could use Salt Creek's high-quality oil without even refining it, but Casper soon had a refinery—Shannon's Pennsylvania Oil and Gas Company built one on South Center Street in 1895. The refinery turned 100 barrels of crude a day into kerosene and lubricating oils. Casper quickly gained a reputation as a rough, but rich, oil town as other refineries opened.

By 1920 oil, cattle, and sheep drove Casper's economy, but later in that decade oil prices fell, and the town took a serious look at its future. Diversification became the key to stability. The first step in that direction took place in 1927, when a horse-rendering plant opened. That led Casper's young men to engage in a strange sort of sport: They took the mufflers off their cars and chased wild horses near Teapot Dome. Once rounded up, the horses went to the rendering plant to be turned into poultry feed, cracklings, grease, and shoe leather.

Casper—Muddy Gap

First White Man's Cabin

In November 1812, Robert Stuart and six companions from Astoria found their way across the Shining Mountains, now known as the Rockies, on their way back to Missouri. The group camped near the spot where Poison Spider Creek empties into the North Platte, west of present-day Casper. The men built a cabin, the first within the present boundaries of Wyoming, and remained for a month, living in relative comfort in the eight-by-eighteen-foot buffalo-skin-covered structure. Stuart intended to spend the winter there, but on December 10 Arapaho Indians found the cabin. The party stayed three more days before abandoning the structure and moving to a site near the future Torrington.

Not until 1888 did a town begin near the location of Stuart's original cabin. The Wyoming Improvement Company surveyed the site, platted forty-nine blocks of town lots, and reserved an area "upon which to erect the future capitol building of Wyoming," according to the WPA history of Wyoming. Developers called the community Bessemer, the "Queen City of the West," but the town failed to live up to its planners' expectations: Bessemer failed even to become a county seat, much less the state capital. In 1891 the county took over the bridge across the North Platte River because of unpaid taxes, and Bessemer soon became a ghost.

Goose Egg Ranch

The Goose Egg Ranch, west of Casper on Wyoming 220, began operating in 1877 when the Seabright brothers brought 27,000 head of Texas cattle to the range and built a large stone house. Their strange brand, shaped like a big egg, gave the ranch its name. Ten years later the Seabrights sold out to Joseph M. Carey, who renamed the ranch the CY. Carey and his brother later became big players in Casper's history, selling lots for the town. Carey also had a role in organizing the 1892 cattle invasion in Johnson County and became Wyoming's senator in 1893 and governor in 1911.

During its heyday, the Goose Egg held popular Saturday-night dances. Once the cowboys playfully exchanged the garments of two infants, and neither family realized it had the wrong baby until both were on the way home. Although many claim this incident is the one about which Owen Wister wrote in *The Virginian*, such baby changes happened often in rural Wyoming—both intentionally, as pranks by cowboys, and unintentionally, when the blankets of sleeping children became mixed and tired parents, who had danced all night, weren't as alert as they perhaps should have been.

Sometimes the cowboys extended their pranks beyond children. Once in the Saratoga area they switched the teams on some wagons parked nearby. Ranchers returning home in the dark didn't realize they had the wrong horses until they got to their own barns.

North Platte Water Project

At a site near Alcova, west of Casper on Wyoming 220, hot springs flow from solid rock. An early analysis showed the water had medicinal quality, and in 1891 an eastern syndicate bought the site for a resort. The owners made plans for $250,000 worth of improvements, but before they could do much the deal fell through.

In 1933 a congressional appropriation provided for an irrigation project that gave Alcova its biggest boost in forty years. The Kendrick Project—named for the Wyoming governor and then U.S. Senator John B. Kendrick—had three main features: Alcova Dam and Reservoir, Seminoe Dam, and a hydroelectric power plant. The main objective of the project was the reclamation and settlement of 66,000 acres of central Wyoming land.

The Kendrick Project was the second cog in a water system involving the North Platte. The first, the massive North Platte Water Project, involved a December 6, 1904, water right granted by the state for Pathfinder Reservoir. That project called for the storage of just over one million acre-feet of water in Seminoe, Pathfinder, Guernsey, and Glendo reservoirs for distribution to farmers in central and eastern Wyoming and western Nebraska.

The North Platte Project, as touted by executives of the Chicago & Northwestern Railroad, would reclaim some 207,000 acres of central Wyoming prairie. The railroad executives got approval to inundate 22,000 acres of privately owned land bordering the North Platte, then went to sell the idea in Douglas and other Wyoming communities.

Apparently, though, the sell job was really a snow job. Casper newspaper editor A. J. Mokler wrote, "The Pathfinder Dam was built under false pretense and Wyoming was thereby deprived of reclaiming a vast amount of acreage which would have been irrigated had the plans been carried out as the people of Wyoming were led to believe."

Many in Wyoming thought the railroad executives worked hand in hand with the Nebraska congressional delegation in an attempt to take Wyoming's water. By far the majority of the water collected in Pathfinder (and the other federally managed reservoirs of the North Platte system developed after 1904) goes to irrigate crops in western Nebraska.

In 1912 Wyoming state engineer Elwood Mead reported, "It was the intention of the Reclamation service to irrigate nearly 700,000 acres of land, the bulk of which was in the State of Wyoming. . . . Reclamation service now reports only 129,270 acres of which 107,521 acres are in Nebraska and 21,749 are in Wyoming." The engineer added that 17,874 of the 21,749 Wyoming acres irrigated in the project were lands of the North Platte Canal and Colonization Company, which operated a viaduct at Whalen Falls, near Guernsey. That meant only about 4,000 additional acres were reclaimed as a result of the new project—"a very small area to reclaim after submerging 22,000 acres with the Pathfinder Reservoir," the engineer concluded.

Pathfinder Dam is named for John C. Frémont, known as the Pathfinder, who once capsized his boats in the Fiery Narrows between the current reservoir and Alcova.

Like the Colorado River, the North Platte is managed under a complex set of regulations. A 1945 U.S. Supreme Court ruling divided water use among Colorado, Wyoming, and Nebraska, allowing each state to irrigate a certain number of acres annually. Wyoming's share is just over 168,000 acres. The court ruling also provides for specific periods of the year when water can be stored and other periods when water is to be used for irrigation.

Management of the North Platte often devolves into a tangled web of lawsuits. In the late 1980s and early 1990s, there were six different ongoing suits involving Wyoming, Nebraska, and the U.S. Bureau of Reclamation. In the major case, *Nebraska v. Wyoming* (1986), Nebraska claimed a water right for the Inland Lakes near Alliance and disputed Wyoming's right to build the Deer Creek Dam near the site of historic Deer Creek Station and to construct the Corn Creek Project on the Laramie River near Torrington. On April 20, 1993, the U.S. Supreme Court ruled that Nebraska did have a right to water for the Inland Lakes, but it left open the questions involving future development at Deer Creek and on the Laramie River.

Other disputes, ranging from the way farmers receive water to a plan for a water trade between the Casper-Alcova Irrigation District near Casper and the Goshen Irrigation District near Torrington, illustrated the intensity of feeling over water use and supply in arid Wyoming.

Pathfinder Dam and Reservoir store water for the North Platte Irrigation Project that serves farmers in eastern Wyoming and western Nebraska. This view is of the dam in December 1937. —Wyoming State Museum

Miracle Mile

A backcountry road from Alcova Reservoir in Natrona County to Seminoe Reservoir in Carbon County provides an alternate route from Casper to Rawlins. Designated as a National Bureau of Land Management Backcountry Byway, the road is partially paved, partially gravel, and suitable for cars in good weather. About seven miles from Alcova the road enters Pathfinder Canyon, also known as Frémont Canyon.

The route follows the North Platte between Seminoe and Pathfinder reservoirs, a stretch of river known as the Miracle Mile. The actual distance ranges from one to six miles, depending on how full Pathfinder Reservoir is. Regardless of length, it it one of Wyoming's best trout fisheries.

Independence Rock

Wyoming 220 heads west out of Casper toward Muddy Gap and Rawlins along the historic Oregon and Mormon trails. The routes stay north of the highway for the most part, but they cross it a few miles east of Independence Rock. That turtle-shaped formation is one of the most noted landmarks on the Oregon Trail west of Fort Laramie. Legend has it that Independence Rock got its name when a party of mountain men celebrated the Fourth of July there in 1830.

In 1834 John K. Townsend mentioned in his diary that he camped at "a large rounded mass of granite, about fifty feet high, called Rock Independence." In 1840 Father Pierre De Smet referred to the "famous rock, Independence . . . that might be called the great registry of the desert, for on it may be read in large characters the names of several travelers who have visited the Rocky Mountains." In 1842, John Frémont described the rock as

> [a]bout 650 yards long and 40 in height. Except in a depression on the summit, where a little soil supported a scanty growth of shrubs with a solitary pine, it was entirely bare. Everywhere within six or eight feet from the ground, where the surface was sufficiently smooth, and in some place sixty or eighty feet above, the rock was inscribed with names of travelers. . . . I engraved on this rock of the far West a symbol of the Christian faith . . . a large cross, which I covered with a black preparation of India rubber well calculated to resist the influence of wind and rain.

In 1847 Brigham Young led the first group of Mormons past the spot, and by 1855 some of Young's followers, who had stone-cutting tools, began engraving travelers' names on the rock, charging $1 to $5 a name. Lt. Caspar Collins commanded the post at the crossing of the Sweetwater River near Independence Rock for a time. Collins wrote to his mother in Ohio, June 16, 1862, "This is the worst country for winds I ever saw. Yesterday . . . it commenced to blow, and it is blowing yet. . . . Major Bridger went off this morning up in the mountains to get out of the wind. He says he is going to get in some canon and make a large fire."

William Henry Jackson's view of a wagon train along the Sweetwater River at Independence Rock with Devil's Gate in the background. —Wyoming State Museum

The first meeting of Ancient Free and Accepted Masons in Wyoming took place at Independence Rock July 4, 1862, and Boy Scouts held many jamborees at the site through the years. Rock markers on the east side of the monument are a reminder of those gatherings.

A Wyoming Lynching

One of the most heinous crimes in the West took place along the Sweetwater River in 1889, not far from Independence Rock. James Averell and Ellen Watson claimed homestead land on the Sweetwater, right in the middle of prime pastureland. Albert Bothwell, one of Wyoming's early-day cattle barons, did not take kindly to the thought of homesteaders living on range he considered his.

Averell first saw the Sweetwater country when he served in Wyoming as a member of Company H of the 13th Infantry, U.S. Army. He joined the army in 1871 when he was twenty and immediately reported to Fort Douglas, Utah, on the outskirts of Salt Lake City. He no sooner had arrived than he was marched off to Fort Fred Steele, Wyoming Territory, fifteen miles east of Rawlins. He spent his first five-year hitch guarding the Union Pacific Railroad and visiting various other military and civilian outposts in the area.

James Averell died at the hand of lynchers on the Sweetwater, July 1889. —Wyoming State Museum

Averell mustered out of the army but reenlisted and served in Company D of the 9th Infantry under Gen. George Crook. During this stint Averell fought both Indians and renegade whites and helped construct Fort Reno and its replacement post, Fort McKinney. There Averell owned a small house and ran afoul of the law when he killed a man. He was arrested and jailed in Buffalo, then released when his prominent friends posted a $2,000 bond. The judge ordered Averell to stand trial in Rawlins, at that time the county seat, but after a series of legal maneuverings authorities dropped the charges against him. The judge ruled that since Averell was in the military, the case should have been heard by a military court.

Averell went free in 1881 and, after leaving the army for good, claimed his homestead on the Sweetwater. He had a road ranch, served as justice of the peace, and wrote scathing letters to newspapers about the rights of homesteaders and the unjust actions taken by wealthy cattlemen, who were trying to run the nesters off the range.

Somewhere along the line Averell met Ellen Watson, an educated young woman from Kansas. Ellen also claimed a homestead on the Sweetwater and began accumulating a small herd of cattle. The two secretly married, but that fact didn't surface—or, at least, wasn't believed—until many years after their deaths.

Ellen Watson, a homesteader who got the nickname Cattle Kate, died on a hot July day in 1889 when six prominent ranchers hanged her and her husband from a tree in central Wyoming. —Wyoming State Museum

Wealthy ranchers, particularly Bothwell, could not tolerate the Averell and Watson homesteads in the middle of their range. They warned the two to leave, then resorted to violence. Six prominent cowmen showed up at the homesteads on July 22, 1889. They grabbed Averell and Watson, put them in a light wagon, and drove to Spring Creek Gulch, about five miles from Averell's saloon. There the cattlemen looped ropes around their necks, pushed them from the rocks, and hanged them.

Ed Towse of the *Cheyenne Daily Leader* quickly reported the incident. His July 23, 1889, story contained a lot of information, most of it inaccurate:

A DOUBLE LYNCHING

Postmaster Averill [sic] and his Wife Hung for Cattle Stealing

They were tireless Maverickers who defied the law.

The man weakened but the woman cursed to the last.

A man and a woman were lynched near historic Independence Rock on the Sweetwater River in Carbon County Sunday night. They were Postmaster James Averill [sic] and a virago who had been living with him as his wife for some months. Their offense was cattle stealing, and they operated on a large scale, recruiting quite a bunch of young steers from the range of that section.

News of the double hanging was brought to Rawlins by a special courier. . . . Averill and the woman were fearless maverickers. The female was the equal of any man on the range. Of robust physique she was a daredevil in the saddle, handy with a six-shooter and adept with the lariat and branding iron. . . . She rode straddle, always had a vicious broncho for a mount and seemed never to tire of dashing across the range.

The thieving pair were ordered to leave the country several times, but paid no attention to the warnings, sending the message that they could take care of themselves, that mavericks were common property and that they would continue to appropriate unmarked cattle.

Towse reported that between ten and twenty ranchers showed up at the Averell road ranch to take the two suspected rustlers into custody. He picks up the tale:

Averill, always feared because he was a murderous coward, showed himself a cur. He begged and whined, and protested innocence, even saying the woman did all the stealing. The female was made of sterner stuff. She exhausted a blasphemous vocabulary upon the visitors, who essayed to stop the vile flow by gagging her, but found the task too great. After applying every imaginable opprobrious epithet to the lynchers, she cursed everything and everybody, challenging the Deity to cheat her enemies by striking her dead if he dared. When preparations for the short trip to the scaffold were made she called for her own horse and vaulted to its back from the ground.

Ropes were hung from the limb of a big cottonwood tree on the south bank of the Sweetwater. Nooses were adjusted to the necks of Averill and his wife and their horses led from under them. The woman died with curses on her foul lips.

A point overlooked by the amateur executioners was tying the limbs of the victims, and the kicking and writhing of these members was something awful.

An inquest may be held over the remains of the thieves, but it is doubtful if any attempt will be made to punish the lynchers. They acted in self protection, feeling that the time to resort to violent measures had arrived.

This is the first hanging of a woman in Wyoming.

Actually, about the only accurate statements in Towse's report dealt with the names of those lynched, the location of the hanging, and the statement that it was "doubtful if any attempt will be made to punish the lynchers." The powerful Wyoming Stock Growers Association pretty much ruled the state at that time, and it certainly had the drop on Ed Towse. He knew that even if an attempt was made to punish the cattlemen, it would not be anything serious.

The court did, in fact, order the six cattlemen—Bothwell, John Durbin, Robert M. Gailbraith, Bob Conner, M. Ernest McLean, and Tom Sun—to answer to the murders, but it returned no indictments because the known witnesses to the incident disappeared or mysteriously died. Most people concluded that the stockmen or the Stock Growers Association had a hand in the disappearances and deaths.

In his subsequent reports on the killing, Towse intentionally confused Ellen Watson, the Sweetwater homesteader, with Ella Wilson, the Hog Ranch prostitute. Later, Towse and other writers deepened the confusion—again, probably intentionally—by dubbing Watson "Cattle Kate" after Kate Maxwell, a notorious whore in Bessemer, a few miles east of where Ellen Watson's moccasin-covered feet kicked their last. The legend of Cattle Kate is one of the best-known in Wyoming, although, like the legend of Rawhide, it is based largely on misinformation.

Bothwell

Albert J. Bothwell, the rancher who led the way in the lynching of Ellen Watson and Jim Averell, built a town on Horse Creek in the vicinity of Independence Rock. There the Sweetwater Land and Improvement Company incorporated, with capital of $300,000. During the summer of the hangings, in 1889, the community of Bothwell had a store, blacksmith shop, post office, saloon, and a newspaper, the *Sweetwater Chief*. Albert Bothwell left the Sweetwater country, as did four of the other men involved in the lynchings. Only the French-Canadian Tom Sun and the graves of Averell and Watson remained.

Devil's Gate

The Sweetwater River got its name from Gen. William H. Ashley in 1823 after his trappers told him that the water left a pleasant taste in their mouths. Tradition tells that a pack mule fell while crossing the stream and spilled its load of sugar into the water.

The first major landmark on the Sweetwater west of Independence Rock is Devil's Gate. Both sites are clearly visible long before you get to them as you travel west from Casper or east from Muddy Gap along Wyoming 220. In the early 1860s, an eighteen-year-old girl climbed to the top of the ridge above Devil's Gate with three companions and fell to her death. Her body is buried in the gorge. The epitaph at her grave says:

Here lies the body of Caroline Todd

Whose soul has lately gone to God

Ere redemption was too late

She was redeemed at Devil's Gate.

Robert Stuart's party of returning Astorians noted Devil's Gate in 1812, and Capt. Hiram M. Chittenden investigated its possibilities as a dam site in

The corrals of the Sun Ranch fill the foreground in this view of Devil's Gate. The road is the old highway, and it lies on the ruts of the Oregon-California-Mormon trails.

1901–2. He pronounced Devil's Gate "one of the most notable features of its kind in the world."

Sun Ranch

Just west of Independence Rock and Devil's Gate lies the Hub and Spoke outfit—the Sun Ranch—homesteaded by Thomas de Beau Soleil, a French-Canadian trapper who Americanized his name to Tom Sun. The east entrance to the Hub and Spoke follows the old highway along the Oregon Trail, past Devil's Gate, and through the rocks in a narrow canyon. Numerous emigrant graves mark the route.

Sun was a contemporary of Buffalo Bill Cody, and some sources claim the French-Canadian trapper taught the famous buffalo hunter how to shoot. They served together at Fort Fred Steele and hunted in the Sweetwater country. Of the six ranchers involved in the 1889 lynching of Ellen Watson and James Averell, Tom Sun was the only one who remained on the Sweetwater after the incident.

Sun proved up, or secured title to, his homestead and reared a family. The ranch remains one of the largest in the state still in the original family of ownership. Covering portions of four counties, the Sun Ranch operation involves many grandchildren and great-grandchildren of patriarch Tom Sun. In the late 1980s, an innovative land-stewardship program that advocated multiple uses and conservation practices started on the Sun Ranch. Known as the Sun Stewardship, this coordinated resource-management project involves the Sun family, federal and state agencies such as the U.S. Bureau of Land Management and Wyoming Game and Fish Department, and conservation groups like Trout Unlimited and the Wyoming Wildlife Federation. Improvements in grazing practices, water development, and other operations helped the ranch increase its production while restoring rangeland and riparian areas.

The French-Canadian Tom Sun homesteaded on the Sweetwater River in the shadow of Devil's Gate. He participated in the lynching of James Averell and Ellen "Cattle Kate" Watson in 1889. —Wyoming State Museum

About eighteen miles of pristine Oregon Trail ruts cross Sun land, and the ranch controls access to Martin's Cove, where many Mormons died in 1856 when their handcart company became stranded in deep snows. Martin's Cove is located a couple of miles west of the Sun Ranch headquarters.

Tragedy of the Martin Company

Edward Martin and his Mormon caravan left Florence, Nebraska, too late in the summer season of 1856 to reach Salt Lake before winter claimed the Plains. Pulling and pushing handcarts across the land, the party (traveling behind another late-starting emigrant train, the Willie Company) struggled with too little food, a lack of warm clothing, and disease. When the Mormons neared Independence Rock, heavy winter snows piled on the ground, making

Gravesites, most of them unmarked, line the route of the Oregon Trail corridor. This marker for T. P. Baker, 1864, lies on the Sun Ranch in central Wyoming.

travel difficult or, in some instances, impossible. The members of Martin's party began dying of exposure, their bodies left in shallow graves all along the trail. Martin and his followers holed up at a sheltered cove until rescue came from Salt Lake. The Willie party was ahead of Martin and pushed on to the west. Even when relief arrived, some of the Mormons remained at Martin's Cove the rest of the winter, where they survived despite poor hunting skills.

Desperate circumstances often lead to desperate measures. The Mormons at Martin's Cove had to resort to boiling the hides of cattle they'd butchered. In one case they even dropped a packsaddle in the pot, but, fortunately, a group of Mormon mail carriers arrived with supplies before they had to eat the thin soup.

US 287
Muddy Gap—Lander
82 miles

Split Rock

Wyoming 220 joins US 287/Wyoming 789 at Muddy Gap. The Sweetwater River swings close to the highway about ten miles northwest of the junction, and the Oregon Trail nearly intercepts the road at Split Rock. It then snakes along the highway to the junction of Wyoming 135 at the Sweetwater Station Rest Area.

Split Rock is a natural feature in the Sweetwater Rocks. Russell, Majors, and Waddell built a station here in 1859 that served stagecoaches, the Pony Express, and the telegraph. Though deep in Shoshone country, Sweetwater Station had no difficulties with Indians until March 1862, when the traditionally friendly Shoshone and some Bannocks stopped movement on the western trails and severed the telegraph lines by striking simultaneously at every station between Platte Bridge and Bear River, Utah. Drivers, station attendants, and guards, taken completely by surprise, saw the Indians capture every horse and mule belonging to the company in this area. The Shoshone—with the loss of only one life—cut communications and temporarily stopped the emigrant encroachment. Mrs. Tom Sun later wrote in the *Rawlins Daily Times*:

> Early in 1862, the 1st Division of the 11th Ohio Volunteer Cavalry with Colonel William Collins in command reached Fort Laramie, and was sent out to guard the stage and emigrant trains. Indians appeared near Sweetwater Station one day, seemingly on the war path. The soldiers left, but the telegraph operator remained at his station. He sent messages to operator John Friend at Split Rock. The Sweetwater operator reported

to the Split Rock station that the Indians were dancing a war dance down on the meadow. Later he warned that they were coming toward the station, then that they were climbing the stockade, and finally that they were coming into the station. Help was sent, but it came too late. The operator was found scalped and pinned to the ground by a peg through his mouth. The station had been burned.

At President Lincoln's request, Brigham Young sent the Mormon Battalion, some 300 volunteers under the command of Capt. Lot Smith, to quiet the Indians. The Shoshone raids resulted in only one killing—a black man who failed to prepare a meal as asked. He likely was the station tender noted by Mrs. Tom Sun in her newspaper article.

Bill Cody's Ride

At Three Crossings Station in the Sweetwater Valley, William F. Cody made history on a ride for the Pony Express. His 322-mile journey (some writers put the distance at 384 miles) is equaled in Wyoming only by Portugee Phillips's several-day trek in 1866 (see page 132).

Cody's adventure started in a routine way. The fifteen-year-old Pony Express rider mounted his horse at Red Buttes, just west of present-day Casper, and headed to Three Crossings, near the town of Jeffrey City. There he was to

Col. William F. Cody started the Buffalo Bill Wild West Show in 1883. He recruited cowboys for his show throughout Wyoming. Cody rode with the Pony Express, scouted for George A. Custer, and earned his famous nickname as a hunter for the railroad. —Wyoming State Museum

turn his mailbag over to a relief rider, who would take it the next eighty-five miles to St. Mary's Station, also called Rocky Ridge. But when Cody arrived at Three Crossings, he found his relief dead—apparently killed by Indians. He mounted a fresh horse and headed toward Rocky Ridge. When he got there he picked up the return mail and, without a break, rode back to Red Buttes. His was the longest recorded ride in the eighteen-month history of the Pony Express, from April 1860 to October 1861.

Jeffrey City

Originally called Home on the Range, this town was renamed for Dr. Charles W. Jeffrey. It became a center of uranium production in the 1960s when Western Nuclear Corporation started operations here. The company employed hundreds of workers, but by 1980 the market for yellowcake uranium had dropped out of sight, and the $50 million processing mill closed. The once-booming town withered, and the modular homes that rolled in during the blast of production now left on flatbeds or tandem axles, headed for some other boomtown.

Besides uranium, this area is known for its jade. In 1943 Verla James found a piece of raw jade weighing 3,366 pounds. James later found other chunks totaling some 7,000 pounds. By 1945 Wyoming led the nation in jade production. Rock hunters also found onyx and moss agates in abundance.

St. Mary's Station

Lt. John C. Frémont painted this picture of the Sweetwater Valley when he passed through in the summer of 1842:

> On either side of the valley, which is four or five miles broad, the mountains rise. . . . On the south side the range is timbered. On the north . . . granite masses rise abruptly from the green swale of the river, terminating in a line of broken summits. Except in the crevices of the rock and here and there on a ledge or bench of mountain, where a few hardy pines have clustered together, they are perfectly bare and destitute of vegetation. Among these masses, where there are sometimes isolated hills and ridges, green valleys open in upon the river, which sweeps the base of these mountains for 36 miles.

In 1859 Russell, Majors, and Waddell of the Pony Express built St. Mary's Stage Station, which because of the rugged hillside nearby is often called Rocky Ridge. A U.S. Bureau of Land Management route, the Atlantic City Road turns off of US 287 a couple of miles west of the Sweetwater Station Rest Area. It heads west directly toward two early settlements in the vicinity of South Pass: Atlantic City and South Pass City. The latter is now a state historic site. You can also reach those towns via Wyoming 28, but the graveled Atlantic City route, which is not good after a heavy rain, most closely follows the Oregon and Mormon trails.

Saga of the Willie Company

The Oregon Trail followed the south bank of the North Platte River to Casper, where emigrants crossed the muddy stream and continued on the north bank. There it was joined by the Mormon Trail, pioneered in 1847 by Brigham Young. On the eastern stretches of the journey the Mormons traveled north of the river to avoid confrontation with those on the south shore. Diaries of the emigration make it clear the two factions had their disagreements, but there were few major conflicts.

The greatest tragedy of the entire western migration occurred between Independence Rock and South Pass in 1856 when two Mormon handcart companies became stranded in winter storms. As described earlier, the Martin Company holed up at a cove on the Sweetwater River just west of Devil's Gate. The James Grey Willie Company trudged ahead across snow-covered Wyoming. "Every death weakened our forces," wrote John Chislett in his journal as the Willie party neared Independence Rock. "In my hundred I could not raise enough men to pitch a tent when we camped."

Willie and his company leaders cut rations to conserve food as the Saints struggled through freezing streams, deep snows, piercing winds, and bitter temperatures. Snowflakes brushed their faces on October 19, the day leaders doled out the last of the flour. Step after step they forced themselves on, finally camping in the willows at the Three Crossings of the Sweetwater. That night eighteen inches of snow fell, and the Mormons' few starving draft animals scattered in the storm.

Dawn broke with five new corpses to be buried. The ground was frozen, so digging graves was an impossible task; instead they buried the dead in a snowdrift and crept on. Chislett wrote, "Finally we were overtaken by a snowstorm which the shrill wind blew furiously about us. The snow fell several inches deep as we travelled along, but we dared not stop, for we had a sixteen-mile journey to make that day, and short of it we could not get wood and water."

As the company huddled and rested that noon a light wagon from the west drove into camp. Its occupants, Joseph A. Young and Stephen Taylor, told the Willie party a relief train was on the way from Salt Lake with supplies for the handcart companies led by Willie and Martin. Young and Taylor told the Willie Company to push on because there were 1,500 emigrants to be rescued and the sixteen loads of provisions on the way from Fort Bridger would not last long.

The Willie party had neither shelter nor wood, and the members had not eaten for two days. They were literally freezing and starving to death. As the Saints made the long, difficult climb out of the Sweetwater Valley and up Rocky Ridge, they were nearly out of provisions again. Many had frostbitten hands, feet, and faces because they didn't have proper clothing for the frigid temperatures.

On the way to Rock Creek, Willie's party again became stranded. Nine people died that night, and the next day, October 22, 1856, fifteen more died at Rock Creek. They are buried in a mass grave that is today marked with a commemorative stone. In all, between 62 and 67 members of the Willie handcart company died, as did an additional 135 to 150 members of the Martin Company.

Wyoming 28
Lander—Farson
68 miles

A Gold Strike at South Pass

The first gold strike at South Pass was reported in 1842 when an anonymous trapper announced he was going east to organize a company to develop a claim at the head of the Sweetwater. On his way Indians killed him. In 1855 other prospectors found limited amounts of gold in the area. In 1861 the last of those men abandoned his diggings to cut poles for William Creighton's telegraph line. Finally, in 1867 a party of miners, returning disappointed from California, prospected the diggings and found abundant placer gold.

South Pass City grew quickly after miners staked claims in 1867, and the following year Atlantic City started, with about 3,000 people living in the vicinity by 1869. Hundreds of placer gold operations dotted Rock Creek, with

Miners at South Pass City. —Wyoming State Museum

work ongoing at the Rose, Buckeye, Diana, Caribou, and Snowbird mines. The largest, near South Pass, went by the name Cariso. Both South Pass City and Atlantic City prospered, each boasting a wide range of businesses.

Like most gold rushes, the South Pass fever quickly subsided, and by 1872 Atlantic City and South Pass City were nearly deserted. Over the next century a number of lesser mining booms rocked the area, but South Pass City didn't survive as a commercial center. It became a ghost town and is now preserved as a state historic site. Atlantic City has done a little better, thanks to a more diversified economy that includes ranching and a few businesses to serve a small population and a larger number of tourists.

Although you can reach both South Pass City and Atlantic City by following the gravel road from near Sweetwater Station, the most popular access is via Wyoming 28 out of Lander.

The Beginning of Women's Suffrage

Esther Hobart Morris is usually credited with getting women the right to vote in Wyoming in 1869. An often-told, but untrue, story about women's suffrage is that E. G. Nickerson and William Bright, candidates to the first Wyoming Territorial Legislature, attended a tea party at Morris's home in South Pass City and promised to submit a bill giving women the right to vote. In fact, the tea party never took place; nevertheless, the story remains a long-lived legend in Wyoming and belongs in the same classification as the legends of Rawhide and of Cattle Kate.

Bright ultimately won the election, and he did introduce legislation giving women equal suffrage. His young wife, Julia, also supported women's voting rights, and she may have influenced her husband. At any rate, Wyoming granted suffrage to women in a law signed December 10, 1869, by Governor John Campbell. It was the first state or territory to grant such status to women, and the law predated the Nineteenth Amendment to the U.S. Constitution by a half century.

In early February 1870 Esther Hobart Morris became the first female justice of the peace anywhere. The man she replaced, J. W. Stillman, refused to turn over his court docket. In her first official action as a justice of the peace, Morris called for the arrest of Stillman, but she later dismissed the case. After about nine months, Morris's term as a justice of the peace ended, and she was not asked to run again. Ironically, the man who replaced her was the same one who preceded her: J. W. Stillman.

Fort Stambaugh

The influx of miners to the South Pass region set off Indian difficulties. Under earlier treaties the Shoshone held territory that included the South Pass area, so when the miners arrived, conflict quickly followed. In 1870 the military established Fort Stambaugh on the Oregon Trail in Smith's Gulch to protect miners at South Pass City. The post was named for Lt. George B. Stambaugh of Fort Brown, who died in a fight with Indians May 10, 1870. Two infantry companies served at Fort Stambaugh, living in four large log barracks.

South Pass

South Pass is the single most important feature on the Oregon Trail in Wyoming; without it, there would have been no trail across Wyoming. South Pass, a treeless, twenty-five-mile-wide plateau broken by low, flat-topped sagebrush hills and pyramidal sand dunes, provided easy passage over the Continental Divide. The incline on both approaches is gradual, making it difficult to discern the divide. Old wagon tracks are so numerous that the pass resembles an aged, plowed field.

The nation's first transcontinental route crossed the land that is now Wyoming because of a low mountain pass—some twenty-five miles wide—found by white men in 1812. South Pass is marked with two stone monuments: one to Narcissa Whitman and Eliza Spalding, the first women to cross the pass in 1836; and this marker for the Oregon Trail.

Robert Stuart and his companions crossed the Rockies in this vicinity in 1812 on their eastward journey from Fort Astoria, Oregon, although they probably did not cross exactly at South Pass. The route saw little use by whites until 1824, when Thomas Fitzpatrick of the Rocky Mountain Fur Company chanced upon the crossing and reported it to Gen. William H. Ashley.

South Pass offered a wide, grassy gateway to the Green River Valley and the various trapping spots of the West: Pierre's Hole, Colter's Hell, the Three Forks of the Missouri, Bear Lake, Cache Valley, Ogden's Hole, and Great Salt Lake Valley. In 1827 Ashley sent a four-pound cannon drawn by four mules through the pass, and in 1832 Captain Benjamin L. E. Bonneville took the first wagons over.

When missionaries Marcus Whitman and Samuel Parker crossed South Pass in 1835, Parker, not dreaming that the most mountainous country lay far west of the divide, noted in his journal that "there will be no difficulty in constructing a railroad from the Atlantic to the Pacific."

A water diversion ditch atop South Pass channeled water from the Atlantic drainage to the Pacific drainage at the turn of the century, but use was discontinued when Sweetwater Valley ranchers complained.

Trappers and traders used the pass throughout the 1830s, and in 1841 the first emigrant train crossed the broad swale. In the late 1850s the stagecoach provided faster transportation over the Oregon Trail route and South Pass. By 1860 the Pony Express was crossing the pass, and the next year Creighton's telegraph followed suit.

Transbasin Water Diversion

Wyoming is somewhat obsessed with water. The state has lots of rivers but little rainfall. At South Pass, sometime around the turn of the century, the first known transbasin water diversion took place. A rancher hand-dug an irrigation ditch to draw water from the Sweetwater River, on the Atlantic side of the Continental Divide, to a homestead near Pacific Spring, on the Pacific side. The diversion worked—at least, until the ranchers on the Sweetwater noticed that their supply had dwindled. Then they made the Pacific rancher stop using his ditch. The evidence still remains: The huge, unused ditch snakes its way along the divide, only a few hundred yards from monuments to the pioneers.

US 287
Lander—Junction US 26/287
22 miles

Lander

The first nonnative people known to travel through the Wind River Valley made up a party led by Pierre Dorion as it headed to Astoria at the mouth of the Columbia River in 1811. Capt. Benjamin Bonneville explored the area in the early 1830s, and Lt. John C. Frémont, from whom the modern-day county gets its name, moved through in 1842. The county seat is named for Frederick West Lander, who engineered the famous road from South Pass. Surveyors from Fort Kearny, Nebraska, spent the winter of 1857–58 in the Popo Agie (pronounced "po-po-sha") Valley, two miles east of present Lander, where they built the first house at what they called Camp McGraw.

This valley and the area west of South Pass long served as home to the Shoshone under Chief Washakie. They objected to Lander's road, but he met with them and bargained for the right-of-way with horses, guns, ammunition, and trinkets. The Shoshone called the Lander Valley "Push Root" because the grasses grew so fast in the spring that it appeared as if their roots were being propelled from underneath. The town of Lander received its name in 1875.

A view of Lander's Main Street, 1883. —Wyoming State Museum

White men first discovered oil in Wyoming in 1824 at a site not far from present-day Lander. Captain Bonneville noticed oil while he was in this area trading furs in 1832, but development didn't take place until the mid-1880s. The local facilities continued producing for more than a century, and the original No. 2 well at Dallas Dome Oil Field was still pumping in the early 1990s.

Wind River Indian Reservation

Unlike the Sioux, Cheyenne, and Arapaho, the Shoshone under Chief Washakie didn't enter into any treaties with the U.S. government to let overland travelers cross their ancestral lands in the early years of the western migration. Their only concession was the unofficial bargain they struck with Lander in the late 1850s. Chief Washakie and his people adopted a policy of assistance to the emigrants.

No major conflict between the Shoshone and the travelers headed west arose until 1862. That year some young Shoshone and Bannock men took the offensive, striking at telegraph stations from the Sweetwater River to Bear River (see page 187). Although the attacks resulted in only one death, they gave the government a reason to demand a meeting—and eventually a formal treaty—with Washakie. At Fort Bridger in July 1863, the government negotiated its first agreement with Washakie allowing whites to cross the ancestral Shoshone lands and to build a railroad over the land. It was one of five trea-

196

ties between the United States and the Shoshone and Bannock tribes that year.

Just five years later, on July 3, 1868, the Treaty of Fort Bridger established the Shoshone and Bannock Indian Reservation, more commonly known as the Wind River Reservation. Originally the preserve included land from the Wind River Valley and extended south to Fort Bridger, but the size was later reduced because of the gold strike at South Pass and the discovery of coal reserves near Rock Springs.

The 1868 treaty led the military to establish Fort (or Camp) Augur on June 28, 1869, on the Middle Fork of the Popo Agie River, to protect the Shoshone and Bannock tribes against their wandering Indian enemies. The protection extended to miners in the Sweetwater region. The post, named for Brig. Gen. Christopher C. Augur, served as a subunit of Fort Bridger and never became an official military fort. It was located within the area of present-day Lander.

In 1870 Fort Augur became Fort Brown, named for Capt. Frederick H. Brown, one of the men killed in the Fetterman fight near Fort Phil Kearny in 1866. A year later Fort Brown moved to the junction of the north and south forks of the Little Wind River. In late June 1871 soldiers began dismantling the original structures and took the usable lumber to the new site, where they built log and adobe buildings. They later added frame and stone buildings at the new camp.

By 1873 the Shoshone had settled on their by-then much smaller reservation. They had annual hunting expeditions and received treaty annuities at Fort Brown (later renamed Fort Washakie). In October 1873 about 1,000 tribal members gathered to get their blankets, coats, pants, socks, red flannel shirts, shoes, bed ticking, and household goods. After receiving these items the Indians immediately started trading and bartering; by the time the sky had darkened, most of the goods were in the hands of agency employees and neighboring ranchmen. Reports are that the red flannel shirts sold for 50 cents and that the hats brought a dime each.

During that period, the Shoshones relied on trade to acquire the goods they needed. Records show that in 1881 the Shoshones and the Arapahoes, who by then shared the Wind River Reservation, sold 2,000 buffalo robes to traders at Fort Washakie. The Bannocks, meanwhile, had moved to their own reservation in Idaho.

During the final wars between Indians and whites, some Shoshone men scouted for the U.S. Army and participated in battles against the Sioux, Cheyenne, and Arapaho. Besides serving in the Bates Battle of July 14, 1874, the Shoshone scouts assisted Gen. George Crook on his second Powder River expedition in June 1876. There they had a head-on collision with Crazy Horse and the Sioux at the Battle of the Rosebud. That fall Shoshone scouts participated in the engagement between troops led by Col. Ranald Mackenzie and Cheyenne braves under Dull Knife.

Chief Washakie's Shoshone encampment on Wind River, 1870. —William H. Jackson/Wyoming State Museum

Shoshone tribal leaders. Front row, from left: Dick Washakie, a sub-chief of the tribe; Chief Washakie; and Tigee. Back row, from left: Per-na-go-shia, Pan-Zook, So-pa-gant, and Mat-ta-vish. —Wyoming State Museum

Under the leadership of Col. Wesley Merritt, 5th U.S. Cavalry, about seventy-five Shoshones led by Dick Washakie, the son of Chief Washakie, prepared in August 1877 to block the flight of the Nez Perce under Chief Joseph. Government officials believed the Nez Perce were just north of the Wind River Reservation. However, Chief Joseph cut through Yellowstone National Park, so the Shoshones and Colonel Merritt had no role in that saga.

Indian Enemies Become Neighbors

The Shoshone and Arapaho are traditional tribal enemies, yet they share a reservation. Of all the tribes whose ancestral lands lay at least partially within Wyoming's current boundaries, only the Shoshone and Arapaho remain in the state.

By late 1877 most Plains tribes lived on reservations established for them by the government. The Southern Arapahoes and Cheyennes went to Oklahoma (although the Northern Cheyenne fled that area and eventually received land in southeastern Montana), and the Sioux had reservations in South Dakota. However, the Northern Arapaho, still landless, found themselves at Fort Laramie as fall turned to winter in 1877. They wanted a reservation on the North Platte River drainage, but settlers had claimed much of that territory.

With no place to put them, the government convinced Washakie to let the Northern Arapaho share the Wind River Reservation for the winter. Setting aside generations of hostility between the tribes, Washakie agreed. The next year he repeatedly demanded that they be moved from his tribe's lands. The government refused and decided to make the temporary solution permanent, leaving the Arapaho on the Wind River.

The tribes hated each other but now became neighbors by force. Nevertheless, the situation has caused few major conflicts. Each tribe has its own leadership, although there are some common activities, including a joint tribal council. Generally, the Shoshones settled in the western portion of the reservation and the Arapahoes lived in the eastern area.

The Wind River Reservation became further eroded at the turn of the century when the tribes ceded much of the area, including land near the present-day communities of Shoshoni and Thermopolis. The current reservation is seventy miles from east to west and fifty-five miles from north to south, covering about 2.2 million acres. Census figures in 1992 showed 2,501 Shoshones and 4,564 Arapahoes, as well as a number of small towns, including St. Stephens, Arapahoe, Ethete, and Crowheart.

Chief Washakie

Chief Washakie had the respect of his own people, white governmental leaders, and even Sioux enemies Red Cloud and Crazy Horse. Born sometime around 1800, Chief Washakie lived the better part of a century, dying on February 20, 1900.

Legend says he was the orphan son of a Shoshone mother and a Flathead father. His name is probably an adaptation of *wau-sik-he* (rawhide rattle). Washakie refused to fight white men on any provocation and kept his tribe at peace during a bloody era. Even so, Washakie was a warrior. Legend says that in the late 1860s, as some tribal members argued about his ability to continue as chief, Washakie left camp and rode alone toward the east. He later returned with seven Sioux scalps and challenged anyone questioning his leadership to duplicate that act.

Fort Washakie

The Wind River Mountains form the western boundary of the Wind River Valley; US 287 follows their eastern flank. The original boundaries of the Wind River Reservation extended beyond those mountains to the Uinta Mountains along the Wyoming and Utah borders and extended east to the North Platte River.

The Treaty of 1868 called for the Shoshone to share their reservation with the Bannock, but the Bannock eventually got their own reservation in Idaho. That tribe had often ranged into western Wyoming, and some members became involved in a dispute over wild game in Jackson Hole in 1895 (see page 57). The tribe had an unusual ability to revive itself, if you believe any of the early stories by trappers. Jim Beckwourth reported them annihilated by enraged trappers in 1826; Joseph L. Meek made a similar report in 1836; and Gen. P. E. Connor reportedly killed 250 of them at Bear River in Idaho. Thereafter, government officials recommended the tribe be quartered where Washakie might "keep a thumb on them," according to the WPA history of Wyoming.

Although the Shoshone agreed to live on a reservation, their enemies—the Sioux, Cheyenne, and Arapaho—roamed freely. In the spring of 1869, Red Cloud's last raiding party killed thirty Shoshone warriors and stole a large band of horses. Washakie refused to settle on his reservation without military protection. He roamed between Fort Bridger and the Salt Lake Valley—as a guest of Brigham Young—until late 1872. That fall government officials called Washakie to Fort Stambaugh, where he learned the Bannock would be transferred to Idaho because the whites wanted the Popo Agie Valley.

Washakie knew his people would not be able to keep all of the Wind River Valley. With great foresight, he decided to bargain for as much as he could get and relinquish gracefully that which would be taken from him anyway. In exchange for 601,120 acres of fertile valley land, he extracted $25,000 in reservation improvements, goods, and the promise of protection. This time the government kept its word, stationing a sizable force at Fort Brown and fulfilling its other obligations. The fort included log buildings, a hospital, a telegraph office, and storehouses. A strong Indian police force organized, and federal soldiers manned the post to protect the Shoshone from their traditional enemies. In 1878 Fort Brown was renamed Fort Washakie in honor of the Shoshone chief.

Religious Activity on the Reservation

In 1883 the Rev. John Roberts, an Episcopal missionary, arrived on the reservation. He spent the remainder of his life working among the Shoshone and Arapaho. The Catholic Church started a mission, St. Stephen's, at the confluence of the Little Wind River and the Wind River in 1883.

The Episcopal Church, encouraged by the Reverend Roberts, established a mission in about 1887 to serve the Arapahoes east of Fort Washakie. The mission received the name St. Michael's, but the church is known as the Church of Our Father's House, and the post office and community are called Ethete. Supposedly, when church officials asked permission to start the mission, the tribe considered the request and the chief replied, "Ethete," which can be translated to mean "good" or "OK."

The earliest mission included a small log church at a site about three miles from the present location of St. Michael's. Between 1910 and 1917 the tribe gave half a section of land, and additional buildings went up in an oval-shaped plan. In addition to St. Michael's Mission and Church of Our Father's House, Mission Circle includes St. Martha's Cottage, which is used as an Arapaho cultural and historical center.

The mission may have received its name from Michael White Hawk, who according to some sources translated the Bible into Arapaho. Others claim the Rev. John Roberts prepared the translation. Roberts spent much of his life among the Wind River Indians.

Sacajawea

The most famous Shoshone woman is Sacajawea. Next to Washakie, she is the most well-known of all Shoshone people. Authorities disagree about her name. She came to be known as the Bird Woman, but "Boat Pusher" might be a better translation, and she went by Porivo when she became the wife of a Comanche in Oklahoma.

Sacajawea accompanied Lewis and Clark on their explorations of the Louisiana Territory in 1804–5, paving the way for the white adventurers because of her heritage. Hidatsa raiders took Sacajawea from her Shoshone family when she was still a child. Jean Baptiste Charbonneau, a French-Canadian trapper, bought her at the Mandan villages on the Missouri River. At the time of the Lewis and Clark expedition she was between sixteen and eighteen years old, having given birth to her first son six weeks before the journey started.

Sacajawea carried her infant son, Baptiste—called "Pomp" in the Lewis and Clark journals—on her back throughout the 3,000-mile journey. The party met her kinsmen, including her brother, Chief Cameahwait, in the Beaverhead Valley of present-day Montana. The chance encounter was instrumental in the expedition's success. Sacajawea's presence gave the white men instant credibility with a potentially hostile tribe and helped them obtain supplies and information about the major rivers of the West. For her part, Sacajawea was reunited with her family; she even adopted Bazil, the orphan son of her sister.

Sacajawea returned to Missouri with Lewis and Clark and eventually left Charbonneau. She lived in Oklahoma before rejoining the Shoshone in the 1840s. When and where she died is shrouded in the cloak of years and uncertainty. Some say she died in April 1884. One story says the Rev. Roberts conducted the burial of Bazil Umbea—Bazil's mother—on the reservation; Sacajawea raised him and no doubt the tribe considered her Bazil's mother, but other sources say she is not interred in Wyoming and that she died much earlier. A grave marker for Sacajawea stands in the Fort Washakie cemetery, beside the grave of her nephew and a monument to her son, Baptiste, who is buried at an unknown spot in the Wind River Mountains.

US 20/26 and Wyoming 789
Casper—Hudson
134 miles

Depending on your perspective, much of Wyoming is either a barren waste or a place of great open spaces and wide vistas. People who have lived here for years adjust to and relish the emptiness. They know it might take a trip of fifty or more miles to reach a doctor, movie theater, or grocery store.

The drive between Casper and Shoshoni on US 20/26 will give you an appreciation for the size and space of Wyoming. The route roughly parallels the trail Jim Bridger pioneered in 1864 from Fort Caspar to Montana's goldfields.

From Casper the highway passes through the tiny towns of Natrona, Powder River, Waltman, Hiland, and Moneta. It provides access to other little places, including Arminto, Lost Cabin, and Lysite. The Bridger Trail headed west from Fort Caspar along Poison Spider Creek, turned northwest to cross the present-day highway at Waltman, then followed Alkali Creek and the southern ridge of the Big Horn Mountains to Lost Cabin, where it turned north and followed Bridger Creek into the Big Horn Basin.

John Broderick Okie came to this area a penniless cowboy and sheepherder in about 1900. He worked hard, obtained land and livestock, then opened a series of general stores. Eventually Okie became a millionaire. His house on Bad Water Creek was known as Big Teepee. Okie had Japanese gardeners, peacocks, a greenhouse, and carbide lamps. Before long, the town of Lost Cabin formed around his home.

Traffic on the Bridger Trail spurred the growth of the town as travelers crossed to the Big Horn Basin. When a route opened through the Wind River Canyon to connect Shoshoni and Thermopolis, the Bridger Trail received only occasional use, and Lost Cabin withered.

The Bates Battle

A rare Indian battle involving Shoshone warriors took place about thirty-three miles north of Moneta at the head of Nowood Creek in 1874. In June, Sioux, Cheyenne, and Arapaho warriors decided to attack the Wind River Shoshones. As the invaders crossed the Big Horn Mountains, they had a disagreement about the purpose of their trip. Some claimed it was a raid for murder and the spoils of war; others said it was to steal horses. Because of the disagreement, the Arapahoes refused to participate.

When word of the situation reached Fort Brown, Capt. Alfred Bates led a 2nd U.S. Cavalry troop of about 60 men, accompanied by about 30 Shoshone scouts and another 160 Shoshones under Chief Washakie, eastward from Fort Washakie. Their target: the Arapaho camp, because the Arapahoes were traditional enemies of the Shoshones. On July 4, 1874, Captain Bates found the Arapahoes settled near a rock ledge. Behind the camp, military and Shoshone guards watched the horses on their pickets. Bates's attack went awry when the Shoshone did not cross over a hill to prevent an Arapaho retreat, as Bates wanted them to do. The Arapahoes reached the ledge, where they had the advantage. After fierce fighting, and with casualties on both sides, Bates ordered his men to withdraw. The Arapahoes could not pursue the retreating whites and Shoshones because the Shoshones had captured their horses.

Meanwhile, the Cheyenne and Sioux, who earlier had split with the Arapahoes, moved through the Big Horn Basin, crossed the Owl Creek Mountains, and topped a hill west of Fort Brown. They met at a hilltop just a mile from the camp, but they apparently had a bad feeling about the situation, because they left without any confrontation. The Cheyennes and Sioux later met the retreating Arapahoes and jeered their former allies for not sticking with the original plan to attack the Shoshones.

Shoshoni Grows from the Reservation

The Chicago & Northwestern Railroad platted Shoshoni in 1904. The community, which now sits at the intersection of US 20/26 and Wyoming 789, really boomed a year later when a portion of the Wind River Indian Reservation—then home to both the Shoshone and Arapaho tribes—opened to homesteaders in 1905. More than 10,500 people registered for the right to draw for 1,600 homesteads on reservation lands. Shoshoni went wild with the onslaught of would-be settlers, and militia from Douglas had to restore order in 1906, at a time when the town had twenty-three saloons and thousands of people.

Riverton and Hudson

Four rivers—the Wind, Little Wind, Popo Agie, and Little Popo Agie—converge at Riverton, site of the 1830 and 1838 mountain rendezvous. The town sits within the borders of the Wind River Indian Reservation. In a treaty that took effect March 3, 1905, the Shoshone and Arapaho relinquished their rights to most of the land north of the Wind River and left more than 1.3 million acres of land available for white settlement. Riverton had a town plat before any buildings went up, which is unusual in Wyoming's history because so many communities started as boomtowns thrown together helter-skelter by the earliest arrivals. But Riverton started with only tents and went by the name Tent City; then it became Wadsworth, for H. E. Wadsworth, an Indian agent at Fort Washakie. Because of the four rivers that converge here, a committee of local residents preferred the name Riverton.

The biggest conflict in the community's early history centered not on the name but on land ownership. The railroad completed its line in 1906, and settlers arrived by August, living at first in tents and wagons. The early residents followed surveyors and filed land claims as soon as the survey lines were laid out. The Wind River Reservation agent told the settlers they couldn't occupy the land until the survey was completed, but the homesteaders refused to move. The agent called in cavalry from Fort Washakie to enforce his decree. A day later a group of about twenty Lander men "jumped" the abandoned claims. Riled, the original homestead claimants marched en masse to take back their plots. They pulled up and burned the jumpers' stakes and put

A wagon crosses the bridge over the Big Wind River. —Arwed N. Holmberg/Wyoming State Museum

204

their own back in place. The Lander men promptly argued that the first survey hadn't been properly conducted. The Riverton homesteaders disagreed, and with rifles at the ready they held the ground.

The Wind River Valley has one of the mildest climates in Wyoming, with hot summer days and less winter wind than most other areas of the state. The fertile valley has been a key agricultural production area dating back to a 1904 Bureau of Reclamation initiative. The Riverton Reclamation Project cost $9 million. It included Diversion Dam, which holds back enough water to irrigate 100,000 acres. The 650-foot-high concrete barrier, completed in 1923, diverts water from the Wind River into the Wyoming Canal.

Hudson, located midway between Riverton and Lander, started on homestead land claimed by George H. Rogers in 1890. After he died, his widow, Emma Hudson Rogers, proved up on the land. In 1905 Emma and her brother, Daniel Hudson, relinquished their homestead rights. Meanwhile, their father, John G. Hudson, a landowner, rancher, and legislator, helped bring in the railroad in 1907–8, and on March 8, 1909, the town incorporated. The community first went by the name Rogersville but was changed to Hudson at the request of the postal service. It served as a trading center for native Americans, coal miners, and oil-field workers.

US 26
Riverton—Dubois
78 miles

The Story of Bull Lake

Just west of the junction of US 287 and US 26 lies Bull Lake, which gets its name from an Indian tale. The native Americans believed that hunters once chased a white buffalo bull into the lake because they wanted its unusual robe. The bull drowned. During the winter the lake ice sometimes wailed, and the Indians said the moaning sound was the white buffalo's spirit, roaring in anger.

Bull Lake and Bull Lake Creek supply part of the water used in the Riverton Reclamation Project. Wind River settlers dug irrigation ditches as early as 1868. When the area was set aside for the Shoshone, the improvements transferred with the land. After 1933 the Public Works Administration built Washakie and Ray Lake reservoirs and several canals to provide irrigation water to the valley. In 1938 the agency built a dam at the Bull Lake outlet to enlarge the lake's storage capacity and expand the region's agricultural area.

Water management in the Wind River Valley spawned a legal fight during the late 1980s, as the Shoshone and Arapaho tribes squared off in court against the State of Wyoming over jurisdiction issues. The Indians wanted a portion of their water right—set aside in the 1868 Fort Bridger treaty—to remain in the river as free-flowing water.

The Legend of Crowheart Butte

One famous story involving Chief Washakie centers on a butte located east of Crowheart and north of US 26/287. The legend goes that Chief Washakie fought Crow chief Big Robber atop this butte in 1866. The winner was supposed to eat the heart of the loser. Washakie won and allegedly ate the Crow's heart. Near this butte in 1857 the Shoshones had a battle with bands of Arapaho, Gros Ventre, and Cheyenne who despised the Shoshone for refusing to make war on the white invaders.

Dubois

In the period after 1868, tough men, and a few equally tough women, lived and worked in Wyoming's mountains, cutting timber in deep winter snow. The logs they felled became ties for the railroads of the West.

Tie hacks, as these workers are known, leveled trees and cut the limbs from them. Then, using a broad ax with a deep, wide blade, they chopped large chips from the edge of the tree, turning it into a roughly square piece. They worked for many companies. Coe and Carter had camps in the Medicine Bow and Sierra Madre mountains of southern Wyoming and in the Green River country. The McShane Timber Company operated in the Big Horns. In the Wind River Mountains and the DuNoir Range near Dubois, the Wyoming Tie and Timber Company cut more than 10 million ties from the early 1900s to 1946.

Most of the hacks were of Scandinavian descent, but some Frenchmen worked the camps. There is a story about a black man named Bill who worked in the Dubois country in the 1920s. When a trainload of men from Sweden arrived to work for Wyoming Tie and Timber, Bill spoke to them in their native language. You *can't* be Swedish, they said; he replied that they'd turn black if they remained in the country long enough. At least one of the new men came close to believing Bill's story; a few days later he asked a camp boss how soon he would begin to turn black.

Most of the tie cutting took place during the deep snows of winter, and workers skied from their cabin homes to the job site. In December 1937 the *Riverton Review* reported:

> Spring Creek, South Fork, Trapper Creek, and all the other small communities above Headquarters have been snowed in since the last storm. From now until spring the residents will have no way of leaving their homes other than by skis or using horse-drawn sleds. There is considerable rueful dismay because the snow came so unusually early this year.

Tie decks near Dubois. —Wyoming State Museum

The stumps the tie hacks left behind are still seen in Wyoming's mountains. Sometimes they stand six or more feet tall, testament to the depth of the snow at the time the hack cut the tree. Workers moved most of the ties chopped during the long winters to landings near streams. When the snow melted in the spring, they released the timbers into the rushing torrents and floated them down creeks and rivers to collection points in the various valleys.

That spring ritual of releasing the timbers down the waterways gave rise to the great tie drives. Men rode the ties, herding them down the rivers. When they got to town—after having been trapped in mountain snows for months—they collected their paychecks and headed for the nearest bar. It's said the hacks quickly learned to "cultivate the three B's—booze, bawds, and brawls."

Although the tie industry, and particularly the tie drives, passed by the wayside in the 1940s—primarily because by then trucks could haul the timber—lumbering continued in the mountains near Dubois. The industry remained a mainstay of the economy for another forty years. In the 1980s the Louisiana-Pacific Lumber Company pulled out of the region because of a low timber supply. Some residents predicted the demise of the community, but by 1994 growth in Jackson Hole spilled over Togwotee (pronounced "toe-ga-dee") Pass into the Dubois region, and the community struggled with growth.

Two Ocean Pass. —Stephen Leek, Teton County Historical Center

A November snow covers Togwotee Trail, probably in the early 1900s. —Wyoming State Museum

Splitting the Water

The region northwest of Dubois is unique in that it holds the headwaters of three major river systems: the Colorado, Missouri, and Columbia. Indians and trappers liked this area and used Union and Togwotee passes to cross into Jackson Hole. Jim Bridger once told a tale of water running two different directions, but few people believed him. Of course, his story related to Two Ocean Pass, where the water splits, some running toward the Atlantic Ocean, the rest heading for the Pacific.

The Whiskey Mountain Bighorns

Wyoming has some of the greatest wildlife herds in the continental United States. One of them, a group of Rocky Mountain bighorn sheep, makes its home on Whiskey Mountain just west of Dubois. Hundreds of animals winter near the community in sheltered valleys to the south and west. In 1993 the community built an interpretive center that explains wild sheep in general and the Whiskey Mountain herd in particular. Often the Wyoming Game and Fish Department catches sheep from the Whiskey Mountain herd and transplants them to other locations in the state.

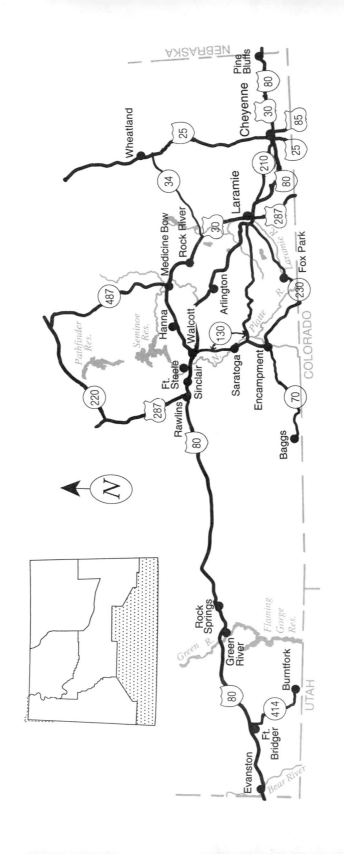

Part 3

Union Pacific Country

Wyoming continued its legacy as a transportation corridor in 1867 when the Union Pacific Railroad (UP) started laying track across it. Work gangs prepared the grade, laid ties, and placed rails, inching across the land. First they covered the prairie east of what is now Cheyenne; then they built through the rugged Laramie Mountain Range, which they knew as a part of the Black Hills. The Union Pacific Railroad crews raced to lay more track than their Central Pacific counterparts, which were headed east from San Francisco.

All along the route, towns appeared overnight at whatever point the end-of-tracks crew found itself. Cheyenne City, Laramie, Carbon, Benton, Tipton, Point of Rocks, Rock Springs, Evanston, and many others got their start as "hell-on-wheels" towns situated about twenty miles apart. In most cases the tracks moved ever westward, and the towns folded and followed. The more prosperous survived and served as railroad supply centers. Now they are county seats: Cheyenne, Laramie, Rawlins, Rock Springs, and Evanston.

Earlier in the 1860s, freight and mail wagons and stagecoaches raced across the land on the Overland Trail, which traversed southern Wyoming on a line roughly parallel to the Union Pacific tracks. The Cherokee forged a trail of their own from Oklahoma through Colorado and southern Wyoming en route to California after the gold strike at Sutter's Mill in 1848.

The government carved Wyoming Territory from Dakota Territory in 1868, simultaneous with the crossing of the Union Pacific. The construction of the railroad gave Wyoming the boost and recognition that made settlement possible. The rail line provided transportation for settlers and opened trade with other areas by providing a way to ship goods such as cattle, sheep, and coal.

US 30 was built in 1913 along the same route as the Union Pacific, following in the footsteps of Indians, mountain men, emigrants, homesteaders, and track layers. Known across the country as the Lincoln Highway, US 30 was the first transcontinental automobile road. On December 13, 1913, a string of bonfires nearly 450 miles long lit the Lincoln Highway across southern Wyoming, heralding the age of coast-to-coast car travel.

When I-80, linking New York and California, was built across Wyoming, it, too, followed the Overland Trail–Union Pacific–Lincoln Highway corridor.

Much of Union Pacific country appears flat and desolate, particularly for those who view it from the major access highway, I-80. But there is much more to this area. It includes prairie near Cheyenne, mountain ranges between Laramie and Rawlins where rivers form, and the Red Desert that lies between Rawlins and Rock Springs. The Uinta Mountains anchor the southwest corner, and the world's largest free-ranging herd of pronghorn antelope roam throughout the western half of Union Pacific country. Our trip through this section begins in the east and heads west.

I-80/US 30
Pine Bluffs—Laramie
90 miles

As you enter Wyoming from the east on US 30/I-80, the first community you'll see is Pine Bluffs. Originally called Rock Ranch, it was established by the Union Pacific in 1867 as tracks pushed across the region. Pine Bluffs also marks the southernmost Wyoming settlement on the Texas Trail. The community became the largest shipping point on the Union Pacific in 1884, as ranches sent hundreds of thousands of head of cattle to eastern markets.

The small towns of Egbert, Burns, and Hillsdale lie just north of I-80 on a series of secondary roads. Like Pine Bluffs, these communities started when the UP laid its tracks. The railroad established Egbert in 1867, and Hillsdale is named for Lathrop Hills, who died in an Indian attack on June 11, 1867, while leading a railroad survey party. Burns was founded in 1907 as Luther by emigrants from Iowa who wanted to establish a Lutheran colony. Its present name honors a railroad engineer. Several other small communities in southeast Wyoming grew as a result of real estate deals and ranching opportunities.

The Checkerboard Begins

Construction of the Union Pacific Railroad was aided by many government incentives. One agreement gave the railroad company alternating sections of land along the route in an area twenty miles north and twenty miles south of the tracks, creating a checkerboard pattern of land ownership. Union Pacific sold much of its land in eastern Wyoming, particularly between Pine Bluffs and Laramie, but it retained the ground farther west. Those land sales

Union Pacific construction train, 1868. —American Heritage Centery/University of Wyoming

led to widespread agricultural development in southeast Wyoming, and the area's small towns, including Albin, Carpenter, and Burns, provide services for ranching and farming families.

The railroad had nearly 12 million acres of land to sell all along the route of the tracks. The land in eastern Nebraska, being more productive and well-watered, sold fairly easily. The land farther west was more difficult and, in many cases, impossible to sell. Much of the land-grant property in Nebraska sold for $4 to $8 per acre, but in central and western Wyoming the price often barely reached $1 per acre.

The Swan Land and Cattle Company purchased 425,000 acres near Fort Steele for 50 cents an acre, and another 575,000 acres near Rock Creek sold for $1 an acre. Railroad officials rapidly accepted the offers because they brought "a fair price for a very large quantity of poor lands," Union Pacific land agent Leavitt Burnham said in a letter to Fred Ames on July 3, 1884.

Much of the land in Wyoming in the area from Fort Steele to Evanston never did sell. Ironically, underlying the land valued at $1 an acre or less were millions of dollars' worth of valuable minerals, which are still being mined by Union Pacific companies today.

Cheyenne

Wyoming's state capital started as a UP hell-on-wheels town. Generals Grenville Dodge and Christopher C. Augur arrived in early July 1867, followed quickly by the first permanent residents—six men and three women—

who set up camp on July 9, 1867. Following a quick townsite survey of an area four miles square, the first lots sold three days later, and Cheyenne's first home went up on July 25, 1867.

One unidentified early resident of the community remarked upon the rapidity of the town's growth: "Well, one fine day, early in July, 1867, four or five hundred of us pitched our tents here, where there wasn't a sign of civilization, and about half of us woke up at daylight the next morning to find that the other half was living in board shanties!" Because of its phenomenal rate of growth, Cheyenne soon became known as the "Magic City" of the Plains.

General Dodge might have selected the townsite location on Crow Creek, although some uncertainty remains on this point. Whoever made the decision chose a strategic location. Cheyenne is midway between Omaha, Nebraska, and Ogden, Utah, along the Union Pacific line and near the base of the mountain range that marks the highest point on the entire transcontinental route. That meant workmen could repair engines and rolling stock at Cheyenne before trains ascended the mountains.

Writing in *A Work of Giants*, historian Wesley Griswold says the site had importance for the U.S. government as well. About six miles west of town, the bond subsidy granted to the UP by the Pacific Railroad Act of May 1862

Union Pacific Roundhouse, Cheyenne. —State Historic Preservation Office

Union Pacific Powerhouse, Cheyenne. —State Historic Preservation Office

jumped from $16,000 a mile to $48,000 a mile because of the increased gradient of the roadbed. That higher pay rate stayed in place for 150 miles, then slacked off to $32,000 a mile until Promontory Point in Utah, where the Union Pacific and the Central Pacific railroads met.

Cheyenne's rapid expansion was apparent from the very start. General Dodge wrote on July 15, 1867:

> People are already flocking here and, like Julesburg, at first it will be a second hell. I have got Gen. Augur to throw his protecting arm over it to keep them from owning town and all. They are coming from all quarters and all expect to make a fortune.
>
> Government itself will alone build up here a large town, as it is to be the depot for all posts north and south and also the distributing point for all points in Colorado. During this winter our trains will stop here and the travel west will here leave; can take stage and other transportation. We shall also build a large workshop, machine shops, round houses, etc.

Quick growth left the city with a carnival atmosphere and little in the way of police control. As a result, vigilante groups took care of lawbreakers for a time until serious businessmen could gain control. Then, on August 16, 1867, authorities established Fort D. A. Russell to protect the coming railroad.

The presence of Camp Carlin, established by the military near Fort D. A. Russell just west of the city as a supply depot, helped foster a more stable

Parade ground, Fort D. A. Russell, Cheyenne, Wyoming, 1935. —Wyoming State Museum

atmosphere. The two military posts soon became the most important in the Rocky Mountain region, in effect replacing Fort Laramie in strategic significance.

Barely four months after the first shanties appeared in Cheyenne, Union Pacific rails reached the community, which already had 4,000 people, a town government, two daily newspapers, and a brass band to welcome the train.

A Military Presence Begins

The first troops based at the new fort were the 30th Infantry and 2nd Cavalry, under the command of Gen. John D. Stevenson. Their chief duty: to protect work gangs and working equipment for Union Pacific construction. The Plains Indians still raised a ruckus at various places in Wyoming during that period, and the troops sometimes became involved in those skirmishes. In time, additional military posts went in farther west along the UP line.

Camp Carlin's official title was Cheyenne Depot, and it became the second largest quartermaster station in the nation. Thousands of mule teams and hundreds of drivers operated from the camp, which featured carpenter, harness, blacksmith, and wheelwright shops as well as corrals, stables, and haystacks. The drab brown wooden buildings also included wagon sheds, stores, cook shacks, and bunkhouses. The upkeep of some 3,000 mules and horses, used to pull the base's 100 wagons or carry supplies in pack trains, kept Camp Carlin's garrison busy. The army closed the post in 1890.

After 1882 the army abandoned many forts used during the Indian wars, but it retained Fort D. A. Russell because of its strategic location and connection to the Union Pacific. In 1885 the War Department made the fort a permanent post and rebuilt it to serve eight infantry companies. In 1906 it enlarged to brigade size. It served as a mobilization center for the Wyoming National Guard during the Spanish-American War and for both cavalry and field artillery during World War I.

On January 1, 1930, Fort D. A. Russell was renamed Fort Francis E. Warren after one of Wyoming's most prominent citizens. Warren ranched in eastern Wyoming, served as territorial governor from 1889 to 1890, became the first governor elected after statehood, represented Wyoming for thirty-seven years in the U.S. Senate, and died in 1929 while in office. During World War II, Fort Warren became a quartermaster training center, and from 1943 until 1946 it housed a prisoner-of-war camp.

In 1947 the Air Force took over Fort Warren and renamed the post Francis E. Warren Air Force Base. The Air Force used it as a training center until 1958, when officials transferred the facility to the Strategic Air Command (SAC). On October 2, 1959, the first Atlas Missile installation took place, and in August of the following year the 564th Strategic Missile Squadron achieved operational status. On July 1, 1963, the SAC 90th Strategic Wing took control with the new Minuteman Missile. Soon 200 missile sites operated within a 150-mile radius in southeastern Wyoming, northeastern Colorado, and western Nebraska.

A Tale of Hospitality

Cheyenne's second mayor, a man named Sloan, operated a dairy. When Duke Alexis of Russia arrived in town with his retinue on his way north on a hunting trip in 1872, the mayor did what any public official would have done: He went to meet the distinguished guest. According to an account by early Cheyenne resident Warren Richardson, Mayor Sloan took the milk cans out of the rear of his wagon, put a board across from side to side as a seat, and went to the train to receive his visitor. The duke, apparently undaunted by the form of his conveyance, got into the wagon and, preceded by a band of four or five horns and a drum, rode through town.

The Cheyenne Club

Cheyenne may have started as a railroad and military town, but it quickly became a center for the state's most powerful cattlemen. After trailing their herds on the Goodnight-Loving Trail, they met down at the Cactus Club for libations and socialization. Built in 1880, the Cactus Club was later renamed the Cheyenne Club because members felt the original moniker didn't exemplify the social importance they wanted to convey.

The Johnson County Invaders planned their foray to Johnson County here, at the Cheyenne Club, an exclusive meeting place for the wealthy cattlemen in Wyoming during the late 1880s. —Wyoming State Museum

The Cheyenne Club's exclusive membership included rich men from the East and Great Britain who were interested in the cattle business and who came periodically to visit their ranches and enjoy western society and scenery. The club initially limited membership to fifty but later expanded. It primarily included cattlemen, but high-ranking military officers from nearby Fort D. A. Russell and Camp Carlin visited without the necessity of formal membership, paying a modest charge per visit.

The club styled itself after an exclusive English men's club and sported the first newly fashionable mansard roof in the city. The main floor included a large, elegant dining room, billiard room, card room, reading lounge, and plush-carpeted sitting room with red velvet floor-to-ceiling drapes. A high, wide veranda on three sides gave a view of Cheyenne. Full-length diamond-shaped mirrors reflected overstuffed leather furniture and the men in their black-tie and formal military dress. Occasionally members wore white-tie outfits— dubbed "herefords" by club members because of the open white front and tails behind. Women invited to social gatherings wore evening gowns.

The basement housed an elaborate kitchen, fully stocked wine cellar, and liquor larder. A French-Canadian chef prepared dishes unparalleled in Wyoming and, because of the clientele, known throughout the world. Upstairs apartments had hand-carved walnut bedsteads, Italian marble–topped dressers, commodes with china water jugs and honey pots, and enormous, ceiling-high walnut wardrobes. The rooms had large fireplaces inscribed with quotations from the works of Shakespeare and topped with white marble mantles.

Members arrived at this showplace for the socially prominent in coaches drawn by three span of perfectly matched thoroughbred horses and tossed large tips to the young men tending the animals. The Cheyenne Club sat on Cattlemen's Row, the most exclusive residential street in the city. Expensive, multistory mansions lined 17th Street, each styled by a different architect. The homes included elaborate livery barns and stables in the back that housed multiple phaetons, buggies, and open and closed carriages of all sorts with the finest blooded horses to pull them.

The owners of these fine houses organized and ran the Wyoming Stock Growers Association, staged a military-style invasion on Powder River, and directed stock detective activities throughout the state—activities that often led to death, even for teenage boys like Willie Nickell (see page 155). They grabbed power and held on with all their might well into the twentieth century.

Cheyenne Frontier Days

Cheyenne's biggest annual celebration, Frontier Days, started in 1897 upon the suggestion of Union Pacific Railroad passenger agent F. W. Angier and *Cheyenne Daily Sun-Leader* editor E. A. Slack. They got the idea from Greeley, Colorado's "Potato Day."

For the first Frontier Day, held on September 23, 1897, special excursion trains brought visitors to the Wyoming capital city. In addition to holding bucking contests, the Frontier Days Committee planned a mock attack on the Deadwood Stagecoach and a mock hanging of *Laramie Boomerang* newspaper editor and humorist Bill Nye. Ida Gilliand Fox of Cheyenne recalled the 1897 Frontier Day in a 1979 newspaper article:

> We met Uncle John and his family and other neighbors and all went to Cheyenne on the 4:30 A.M. train. I remember only a little of that day—how we had to stand along the railing around the race track at the old Frontier Park all afternoon, Mama grabbing Helen and running, me following, whenever a bucking horse or a steer headed our way.

Hundreds of visitors attended one particular show that started with the firing of cannons by Fort D. A. Russell troops and the sound of hundreds of citizens shooting rifles, pistols, and shotguns. "Horses jumped fences, men were knocked down and were thought killed, but we are happy to announce that no death resulted," the press reported. The event was strongly criticized by some newspapers as a "rough-neck show seeking to perpetuate the spirit of western rowdyism through which the west is passing."

The Cheyenne organizers didn't heed the press's suggestion that the event should be a one-time-only affair, and Frontier Day soon expanded into a multiday event that included parades, cowboy contests and races, Indian displays, and fake stagecoach holdups. The bronco riding was always a major attraction. Cowboys who participated spent their lives on the range working cattle; when they got to Frontier Days, the owners of the ranches for which they worked often wagered on them. The bucking-horse contest pitted man against beast and gave ranchers a chance to see who had the best cowboys.

The cowboys rode with saddles, and to win first place they had to stay aboard until the horse came to a standstill. They weren't allowed to "pull leather" or grab any portion of the saddle, but they could fan the horse with their hat, whip it with a rawhide quirt, and, in most years, use their spurs. Definite rules for the rodeo events started developing in 1905, when judges and contestants agreed the winner should be determined on the basis of averages, rather than on the fastest time for one performance or the best ride on one bucking horse.

There were no chutes in those days, so cowboys led horses to the middle of the arena and saddled in the open. That process took lots of time, but the spectators didn't mind; it was part of the show. Generally the horses were blindfolded, or "eared down," while cowboys tightened their rigging. It became an unwritten rule of the arena that a cowboy saddled his own mount. That way, if something went wrong with the rigging during the ride, he had nobody to blame but himself. After saddling up, a cowboy lightly stepped aboard, and the horse handlers stepped back. There was no time to measure the buck rein before the wild bronco started to pitch. The cowboys of that era used a different bucking rein than modern cowboys do; the horses wore a hackamore with double reins, and many cowboys would ride holding onto the reins with both hands, one on either side of the horse.

The cowboys themselves often supplied the horses used in the rodeos. Range animals rounded up on the prairie had strength and stamina from their mustang breeding. Because these horses saw little use on the ranch, they generally were strong and powerful. They often also were vicious and dangerous, apt to kick or strike a rider thrown from the saddle.

From 1901 to 1912, a big black horse named Steamboat thrashed with unequaled fury when a rider climbed aboard. Although many of the top cowboys of his era challenged Steamboat's hurricane deck, very few managed to ride him successfully. His power and skill in unseating crack riders made Steamboat a legend in his own time, and he is remembered as the symbol of Wyoming on the state's license plates.

Frontier Days gave cowboys a chance to show thousands of spectators their skill on the back of a bucking bronc. In 1903 the bleachers were already full by the time the Denver excursion train arrived, and there was no seating left for the Colorado visitors. "A great number of carriages lined the outer edge of the half-mile track, while every man who could beg or borrow a horse was mounted and occupied a coveted position inside the ring," the *Wyoming Tribune* reported.

At another early Frontier Day celebration, a cloudburst turned the racetrack in front of the grandstand into a quagmire. The cowboys said it was too dangerous to ride in the deep mud and argued that the show should be postponed. Such an action was unthinkable to the show promoters, who didn't know how they would appease the disappointed crowd. After a delay, the organizers decided to have Bertha Keppernick, a promising rodeo contestant, ride a wild horse in front of the grandstand. Warren Richardson, chairman of the first Frontier Days Committee, later recalled:

> This she did, one of the worst buckers I have ever seen, and she stayed on him all the time. Part of the time he was up in the air on his hind feet; once he fell backward, and the girl deftly slid to one side only to mount him again as he got up. She rode him in the mud to a finish, and the crowd went wild with enthusiasm. Result, the cowboys thought that if a girl can ride in the mud, we can too, and the show was pulled off.
>
> The real active idea of Woman Suffrage was thus demonstrated in Wyoming at a Frontier Days Celebration. . . . Hurrah for the Wyoming gals! They lead in everything!

Cheyenne Frontier Days expanded through the decades. Today it is a nine-day celebration drawing the top competitors in the Professional Rodeo Cowboys Association, who rope, ride, wrestle, and race for hundreds of thousands of dollars in prize money.

Through the years the cowboys and cowgirls cheered each other for record-setting rides, commiserated over disappointments, and grieved together when one of their own died, as happened in 1989 when a bull blasted Lane Frost during the final rodeo performance. The young world champion died in the dirt at Cheyenne, but his legacy is marked at Frontier Park with a life-size monument by Casper artist Chris Navaroo, dedicated in 1993.

The largest collection of horse-drawn vehicles in Wyoming winds through the streets of Cheyenne the last full week in July as part of Cheyenne Frontier Days celebration, which started in 1897.

Just a Little Politics

With Indian wars and cattle wars and sheep wars dotting the state's history, it might seem surprising that Wyoming got started on the road to statehood by women. Well, not exactly . . . but that caught your attention, didn't it?

The story is this. In the 1860s darned few people lived in Wyoming, which until then had been part of the territories of Idaho, Oregon, Utah, Nebraska, and Dakota. The region had an unknown number of Indians of various tribes: Arapaho, Shoshone, Cheyenne, Sioux, and occasionally Crow and Ute. The white population consisted primarily of military troops, mountain men turned traders or guides, and, by 1867, a few low-class women and camp followers associated with construction of the Union Pacific Railroad. Then a pretty decent gold strike took place near South Pass, and a number of families started moving to the area (see page 191).

At the South Pass gold mines, efforts to organize Wyoming Territory began in earnest, and on July 25, 1868, the federal government carved it from Dakota Territory. Then territorial legislator William H. Bright sponsored a bill giving women the right to vote, hold office, and serve on juries. Many people encouraged Bright, and the legislature approved the measure, which Governor John Campbell signed into law on December 10, 1869. That move brought more women to the state, bolstered the low population (which grew to 9,118 by 1870), and, two decades later, gave Wyoming the right to call itself the Equality State. Also known as the Cowboy State, Wyoming may be the only state to have two well-known nicknames.

By the time Wyoming attained statehood, becoming the forty-fourth star on the American flag on July 10, 1890, its population had reached 62,555. In 1990, when Wyoming celebrated its centennial, the state ranked last in the union in population, with a census count of 453,588.

Despite its low population, Wyoming often did pave the way in guaranteeing rights for women. Besides being the first state to give women the right to vote and hold office, Wyoming was the first to have a woman governor, electing Nellie Tayloe Ross on November 24, 1924, to serve out the remainder of her husband's two-year term after his death in office. In 1870 a Laramie judge impaneled the world's first juries with women jurors, and in the 1920s Jackson became the first community in the state, and perhaps in the nation, to elect an all-women municipal council (see page 71).

Wyoming is largely Republican—at least, it supports Republican candidates more often than not, with twenty-one of the thirty-five governors' terms since statehood served by Republicans. The GOP also consistently dominates both houses of the state legislature. In presidential elections since 1892, Wyoming residents have chosen Republican candidates fourteen times and Democratic candidates eleven times. The southern counties along the UP line tend to be labor oriented and Democratic in persuasion, while those farther north are predominantly Republican.

Heading over Sherman Hill

From Cheyenne to Laramie, I-80 parallels the Union Pacific Railroad and matches or runs near the route of US 30. Westbound travelers hit their first national forest since the Mississippi River—the Medicine Bow. Those headed east may find the climb up Sherman Hill out of Laramie a bit slow, but once the ascent ends, the interstate rolls in a four-lane ribbon across Wyoming's eastern plains.

During winter this forty-five-mile stretch has a split personality. At times it offers a scenic journey through a wonderland of snow, pine trees, and huge granite formations. At others it presents a white wall of blowing and drifting snow, rushing winds, and fog or ice.

It's not true, but some people claim the wind *always* blows in southern Wyoming, particularly along this highway. Natives joke that the snow never lands, it just blows by on its way from Utah to Nebraska. Some claim that people born in Wyoming always stand at a tilt from leaning into the wind; the story goes that one day the wind quit and everyone fell down. Of course, there are hot days when the temperature soars to 90 (that's a hot day in Wyoming, anyway) and people become irritated and wish for just a little breeze to cool things down. . . .

Between Cheyenne and the top of Sherman Hill, US 30, I-80, and the old Union Pacific roadbed all run together. Gen. Grenville M. Dodge and a party

Original railroad grade near Dale Creek Crossing. —State Historic Preservation Office

Construction of Dale Creek Bridge, Union Pacific Railroad.
—J. E. Stimson Collection/Wyoming State Museum

of railroad surveyors discovered the route as they fled to escape an Indian attack. Construction of the UP through this country didn't come easily, so for a 150-mile segment railroad builders received triple payment. The wooden Dale Creek Bridge is one example of the hard work laborers expended in building this stretch of the line. Constructed in 1868–69, Dale Creek Bridge spanned a chasm 650 feet long and 135 feet high, making it the highest railway bridge in the world at the time. A new grade for the line, combined with a long tunnel, eventually made the Dale Creek crossing unnecessary.

Although much of the Indian threat subsided before construction of the Union Pacific, raids still occurred. As a result, every mile of the UP went in under military escort. Workers adhered to military drill and had orders to stand and fight if attacked.

Two Monuments

On the high plains midway between Cheyenne and Laramie stands a monument to tenacity. In this case, it's a pine tree that appears to grow out of a large granite boulder. I-80 splits around the tree, with pull-outs for people who want a closer look. It's not certain how old the tree is, but the Wyoming Writers Program guide, written in the 1930s, reported that Union Pacific firemen drenched its roots with water as they passed by every day. The trunk grows through a great crack in the rock; the roots are in the soil beneath the boulder.

Another monument stands two miles west of the lone tree, just off the interstate highway. This one, built in 1882 at the highest point on the transcontinental railroad, recognizes the Ames brothers. Oliver Ames was president of the road, and Oakes assumed virtual control of the construction. The monument is 60 feet square at the base and 60 feet high, with relief medallions of both men placed on its sides. Located about 600 feet from the original roadbed, it marks the highest elevation on the entire UP route.

According to the Writers Program, some years after construction of the Ames monument a Laramie justice of the peace named Murphy found that it was on public land. He filed a homestead claim and ordered the railroad to take the pile of stones off his farm. The railroad attorneys countered by threatening to have Murphy impeached for conspiracy. The monument remained.

This quarry supplied stone for the monument built as a memorial to Oliver and Oakes Ames, brothers who played a major role in constructing the Union Pacific Railroad across southern Wyoming in 1867–68. —J. E. Stimson Collection/Wyoming State Museum

Ames Monument. —State Historic Preservation Office

Bill Carlisle, the Last Train Robber

Spring Creek Camp, a one-time tourist facility at the east end of Laramie, featured cabins built of local red sandstone. Bill Carlisle, often called the last train robber, bought the cabins after his career as an outlaw and a long stint in the Wyoming State Penitentiary.

Carlisle robbed his first train, the Portland Rose, near Green River on February 9, 1916, years after Union Pacific officials thought they'd brought such banditry to a halt. After taking what he could from the well-dressed men on the train, Carlisle climbed to the top of the sleeping cars, ran forward to the baggage car, and then dropped between it and the mail car. When the train slowed, he jumped to the ground and hid behind the right-of-way fence.

It didn't take long for the train to reach Rock Springs and sound the alarm. An initial search turned up nothing, and the railroad quickly offered a reward of $1,500 for Carlisle, dead or alive. The fugitive eventually made his way to the Laramie Peak country, where he lay low for a period. Carlisle hadn't netted much in that first looting, only $52.35, so he worked on ranches and made plans to rob another train to get enough money to head to Alaska.

The second holdup happened April 4, 1916. Carlisle climbed aboard the westbound Overland Limited as it pulled out of Cheyenne and, as he had on the Portland Rose, pulled a white silk bandanna over his face and made his haul. As before, he collected money only from the male passengers on board and took no jewelry except for one watch and chain. This time, however, train crew members managed to get a message to railroad officials as the robbery took place, and an immediate manhunt began.

Because he'd perpetrated the second crime between Cheyenne and Laramie, Carlisle found himself off the train in familiar and friendly territory, with $506.07 in his pockets from the robbery. He wandered from the Laramie plains to Douglas and Casper, where he learned Union Pacific officials had a number of men in custody, suspected of the theft. To prove that none of the men under arrest had committed the crimes, Carlisle sent a letter to the *Denver Post*. In it he said he would hold up another train somewhere west of Laramie and enclosed a watch chain he'd commandeered in his second robbery.

True to his word, on April 21 Carlisle bought a ticket in Greeley, Colorado, for the Pacific Limited on its run from Greeley to Rawlins. Just after the train pulled out of Hanna and started the forty-mile stretch into Rawlins, Carlisle made his move. He plundered the men's valuables, took special railroad agent Fred Dudley's guns and wallet, then jumped from the train not far from the North Platte River.

But Carlisle's luck went bad with his leap from the train. He badly twisted an ankle, fell on his face, and blackened an eye. The bandit made it to the river and waited for morning, but with the dawn came the posse. Carlisle gave himself up and less than a month later started a life sentence at the state penitentiary in Rawlins.

Initially, Carlisle tried to conform to penitentiary regulations but, true to his nature, he eventually formed an escape plan. During a stint in the prison shirt factory, Carlisle designed a packing crate in which he could hide. One Saturday in November 1919 he prepared some shirts for shipment from the prison, crawled into his special box, and got a quick ride beyond the stone prison walls.

Carlisle walked west almost twenty miles to the Creston Siding, where he imposed upon the section crew by spending the night and having breakfast. Then he visited a sheep wagon, where the herder and camp tender willingly provided clothing and a rifle.

No longer dressed in prison garb, Carlisle then boldly hitched a ride on an eastbound freight train. In a series of enterprising maneuvers, he rode the rails east and west between Laramie and Rawlins, always making sure to get on the train that wasn't being checked by authorities. Satisfied that his trail was cold, he targeted a westbound train heading out of Rock River. But as he looted the train, Carlisle got shot in the hand. He fled toward the ranch country in the

Laramie Mountains, where he got help from local residents. At Esterbrook, southwest of Douglas, a posse caught up to Carlisle, and before long he was back behind bars in Rawlins. This time he served until his parole, January 9, 1936.

Upon his release from prison, Carlisle worked in Kemmerer, married, adopted a daughter, and then bought the tourist court at Laramie. Throughout his career as a train robber, Carlisle had enjoyed the sympathy of rural residents and the press. For a time he sold newspaper subscriptions to ranchers in southeastern Wyoming, and in 1946 he wrote the story of his life, *Bill Carlisle, Lone Bandit*. He died at the home of a niece in Pennsylvania on June 19, 1964, nearly half a century after he robbed his first train.

Laramie

Fort John Buford was the first permanent settlement in the basin formed by the Laramie Mountains to the northeast and the Medicine Bows to the southwest. Its construction in July 1866 came a year before the Union Pacific railroad moved through the Laramie Valley. Eventually the outpost became Fort Sanders, named for Brig. Gen. William P. Sanders. It included log, stone, and frame buildings. Workers set type for Wyoming's first newspaper, the *Frontier Index*, in an equipment train car at the fort.

Like other major cities across southern Wyoming, Laramie attained permanent status when it became railroad division headquarters in 1868. That

Fort Sanders guardhouse, at the south edge of Laramie. —State Historic Preservation Office

summer Gen. Ulysses S. Grant, Gen. Philip H. Sheridan, and Gen. William T. Sherman met at Fort Sanders to discuss gradients and curvatures with railroad officials.

Handling the Lawbreakers

Like Cheyenne before it, Laramie had wild early days, so vigilance committees formed to provide some measure of control. One night the vigilantes decided to raid every gambling hall simultaneously, but the raid went awry when the attack on the Belle of the West dance hall took place too early. Nevertheless, that night of fighting left several dead, including a member of the vigilance committee, a member of the dance hall band, and a desperado. About fifteen people received wounds, and three known troublemakers—Con Wagner, Asa Moore, and Big Ed—swung from a pole. The following morning vigilantes hanged another bad man, "Big Steve," from a nearby telegraph pole. That action restored order for a time. Eventually N. K. Boswell became sheriff, and he maintained control with an iron fist.

Initially, those who defied authority when in the vicinity of Laramie landed behind bars at Fort Sanders. Before long, though, it became evident that the military post didn't have the room or the guards necessary to control the lawbreakers, and efforts to establish a territorial penitentiary on the west bank of the Laramie River began. Like Fort Laramie, the local sites get their name from the trapper Jacques La Ramee.

Workers constructed the first prison wing in about six months, completing the building by October 15, 1872. A fire ripped through the facility the next year, but repairs soon put it back into operation. During its tenure as a federal and state penal institution from 1872 until 1902, it housed the likes of Butch Cassidy, "Big Nose George" Parrott, and Clark Pelton (alias "the Kid"), a member of the Bevins and Blackburn gang of road agents who robbed the Cheyenne and Deadwood stages. It also held women, including Minnie Snyder, convicted of manslaughter in 1896 after she killed a man who reportedly wanted to take land she and her husband owned.

The prison included separate quarters for men and women. The women's area consisted of two cells, a washroom with hot running water, and a large sewing room. The prison complex also included a broom factory, blacksmith's shop, barns and livestock pens, boiler houses, icehouses, and a bakery.

When Wyoming became a state in 1890, prison control transferred to state officials. In 1902 a new facility in Rawlins started taking the prisoners from Laramie, and by 1903 the Wyoming Territorial Prison closed its doors as a penal facility. Before long the doors opened again, as the territorial prison became a barn for the University of Wyoming's experimental stock farm. For more than sixty years, cattle and sheep found refuge within the prison walls, but in the mid-1970s the barn's deteriorating condition led UW officials to vacate it, although they continued to use other prison facilities for the stock farm.

Wyoming's territorial prison in use as the University of Wyoming Livestock Farm. —State Historic Preservation Office

Finally, in 1986, the Wyoming Territorial Prison Corporation formed to preserve and restore the complex to near its original condition and to create the Wyoming Territorial Park. Using funds provided by the state and generated through a local capital facilities tax, the corporation began the restoration process in the winter of 1989. It completed the renovation two years and $5 million later. Wyoming Territorial Park opened to the public on July 1, 1991, with displays that bring the territorial prison period to life. In 1992 the U.S. Marshal's Museum opened in the restored horse barn. It details the history of the nation's oldest federal law-enforcement agency. A re-created hell-on-wheels town completes the territorial park.

Wyoming's Only University and Women's Rights

In 1887 the University of Wyoming, then called Wyoming University, opened its doors in the heart of Laramie. From the very first, the land-grant university accepted women students. That equality for women mirrored other opportunities for women in Wyoming Territory, particularly in Laramie.

The first woman in the nation to cast a ballot did so in Laramie on September 6, 1870. Seventy-year-old Louisa A. Swain, called Grandma Swain, deposited her vote "at just as early an hour, as by the fastest time, the law would permit," the *Laramie Daily Sentinel* reported. In addition to Grandma Swain, ninety-five other women cast their votes.

Even before that historic election, women had served on both a grand jury and a petit jury. Among those seated on the common law grand jury were Elisa Stewart, a teacher; Amelia Hatcher, a widow; Mrs. G. F. Hilton, wife of a physician; Mary Mackel, wife of a clerk at Fort Sanders; Agnes Baker, wife of a merchant; and Sarah W. Pease, wife of the deputy clerk of the court. During their three-week session, they reviewed cases involving horse theft, cattle rustling, and murder.

Union Pacific Opens a Rolling Mill

Laramie leaders took the initiative in the early 1870s when they heard the Union Pacific intended to open a mill to work over iron somewhere in the territory. Knowing the location had to be along the UP line, local leaders figured it might just as well be in their city, and they began campaigning for the facility. The *Cheyenne Leader* reported, "They are not asleep, but actively at work developing their resources; and if they do not succeed in getting the rolling-mills located at or near Laramie City, they will have nothing to upbraid themselves with for lack of effort and enterprise."

As assets, Laramie touted nearby coal mines, Iron Mountain, and a steady water source from a local spring. In September 1874 Laramie's campaign bore fruit when construction of the new rolling mill started. A huge masonry building more than 100 feet wide and 230 feet long housed nine furnaces, huge boilers, and engines. Other large pieces of equipment included shears for cutting old rails and new rails, double saws to cut the completed rails, and a six-ton crane needed to lift the rolls to the lathe.

Advantages to Laramie became evident almost immediately after the rolling mill began operation. Water delivery improved, which caused a drop in

Rolling Mills, Laramie. —J. E. Stimson Collection/Wyoming State Museum

insurance rates because of the city's better fire-fighting capability. Housing shortages created problems, but real estate values jumped as a result. The tax rolls swelled, and businesses saw increased traffic. By April 1875 about 150 men worked at the rolling mill, which then had a capacity of 120 tons per day, the equivalent of three miles of regular gauge railroad ties. Just after the rolling mill opened, the Union Pacific started building a foundry capable of casting anything from a car wheel to a door handle or stove door. Besides making items for the UP itself, the foundry also produced goods for the public ranging "from a stove griddle to an iron front for a brick block," Lola Homsher wrote in *The History of Albany County, Wyoming, to 1880.*

An explosion ripped through the rolling mill on March 27, 1876, killing eight men and injuring another four. Although the facility was heavily damaged, the company repaired it and continued to provide rails for its own line and others, including the Utah Northern and Republican Valley railroads.

Wyoming 210

Cheyenne—Junction with I-80 (east of Laramie)

38 miles

Locals call Wyoming 210, an alternate route between Cheyenne and Laramie, Happy Jack Road for "Happy Jack" Hollingsworth, a rancher who settled near the foothills of the Laramie Mountains in 1884. Hollingsworth ranched and cut wood in the Laramies and hauled it to Cheyenne, where he had a ready market. Some sources say Jack often sang as he worked; perhaps that's how he got the nickname "Happy Jack."

The highway that bears his name heads west from Cheyenne, diverging from I-25 near Warren Air Force Base. It winds through the mountains past small ranches, recreation areas, and remnants of mining ventures to join I-80 about seven miles east of Laramie at the Lincoln Monument, a large sculpture by Robert Russin commemorating Abraham Lincoln, for whom US 30 is named.

About a dozen miles west of Cheyenne the highway provides access to Silver Crown Hills, a would-be gold-mining boomtown. In 1885 a University of Wyoming professor said the Carbonate Belle claim promised to be the greatest bonanza since the Comstock Lode in Nevada. Impressed, Cheyenne businessmen agreed to put up $500,000 for development if the assays were satisfactory. The professor had good reason to believe the assays would show plenty of color—he salted them. However, another University of Wyoming professor, Wilbur C. Knight, exposed the fraud. A legitimate vein later turned up on Middle Crow Creek, and gold, silver, and copper mining took place from the 1880s until the 1940s.

Water for Cheyenne

Two reservoirs, Granite and Crystal, store water for Cheyenne in the Laramie Mountains. As early as 1867, Cheyenne residents raised concern about the municipal water supply. According to early-day resident Warren Richardson, Cheyenne's initial water system consisted of a fellow called Old Bates, who filled barrels at Crow Creek and sold them in town, charging 25 cents a barrel. The next system comprised four wells, one at each corner of town, each with a wooden bucket and rope to collect water.

In the early 1900s, the city obtained water rights in Crow Creek by proving the municipal need was greater than the agricultural need of the nearby Thomas D. Holt family. A pipeline brought the water from Crow Creek to the Union Pacific shops in town. By 1910 Crystal and Granite reservoirs stored the Crow Creek water, and by the 1950s a pipeline carried it twenty-five miles to the city. Cheyenne showed great foresight in 1954 when the city claimed water rights in the Little Snake River drainage, more than 150 miles—and three mountain ranges—to the west.

In the early 1960s, Cheyenne started a massive water-development program involving those water rights. The first portion of the project involved

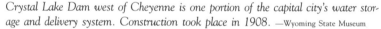

Crystal Lake Dam west of Cheyenne is one portion of the capital city's water storage and delivery system. Construction took place in 1908. —Wyoming State Museum

construction of two additional reservoirs: Rob Roy in the Medicine Bow Mountains and Hog Park in the Sierra Madres. The city then began diverting water from the west side of the Continental Divide, taking it out of the Little Snake River drainage and transporting it via an underground tunnel to the east side of the divide.

Physically, the system worked like this: First, the water diverted from Little Snake tributaries flowed through a tunnel under the Continental Divide into Hog Park Reservoir and eventually into the Encampment River. That water then flowed into the North Platte River. At the same time, Cheyenne diverted water from the North Platte River drainage into Rob Roy Reservoir, then moved it through a different underground pipeline to Crystal and Granite reservoirs in the Laramie Range. Yet another pipeline transferred it from there to the city itself. Water from the Little Snake River never reaches Cheyenne. Instead, it replaces water taken from the North Platte drainage for the city.

Stage one of Cheyenne's water project went into service in 1964. Stage two cost $107 million and started operating in the late 1980s. Stage three, if it's ever built, will collect even more water from the Sierra Madre Range and Little Snake River drainage for use in Cheyenne.

The U.S. Army's Fort Warren Maneuver Reservation once lay in the vicinity of Crow Creek and Cheyenne's reservoirs. From mid-July to mid-August, troops tested and practiced with field artillery and small arms. The army selected the site for its varied terrain and had a camp five miles west of the military maneuver reservation.

The Overland Trail

Jacques La Ramee and other trappers came to this region and worked the streams for beaver from 1817 until 1843. Gen. William Ashley's trappers traveled part of the future Overland Trail route in 1824–25, Jim Bridger knew of the route by 1835, John C. Frémont camped along it in 1843, and the Cherokee used it to travel from Oklahoma to California in 1849, for which it became known as the Cherokee Trail. Local tribes gathered ash for bows and held ceremonial dances in the nearby mountains to cure diseases. The use of ash for bows was said to be "good medicine," and this phrase gave the mountains, and later the national forest, their name: Medicine Bow.

In 1862 Ben Holladay established his stagecoach line on this road, with stations located between ten and sixteen miles apart. Despite frequent attacks by Indians, Holladay set up permanent stage stops. His coaches mostly carried mail, along with an occasional passenger. The route left Julesburg, Colorado, crossed northern Colorado, and entered Wyoming just north of Virginia Dale, which is named for Jack Slade's wife. It roughly followed today's US 287 from Tie Siding to Laramie, crossing the Laramie Plains to Fort Sanders, at the south edge of Laramie. The Overland Trail then headed northwest, along a line now marked by Wyoming 130 and I-80, to Arlington, Elk Mountain, and Fort Halleck before veering due west to Bridger's Pass, Fort Bridger, and, eventually, Utah.

Most Overland Trail use after 1865 resulted from fighting between the military and the Plains Indians in northern Wyoming. The various tribes attacked the Oregon Trail in order to stop the western migration and to cut off communications such as the Creighton telegraph. Those hostilities along and north of the North Platte River to Independence Rock led westbound travelers to seek safer passage elsewhere. They moved south and used the Overland, which had the disadvantages of more mountains and less water.

Wyoming 130
Laramie—Saratoga
71 miles

One of the most scenic drives in southern Wyoming crosses the open plains west of Laramie, climbs into the Medicine Bow Mountains, and then drops into the North Platte Valley. Wyoming 130 intersects the Overland Trail and follows the path of the Laramie-Centennial-Rambler Mine Stage Route for several miles as it leaves Laramie, but then the Overland swings toward Rock Creek and around the mountain range, whereas the highway forges over the top. Wyoming 130 rims a basin known as Big Hollow.

Centennial

The ranching community that sits just where the road starts its ascent got its start in 1876 when prospectors discovered gold. The locals dubbed the community Centennial for the nation's celebration that year.

The lost Centennial lode is a part of Wyoming lore and legend. In the 1870s Col. Stephen W. Downey refused $100,000 for a rich gold lode near the town and opened his own mine. He should have sold, because the vein pinched out. Nevertheless, in the early 1900s a Boston syndicate heavily invested in the town, anticipating a rediscovery of the gold and the construction of a railroad spur line. They, too, were disappointed.

Just west of Centennial lies the site of Platinum City, where prospectors searching for the lost Downey lode in the late 1920s found traces of platinum among the fine grains of gold, copper, and silver. Promoters imported mining machinery, bought the meadows at the foot of Centennial Ridge, platted Platinum City, and offered building lots for sale. But, as always, it soon became apparent there weren't pots of gold at the Centennial rainbow's end. Furthermore, the railroad rerouted, bypassing the area. In 1938 government officials confiscated the property. Meadowland, machinery, camp equipment, and household articles once valued at more than $100,000 sold at public auction for $7,000.

In 1992 prospectors returned to the Centennial Valley, once again looking for gold—perhaps the lost Downey lode. By 1995 they still had not begun any development. However, Centennial did experience a boom of sorts, as people seeking a quiet location of great scenic value discovered this spot at the base of the Snowy Range.

Miss Rodeo America

Centennial's one real claim to fame could be a beautiful young cowgirl who worked cattle on her family's ranch and represented the Professional Rodeo Cowboys Association as Miss Rodeo America in 1992. A huge billboard proclaimed Centennial as the home of Miss Rodeo America during Stacey Talbott's reign. The sign welcomed visitors in the same folksy way a "police car" at the edge of town warned speeders. That vehicle probably fooled very few drivers—it was an abandoned car painted to look like a police vehicle, complete with tin-can red lights on top.

The Snowies

The glacially carved peaks that rise above the Medicine Bow Mountains got the name Snowy Range from local residents because the snowfields on the east face, remnants of winter blizzards, remain all summer. Atop Libby Flats, at an elevation of nearly 11,000 feet, the pine forest gives way to alpine tundra, where trees are stubby and stunted by the harsh climate. The view from the Libby Flats observation point includes the Centennial and Laramie valleys to the east and the Snowy Range to the west.

These mountains are sprinkled with abandoned cabins, the legacy of tie hacks who cut their living from the forests from the 1860s to the 1940s. One tie-hack camp is located at Turpin, north of Medicine Bow Peak. The tie hacks chopped trees during the winter months and hauled them to decks near streams. When the creeks swelled with spring snowmelt, the men pushed the ties into the water and floated them down the rivers to landing stations and eventual use by local railroads.

A Place for War Prisoners

The Ryan Park National Forest campground on the west side of the Snowies, just a mile east of Ryan Park, was a Civilian Conservation Corps camp during the 1930s and a prisoner-of-war camp for Italians and Germans during World War II. The POWs logged for R. R. Crow and Company from 1943 to 1945.

Most of them first came to a camp at Douglas before being sent to other locations in Wyoming. The prisoners at Ryan Park were "one of several groups which are being fanned out from these camps into areas where there is a definite labor shortage," the *Saratoga Sun* reported October 28, 1943. It added, "The Crow Company has found the procurement of manpower an almost insurmountable obstacle to production for some months past, and it is thought that the securing of war prisoner labor will result in the much-desired stepping-up of production at the company's local sawmill."

The Ryan Park POW camp held up to 200 prisoners at any given time, with only minimal security at the site. Once four prisoners escaped from the camp and got to Saratoga, where authorities found them near the rodeo grounds on the east side of town. Perhaps because of the isolation of Ryan Park and the fact that the prisoners' homeland lay across an ocean, the facility didn't need heavy security. The former camp is now a national forest campground with an interpretive sign and markings at some of the POW building locations.

A marker at the Ryan Park POW camp is now cracked with age.

A Century or More on the Land

The Brush Creek area, east of the intersection of Wyoming 130 and Wyoming 230, has a long-standing ranching tradition. Winthrop Condict, an Illinois boot and shoe salesman, and Jonathan Dickinson Condict, a New York attorney, started a family ranch on Brush Creek in 1884. The Condicts liked the area and envisioned lush pastoral settings with cattle grazing on the immense sagebrush flats. Early arrangements called for Winthrop to retire from the footwear business and remain in the Platte Valley to run the ranch. After constructing the first buildings, he returned to Illinois to marry Hattie Young on May 1, 1884. Her brother, Charles Young, would soon be a Brush Creek rancher as well.

Charles Young settled on Brush Creek in 1886 at the urging of his sister. He worked for the Condicts a couple of years, then bought land a few miles up the creek. The Young ranch became the site of the Brush Creek School, which also served as a local community center, a place for book learning, dances, church services, funerals, Ladies Aid suppers, and plays.

G. H. "Gus" Barkhurst settled his property, which sat between the Condict and Young ranches, in 1887. A couple of years later, in need of more money to take care of his growing family, Gus went to work as Union Pacific track foreman at Fort Steele. While Gus worked for the railroad, his eldest son, Jess, took care of things at the ranch, training hounds to chase coyotes and breaking horses. All of this was good training for his later work as a member of Buffalo Bill Cody's Wild West Show.

Those three ranches remain with the Condict, Young, and Barkhurst families, now operated by grandchildren or great-grandchildren of the early settlers. Just up the river the Sanger Ranch, settled by Isaac and Clara Sanger in 1892, and downstream the Ryan Ranch, settled by B. T. Ryan in 1873, continued under family ownership as well.

As property values increased after the 1970s, it became more difficult for young men and women to ranch with their parents, and most of the family outfits in this part of Wyoming sold to outside owners. Corporate owners ranging from TCI Telecommunications Inc., the huge cable television conglomerate, to Gates Rubber Company and the heirs to 3M Corporation bought property in the Platte Valley. For the most part they kept the ranches in agricultural production and employed local managers, farmhands, and cowboys. Many other parts of Wyoming saw the same type of ownership changes; often the land became subdivided for homes of wealthy part-time residents. It became more difficult to pass the land from father to son or daughter as land values increased, making the five 100-year-old, family-owned ranches on Brush Creek and the North Platte all the more unusual.

Laramie—Colorado Line
43 miles

Albany County is known for its wide-open ranching country and mining swindles—or, at least, attempts to swindle. A scam similar to the salted mines at Silver Crown Hills (see page 228) took place west of Laramie at Jelm. There John Cummins laid out a 170-block city in the 1870s. He promoted the community throughout the region, displaying ore samples he said came from the nearby mountains. A Denver company paid Cummins $10,000 for mineral rights, only to later learn the promoter was a scoundrel. He'd salted the mine.

Fox Park, midway between Laramie and the Colorado state line on Wyoming 230, has a past, present, and perhaps future tied to the timber industry. The first lumber workers in the area were several hundred Swedish tie hacks who chopped for the railroads. During the 1960s and 1970s, a lumber company owned by Marvin Brandt and Dean Wickland produced pine boards. Increasing pressure from environmental groups led to reduced harvest from the Medicine Bow National Forest, so Brandt and Wickland closed their operation in 1992. Firms from Laramie, Saratoga, and Encampment continue to log in the area.

I-80
Laramie—Rawlins
100 miles

Sno Chi Minh Trail

Two highways parallel each other from Laramie to Walcott Junction: old US 30, which runs past Rock River, Medicine Bow, and Hanna, and I-80, located farther south and closer to Arlington, McFadden, and Elk Mountain. Two-lane US 30/287 is the best winter route. It seldom closes, even though at times blinding blizzards make it impossible to see and most people have to hole up somewhere along the route.

This area of Wyoming is like a big funnel. The western winds coming from the wide-open Red Desert country west of Rawlins are squeezed between Elk Mountain and the Hanna Basin uplift. That narrowing of the channel, much like a gorge on a river, forces a concentration of the air, which means the wind can get pretty intense in this section of Wyoming.

When highway engineers started planning I-80, they settled on a line fairly close to Elk Mountain, pretty near the historic Overland Trail. Long-time local ranchers knew how the wind blew and how blinding blizzards swept off the Snowy Range. They told the planners to move the route farther north, more along the line of US 30/287.

The engineers ignored the warnings and built the four-lane highway. They soon found, however, that I-80 is one of the first routes to close when a winter storm sweeps across southern Wyoming's landscape. Because its construction took place during the Vietnam War, ranchers quickly dubbed the highway the Sno Chi Minh Trail. Sometimes drifts pile up, and other times the highway is a sheet of ice, but the greatest problem is poor visibility. During storms the snow comes rushing and swirling off the mountains. Complete whiteout conditions aren't uncommon.

At such times the best options are to wait out the weather at Rawlins or Laramie, take US 30/287, or travel on Wyoming 130/230 through Saratoga and Encampment. When howling blizzards make it impossible to see on I-80, the conditions in the mountains themselves often aren't nearly as bad.

Arlington

Two trails marked this area in the 1800s. The Overland entered Wyoming north of Virginia Dale, Colorado, crossed the Laramie Plains, swung around Elk Mountain, and headed west. A separate trail to Fort Fetterman started here as well.

Freighters from Medicine Bow wanted a new route to avoid the numerous river crossings between the Union Pacific Railroad and Fort Fetterman. Their road led to a new stage station on the bank of Rock Creek, complete with a warehouse, general store, blacksmith shop, mess hall, three saloons, two hotels, and, later, a large stockyard.

Joe Bush homesteaded the area in the early 1860s and operated the stage station. He built a toll bridge across Rock Creek and defended his post against Indians when necessary. Early-day Wyoming surveyor W. O. Owen once recalled:

> I made many surveys for Mr. Bush, and found him four-square to the world all the time. . . . Bush had fought Indians for years and when they attacked his station it was no new experience for him. The stage station at this point was repeatedly attacked by Indians and Bush fought the savages valiantly. He had a score of wounds from arrows and many times have I seen the scars.

Bush didn't hold his homestead claim, which passed to Sadie and Bill Williams. They raised a large garden and sold the produce to miners, emigrants, and passersby. Bill met an untimely end when his horse pitched him and dragged him to death. Sadie then operated the station alone, and she proved to be an able businesswoman. According to one report, she was an efficient, practical nurse, always ready to help friends in times of illness. She also ran a card game at the saloon and "had a ready tongue and could handle a six-shooter as well as most men." Sadie eventually remarried and sold the station. It fell into the hands of Alvy Dixon, a former freighter between Rock Creek, Fort Fetterman, and Fort McKinney.

In 1882 the government established a post office called Rock Dale, but the station was always called Rock Creek. By the next year 175 teams were regularly freighting out of Rock Creek Station, which became a major terminus for cattle entering Wyoming and Montana. According to one report by the railroad agent, during the fall of 1883 an average of 100 carloads of cattle were shipped every twenty-four hours. A stage line from Rock Creek to Junction City, Montana, soon developed; spanning 400 miles, it followed the freighter trail's route to Fort Fetterman, then headed northwest past Buffalo and Sheridan.

The Union Pacific Railroad abandoned Rock Creek Station on April 1, 1900, and a new town, Rock River, soon thrived a few miles north. Alvy Dixon's family retained the facilities at Rock Creek Station—known as Arlington by the early 1900s—and turned to ranching, which continued in the 1990s under the direction of Dixon's stepson, Chet Pitcher.

An Indian Raid

Cheyenne Indians attacked a train of seventy-five wagons between Arlington and Elk Mountain in 1865. One family on the wagon train, the Fletcher family, suffered badly in the conflict. Indians killed Mrs. Fletcher, wounded her husband, and captured two daughters, Mary, thirteen, and Lizzie, two. Three Fletcher sons escaped the fight unharmed.

Although hit with several arrows, Mary Fletcher managed to pull them free, and she watched the wagons burn in the valley before the Indian women forced her to follow them. Mary became separated from her younger sister and a year later contacted a white trader, who is said to have paid a horse, a gun, and $1,600 for her release. She eventually rejoined her father in Salt Lake City.

Thirty-five years after the raid, a white woman who spoke only Arapaho visited Casper with some Indians from the Wind River Reservation. Mary Fletcher read about her in a newspaper, returned to Wyoming, and identified her as Lizzie. The younger sister remembered nothing of her capture as a toddler and refused to leave her Arapaho husband, John Brokenhorn, and go with Mary. Several years later, when the government made tribal land allotments, Brokenhorn refused his share, saying that the white man's government had no right to confine Indians to a part of the land that was wholly their own, according to the Wyoming Writers Program guide.

Carbon

First Coal Town on the Union Pacific Line

A few miles east of Hanna and north of I-80 lie the remains of Carbon, built in 1868 as the first coal production center on the Union Pacific Railroad line. Houses "sprang up as from the earth itself, as miners dug caves into the side of the nearby ravine and covered the fronts with boards and earth, with a stovepipe poked thru a hole in the top of each roof," according to the 1940 *History of the Union Pacific Coal Mines.*

Although more substantial buildings later went up, living conditions remained harsh. The town had no water, relying on a large cistern the railroad filled from large tank cars. Seven mines opened in the area, worked by big, raw-boned men from England, Ireland, Scotland, Denmark, and Finland. Carbon's main street became a melting pot.

An early threat came from Cheyenne and Arapaho Indians, who once attacked the stable boss as he searched for some wandering mules. Other men

Sandstone ruins of a building at Carbon, the first coal mining town on the Union Pacific line in Wyoming.

found the stricken man and carried him to the mine while miners "ran from door to door gathering the grim-faced women and their frightened children. Soon all living in the camp were inside or at the mine, the women and children huddled inside, while the men, above ground, tramped back and forth with their hunting rifles swung over their arms," the UP account said.

The lack of a good water source created the greatest problems. Many of the town's children died of cholera when the water became contaminated, and in 1890 fire burned most of the business district because there was no water for fire fighting. Carbon's 1,500 residents and businessmen quickly rebuilt.

The *Black Diamond* newspaper kept up with town happenings, including school activities, events at the Finnish Temperance Hall and the "Coming Men of America" lodge, and performances of the town's two brass bands. Most men worked in the seven underground coal mines, digging an estimated 4.7 million tons of coal from 1868 until 1902. Carbon became a ghost town after the turn of the century because the Union Pacific shifted its main line from the center of town to a route farther north with an easier grade. Some said the coal mines had played out anyway.

Many children died in Carbon of cholera because the town had no good water supply. They lie in graves nearly obscured by sagebrush.

Death to Lawmen

In August 1878, Big Nose George Parrott, "Dutch Charley" Burris, and several accomplices tried to derail a westbound Union Pacific train east of Carbon by drawing the spikes that held the rails. The would-be bandits fled when a section boss noticed the loosed rails and flagged the train. He then notified the sheriff.

Carbon County deputy sheriffs Tip Vincent and Robert Widdowfield joined a posse and gave pursuit, but the bad men eluded the group, and eventually Vincent and Widdowfield went on their own. They tracked the outlaws around the west base of Elk Mountain to an aspen grove, where they found a warm campfire. As the deputies checked the fire, the bandits fired from ambush, killing both. Widdowfield fell with a bullet in the back of his head. Vincent had an opportunity to fire a few return rounds before he also fell, dying some fifty feet from his companion with several gunshot wounds to his chest and legs.

In addition to having attempted to rob a Union Pacific train, the gang now had to answer for the murders of two sheriff's deputies—the first two lawmen to die on the job in Wyoming Territory. They mounted their horses and headed north toward the Hole-in-the-Wall country west of Kaycee, eventually reaching Montana.

Big Nose George Parrott.
—Wyoming State Museum

When Vincent and Widdowfield failed to return, Sheriff James G. Rankin organized a search party. The men rode a cold trail from Carbon, over Rattle Snake Pass and along the fringes of Elk Mountain, where they found the bodies, nine days dead, on August 27, 1878. The search party obtained coffins and took the two deputies to Rawlins for burial.

The cold trail grew colder, and the outlaws seemed to disappear. Then, more than two years later, during a drunken gambling spree in Montana, Big Nose George and Dutch Charley boasted of killing the two Wyoming lawmen. Rankin had the news before long, and just as quickly they were in custody and on the way to Rawlins for a trial.

Dutch Charley was the first to return to Wyoming with the long arm of the law around his shoulders. Rankin intended to take Dutch Charley to Rawlins for a trial, but when the UP train they were riding got to Carbon, vigilantes stopped it and started a methodical search of the cars. They found Charley hidden under a pile of buffalo robes.

The mob grabbed Dutch Charley, a six-foot-tall man weighing well over 200 pounds, dragged him from the train, and put him on a barrel with a rope knotted securely around his neck. Asked to confess, Charley refused. The men threw the rope over a telegraph pole and again asked him to confess. Still he refused, and the men pulled the rope, dragging him from his perch on the barrel. They let him down to his toes and asked for a confession. Charley— brave or stupid to the end—would not oblige, and they pulled the rope. Up and down, up and down, the process was repeated, with Robert Widdowfield's mother and brother Joe watching from the sidelines. Eventually the mob tied the rope, strangling Charley to death.

Carbon miner John Milliken watched the proceedings. "They left him hanging there until the next day," he wrote many years later. "The wind was blowing hard all night, and the body swung back and forth, back and forth all night, hitting the [telegraph] pole each time with such force that by morning the face was horrible mashed."

As a morning passenger train rolled through Carbon early the next day, Union Pacific conductors quickly pulled the shades to shield their passengers from the grisly sight of Dutch Charley swinging in the wind. Late that same day Sheriff Rankin arrived in Carbon, cut down Burris's body, and took it back to Rawlins.

The arrest of Big Nose George took place near Miles City, Montana, at the hand of U.S. Marshal John X. Beidler, known simply as X throughout Montana. As deputies returned with the prisoner, the reminder of Dutch Charley's end stuck with them all, and the scene almost repeated itself. Vigilantes once again stopped the train at Carbon, grabbed Parrott, and made preparations for a necktie party. But Parrott desired to preserve his hide, if only for a while longer, and he told the crowd how he and his cohorts had planned to rob the train. He explained the use of a wire across the tracks to try to derail the train and how they shot the deputies from ambush near their camp on Rattle Snake Pass.

Parrott made it to Rawlins alive on August 7, 1880, and pleaded guilty on September 13, 1880. Four days later he changed his plea to not guilty, only to switch his plea again on November 18. His sentence was handed down on December 15: Parrott would hang between the hours of 10 A.M. and 4 P.M. on April 2, 1881.

But Parrott didn't keep the date. On March 22, 1881, he attempted to escape, using an old case knife to remove the rivets from the handmade shackles that bound him. He hid in the toilet at the jail, and when Sheriff Rankin entered the cell to check the prisoners, Parrott attacked from behind. He struck Rankin with the shackles and cut his scalp in three places. Rankin landed a blow to the prisoner's head and yelled for his wife, Rosa—who lived at the jail with her husband and cooked for the prisoners—to bring his pistol. She first slammed the heavy cell-house door to prevent an escape.

The good citizens of Rawlins had had enough of Big Nose George Parrott. By twos and threes they gathered outside the jail while Sheriff Rankin rested in his room and a guard named Simms watched the jail. Between 10 and 11 P.M., a rap on the door preceded a demand that "friends" wanted inside the jail. Simms told them it was too late to visit, but the men broke through the door and covered the guard with several pistols.

Once inside, they went to the room where Rankin lay. There was little he could do; the vigilantes held a pistol on him and took the keys from his pocket. They had some difficulty in locating the key to Parrott's cell, but eventually they did so and took the condemned man from the jail, headed toward the southeast part of town.

By the time the group reached a telegraph pole in front of the J. W. Hugus store on Front Street, a crowd of seventy-five to one hundred people had gathered. The masked men who had taken the prisoner from the jail fastened a rope to the pole. They pushed a barrel under the pole and helped George climb on it. A man wearing a white mask fastened the rope around Parrott's neck and gave the word. "All right," he said, and someone else added, "Kick the barrel." But Parrott fell to the ground, and someone said, "Hang him over and make a good job of it this time."

The mob found a ladder and started the process anew. Some reports claim Parrott told them, "It is a shame to take a man's life in this way. . . . [G]ive [me] time and I will climb the ladder myself, and when I get high enough I will jump off." The vigilantes refused him this courtesy, however, and on the second try they succeeded in hanging their prisoner.

Dr. John Osborne, who served as Union Pacific surgeon from 1881 to 1887, answered the summons of Rawlins residents the night they hanged George Parrott. "I was called to the door and requested to go with a mob that had formed to lynch 'Big Nose George' for the purpose of telling them when the prisoner was dead, as they did not want to run the slightest risk," Osborne wrote later.

Artist's drawing of the hanging of Big Nose George Parrott, 1881.
—Wyoming State Museum

The Lynching of Big Nose George at Rawlins Wyo. in the Year of 1881 This Drawing is From a Description of the Lynching by a Witness.

After hanging in the cold Rawlins wind for about two hours, Parrott's body was finally cut down and turned over to William Daley, the only undertaker in town. Daley removed the shackles from the dead man's limbs and gave them to Osborne, who later gave them to the Union Pacific museum in Omaha.

The doctor and two of his companions—Dr. Thomas G. Maghee, a UP surgeon-physician, and Lillian Heath, a young woman studying under Dr. Maghee—took even more gruesome reminders of George Parrott. Osborne made a plaster of Paris death mask of the outlaw and peeled skin from Parrott's chest, which he had tanned and made into a pair of shoes. A part of Parrott's skull became a doorstop, many of his bones ended as paperweights, and others finally wound up in a whiskey barrel, which was buried on Front Street in Rawlins. When builders excavated the barrel in 1950, they compared Miss Heath's skull-piece doorstop to the remains and concluded the bones in the barrel were those of Parrott. After a sojourn at the Carbon County Museum, the bones eventually were scattered to the winds in Utah.

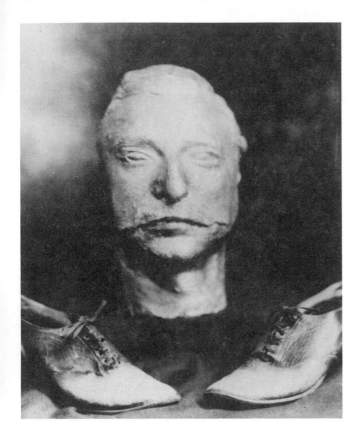

A plaster cast of the head of Big Nose George Parrott and the shoes made from his skin.
—Wyoming State Museum

A Mountain Marker

Elk Mountain looms large and awesome on the plains of Wyoming, rising at the end of the Medicine Bows and acting as a beacon for drivers and airplane pilots. It is named either for Sioux chief Standing Elk or for the animal. If the old mountain could talk, it would have great tales to tell. Fort Halleck sat at its base to protect travelers on the Overland Trail, Dutch Charley and Big Nose George ambushed lawmen on its west side, tie cutters felled hundreds of trees for construction of the Union Pacific Railroad, and a land-use fight occurred over its slopes.

A couple of miles south of the highway, at the point where I-80 swings closest to the mountain, the army established Fort Halleck in 1862 to protect the Overland Trail. Named for Maj. Gen. H. W. Halleck, the fort operated only from 1862 until 1866. Company A of the 11th Ohio Volunteer Cavalry selected the site and built the post, and the infamous Jack Slade frequently visited as superintendent of the stage line. Winter winds howled off Elk Mountain, hammering the soldiers. In February 1864 a blizzard caught a party of

Fort Halleck soldiers away from the post. Col. William O. Collins wrote of conditions as the troop became stranded in a sea of white during a winter storm:

> The air was so filled with snow that it was very often impossible to see ten yards. . . . Any track was obliterated in a very few minutes. . . . Some of the men became much benumbed. . . . About ten men stopped and I remained with them but it was impossible to kindle a fire on account of the violence of the wind. . . . When I dismounted I could not walk [and] had no feeling until being rubbed with snow for some time. . . . It is difficult to form an idea of the storm. The snow, moving horizontally, struck the face like shot, perfectly blinding the eyes.

Tie hacks cut thousands of trees on Elk Mountain and other nearby forested areas during construction of the Union Pacific Railroad. The high stumps of those trees cut for ties remained in the 1980s as a monument to the work. That's when a major land-access fight broke out over Elk Mountain.

The east face of Elk Mountain with horses grazing on the Pete McKee Ranch.

Fighting over the Checkerboard

By the 1980s, the Union Pacific Railroad had sold many of the alternating sections of land granted to it by the federal government at the time of construction. In eastern Wyoming, private landowners held most of the former public lands. From Elk Mountain west, however, there was still unclaimed public land, and the so-called checkerboard remained. This situation created tremendous problems for both federal and private land managers. Ranchers who owned or controlled the private land sections also controlled access to the federal sections, which no one wanted during the homesteading era because of the lack of water.

A major dispute occurred over Elk Mountain when rancher Norm Palm refused public access across one of his private land sections. He granted a crossing right to the U.S. Bureau of Land Management (BLM) and the University of Wyoming—which has a weather monitoring station on top of the mountain—but refused to let individuals do the same.

The big issue was access, but it was tied to economics. Palm and a group of other area landowners banded together and charged a $250 fee for hunting privileges on their land. The Wyoming Wildlife Federation (WWF) argued that the ranchers' policy of charging a fee restricted public use of public land. The WWF filed suit against Palm to force him to allow people to cross his land so they could reach three sections—1,920 acres—on top of the mountain.

A federal judge ordered this road providing access to the top of Elk Mountain closed in 1987 after Elk Mountain rancher Norm Palm successfully showed he had never granted a public easement across his private land.

In October 1986, U.S. District Judge Ewing Kerr said the 1957 easement Palm gave to the BLM was never intended to allow public access to the mountain. Kerr wrote:

> No grant of public access was ever intended by the parties. . . . The BLM originally requested the easement for the purpose of establishing a fire lookout tower on top of Elk Mountain. The easement for right-of-way granted to the United States and crossing Palm Livestock lands is unambiguous and clearly limited in scope. It does not provide a right of public access across Palm's private land.

U.S. Attorney Richard Stacy, who argued the BLM's side of the case before Kerr, called the ruling "a big victory for people who use public lands for private profit and a big defeat for the citizens of this state."

But the WWF made its point when about twenty-five people hiked up the mountain on a hot August day in 1987. The hikers left their cars parked on the Rattle Snake Pass road, then—dodging rattlesnakes and Palm's private land—walked three miles up the mountain, staying on public land by stepping across section corners.

Walcott

There isn't much at Walcott today, but this area at the junction of I-80, US 30, and Wyoming 130 once served as a bustling UP railroad station. During the copper boom at Grand Encampment from 1898 to 1908, this station handled more freight than any other on the UP line between Omaha and Ogden. A major Australian-style wool-shearing and -processing center saw use near Walcott during the period, when Carbon County was the third-leading sheep and wool producer in the nation. When coal development boomed in the Hanna Basin in the 1970s and 1980s, hundreds of people lived here in trailer homes, quickly moving in and just as quickly moving out when the boom went bust.

Fort Steele

In 1843 John C. Frémont camped on the North Platte River near the site of the present-day Fort Steele State Rest Area and historic Fort Fred Steele. Frémont's men killed a large number of buffalo and built scaffolds on which to dry the meat. Just as the work started, however, about seventy mounted Cheyenne and Arapaho attacked. Frémont's men rushed into a grove, and that brought the Indians to a halt. The Cheyenne and Arapaho explained that they thought the military men were enemy Indians. Frémont and the chiefs smoked a pipe of peace and exchanged gifts, with no apparent hard feelings on either side.

Fort Fred Steele was established in 1868 to protect construction crews building the Union Pacific Railroad from Indian raids. But native Americans threat-

Agriculture is a mainstay industry of Wyoming, and sheep raising is just one spoke in its wheel. The occupation caused deadly conflict over the range, but at one time millions of head of sheep roamed the state. This is a view of a sheep-shearing "steam plant." —Wyoming State Museum

Workers lounge on a pile of wool bags near Lance Creek. Each of the big bags can hold 300–400 pounds of wool, depending on how good a job the "tromper" does in filling it. —Wyoming State Museum

ened more than train workers. In 1874 a large party of Indians attacked ranchers Boney Earnest and Yank Sullivan about three miles downstream from Fort Fred Steele. In an August 16, 1939, reminiscence of the incident, Earnest wrote:

> Sullivan had just been discharge [sic] out of A. Company of the United States Cavalry and was building a ranch just over the line of the military reservation. He got me to go down and help him. The next morning after we got to the ranch site and before we were out of bed in the morning we heard the war whoop and found that we were surrounded by two hundred Indians. In less time than it takes to tell it we both grabbed our guns and were in action as we slept with our guns. We poured such withering fire into the Indians which they returned and the fight was on. Although both sides were badly embarrassed by the tall sage brush, and no doubt that was all that saved us and the Indians also.

The native Americans then launched an attack on Fort Fred Steele before heading west along the Union Pacific line to the Granville section house at the site of Parco, which is now Sinclair. There the Indians dispersed.

Joe Rankin's Ride

Another of Wyoming's storied horseback rides ended at Fort Fred Steele. It started on the White River in northwestern Colorado.

Nathan C. Meeker served as agent on the Ute Indian White River Reservation in September 1879. He was not the best Indian agent, and when he attempted to force the Utes to adopt a government farming policy, the tribe revolted and killed him. Maj. Thomas Thornburg led a relief party from Fort Steele to White River, but about 250 Indians ambushed the soldiers, killing Thornburg and a dozen other men and wounding forty-seven troopers. Scout Joe Rankin slipped away during the night of the Indian ambush, riding 164 miles to Rawlins and eventually reaching Fort Fred Steele with the news.

Sinclair

This is a town of many names. Originally a Union Pacific depot called Granville Station, it became Parco in the 1920s when the Producers and Refining Corporation moved in. It is now Sinclair, named after Sinclair Refiners Company. Its owes its life as a town primarily to oil development and refining.

Parco/Sinclair differs from other company towns in the stylish design of its streets and buildings. Oil magnate Frank Kistler, the founder of the Producers and Refiners Corporation, hired the prominent Denver architectural firm of Fisher and Fisher to design the town. The firm used a Spanish colonial motif, with a central plaza and fountain surrounded by public buildings and residential areas.

Parco/Sinclair quickly became a model company town, thoroughly distinct from the cookie-cutter continuity of company towns such as Hanna and Rock

Springs. Kistler sold Parco in 1934, but the community survived under the ownership of Sinclair Refining and got its new name in 1942. Supplies come to the refinery in a pipeline from the Wertz and Lost Soldier oil fields developed in the 1920s near Bairoil, about thirty miles north of Rawlins.

Just south of Sinclair is the former site of Benton, the first town established by the Union Pacific Railroad west of Laramie. Within two weeks the community had a population of 3,000, a city government, and a daily paper. At the time of its prosperity Benton was the end of the line for the UP, as well as the headquarters for the construction division. Twice a day trains arrived and departed, and stages left for Utah, Montana, and Idaho.

Goods once freighted across the plains now came by rail to Benton, where they were reshipped. The streets filled with Indians, gamblers, "cappers," saloon keepers, merchants, miners, and mule whackers. Benton's "great institution" was the Big Tent, a frame building 100 feet long and 40 feet wide. It had a canvas cover and a floor so people could dance and gamble.

Like many another boomtown, Benton died almost as quickly as it grew. It was replaced by Rawlins, six miles farther west.

Rawlins

As the Union Pacific chugged westward, military men and railroad engineers preceded track-laying crews, establishing stations roughly twenty miles apart. In 1867, on just such a mission, Gen. John A. Rawlins discovered a spring in a draw, "the most gracious and acceptable of anything" he found in the area. He told Gen. Grenville M. Dodge that if anything were ever named for him, he should prefer it to be a spring. When General Dodge established a town near the site in 1868, he called it Rawlins Spring.

Eight years later, John C. Friend shipped a carload of pigment from the paint mines near the new town. The paint, called Rawlins Red, covered many structures, the most well-known being the Brooklyn Bridge.

Rawlins has a turbulent history of economic booms and busts. It started as a UP hell-on-wheels town and gained prominence as a sheep production center. Thousands of head of sheep ranged on the Red Desert and in the Great Divide Basin. The sheep moguls' stately homes contrasted with the low-rent dwellings of the railroad workers, and Rawlins became very much a town divided. The wealthy white sheep owners lived north of the Union Pacific line, while the working-class railroad workers, often of Mexican descent, lived on the south side.

In 1898 work started on a new state penitentiary in Rawlins, and by 1902 the facility housed its first prisoners. Located on the north side of town, the stone and steel structure sat just a couple of blocks from the mansion of sheepman George Ferris. It served as the state's prison until 1981, when Wyoming erected a new facility about a mile south of town, over the hill and out of

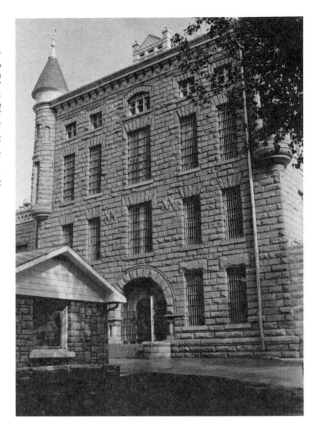

The Wyoming State Prison moved from Laramie to Rawlins by 1903 and prisoners were housed in this stone and steel facility until late in the century, when they moved to a new prison built just east of Rawlins. The Frontier Prison, shown here, is now operated as a tourist attraction.

sight. The older facility—called the Frontier Prison even though it was built after the attainment of statehood—fell under the auspices of a promotional group, which restored and opened it as a tourist attraction.

The new prison, meanwhile, witnessed a dramatic confrontation. In December 1988 two prisoners grabbed two women working as prison counselors and held them hostage for eleven hours. The inmates, Abdulah Amin and Donald Calkins, demanded to speak to the news media, saying they wanted to outline grievances related to prison policies. In particular, they alleged that staff allowed racist activities to take place at the facility. Warden Duane Shillinger refused the prisoners access to the news media during the time they held the counselors at knifepoint, but once the women went free, Amin was permitted to speak to three photographers, one each from the Associated Press, the *Casper Star-Tribune*, and Casper's KTWO television station. Fortunately one of the photographers had a tape recorder. In his statement, Amin said:

> We got a lot of racists here. . . . We have no black officers here, we have
> no black counselors here, we have no black administrators here, we have
> nobody to relate to. . . . The prison systems are based on the definition
> (of) exactly what racism is—oppression, segregation and suppression.

> Anytime you take any human being or you take any human mind and you suppress it and you try to destroy that mind, well then you also destroy anything that comes out of it and anything that comes around it. That's what happened in our situation today. We want the world to know.

A jury later found Amin and Calkins guilty of aggravated assault and kidnapping and sentenced them to additional life terms in prison. However, the story has an unusual twist. After Amin and Calkins received their sentences, new information showed one of the prison counselors may have helped plan and stage the kidnapping. Even so, District Court Judge Larry Lehman denied a motion for a new hearing in May 1992.

US 30/287
Laramie—Walcott
80 miles

Rock River

Confusion surrounds the origin of Rock River. In the late 1860s Rock Creek Stage Station began operating upstream from the present town; that post became Arlington. The Union Pacific also had a Rock Creek Station, which it abandoned in 1901. At that time the railroad moved the community downstream on Rock Creek and renamed it Rock River. The railroad built large concrete snow sheds over the railroad tracks near Rock River after a 1916 blizzard tied up overland trains for more than a week.

A couple of cowboys excavated a cellar at the site of the UP Rock Creek Station that year and found a treasure, unearthing several thousand dollars in old gold coins stored in glass jars. William Taylor, who once owned the property, claimed the money, and the Wyoming Supreme Court agreed with his petition. Locals speculated that the coins represented loot from a stagecoach robbery or that they were hidden by a German innkeeper who once lived on the place and disappeared after setting out to visit Germany.

One robbery did take place near Rock Creek involving a Union Pacific train. Wilcox Station stood about six miles west of Rock Creek. There, on June 2, 1899, two pistol-packing men flagged down the westbound train, ordered the engineer to cross the bridge beyond Wilcox, then blew the bridge up. Using a plan they might have borrowed from Butch Cassidy and another well-known Wyoming outlaw, "Flat Nose" George Curry, they forced the engineer to run the train two miles farther west before they looted the express cars. They then grabbed horses they'd staked earlier and rode north with $60,000 in unsigned bank notes.

Como Bluff, a Dinosaur Graveyard

Northwest of Rock River and north of US 30, Como Bluff extends from east to west. This bluff became the site of significant paleontological research in the 1870s. O. C. Marsh, the first professor of paleontology in the United States, came to Wyoming and made an unusual discovery.

During the Cretaceous and Jurassic periods, from 70 to 180 million years ago, the Laramie plain had a torrid-zone climate and was a flat, marshy sea coast. A wide variety of dinosaurs lived in the region. At some point in the past, a great upheaval took place, pushing ancient strata into the Sundance and Morrison geological formations and laying them open to scientific investigation.

During his visit to Wyoming in 1877, Marsh found perfect fossil specimens of the largest land-dwelling creatures ever known. Como Bluff yielded the first major discovery of dinosaur remains in the world, and skeletons recovered here reside in the Peabody Museum at Yale, the National Museum of the Smithsonian Institution in Washington, D.C., and the American Museum of Natural History in New York.

Owners of this cabin claim it is the oldest building in the world because it is made from fossilized dinosaur bones quarried from the nearby Como Bluff, where paleontological studies found a wide array of early animals.

Other scientists from esteemed educational institutions, including the Philadelphia Academy of Sciences, Harvard College, the Carnegie Museum in Pittsburgh, the University of Wyoming, the Royal Ontario Museum in Toronto, and the National Museum of Canada in Ottawa, searched for specimens at Como Bluff. Not all the remains found were dinosaurs—some were mammals. More than a century after Marsh excavated at Como Bluff, Casper geologist John Albanese said:

> Marsh's legacy is still bearing fruit. A recent examination of his original collection from Como Bluff, stored for decades in the basement of the Peabody Museum, revealed the presence of some mammal bones. Next to a locale in Wales, these are the oldest mammal remains yet found on earth. These mammals were tiny creatures, no larger than a small mouse.

In all, scientists removed fourteen complete dinosaur skeletons from Como Bluff. The two-house town includes a cabin built of dinosaur bones. Its owners say it is the oldest house in the world, with building materials millions of years old.

Medicine Bow

In 1885 Owen Wister visited Wyoming and Medicine Bow for the first time. The description of the town he wrote in his journal on July 19, 1885, is almost identical to a passage from *The Virginian*, the classic Western he wrote in 1902. The journal entry said:

> This place is called a town. "Town" will do very well until the language stretches itself and takes in a new word that fits. Medicine Bow, Wyoming, consists of 1 Depot house and baggage room, 1 Coal shooter, 1 water tank, 1 Store, 2 Eating houses, 1 Billiard hall, 6 Shanties, 8 Gents and Ladies Walks, 2 Tool houses, 1 Feed Stable, 5 Too late for classification, 29 Buildings in all.

The town is little bigger now. It has a new school for its 100 or so students, a convenience store and gas station, a post office, a motel with a restaurant and bar, a museum in the abandoned Union Pacific Railroad depot, and the Virginian Hotel, which triples as a bar and cafe.

Medicine Bow also has a newspaper, the *Medicine Bow Post*, started in 1977 by the intrepid David Roberts during a coal- and uranium-mining boom. Roberts cranked out a winning journalistic effort for a decade, exchanged places with a *Washington Post* reporter for a couple of weeks, then donated the paper to the University of Wyoming to train community journalists.

Let the Wind Blow

"Strewn there by the wind" is how Wister described Medicine Bow. The wind blows here most of the time as it comes through the funnel formed by Elk Mountain and the Hanna Basin uplift. During the energy crisis of the

"As if strewn there by the wind . . ." is how novelist Owen Wister described Medicine Bow when he first saw the town. Today a sign near the town's museum reminds people of the Virginian's connection to Medicine Bow.

1970s, Americans started exploring alternative energy sources, and Wyoming's wind seemed a likely candidate. The U.S. Department of Energy, in conjunction with the National Aeronautics and Space Administration and U.S. Bureau of Reclamation, undertook a multimillion-dollar project that involved construction of two massive wind turbines.

Bureau of Reclamation scientists first verified Medicine Bow's windy reputation—the average wind speed is twenty miles per hour. Then, using aerial photographs and data gathered by the University of Wyoming, they identified five sites as potential locations for wind generators. By 1977 instruments had gathered sufficient data, and a year later the first wind turbine was up and running at a site five miles south of Medicine Bow. By 1982 there were two— a Boeing MOD-2 and a Hamilton Standard WTS-4, the world's most powerful turbine.

It was a long way to the top of the Hamilton Standard. An elevator covered part of the distance, but the final ascent required a hand-over-hand climb up a steel rung ladder. At the summit the metal floor, slick with oil, pitched like a ship upon a sea as waves of wind blew the turbine from side to side, even on a seemingly still day. Only project officials dared go to the top when the wind was really howling.

The U. S. Bureau of Reclamation built the $10.8 million Hamilton Standard WTS-4 wind turbine as part of a wind energy study in the 1980s, but the huge turbine (the rotor is 257 feet) sold for the salvage price of $50,000 to a project engineer when the Bureau of Reclamation and the Department of Energy abandoned the project. The engineer repaired the turbine and set it spinning again, but high winds in 1994 damaged the rotor, leaving it inoperable.

Both turbines generated electricity for several years, but then the federal government withdrew funding, and structural problems led to abandonment of the project. In early September 1987 a dynamite charge brought down the $4 million Boeing MOD-2. The government also wanted to get rid of the $10.8 million Hamilton Standard. When no other governmental agency or the University of Wyoming wanted the turbine, it went out for public bid. Bill Young, a former Bureau of Reclamation project engineer, bought the turbine for $50,000.

The government had estimated it would cost more than $1 million to repair the turbine, but Young did it for less than $100,000. By Christmas 1992, Young had his turbine back in working order, and the huge, 257-foot rotor blades again turned in the wind, generating power for Young to sell to the Western Area Power Administration. But on January 14, 1994, the wind bent the blades into the turbine and wrecked the machine. Debris flew hundreds of feet into the air.

In early 1995 Young's huge turbine remained inoperable, but a new wind-power project appeared likely to start in the windy area between Arlington and Hanna. Kenetech proposed the project in cooperation with Bonneville Power Administration and Pacific Power & Light Company. Plans call for 200 wind turbines initially and 1,320 turbines if full development occurs.

Shirley Basin

A half hour's drive north of Medicine Bow on Wyoming 487 will bring you to Shirley Basin. If you take the drive, you probably won't see much traffic. This country seems almost abandoned, with only a few isolated ranches dotting the landscape. That wasn't always the case. During the 1970s hundreds of people lived at Shirley Basin, a company town north of Medicine Bow. Uranium mining sustained the community, but over time the market declined, production ceased, and, in 1992, the town closed. Officials abandoned the local school and sold the buildings and the land. By then almost everything and everyone else had already vacated the site.

Not far from Shirley Basin the Wyoming Game and Fish Department reintroduced to the wild the first captive-bred and -raised black-footed ferrets. A bevy of newsmen and game managers wearing surgical masks watched as the rare animals ran free in the fall of 1992. The next spring ferret watchers rejoiced when they spotted the first ferret kits born in the wild in more than a decade.

Hanna

Named for UP Railroad executive, financier, and politician Mark Hanna, this coal-mining center started as a stage station in 1886. With the demise of Carbon, a few miles south (see page 242), it became a major point on the Union Pacific Railroad. Mining has always driven this town's fortunes; some of the nation's best low-sulphur, high-heat-content coal underlies the entire Hanna Basin. Mining started as early as 1880 but suffered major setbacks in 1903 and 1908 when underground explosions claimed hundreds of lives.

The first major tragedy struck in late June 1903 when a blast ripped through the coal mines, killing 171 miners. The *Laramie Boomerang* reported three great cave-ins, and an underground fire hindered rescue attempts and even delayed the effort to remove bodies. Newspapers reported on recovery attempts for weeks; one dispatch in the *Denver News* said:

> Hanna, Wyo., July 2—The most conspicuous hero of the catastrophe is a black man—Will Christian. Of all the men in the mine he seems to have retained his wits best and to him three other men can give thanks for their lives. Christian and three companions were working in a room of the seventeenth entry when the explosion came, and were blown violently along. Christian alone maintained his feet. After the blast passed his fellow workmen were panic stricken and rushed blindly about in the dark. Christian quieted them with encouraging words, and in a few minutes cast light on the situation with a crude safety lamp improvised from a piece of canvas and an ordinary helmet lamp. When the light shone in the darkness two other men joined the group. Telling the crowd to follow him, Christian set out along the entry. One man did not come and

another Finn, Isaac, after going a short distance called that he might as well die then and casting himself into a deep pool, perished miserably. Christian, Andro Hoe, Frank Massia and Robert Carlin, wandered from room to room for some time . . . and then despairing sat down . . . and gradually overcome by gas [they] dropped asleep. Christian was the first to awaken and leaving his companions stupefied, started out again. Within a short distance he found a door . . . culminating at the surface in a forty-five-foot air shaft. . . . Crawling on their hands and knees for the greater part of the distance, they at length reached the air shaft and climbed to the free, pure air.

Although other disasters left hundreds of miners buried permanently in the coal seams, coal mining continued at Hanna. In the 1970s a boom swelled the town as energy-hungry America turned to domestic reserves for its supply. The Hanna mines utilized both open-pit and underground methods, and the region became the leading coal-producing section of the state. Hundreds of miners flocked to the area, where they built homes or hauled modular housing in on their own undercarriages. Hundreds more commuted from Medicine Bow, Saratoga, Encampment, Rawlins, and even Laramie.

Local governments couldn't build fast enough. By the time a new school for Medicine Bow opened its doors, the boom had gone bust, and a facility adequate for 400 students served only about 100. The miners moved to the next strike—which might have been the Powder River Basin mines near Gillette or the gold operations in Elko, Nevada—and the houses rolled out of town on their wheels, following their owners in their quest for wealth.

Wyoming 130 and 230
Walcott—Encampment
40 miles

Midway between Walcott Junction and Saratoga, Wyoming 130 crosses the Overland Trail. Two-track hunting and ranch roads mark the ruts in the sagebrush. West of the highway the trail meets the North Platte River at Bennett's Ferry, where many emigrants camped for days waiting their turn to cross the stream. Cliffs above the river bear reminders of the emigrants, who carved their names on the rock much as the Oregon Trail travelers did at Register Cliff, Independence Rock, and Names Hill.

The crossing is also the location of a pioneer cemetery for those who lost their lives while attempting to traverse the Platte or in Indian raids. A stairway of sorts leads to the top of the cliff, where, area residents believe, emigrants posted lookouts for Indians.

Saratoga

Although native Americans did attack emigrants and stagecoaches on the Overland Trail, they considered the area south of the trail neutral ground. Where Saratoga now sits, the Indians soaked in mineral hot springs. Early inhabitants obtained materials for stone tools near here, and local legend has it that the Indians attempted to effect a cure for smallpox in 1874 by soaking stricken individuals in the hot springs, then immersing them in the cold waters of the North Platte. The story goes that the "cure" often proved fatal, and for many years the tribes refused to visit the springs.

The State of Wyoming eventually gained control of the Saratoga hot springs and built a free mineral pool. Since 1982 the town of Saratoga has managed the pool, and local residents still soak in the hot water and jump into the cold river. This action is particularly exhilarating during the winter, when steam from the hot mineral pool obscures the river, making it seem as if it's part of an impressionist painting.

The first permanent community at the hot springs took the name Warm Springs, but in 1884 residents called that a "so-so name" and changed it to Saratoga after the resort community of Saratoga Springs, New York. An upscale population comprising prominent cattlemen set the social tone for the town, and a decade later the elegant Hotel Wolf opened at the corner of First and Bridge streets. It remains in business a century later, still sporting Victorian charm.

A Fish Story

From 1850 to 1870 trappers said the North Platte River and its tributaries had no game fish. William Turnbull, a pioneer in the area, confirmed that situation. He spent his younger days as a hunter, furnishing deer and antelope meat for Fort Fred Steele. Occasionally, in order to vary the diet, Turnbull tried to catch a mess of fish, but there were none in the river.

In the 1880s, however, residents at Warm Springs discovered that the river did have game fish—thousands of them. In fact, the water was simply alive with them. For a long time the sudden appearance of fish remained a mystery. Then a man drifted into the area and told the following tale, as chronicled by Saratoga newspaper publisher Robert D. Martin, in an unpublished manuscript.

The man's story went this way: In 1871 or 1872 a westbound Union Pacific express train was held up at Fort Fred Steele because of a wreck or some other obstruction of the line farther west. As part of its express cargo, the train carried a large shipment of small trout stored in big cans. The fish were being sent from an eastern fish hatchery to some western destination. After the train sat idle for many hours, the fish began dying in the cans. Not knowing how long the train might be stalled there and not wanting thousands of dead fish on their hands, the crew backed the train a short distance onto the bridge

Saratoga fish fry. —Historical Reproductions by Perue

over the North Platte and dumped all the fish into the river. No one knew about it except the train crews.

The brook and rainbow trout had the entire channel to themselves, with no settlements, no ranches, and nothing to disturb them in a thirty-mile stretch upstream from Fort Steele. The fish multiplied and grew until the 1890s, Martin said, when fishermen landed rainbow trout weighing between ten and thirteen pounds and brook trout averaging five to six pounds. With no limit imposed, it was not unusual for an angler to catch 100 trout in a day, and many did. At the Saratoga Railroad Day Celebration and Fish Fry in August 1907, local anglers took to the river and really "did their stuff," bringing in 3,100 trout to feed the visitors. The supply of fish in the river seemed inexhaustible, and they were taken by the thousands during a twenty-year period—roughly from 1890 to 1910.

Martin reported that a fisherman from the East coined the slogan, "Saratoga, Where the Trout Leap in Main Street"—which was no exaggeration. Trout were just about as plentiful within the town limits as they were in the river outside of town. In its report of the 1907 celebration, the *Saratoga Sun* said: "Many of our visitors found it of interest to stand on the bridge and watch and try to count the big trout that were visible in the clear water of the river— above, below and under the bridge. Of course they couldn't get a count on them, but it was estimated that there were more than 300 in sight."

About 1910, the effects of no-limit fishing started becoming apparent, but the real disaster, according to Martin, happened when the state stocked brown trout in the river. National fish hatchery workers said the species shouldn't be mixed, but the state put them in anyway, and the rainbow fishing rapidly deteriorated. By 1970, about a century after the first trout swam freely in the North Platte, the river had again become a prime fishery, one of the state's "blue ribbon" trout streams. Floating and fishing are major river pastimes for locals and tourists every summer.

Encampment

As early as 1834, some trappers regularly worked the streams on both the Atlantic and Pacific drainages of the Sierra Madres, gathering pelts for the Rocky Mountain and American Fur Companies. They held a rendezvous at the upper end of the North Platte Valley and called the area at the foot of the Sierra Madres Camp le Grand, which later became Grand Encampment.

After the mountain fur trade dwindled to a close in the early 1840s, the Grand Encampment Valley saw little use. Colorado Utes ranged into the area, and one branch of the Cherokee Trail brought travelers through on their way to California during the 1849 gold rush. Cherokee followed the trail late into the 1800s, carving travois ruts still clearly visible in many locations.

The main branch of the Cherokee Trail followed the same general route as the Overland Trail, but one southern fork turned west near Fort Collins, Colorado, followed the Cache La Poudre River into North Park, and then edged the flank of the Sierra Madres over the North Platte River, spanning various

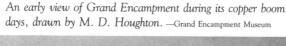

An early view of Grand Encampment during its copper boom days, drawn by M. D. Houghton. —Grand Encampment Museum

creeks—Big, Bear, Beaver, Antelope, and Indian—before crossing the Grand Encampment River just north of the present-day town of Riverside. Then the trail headed toward Three Peaks, crossing Cow and Calf creeks, rounding the peaks, and joining the main branch of the Cherokee Trail southwest of Rawlins.

The first permanent white settlers moved into the Grand Encampment Valley in the 1870s. Burly men worked in mountain logging camps cutting ties for the Union Pacific Railroad. About the same time ranchers arrived, driving Texas longhorns and other cattle breeds to the high mountain lands.

The Tomahawk, Home of Swan

Swan was little more than a wide spot in the road. Though seemingly named for a graceful bird, the town actually honored one of the largest landholding families in southeastern Wyoming before the turn of the century. Swan sat just west of the Encampment River and about a mile north of Riverside. Postal officials established the Swan post office June 27, 1881, on the Tomahawk Ranch, owned by four brothers: Thomas, Lewis, William, and Obadiah Swan. They were cousins of William F., Alex, and Black Tom Swan, who owned the huge Swan Land and Cattle Company and the local Ell 7, which extended from Chugwater to near Baggs (see page 152).

After fighting in the Civil War, the brothers came to Cheyenne and entered the cattle business. By 1882 they had trailed their first herd of longhorns into the Encampment Valley, where they ran up to 10,000 head of cattle until 1886. The weather eventually took its toll, and they griped that "the only thing that the country was good for was buffalo and Indians and they both knew enough to leave in the winter." The Swans sold their land and went to Cheyenne.

The Grand Encampment Copper District

The mining boom at Grand Encampment started in 1897, when sheep-herder Ed Haggarty found copper several miles west of town, on the west side of the Continental Divide. Hordes of miners and speculators flocked to the area, raising a town (Grand Encampment) on the hillside above Doggett (which later became Riverside). Hundreds of mine shafts went down into the rocky soil.

Haggarty's find became the richest of them all. He dubbed it the Rudefeha for the first letters of the mining venture's backers—Rumsey, Deal, Ferris, and Haggarty. Before long, only George Ferris and Haggarty remained as active partners, so the mine was best known as the Ferris-Haggarty.

In 1899 Haggarty sold his initial interest in the mine for $30,000 to Ferris, a prominent Rawlins sheepman who died later that year at Snowslide Hill when a team of horses ran away with the wagon in which he was riding. In a 1972 history of the Grand Encampment mining district for the Wyoming Recreation Commission, Mark Junge wrote:

The ownership of the mine was not completely destroyed, however, because by that time another important individual—Willis George Emerson—had taken an active interest in the Ferris-Haggarty property. With Haggarty, Ferris, a man named Bernard McCaffrey and himself as principals, Emerson had organized the Ferris-Haggarty Copper Mining Company in January 1899. The promotion of the Ferris-Haggarty company by Emerson is probably one reason why there was soon a rush to the Grand Encampment region.

Emerson enticed journalist Grant Jones to Grand Encampment. Jones was born in 1870 in Kentucky and attended high school in Wichita, Kansas. His family, reported to be well-to-do, later settled in Chicago, and in 1893 Jones enrolled in Northwestern University in Evanston, Illinois, as a special student in the College of Liberal Arts. He then wrote for both the *Chicago Daily Mail* and the *Chicago Times-Herald* before heading west and eventually landing in Grand Encampment.

In Wyoming, Jones put his prolific pen to work. Within a week he had half a column on Grand Encampment in newspapers throughout the country. His stories appeared in the *New York Herald*, *New York Sun*, *Philadelphia North American*, and *Atlanta Constitution*, as well as papers in Cleveland, Cincinnati, Pittsburgh, Chicago, Kansas City, Omaha, Denver, and Colorado Springs. "I have often been assured, by people in this country, that those first published articles on Grand Encampment were the means of bringing several hundred active workers to Wyoming," Jones wrote in his own newspaper, the *Dillon Doublejack*, started in 1902.

Peryam Roadhouse

The route between Riverside and the Colorado state line on Wyoming 230 passes by the oldest ranches in the Encampment Valley. William T. and Alice R. Peryam, along with two small children, arrived from Colorado in 1879 to claim land along the Encampment River. Some say they were the third family—after the Amos Baggott and Guy Nichols families—to settle the upper valley.

Two things happened in the mid-1890s that changed life forever for the area near Peryam's house. In the fall of 1896 Ben Culleton rode for cattle on Purgatory Gulch and took a break. He sat on an outcropping of quartz rock and found gold. Less than a year later, sheepherder Ed Haggarty struck copper in the nearby mountains. The boom was on, and the Peryams, living on the road by the river ford, bore the brunt of the flood of visitors. Before long Rawlins friends prevailed upon them to hang out a shingle and charge 35 cents for a meal. They added cots, putting them everyplace but in the chicken coop, and eventually moved in some houses from other ranches and rented them out.

In 1899 George Doane of the Doane-Rambler mine at Battle Lake sold his holdings to the owners of the Ferris-Haggarty copper mine and moved in next to the Peryams. A former contractor and builder from Boston, former manager of Union Pacific stores at Carbon, and old Peryam family friend, Doane convinced William and Alice to build a road ranch plastered inside and finished with wainscoting. Construction started in 1899 and concluded a year later. In 1901 Peryam added a toll bridge over the Encampment River, charging a 25 cents for a team and wagon and 10 cents for a single rider.

The road ranch became a resounding success, and many of the prominent mining men of early days headquartered there. The white two-story house had green trim and nine upstairs bedrooms. The downstairs contained a large kitchen, a parlor, a huge dining room that ran the length of the house, a storeroom, a library, and the master bedroom. Guests walked on oak floors, climbed an oak staircase, and enjoyed cool evenings on a wide, covered porch. The outbuildings consisted of the Peryam's original log cabin (which served as a garage, bunkhouse, and washhouse), additional bunkhouse rooms, a root cellar, a granary, a chicken house, and livestock barns. Today, huge old cottonwood trees surround the Peryam roadhouse as it sits by the river, no longer in use.

Copper Smelter

By 1902 a smelter reduction works stood on the hillside above the Encampment River. The plant, operated by the North American Copper Company, transformed copper ore into consumable metal. The company's payroll soon rose to about $40,000 a month, and Grand Encampment became the principal commercial center of the mining district. The *Saratoga Sun* reported, "Optimistic opinions were voiced predicting that Encampment would be the new 'Pittsburgh of the West,' or a second Denver, and the hope was even expressed that the town would serve as the location of the new Wyoming State Capital."

Businesses opened almost daily in the town of 1,000 residents. Encampment had a gravity-based water system, an electric plant, a school, and two churches. Said the *Sun*, "The town is surrounded by a rich agricultural district that is rapidly filing up on one hand with farmers and a mineral district surrounding and reaching out like the spokes of a wagon wheel from the hub."

That district included towns at Elwood, Copperton, Rambler, Battle, and Dillon. All were thriving in 1903, the year Willis George Emerson promoted construction of a sixteen-mile-long aerial tramway from the Ferris-Haggarty mine to the Grand Encampment smelter. It was the longest aerial tramway in the world at that time and an unprecedented engineering feat. The tramway had 270 towers with 840 buckets that could hold 700 pounds of ore swinging from the heavy cables.

Fires at the smelter, delays in getting a railroad line to the community, and falling copper prices stalled the boom, and in 1908 the copper bubble started to deflate. By 1913 the smelter had completely shut down, and the population of Grand Encampment fell by half.

Shannon Vyvey, 3, works on the laundry at the Grand Encampment Museum living history display Memorial Day weekend, 1993.

Today the "Grand" has been dropped due to postal regulations, and Encampment has about 400 residents and, some say, a similar number of dogs. Principal industries center on ranching and timbering. Encampment has been officially designated an Endangered Community by the U.S. Association of County Governments. Remnants of the copper-mining era and other periods of local history are preserved at the Grand Encampment museum, which includes a pioneer town of more than a dozen authentic buildings. These include a one-room schoolhouse, a stage station, a tie-hack cabin, and a two-story outhouse of the kind needed in high mountain country, where winter snows pile incredibly deep.

Encampment—Baggs

51 miles

One of Wyoming's most spectacular mountain roads leads from Encampment through the historic copper district and the Medicine Bow National Forest to the Little Snake River Valley and the town of Baggs. The first primitive road served mining camps by 1898, and in the 1920s the U.S. Bureau of Public Roads constructed a better route over the mountain. Civilian Conservation Corps workers pioneered the sixty-mile route in the 1930s, and workers paved it through the Medicine Bow National Forest during the 1990s.

The highway crosses the Continental Divide at Battle Pass, near the townsite of Battle and the mountain lake where, according to a story of doubtful veracity, Thomas Edison conceived the idea for the filament in the incandescent light bulb. Edison, who came to the area as a member of the Henry Draper Astronomical Expedition to witness a solar eclipse in 1878, hunted in the

Battle Lake, in the Sierra Madres, where Thomas Edison fished in 1878.

area and fished at Battle Lake. As he sat near the lake and stripped the tough, pliable strands of bamboo from a fishing rod, the story goes, he got the idea for the filament. He later used bamboo in his first experimental lamps.

Dillon

About five miles west of the Continental Divide, Wyoming 70 crosses Haggarty Creek, near which the town of Copperton stood during the mining boom. Upstream about two miles, on a rough forest road, lie the remains of Dillon. This settlement sprang up before 1900 when owners of the Ferris-Haggarty mine declared that no more booze could be sold at Rudefeha, a mile farther upstream. Dillon became a wild camp with about 250 residents, two well-stocked general stores, two meat markets, and good restaurants, as well as several saloons. It's commonly accepted that the town was named for Malachi Dillon, the boardinghouse owner who, according to local legend, threw meals in for nothing if customers patronized his bar.

At Dillon's boardinghouse on October 16, 1902, Grant Jones "told the boys that I was going to publish a newspaper here." His goals were twofold:

> I hope to bring men and money into Wyoming to develop our vast and latent resources and to help build up our state to a commercial importance commensurate with its natural greatness. I hope to be able to tell of some of the sacrifices and struggles—of some of the romances—in the lives of those who have carved their ways in awful singleness through the wilderness of Wyoming, as path-finders and history makers.

The optimistic Jones published 7,000 copies of the first issue, with about 4,500 distributed throughout the country. The papers crossed the Continental Divide on sleds dragged over snow averaging more than four feet in depth during winter, with drifts some twenty feet deep. Though he sent his paper all over the United States, it was aimed primarily at the hardworking miners in the region. He wrote in the premiere issue:

> To the most distinctly unique brotherhood in the world I herewith dedicate the *Dillon Doublejack*. To the brotherhood whose members see the word "welcome" on fewer doormats, and know more about hospitality, travel over more miles of land and see fewer railroad tracks, eat more bacon and see fewer hogs, drink more milk, condensed, and see fewer cows, worship nature more and see fewer churches, regard women with more chivalry and see fewer of them, judge men better and wear fewer starched shirts, undergo more disappointments and retain more hope— than any other class of men in the whole wide world—to the brotherhood of quartz, and placer prospectors and miners—I dedicate the *Dillon Doublejack*.

Jones made all the miners special correspondents and printed their stories. "The plain truth shall be entirely sufficient," he announced, "and I shall be grateful to those who will furnish this paper with accurate information pertaining to the assured and productive resources of this state." He added that the *Doublejack* would be of special interest to "bad men who have roamed and to good men who have learned to chew tobacco."

Jones only edited the *Doublejack* for six months before he died on June 19, 1903, at a cabin in Battle, most likely from the deadly combination of exposure, alcohol, and morphine.

Little Snake River Valley

West of the Medicine Bow National Forest, Wyoming 70 crosses the low country of the Little Snake River. A few miles from the forest boundary, a country road provides access to ranches, to Colorado, and the site where some of the first white men in the region were attacked by Indians. In 1841 American Fur Company trappers Henry Fraeb and Jim Baker, along with several companions, had to defend themselves against a party of Utes near the confluence of Battle Creek and the Little Snake River. Fraeb and several other trappers died. The incident gave the creek, Battle Mountain, and many other local features their names.

Baker remained in the Little Snake River Valley and built a three-level log blockhouse in 1873, where he settled with his two Indian wives. He adopted certain Indian tribal customs—in particular, having his wives tend his trapline on the Little Snake River. He liked to sit and smoke in the clearing before his blockhouse while his wives combed and curled his flowing hair and beard. He died in 1898 and is buried near Savery. In 1917 officials moved Baker's cabin to Cheyenne, but Savery-area residents retrieved it in the 1970s. It is now part of the Little Snake River Valley Museum at Savery.

The outlaw Butch Cassidy also spent much time in this isolated valley. It worked well as a hideout for his wild bunch, whose members held up Union Pacific trains. Cassidy, considered a "gentleman outlaw," claimed never to have killed anyone during his holdups. Once, returning from Winnemucca, Nevada, with a $35,000 haul, Butch and his cohorts—often called the "Hole-in-the-Wall Gang" or the "wild bunch"—rode into Baggs, throwing money and bullets about with abandon.

When absent from their headquarters—which was near Powder Mountain, forty miles west of Baggs—the gang kept its swift, sturdy horses under guard and at the ready, its arms and ammunition stacked in military fashion. Cassidy and his sidekick, Harry Longabaugh, the "Sundance Kid," eventually escaped to South America, where they continued to rob trains and banks. Whether they met their maker in Bolivia or returned to Wyoming is a question that has never been conclusively answered.

A Dam for the Little Snake

When Cheyenne began constructing stage two of its water-delivery system in the 1980s (see page 229), residents of Little Snake River were promised that the state would provide in-basin storage to help meet their own irrigation and municipal needs. After studying a number of alternatives, the state finally settled on development of Sandstone Dam, north of Savery.

Project proponents such as State Representative George Salisbury and his son-in-law, Pat O'Toole—who earned the nickname H$_2$O O'Toole because of his unfailing support of Wyoming's water development projects—said the Sandstone Project would satisfy the commitment lawmakers had made to the valley population. But residents such as Joyce Saer and John Boyer, whose family-ranching operation would be significantly changed if a dam is placed in their backyard, fought Sandstone, saying that geologic conditions make it unsafe. As of this writing, the dam remains unbuilt and the debate continues.

I-80
Rawlins—Evanston
208 miles

Many drivers say the most boring stretch of highway in Wyoming is I-80 between Rawlins and Evanston. The route runs parallel to and often in sight of the Union Pacific Railroad, which gave the area towns their start. It lies north of the Overland Trail from Rawlins to Point of Rocks, then runs south of the trail to Lyman.

This is Wyoming's most arid land. Known as the Red Desert, sometimes the Little Colorado Desert, it receives less than ten inches of rain annually. The region is home to the world's largest herd of pronghorn antelope and thousands of head of sheep. The Continental Divide cuts through the state here. It splits at a location about fifteen miles southwest of Rawlins. One fork loops north to the Seminoe Mountains, then west along the Green Mountains and Antelope Hills. The other fork heads west on a line parallel to I-80, which it crosses just east of Table Rock, then angles west and north. The two branches rejoin just south of South Pass. The circular depression formed by that splitting of the divide, known as Great Divide Basin, constitutes the largest portion of the Red Desert.

Checkerboard Range

The checkerboard land pattern created by the federal government's concessions to the Union Pacific railroad (see pages 212 and 250) facilitated mineral development in southern Wyoming and made it possible for ranchers to control thousands of acres of rangeland while owning only half of the ground. However, few claimed homesteads on the public lands west of Rawlins. To do so was completely impractical; the arid soil produced too little forage for ani-

Wild horses race across Bureau of Land Management lands near Adobe Town in south central Wyoming in May 1994.

mals. When range managers say the land is poor, they do not blame this condition on overgrazing and excess use. The soil simply lacks nutrients, and there is not enough water. Under existing natural circumstances it can never be good range.

Driving west from Rawlins on I-80, the first town of any consequence is Wamsutter, originally called Washakie but later renamed to honor a UP bridge builder. A sea once covered this area, leaving behind the many *turritella* agates (fossilized turtle shells) found in the region. About fifteen miles south of town is the site of the Overland Trail's Barrel Springs Station. The spring, located in a vast expanse of sagebrush and greasewood, yielded early travelers crystal-clear, almost ice-cold water that was very different from the usual vile-tasting supply of the Bitter Creek country. The spring got its name when the station keeper knocked the ends out of a 50-gallon whiskey barrel and set it in the ground nearby.

The towns west of Wamsutter, with picturesque names such as Red Desert, Table Rock, Bitter Creek, Point of Rocks, and Superior, have their own engaging stories. Red Desert started as a UP siding but attracted attention when Rawlins photographer Verne Wood captured on film a classic picture of a palomino stallion named Desert Dust.

Hundreds of wild horses—mostly descendants of those that escaped from emigrants, ranchers, and the like—still race through this country, ranging from the Colorado border to the Lander Valley. Since the Wild Horse and Burro

Act became law in 1971, some 141,762 animals have been removed from public lands in Colorado, Oregon, California, New Mexico, Idaho, Montana, Utah, and Wyoming. Of that total, 122,627 have been adopted. The U.S. Bureau of Land Management has set a target of allowing only 30,000 wild horses on the range by the year 2000.

The agency captures between 800 and 1,000 horses a year, using helicopters and cowboys on horseback to drive the animals into cleverly set traps. Roundups begin before dawn, with cowboys riding to predesignated sites while a helicopter flies into the sunrise looking for the scattered herds. The pilot twists and turns, guiding the horses toward the hidden cowboys, who funnel them down draws and coulees into jute and metal corrals. The old mares and stallions race across the sagebrush hillsides trying to outmaneuver the machine in the air but ultimately find themselves behind bars.

After letting the wild horses settle, the cowboys tie their own mounts and transfer the wild animals to stock trucks for transportation to adoption centers, including one in Rock Springs. There, people can view the wild horses and take one home. Not all animals are kept for adoption; older mares and stallions return to their native range or are shipped to market. Only the younger ones are included in the giveaway program.

Pulpit Rock Hoax

Table Rock initially went by the name Pulpit Rock after Brigham Young delivered a sermon to some of his Mormon followers in 1847. In 1876 two old prospectors salted the mesa with precious stones they'd obtained in Holland. They blindfolded potential investors and brought them to "Diamond Mesa," where they removed the eyeshades so to reveal the great discovery. The miners fooled such men as Horace Greeley, the Rothschilds, and Louis Tiffany, raising more than $500,000 for a promotion company. A geological survey party cook blew the lid off the fraud when he kicked up an ant hill that yielded a diamond and found traces of a lapidary tool.

One report on the scandal said, "This rock has produced four distinct types of diamonds, oriental rubies, garnets, spinels, sapphires, emeralds and amethysts, an association [that is] impossible in nature."

Point of Rocks

There isn't much at Point of Rocks to suggest the significant role it played in Wyoming during the 1860s. It was originally a Pony Express relay station, then served as the gateway to South Pass City during the gold rush that began in 1867 (see page 191), as miners arriving via the Union Pacific or Overland Stage got off at Point of Rocks. Most of the buildings were of adobe. Point of Rocks eventually became an important shipping point for western stockmen wanting to send sheep and cattle to markets in Omaha or Chicago.

Union Pacific Coal Mine No. 16. —Wyoming State Museum

Rock Springs

Rock Springs got its start at a different location from its current one. It originally sat just west of Killpecker Creek (which got its name when soldiers drank the water and it had a distinct effect) at the site of Blair's stockade and the old Rock Spring, for which the city is named. In 1861 a Pony Express rider discovered the spring flowing out of rock when Indians forced him from his regular route. The Overland Trail passed nearby, and a regular stage station operated there. In 1866 Archie and Duncan Blair built a stone cabin, trading post, and stockade, and before long the site became Blairtown.

According to popular legend, Jim Bridger first discovered the coal deposits near Blairtown. He reportedly told the French Canadian who then operated the Rock Springs Stage Station, but that unfortunate person died in an Indian fight near Boar's Tusk about twenty-five miles northeast of Rock Springs; the Blair brothers then took over the stage station and learned of the coal vein.

Recognizing its value, they pondered ways to develop the coal. Once the Union Pacific Railroad moved through the area in 1867–68, they started mining coal and shipping it from a station at Blairtown. Before long, however, the mining operation became a losing proposition. Because the UP got land in exchange for building the line, it soon located its own coal deposits. When the company began developing mines—first at Carbon and later near Rock Springs and Evanston—it put the squeeze on independent operators such as the Blairs by charging high freight rates. That made the independent coal almost twice as costly as the UP product and effectively created a monopoly for the railroad mines.

Company mine production soared from a combined total of 7,000 tons at Carbon, Rock Springs, and Evanston during 1868 to 50,000 tons the next year and 200,000 tons in 1875. Rock Springs soon became the biggest coal producer west of the Missouri. Its mines supplied much of the coal that powered UP trains and provided a surplus available for use by other railroads.

In the early 1900s miners dug coal from beneath their homes at Rock Springs, and the high school stadium sat on the leveled-off mine dump of the old Union Pacific mine. The extensive mining became a concern for Rock Springs in the 1980s, when buildings throughout the community started to sink into abandoned mine shafts. The U.S. Abandoned Mine Lands program poured millions of dollars into Rock Springs, Hanna, and other Wyoming communities to alleviate problems with coal mine subsidence.

The bald peak south of Rock Springs is known as Burning Hill or Burning Mountain because of a fire in the old coal mine beneath the promontory. Some old-timers said white coal miners in the 1870s broke open a carload of tea consigned to the Chinese and hid it in the old workings. They took the action to discourage the Chinese from continuing to dig coal in Rock Springs. The story goes that when the Chinese almost discovered the tea, the white men set it on fire, and it continued to burn in 1950.

Miners sometimes do dumb things. For example, on July 17, 1891, two drunk men fired their guns into 1,200 kegs of blasting powder and 700 pounds of dynamite near Rock Springs. The building in which the explosives sat quickly disappeared, leaving a great ragged hole. Four men died.

A Racist Conflict

Until 1875, all the miners in Rock Springs were white men. But when mine workers went out on strike that year, the Union Pacific hired Chinese replacements. The UP couldn't allow the mines to cease production; if they did, the trains wouldn't have a fuel supply, which would cripple the company. Strikes are never easy, and the situation in Rock Springs dragged on from 1875 until 1885. Over time it came to resemble a festering abscess that occasionally oozed, always hurt, and eventually broke.

This ugly chapter in Wyoming's history began when miners at Carbon and Rock Springs organized into local chapters of the Miners National Association and demanded better pay in the fall of 1875. The company refused and fired some of the union organizers. The Union Pacific had to continue mining coal in Rock Springs to keep the railroad operating; in the process, it struck a blow at unionism and helped other railroads neutralize threats from unions at their operations. The coal supply in Rock Springs could meet all needs as long as production there continued.

But on November 8, 1875, some 500 miners at Rock Springs and Carbon walked off the job, closing the two largest coal mines on the entire UP system. Amid threats that miners would set the coal mines on fire, the UP asked Governor John Thayer for protection, and he responded by ordering U.S. soldiers to both Carbon and Rock Springs. The troops immediately positioned themselves at the mine entries, coal sheds, engine houses, and other company facilities.

During the next two weeks, the striking miners saw their money and food supplies diminish; then they heard that the UP had 150 Chinese workers on the way to Rock Springs. By November 22, the Chinese had set up camp near the Number Three mine, a quarter of a mile from the center of town. The governor warned the strikers that the new laborers, no matter what their nationality might be, were not to be interfered with and that the entire U.S. Army would enforce the law in Rock Springs if necessary. The *Laramie Daily Sentinel* reported on November 25, 1875:

> The Chinese have commenced their labor and are running out the coal in as good a condition as in days gone by. . . . The Excelsior Coal Company today notified all miners that had been previously employed by them that they could obtain passes until tomorrow at 6:00 p.m. by calling upon Mr. Snow. This move on their part would seem to indicate that they too do not propose to trade any longer with strikers. . . . Much as this step is to be regretted by all interested in the welfare of our young Territory, it may be and probably is the only way to a successful solution of this vexed question at the present time; but we do sincerely hope and anxiously look forward to the day when capital and labor shall find its equilibrium and the Caucasian race be the only laborers employed throughout our borders.

Interior of Union Pacific coal mine. —Wyoming State Museum

Chinese workers returned to Rock Springs to work the coal mines after the 1885 massacre. —Wyoming State Museum

Tensions eased, and within days troops had withdrawn from Rock Springs. Mining operations continued, with the majority of the work done by Chinese, although some of the striking miners returned to the pits. For nearly a decade, coal production continued with few major problems. Then another strike situation developed, and sentiment against Chinese rose to fever pitch. Finally, a labor riot exploded September 2, 1885, between white and Chinese miners. At the time, Chinese miners outnumbered white ones by a two-to-one margin (331 to 150).

A white mob took control of Rock Springs's Chinatown that September day, torching homes and killing between twenty-eight and fifty-one Chinese miners (the commonly accepted number is the smaller of the two). Some of the victims perished in the fighting, and others died of exposure as the whites forced them to seek refuge in the desert country surrounding Rock Springs. One riot witness said the mob set fire to every building and fired thousands of rounds of ammunition "while the burning houses roared in the night."

Governor Francis E. Warren wired President Grover Cleveland for aid, informing him that the white men had attacked the Chinese coal miners and driven them out into the desert hills. The governor's telegram said: "Mob now preventing some five-hundred Chinamen from reaching food or shelter. Sheriff of county powerless to suppress riot and asks for two companies of United States troops. I believe immediate assistance imperative to preserve life and property." Federal troops again marched into Rock Springs to restore order.

This time they remained for thirteen years, until the start of the Spanish-American War.

Although Warren himself opposed the use of Chinese labor, he fulfilled his duty as a state official, telling Cheyenne's *Democratic Leader* on September 17, 1885, "It is not necessary for me to say to those who know me that I have no fondness for Chinese . . . but I do have an interest in protecting, as far as in my power lies, the lives, liberty, and property of every human being in this territory . . . and so long as I am governor, I shall act in the spirit of that idea."

A grand jury convened in Green River but failed to return any indictments in connection with the riot and massacre of September 2, 1885. As in the later invasion on Powder River by the Wyoming Stock Growers Association (see page 304), there was no public hue and cry over the failure to prosecute those responsible for the deaths. Most people just breathed a sigh of relief that the incident could be put behind them.

The breakout at Rock Springs precipitated problems throughout the West between Chinese miners and white workers. The worst violence erupted in the Pacific Northwest, but other problems flared in Idaho, California, and even in Washington, D.C. Anti-Chinese sentiment in Wyoming drove the Asian residents from Laramie, Cheyenne, and other communities. The trouble also spilled across the ocean, as Chinese threatened reprisals against Americans living in China.

Although many Chinese fled Rock Springs, not all left. Those who remained rebuilt Chinatown, where they displayed their 100-foot-long silk dragon frequently. The dragon's frame was made of bows similar to those of a covered sheep wagon. Its head resembled a long-horned Texas steer, with a mouth like that of a mad bull and a forked tongue. The red and green eyes

Chinese New Year's Eve celebration, Rock Springs, Wyoming, 1899. —Wyoming State Museum

bulged. The dragon, which was carried by from thirty to forty men, stopped in front of each Chinese business and made several bows. A band provided music, peppered with the sounds of thousands of firecrackers.

Modern Rock Springs

In 1969 the Pacific Power & Light and Idaho Power & Light companies started planning the construction of Jim Bridger Power Plant, a major electricity-generating facility to be located near Rock Springs. The utilities said the project would take several years, with peak employment of 1,500 workers. Rock Springs officials welcomed the plant, which would bring sorely needed jobs and economic development to their area. After a year or so, the two power companies decided to step up the construction schedule—instead of 1,500 workers, they now needed 3,000. Rock Springs, with no time to prepare for the onslaught of new residents, reeled from the impact. Just when it started to cope with that situation, a major energy boom struck southwestern Wyoming, and the population rocketed again.

Construction of Jim Bridger Power Plant roughly coincided with the decision by the Organization of Petroleum Exporting Countries (OPEC) and other Middle Eastern nations to slap an oil embargo on the United States. As a result, the price of oil supplies quadrupled, and the United States turned to development of domestic reserves. Petroleum companies began eyeing southwestern Wyoming oil and natural gas supplies, and demand dramatically increased for coal.

As it had a century earlier, Rock Springs provided much of the nation's supply. The open-pit Black Butte Mine east of town, located along the route of the Overland Trail, had a nearly four-mile-long conveyor belt connecting the sixty-square-mile coalfield to a railroad spur line. At the rail line, workers filled each 100-car coal train with 10,000 tons of coal within a two-hour period.

The rising demand for coal, increased production of trona (used in the manufacture of glass and as baking soda), and burgeoning oil and natural gas development created a boom the likes of which Wyoming had never before seen. The state held about 30 percent of the nation's uranium ore reserves, ranked fourth in coal reserves, fifth in crude oil reserves, and seventh in gas reserves. It became the hottest spot in the Rocky Mountains for mineral development.

All that development brought in thousands of workers and a slew of problems. Rock Springs grabbed national media attention when stories circulated of corruption at the highest level of city government. Prostitutes openly solicited on K Street. Police tried to gain control but failed, perhaps partly because some of the cops themselves became involved in the criminal activity.

In the lowest period of the city's sinful period, a grand jury sat for more than a year, then disbanded without having handed down a single indictment. Rumors ran rampant though Wyoming that people in the highest levels of local, county, and possibly even state government were involved in criminal activities in southwestern Wyoming. Eventually Ed Cantrell took over as Rock Springs's director of safety. He hired a young Puerto Rican undercover cop, Michael Rosa, and started the effort to regain some control. Rosa did his work well and arrested numerous people for narcotics offenses. Then the grand jury called him to testify.

Immediate speculation arose about why Rosa got the summons. The night before his scheduled appearance, Rosa spent time at the Silver Dollar Bar in Rock Springs. Cantrell and another police officer contacted him there, and the three men drove away in Cantrell's vehicle. Michael Rosa never got to testify—Cantrell shot him that night at short range between the eyes. When he faced murder charges for Rosa's death, Cantrell convinced flamboyant Jackson attorney Gerry Spence to take his case. He claimed self-defense, saying he was forced to shoot when Rosa made a move for his gun. But the prosecution argued that Rosa's gun never left its holster. Spence won the case, and Cantrell was acquitted.

In later years, Cantrell worked as a range detective for ranchers throughout southern Wyoming. Spence continued winning landmark cases for such notorious clients as exiled Philippine president Ferdinand Marcos's wife Imelda, former Miss Wyoming Kimberly Pring, and white supremacist Randy Weaver. But he didn't always defend—sometimes he prosecuted, as we'll see a bit later.

Green River

Green River, the Sweetwater County seat, started as a station on the Overland and Pony Express routes. Settlement came with the Union Pacific in July 1869, when developers hoping to profit from the railroad boom laid out a town. By September 2,000 people occupied the site. The Union Pacific paid the speculators no attention, bridged the river, and moved on as fast as possible to start a new town on down the line. People settled at Green River anyway.

The Union Pacific lent early Green River its stability, particularly after the town became a major division point. Because so many of its citizens worked for the railroad, the community prohibited door-to-door salesmen from soliciting during daytime hours. Known as the Green River Ordinance and later adopted by other towns, the ban ensured peace and quiet so men and women who worked irregular shifts could sleep during the day.

Green River's first work force labored for the Union Pacific, but by the 1990s many residents also worked for nearby mining companies. A labor strike in the area in 1994 divided the community, but it presented a united front in February 1995 when a mine cave-in triggered an earthquake that rocked the nearby Solvay Minerals trona mine. The February 3 mishap trapped two miners underground, and highly skilled mine rescue teams worked around the

A group of tie hacks posed for this photo before taking to the rivers to move ties in southern Wyoming. The pike poles they hold are for moving and turning ties in the water. —Grand Encampment Museum

clock to reach the men. Within days they found both alive, but one man, twenty-six-year-old Mike Anderson, died of toxic fumes before rescuers could get him out of the mine.

The stream from which the community takes its name was called Seedske-dee by the Indians and Rio Verde, Spanish River, or other names by early white explorers. The Green forms the headwaters of the massive Colorado River system, which supplies water to millions of residents in Nevada, California, Arizona, and Mexico (see page 38). As the Union Pacific tracks pushed west, timbermen cut ties in the mountains near Pinedale and Dubois, then floated them down the Green for eventual use on the line. During the annual spring tie drives some 300,000 logs moved down the river. Daring youngsters amused themselves by walking up the bank a mile or so and riding the ties down the swollen stream.

Expedition Island

Maj. John Wesley Powell's expeditions down the Green and Colorado rivers in 1869 and 1871 started near the town of Green River.

No conclusive evidence pinpoints the exact launch point of Powell's first trip, but the second one departed from a campsite at Expedition Island on May 22, 1871. As he embarked on exploration of the last large unknown area in the continental United States, Powell opened a new era for the nation. His voyages led to innovative concepts in conservation, land reclamation, forestry, water management, geology, and geographic surveys as well as a new approach to western land uses.

Powell was reared in New York but lived much of his early life in Ohio, where he became interested in natural history. After losing an arm at the Battle of Shiloh during the Civil War, he studied and taught natural history but soon grew restless. Powell then organized scientific explorations of the Colorado River drainage system. When he found that the new transcontinental railroad would cross the Green River in western Wyoming Territory, he decided to begin his journey there.

Powell and his crew left in May 1869 on their first foray into the unknown canyons of the Green and Colorado rivers. Fifteen days into the trip one of their four boats wrecked, and they lost one-third of their provisions and all of Powell's notebooks. Just a week later, fire destroyed their mess kit, and heavy rains eventually spoiled the remaining food. Beset with unbelievable hardships, the party continued downstream. In the depths of the Grand Canyon, three men left the expedition and headed on foot for the Mormon settlements of Utah; all were killed by Indians. At the end of August, Powell and his remaining crew emerged from the Grand Canyon at the mouth of the Virgin River. His party lost all of its provisions and most of the scientific data it collected on that first wild ride through the Grand Canyon. Nevertheless, Powell repeated the journey two years later to gather more information.

Riding the rugged rapids of the Colorado through the magnificent chasms carved by millions of gallons of water, Powell clearly saw the need to develop land-use policies to prevent a breakdown of the ecological diversity of the region. In 1881 he became director of the newly formed U.S. Geological Survey and for three years fought for land and water use programs in the arid West. Powell's efforts went largely unheeded until shortly before his death in 1902, when President Theodore Roosevelt approved legislation creating the U.S. Bureau of Reclamation. That agency immediately started controlling water in the West, building more than 250 dams on rivers and streams to provide irrigation water throughout the region.

Sweetwater Brewery

One of Wyoming's pioneer industries began in Green River when German emigrants opened the Green River Brewery, which eventually became the Sweetwater Brewery. The building in which the business operated, a cross between a Rhineland castle and the Chicago water tower, attracted plenty of attention on its own.

The first brewery opened under the supervision of Adam Braun in 1872, before the town had even a school or a courthouse, but it washed away in a flood shortly thereafter. In 1875 Otto Rauch obtained control of the business and built a one-story wooden structure. Finally, in 1879, Karl Spinner became brewmaster, and the beer's reputation soared. It became known as Green River Beer, then as Columbia Beer after placing second in the 1890 Columbia Exposition.

In 1891 Hugo Gaensslen purchased the brewery and raised a new three-story frame building; then, in 1900, he built the unique stone Sweetwater Brewery. The native sandstone used in the construction came from behind Tollgate Rock—where Mormons once extracted a charge from passersby—and from Spring Canyon, north of town.

In 1919 the Volstead Act ushered in the Prohibition era, and beer making ceased. Sweetwater Brewery started making a nonalcoholic "near beer" known as Wyoming Beverage and a lemon-lime drink called simply a Green River.

Sweetwater Brewery, Green River. —State Historic Preservation Office

Fort Bridger

Now a state historic site, Fort Bridger, like Fort Laramie in eastern Wyoming, played a significant role in the state's development. Long before any Euro-Americans lived permanently in Wyoming, Indians gathered along the Black's Fork of the Green River. The Shoshone and Bannock Indians claimed this as part of their territory, and mountain men gathered here for the 1834 rendezvous.

This location particularly appealed to Jim Bridger, who started building a trading post in 1842 "in the path of the emigrants," as he put it. Bridger's post opened in 1843 and consisted of two houses joined together, surrounded by an eight-foot-high fence. Louis Vasquez became Bridger's partner at the post, and they did a brisk business when heavy migration started on the Oregon Trail in 1843 and the Mormon Trail in 1847. The trails split at Fort Bridger, with the north fork leading to Fort Hall, Idaho, and eventually to Oregon or California, and the south fork providing access to the Salt Lake Valley.

In his Oregon Trail journal, Joel Palmer wrote on July 25, 1845:

> Traveled about 16 miles, crossed the creek several times, and encamped near Fort Bridger. . . . It is built of poles and daubed with mud . . . a shabby concern. Here are about 25 lodges of Indians, or rather white

Jim Bridger started a trading post on the Black's Fork of the Green River in 1842 "in the path of the emigrants." Although Mormons burned his original post, a new log version, complete with sod roof, has been constructed at modern-day Fort Bridger.

The commissary at Fort Bridger has goods on the shelves and hardtack in the bin, but these days the fort is operated solely as an attraction. It is one of Wyoming's state parks.

trappers' lodges occupied by their Indian wives. They have a good supply of robes, dressed deer, elk and antelope skins, coats, pants, pork, powder, lead, blankets, butcher-knives, spirits, hats, ready-made clothes, coffee, sugar, etc. They ask for a horse from twenty-five to fifty dollars in trade. . . . At this place the bottoms are wide, and covered with good grass. Cotton-wood timber in plenty. The stream abounds with trout.

At the time of early westward emigration, the future boundaries of Wyoming held only two permanent settlements: Fort Laramie and—some 450 miles farther west—Fort Bridger. Travelers relied on both posts to rest, recuperate, restock, and repair before continuing their journey.

In 1847 Brigham Young stopped at Fort Bridger as he led his people toward the Salt Lake Valley. Five years later Young sent some of his Mormon followers to Willow Creek, about a dozen miles south of Fort Bridger, to farm and to establish a rival trading post, called Fort Supply. Shortly after Fort Supply opened for business, Bridger left his fort on the Black's Fork, and the Mormons took possession. He later claimed the Mormons forced him to leave, and stories circulated that Bridger hid out with his Indian friends as the Mormons searched for him. The Mormons, for their part, always claimed Bridger sold the fort to them.

At any rate, Lewis Robinson, quartermaster of the Utah militia, which operated under the auspices of the Mormon Church, took over Fort Bridger, built several stone houses, and enclosed them with a stone wall 400 feet long and 14 feet high. The Mormons retained control until the 1857 Mormon War. As Col. Albert S. Johnston and his troops advanced on Fort Bridger, the Mormons retreated to Salt Lake. Before leaving, they burned both Fort Supply and Fort Bridger.

Johnston temporarily established Camp Scott about two miles south of Fort Bridger. Federal troops, subsequently stationed at Fort Bridger, guarded the Overland Stage Route and the Union Pacific Railroad. After Shoshone chief Washakie signed a treaty at Fort Bridger establishing new boundaries for the Wind River Reservation in 1868, the fort became a base for troops at the Wind River Agency and in the Sweetwater mining district.

From May 23, 1878, until June 1880, Fort Bridger had no garrison. Troops reoccupied the post after an uprising on the Uinta Reservation and the Meeker Massacre on the Utes' White River Agency in Colorado. The army abandoned Fort Bridger as a military post November 6, 1890.

The state of Wyoming now operates Fort Bridger as a state historic site. The fort hosts one of the largest rendezvous reenactments in the West, attended every Labor Day weekend by hundreds of modern-day mountain men and Indians, and thousands of spectators.

Burntfork

South of Fort Bridger, Wyoming 414 provides access to Lyman, a strongly Mormon community near the former site of Fort Supply, and the small towns of Lonetree, Burntfork, and McKinnon. The highway crosses through some of the lush Bridger Valley before swinging up and over badlands where nothing seems to grow. The highway turns east at Lonetree along the Henry's Fork of the Green River, and the land again becomes lush and pastoral.

The first mountain-man rendezvous, organized by William Ashley in 1825, took place along the Henry's Fork near the present town of Burntfork, which is really just a couple of houses nestled in an agricultural valley. The area is best known as the home of Elinore Pruitt Stewart, a Denver widow who left the city with her young daughter to work for a homesteader. Elinore soon married the man for whom she worked and claimed a homestead of her own. Much of her story is told in the books she wrote, including *Letters of a Woman Homesteader* and *Letters on an Elk Hunt*.

Stuart presented homesteading as a panacea for the poor, particularly poor women. In *Letters of a Woman Homesteader* she wrote:

> When I read of the hard time among the Denver poor, particularly the women, I feel like urging them every one to get out and file on land. . . . [A]ny woman who can stand her own company, can see the beauty of the sunset, loves growing things, and is willing to put in as much time and careful labor as she does over the washtub, will certainly succeed; will have independence, plenty to eat all the time, and a home of her own in the end.

Downtown Evanston. —State Historic Preservation Office

Evanston

Situated just inside Wyoming's border with Utah, Evanston is in many respects more strongly attached to the Beehive State. At one time this area was a part of Utah Territory, and many of Brigham Young's followers settled here during the 1850s. The entire area of southwestern Wyoming west of Lyman continues to have a strong Mormon influence.

Like most of the other communities in southern Wyoming, Evanston grew primarily because of the Union Pacific Railroad, which arrived December 1, 1868. Harvey Booth preceded the line by a couple of weeks and pitched a tent November 23, 1868, opening a restaurant, saloon, and hotel. By the time the UP line came through, more than 600 "camp followers" and construction workers had landed in the vicinity of Booth's tent.

Before many days passed, "raghouses" of canvas and wood had gone up. But then the railroad decided to move division headquarters to Wasatch, Utah, twelve miles west. Twenty-four hours later, only Booth and saloon keeper Frank Moore remained in Evanston. In June 1869 railroad executives changed their minds and moved division headquarters back to Evanston, where the Bear River provided a necessary water supply for the railroad. The site became a major maintenance facility for the railroad between Green River and Ogden, Utah.

Union Pacific civil engineer Charles Almy located coal north of Evanston in 1868, and when the Central Pacific's Rocky Mountain Coal and Iron Company opened a mine, the town of Almy grew up around it.

Coal mines quickly opened in the rich Almy veins, and Evanston, like Rock Springs to the east, soon had a large Chinese population with its own version of Chinatown: a huddle of shanties north of the railroad tracks. The Chinese used scrap lumber, packing boxes, tar paper, and flattened oil cans for their homes, which resembled children's playhouses. Early on, some shanties became opium dens and gambling houses.

After 1870 most of the Chinese toiled at the Almy coal mines, although some worked as merchants, laundrymen, and vegetable peddlers who cultivated gardens near Bear River. White men in the region doubted much of anything could grow here, but the Chinese diverted water from the Bear River with waterwheels resembling those used in their native land and raised a crop that supplied the town.

Evanston had a joss house—one of three in the United States at that time—where the Chinese could practice their religion. The shrine featured carved panels flanking the door, and fragrant joss sticks burned before a placid idol behind gates of curved teakwood. Chinese came long distances to worship in the ornate two-story building, but after the massacre in Rock Springs and other incidents of discrimination toward the Asian population, many Chinese left the area. The joss house burned in 1922. Evanston residents have built a replica of the structure to serve as a tourist attraction.

Oil, Gas, and Another Boom

Early pioneers knew of oil in the Evanston area, but no profitable development and marketing took place until 1900, when the Union Pacific Coal Company struck oil while drilling a water well. Speculators rushed to the area, and extensive development followed. Agriculture—particularly sheep production—timbering, and railroad operations rounded out Evanston's economic profile, and its population grew to 4,000, then hovered near that mark for decades.

The Arab oil embargo and subsequent rise in oil prices in 1973 made it financially attractive to begin more extensive exploration in the Evanston area, known as the Overthrust Belt. Wyoming crude oil prices jumped to all-time highs, and the area's low-grade coal and natural gas became popular domestic fuel sources. By 1980 Evanston's population had reached 7,000, and the region enjoyed its biggest boom since the arrival of the railroad and the discovery of the Almy coal mines.

Like the extensive development at Rock Springs a century earlier, this boom also had its violent moments. From Rock Springs to Evanston, more people moved in than the communities could handle. Developers rushed to provide services, but one of those projects turned terribly sour in Evanston when a local attorney, his wife, and son died in an explosion in their home.

Vincent Vehar served on the Uinta County Planning Commission, which denied a building permit to Mark Hopkinson, a Bridger Valley resident. Hopkinson played college football in Arizona until he injured his knee; he jumped heavily into drugs, then straightened himself out and turned his attention to development in the Overthrust Belt. But when Vehar thwarted his planned housing project in the Bridger Valley, Hopkinson ordered the bombing of the attorney's home. The 1979 blast leveled the building, killing the three Vehars.

At Hopkinson's trial, Jackson attorney Gerry Spence, a personal friend of the Vehars, acted as special prosecutor. A jury convicted Hopkinson of the murders. Later Hopkinson was convicted of arranging the torture slaying of Jeff Green, an associate who was scheduled to testify against Hopkinson in the Vehar case, from his federal prison cell in California. The person who actually tortured and killed Green was never identified. Hopkinson received a death sentence for ordering the murder.

A dozen years after his initial conviction, and despite a dogged effort by Wyoming public defender Leonard Munker to save him, Hopkinson was executed at the Wyoming State Penitentiary in Rawlins on a bitterly cold, terribly windy night in January 1992. His death by lethal injection came in spite of pleas from members of the Vehar family and Spence that the death sentence be set aside. For his part, Hopkinson remained calm and quiet to the end. He maintained his innocence and died without naming Green's killer.

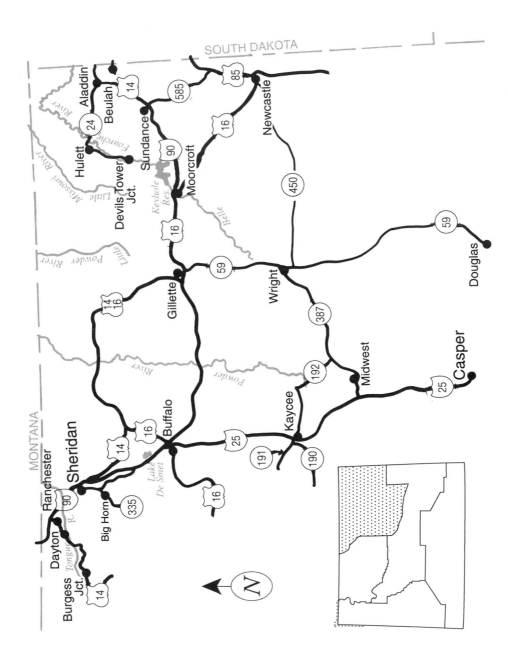

Part 4

Powder River Country

The rolling hills of the Powder River Basin have been a battleground for as long as people have been living here. For a time the Crow claimed this region; then the Sioux drove them north; and eventually the Cheyenne and Arapaho shared the country with the Sioux. Those three tribes rallied against the incoming gold miners and military after 1864, the year John Jacobs and John Bozeman forged a pathway across the Powder River Basin along the east face of the Bighorn Mountains. The road, which became known as the Bloody Bozeman, provided the fastest route from the settlements of Wyoming and Colorado to Montana's goldfields. The Sioux fought harder to hold Powder River than they did to hold any other place in Wyoming. They managed to force out the military for a time but ultimately found themselves on reservations anyway.

A second confrontation occurred in the basin in 1892 when powerful cattlemen hired an army to drive out homesteaders and rustlers who had moved in on the range. That saga took place between Casper and Buffalo. The region also saw coal development at Cambria, Gillette, and Sheridan.

Cattle and sheep still graze in this dry country, relying on isolated watering holes formed by rain and snowmelt. Driving through the area, you sometimes feel as if it's forever to anywhere, as the hills and breaks seem to have no end.

The Bighorn Mountains form the western boundary of Powder River country, and the Black Hills spill over from South Dakota to frame the northesastern corner of Wyoming. There, the nation's first national monument, Devils Tower, rises from the Belle Fourche river bottoms. Various Indian legends surround the tower, which is sacred to local tribes.

For our journey through this land of rolling hills, we begin along I-25 at the southern edge of the region and travel north, then we'll follow I-90 from east to west.

Salt Creek Oil

Since the drilling of Natrona County's first oil well in 1887 a few miles northwest of Casper, this region's fortunes always have been tied to the underground liquid. Wildcatter Mark Shannon brought in the first oil well at the legendary Salt Creek Oil Field near present-day Edgerton, off I-25 north of Casper. Wyoming 259 and Wyoming 387 provide access to the Salt Creek Field and the Teapot Dome area.

Prospecting started in 1882, and the first well drilling took place there in 1887. Shannon was working for the Pennsylvania Oil and Gas Company in the fall of 1889 about a mile north of Salt Creek Field when he hit the gusher, which flew to 1,090 feet. A shooter like that is hard to keep a secret, even though Shannon and the company tried. The oil had barely settled before speculators rushed to Natrona County.

Investors from France, England, Holland, and Belgium poured funds into development and drilling ventures. The trail between Salt Creek and Casper filled with freighters hauling wagon loads of oil. The trip took a week in good weather and a fortnight when it stormed. The rough and ready teamsters lost their oil-hauling position in 1910 when the Franco-Wyoming Company laid the first pipeline from Salt Creek to the Casper refineries.

Railroads could use Salt Creek's high-quality oil without refining it, but refineries processed the raw petroleum for other uses. Pennsylvania Oil and Gas built a refinery on South Center Street in 1895. The facility turned 100 barrels of oil a day into kerosene and lubricating oils. Casper quickly gained a reputation as a rough, but rich, oil town as other refineries opened.

Vague language in land-lease agreements contributed to rampant claim jumping until more restrictive wording appeared in 1920 in the Land Leasing Act. During the early years of development, armed men patrolled individual claims. Violence often erupted, and those holding claims found themselves embroiled in battles on the ground and in the courts when professional claim jumpers tried to seize properties.

Teapot Dome

The biggest scandal of all didn't relate to claim jumping. It occurred near Midwest at Teapot Dome, where officials allowed oil leasing without competitive bidding. Various companies claimed U.S. Petroleum Reserve No. 3, first known as Irish Park and later as Teapot Dome, before 1910. When extensive development of the field started, President William H. Taft made the tract a naval reserve and closed it to private exploitation.

The countryside near Midwest is dotted with the pumpjacks of hundreds of oil wells. This area came under scrutiny by the U. S. Government in the 1920s when a major scandal broke over the Teapot Dome, where leasing had been improperly allowed without competitive bidding.

Early in his administration, President Warren G. Harding transferred the reserves from the navy to the Department of the Interior. In 1922 the government charged that Secretary of the Interior Albert B. Fall had leased the Teapot reserve secretly and without competitive bids. The deal might have gone unnoticed had not the lessee, Harry F. Sinclair's Mammoth Crude Oil Company, opened the largest gusher ever seen in Wyoming. "It came to life with a tornado's force, hurling tools against the crown block and showering crude oil for several hundred yards," Jean Mead wrote in *Casper Country: Wyoming's Heartland.* Initially, about 28,000 barrels of oil flowed daily, but the volume soon tapered to a steady pouring of 100 barrels a day. The Teapot Field continued expansion, and soon sixty-five wells were producing on a regular basis; by 1923, output had reached an average of 273 barrels a day.

A Senate investigation of the questionable leases ensued, and allegations flew that Sinclair and other oilmen had bribed Fall for access to the rich Teapot Field. Sinclair got a minor tap on the fingers: a three-month prison sentence and a $500 fine. Secretary Fall's punishment was more severe: three years in prison and a $300,000 fine. In 1927 the U.S. Supreme Court invalidated the leases and restored control of the land to the navy. The transfer included the improvements made by Mammoth Crude.

Kaycee

Like Jay Em (see page 136), Kaycee gets its name from a brand—in this case, the mark of the KC Ranch, which itself has a significant place in Wyoming's history.

In the spring of 1860, long before the ranching era, four missionaries from the Iowa Synod of the German Lutheran Church at St. Sebald, Iowa, established an Indian mission east of the future site of Kaycee and about 100 miles north of Deer Creek Station. According to the WPA history of Wyoming, the missionaries said they corralled their wagons and blessed the ground "where the ground was level and the grass was thick and luxuriant for the tired oxen, and the soil adaptable to agriculture."

The Lutherans erected a temporary hut for shelter, broke the ground with their plow, and planted corn and grain. They then built a sturdy log mission station, sunk a well, and looked for the Crow Indians, whom they had come to instruct. But they quickly found the country was no longer "Absaroka, the Land of the Crow." The Sioux and Cheyenne had pushed the tribe out.

Missionaries always have a lot of faith, and these four still believed the Crow would come to them for instruction. "We will see and converse with our dear Crows, which will take place very shortly, as they are to receive their annuities at Deer Creek this year and their road leads directly by our station," they wrote. But no Crows came. Then one missionary deserted, and a request went back to the synod for additional volunteer workers. But some Sioux killed another missionary before the message had time to reach its destination, and the remaining pair hightailed it back to Deer Creek. They had barely left the station before the Sioux burned the buildings.

The native Americans felt they had every right to drive white missionaries out of the area. Treaties with the government at Fort Laramie in 1851 reserved land for the tribes north of the North Platte River and east of the Bighorn Mountains extending all the way to the Black Hills. White men had permission only to pass through the land, not to settle and build structures.

Other than those four missionaries, few people ventured into the Powder River Basin during the 1850s and early 1860s. When prospectors found gold in Alder Gulch, Montana, in the 1860s, miners prudently avoided the Powder River country on their way to the new goldfields. They followed the Oregon-California Trail to Idaho—either from the east or the west—then headed north. But miners, who would head for any new strike they heard about that might outshine their current claims, wanted to get there *fast*. So it seemed pretty logical that they'd eye the Powder River Basin. By skirting the east face of the Bighorns to Montana and then heading west, they could cut many days off their travel time.

Jacobs and Bozeman Forge a Trail

Intrepid mountain men John Jacobs and John Bozeman found the first route across the Powder River Basin in 1864. They started in Montana and headed south, taking care to stay out of sight of the Sioux and Cheyenne, although on that score they had only partial success. The Indians stopped them, took most of their provisions, and beat the young girl with them—Jacobs's daughter—because she was half-Indian and traveling with white men. Undaunted, the following spring Jacobs and Bozeman started leading caravans of miners through the territory toward Montana.

From 1865 until 1868 that country was aflame in a conflict often called the first Sioux War. Most of the major Indian battles fought on Wyoming ground took place during that period at sites on the Powder River, Crazy Woman Creek, and Tongue River. The first Sioux War climaxed in 1868 when Lakota chief Red Cloud agreed to peace terms in a parley at Fort Laramie. The second Sioux War began with the discovery of gold in the Black Hills in 1874 and ended in 1876 when Crazy Horse finally surrendered near Hat Creek Station in eastern Wyoming. But not until after the fight at Wounded Knee, South Dakota, in 1890 did the Sioux truly relent and give up their nomadic lifestyle.

John M. Bozeman left his name on a trail he blazed through the Powder River Basin in 1864 with John Jacobs. The Sioux hated the trail through their hunting grounds. They fought those who used it, earning it the nickname Bloody Bozeman.
—Wyoming State Museum

Sioux chief Red Cloud.
—Wyoming State Museum

Red Cloud fought in the Battle of Platte Bridge in July 1865 (see page 169), after which the Sioux, Cheyenne, and Arapaho returned north. He also took a leading role in the mid-August harassment near Pumpkin Buttes of James A. Sawyer's party, which was surveying a wagon road from the mouth of the Niobrara River to Virginia City, Montana, as an official route to complement Bozeman's road. In early 1866 the military expressed optimism that a lasting peace could be negotiated with the Indians at Fort Laramie. Little real change had taken place since the 1851 treaty, but the army couldn't gain control of the tribes, so it tried instead to persuade them to keep the peace themselves.

An official government peace conference finally started on June 5, 1866, but eight days later it collapsed when Col. H. B. Carrington arrived. Red Cloud refused to meet Carrington, telling authorities he believed Carrington's troops wanted to steal the Bozeman road before the Indians had an opportunity to decide whether to sell the land. Instead Red Cloud gathered his blanket and people and held up his gun, saying, "In this and the Great Spirit I trust for the right." Then he headed to Powder River.

Even with Red Cloud's reaction fresh in his mind, Carrington remained optimistic. On June 16, 1866, the day before he left for the Powder River country, Carrington wrote Lt. Col. H. G. Litchfield:

*Col. H. B. Carrington,
commander of Fort Phil
Kearny, February 1902.*
—Wyoming State Museum

All the commissioners agree that I go to occupy a region which the Indians will only surrender for a great equivalent; even my arrival has started
among them many absurd rumors, but I apprehend no serious difficulty.
Patience, forbearing, and common sense in dealing with the Sioux and
Cheyennes will do much with all who really desire peace, but it is indis-
pensable that ample supplies of ammunition come promptly.

The Cheyenne under Dull Knife and Black Horse warned Carrington that
the Sioux were prepared to fight. They offered him 100 young men to fight
the Sioux if he would give them provisions. Carrington arrogantly declined
the offer. The next day the Lakota attacked one of Carrington's wagon trains,
running off 187 head of stock, killing two men, and wounding two others.
Thereafter, as Grace Raymond Hebard wrote in *The Bozeman Trail*, "there
never was a day, never an hour, but that the Indians attacked, or would have
attacked if not properly watched."

Carrington, as he pointed out himself, needed a great supply of ammunition, cavalry troops, and seasoned fighters. He got none of that. Ammunition,
and even food, came in short supply, there were never enough horses, and his
troops were more often than not raw recruits who had no conception of military discipline or who arrogantly looked upon the Plains Indians as inadequate

foes. The soldiers thought they'd quickly take the starch out of the Indians, but the Lakota hammered the troops instead.

Today, I-25 between Casper and Buffalo and, from there, I-90 to Sheridan, Ranchester, and the Montana state line give access to many Powder River battle sites, although travelers do not encounter the sites in any semblance of chronological order.

Dull Knife Battle, 1876

Following the Sioux-Custer fight on the Little Bighorn in June 1876, Dull Knife and Little Wolf led the Cheyenne and Arapaho to an area west of Kaycee, where they camped south of Fraker Mountain, a rock barrier named for early settler Augustus Fraker, in a deep valley on the Red Fork of the Powder River. The campsite now sits on private land about midway between Barnum, on Wyoming 190, and Mayoworth, on Wyoming 191.

On the evening of November 25, 1876, Gen. Ranald Mackenzie and his approximately 1,100 troops, including a large number of Pawnee, Shoshone, Sioux, Arapaho, and even Cheyenne braves, surrounded Dull Knife's camp. After the battles on the Rosebud, the Little Bighorn, and at Slim Buttes, the U.S. military changed its strategy from one of open confrontation with the Indians to one of seeking out the various bands in their winter camps. During that time of the year Indians seldom fought; they had women and children with them and needed to prepare for the cold season. Gen. George Crook ordered his men to attack these unsuspecting villages, capturing horses and destroying food, tipis, weapons, and utensils. Such losses, he calculated, would force the tribes to surrender and adopt reservation life. Mackenzie, operating

The valley where the fight between Dull Knife's Cheyennes and Gen. Ranald Mackenzie took place in 1876. —State Historic Preservation Office

on Crook's orders, turned his troops loose upon the sleeping Cheyenne under Dull Knife and Little Wolf.

Driven from their lodges, the Cheyenne put up a strong defense, fighting until midafternoon of the next day, but Mackenzie destroyed their camp and supplies. Left almost naked, the surviving Cheyenne escaped to the north through Fraker Pass and sought refuge with Crazy Horse, seventy miles away. Men, women, and children walked through deep snow, leaving a trail of blood. An account by Capt. John G. Bourke, 3rd Cavalry, gives a glimpse into the battle scene:

> The Cheyennes' talk was still fierce enough and their courage unabated; had we attempted to force them out of their improvised rifle pits in the crevices and behind the rocks on the hillside, there would have been fearful loss of life.
>
> Prudence suggested that we make sure of what has been gained, move off all the pony herd rounded up by our Indian scouts, burn and destroy every vestige of the village, meanwhile sending back to General Crook for the infantry, whose more powerful rifles could be brought to bear upon the hostiles in the morning in case they did not withdraw to another position during the night. Our own losses were, of course, known— one commissioned officer, Lieutenant McKinney, and six enlisted men killed, and twenty-six wounded.
>
> The full loss of the Cheyennes was not determined until their surrender at Red Cloud agency several weeks later, when they submitted a list of forty killed . . . never mentioned the number of wounded. From the desperate cold of the following night they suffered as much as from the fight . . . that night was unusually severe, the spirit thermometer in our supply camp registering nearly but not quite 30 degrees below zero.

The soldiers set about the mass destruction of the 200-lodge Cheyenne village. They piled fat and marrow preserved by the Indian women in the middle of lodges, heaped wood onto the pile, and struck a match. Bourke wrote:

> Crackling flames roared and bellowed in their upward rush through the hide and canvas covering; but before the lodge poles were actually ignited, explosions of powder kegs and cans sent most of the belongings of Cheyenne domestic life rocket-like into the air. Never were orders more thoroughly executed. Experience had taught us in bitter lessons the preceding winter that villages only half destroyed were scarcely to be considered injured at all; on this occasion it was determined not to let a square inch of canvas, hide, robe or even gunnysack be left for use by the discomfited enemy.
>
> Lodge poles not more than half burned were broken into smaller pieces and thrown upon what is no rhetorical flourish to call the funeral pyres of Cheyenne glory.

For the troops, the attack on Dull Knife's village was a chance to avenge the Custer defeat of six months earlier. They found among the Cheyenne lodges much evidence that Dull Knife's warriors had fought at the battles of the Little Bighorn and the Rosebud. Just as the Little Bighorn fight with Custer was a significant victory for the Indians, the Dull Knife fight became a complete triumph for the army. It finally broke the spirit of the free-ranging Cheyenne, who later surrendered at reservations in South Dakota.

Hole-in-the-Wall

To the south from the site of the Dull Knife battle is the rugged canyon country called Hole-in-the-Wall. The well-known hunting ground includes tributaries of the Powder and Bighorn rivers and streams with names such as Otter, Trout, Beartrap, and Buffalo. Besides having a reputation for good hunting, Hole-in-the-Wall was once notorious as an outlaw hideout. The area is about thirty-five miles long and has only one eastern entrance, which a few men could easily defend.

On the west side of the hole, trails led to Montana, Idaho, Utah, and Colorado. All manner of bad men used the Hole-in-the-Wall country as an important station on the Outlaw Trail, including the James Gang, Butch Cassidy, and Flat Nose George Curry. An elaborate system of hollow-tree or hole-in-a-rock post offices kept Cassidy's gang members in communication. Flat Nose George Curry and Harvey Logan, with their spectacular robberies and cold-blooded killings, drew lots of attention from the press and coined the "hole-in-the-wall" moniker. Newspapermen seized upon the name and soon had every fugitive west of the Mississippi headed toward the canyon along the 300-foot-high north-south wall of sandstone known as the Red Wall. It's unlikely that all of the outlaws said by the press to be holed up in Hole-in-the-Wall actually spent time there, although some certainly hid out in the canyon country. Hole-in-the-Wall probably sheltered more cattle rustlers than train-robbing bandits.

Wyoming 192 and 387
Kaycee—Wright
75 miles

Fort Reno and Cantonment Reno

Fort Reno, one of three forts located along the Bozeman Trail, was named for Maj. Jesse L. Reno, who died in the Civil War at the Battle of South Mountain on September 14, 1862. The military established Fort Reno on the Powder River just west of the Pumpkin Buttes, about twenty-eight miles east of present-day Kaycee and about five miles northwest of Sussex.

Fort Reno, established on the Powder River in 1865, first went by the name Camp Connor, but Col. H. B. Carrington renamed it Fort Reno. The military abandoned the fort in 1868 and the Sioux immediately burned it. —Wyoming State Museum

The military built Fort Reno to protect travelers on the Bozeman Trail but garrisoned it only from 1866 to 1868. The Sioux burned the fort immediately after the military abandoned it under terms of a peace treaty between Red Cloud and the government in 1868.

Nearly a decade after abandoning Fort Reno, the military established Cantonment Reno three miles south of the former post. Also called Camp McKinney, Fort McKinney, and Depot McKinney, it should not be confused with the earlier Fort Reno, nor with the Fort McKinney later established west of Buffalo. From 1876 to 1878 Cantonment Reno served as a supply post for the U.S. Army in its final campaign to force native Americans onto reservations. Located near the confluence of the Powder River and Dry Creek, Cantonment Reno had no stockade, but the army built more than forty major log structures at the site.

The post offered little in the way of luxury, but it served better than the tents and dugouts men used prior to its construction. It played a role in the army's winter campaign of 1876–77; when the army attacked Dull Knife and his band of Cheyenne, part of the regiment drew supplies from the post. The cantonment later took the name Fort McKinney for Lt. John McKinney, who died in the Dull Knife fight. It became Depot McKinney when the army established a new Fort McKinney near Buffalo. Except for a small number of men who cared for the post and provided service on the telegraph line, the army had deserted the site by 1878.

After that period, about 100 people lived on the east side of the river, across from the post, at a settlement known as Powder River Crossing. Like the army post, the settlement shrank into obscurity, and now both locations are part of a ranching operation.

A Wyoming Range Fight

No sooner had the military and Indian wars on the Powder River ceased than another conflict started. This time the antagonists were powerful, wealthy, free-range cattlemen and hardscrabble homesteader-settlers.

Hundreds of thousands of head of Texas cattle moved into and through Wyoming on the Texas and Goodnight-Loving trails from 1875 to 1884. The rolling prairies of the Powder River Basin, long prized by the Indians, became populated with longhorns as cowmen realized that the nutritious native grasses put weight on the animals. But the great herds soon had company. Settlers moving west in search of land to claim under the Homestead Act found the Powder River country particularly appealing, and many staked out a quarter-section, broke ground for crops, and raised a few head of cattle.

Over time, the settler influx became a great thorn in the cattlemen's side. During the 1870s and early 1880s, those men ran their stock on the open range. They had no need to worry about grass or water, because it seemed to be in endless supply. But then the homesteaders built fences around their land, often limiting water holes for free-ranging cattle.

Even so, the cattlemen, with greedy disregard for the land, brought more and more animals to run on the range. Eastern Wyoming soon had too many cattle, and the land began to show the effects of overuse; in places the damage is still evident a century later. Then good old Mother Nature started to stir the pot. First it didn't rain; then it snowed and snowed and snowed; and finally it got so damn cold the cattle literally froze on their feet.

The weather first turned hostile during the summer of 1886. Hundreds of thousands of head of cattle ranged over Wyoming's grasslands, like they'd done in previous years. But this summer no rain showers rejuvenated the land; the hot sun baked the grasses, curing them long before their time, then burning them from the stalks. The stock went hungry into the fall.

Winter didn't start particularly early; the first major storm of the season blew in from the west on January 9, 1887. Another hit January 11. Three days later stockmen rode through sixteen inches of snow, forging through and around drifts twelve to fifteen feet high, wondering how their cattle were faring. However, before any complete damage assessment could take place the bottom dropped out of the thermometer, and the Great Plains—from Canada to Texas—went into a deep freeze, with temperatures plunging to 46 degrees below zero and remaining in that vicinity for ten long, bitter days.

At the end of January the temperature rose and the snow began to soften, but it stayed warm only long enough for some of the snow to melt and form pools of water. Then the temperature plummeted again, freezing the water and covering the land with a sheet of ice that made it nearly impossible for cattle to eat. February was just as cold and snowy as January, and not until late

March did the storms abate. Cowboys called that miserable winter the Great Die-Up. Thousands of head of cattle perished—stacked frozen against the fences put in place by homesteaders—and so did a way of life. John Clay, a Chicago businessman who later managed the Swan Land and Cattle Company, wrote of the disaster: "Three great streams of ill-luck, mismanagement and greed now culminated in the most appalling slaughter of animals the west had ever seen or would see again, second only to the slaughter of the buffalo."

With that tragic winter fresh in their minds, the big cattlemen soon realized they had other concerns to deal with: settlers and rustlers. The terms became synonymous in Wyoming from 1888 until at least 1892, when the most infamous event of Wyoming's range history occurred. It took place in the Powder River Basin, where echoes of earlier battles with Indians still reverberated across the hills.

Johnson County Invasion

Two men died in late fall 1891, in the first incidents of a range struggle that clearly demonstrated the arrogance of wealthy men. The victims were Orley E. Jones, known as Ranger Jones, a popular cowboy and bronc buster who homesteaded on the Red Fork of the Powder River west of Kaycee; and John Tisdale, an outspoken homesteader known for condemning the big cattlemen for their treatment of small landholders. Both died in ambushes. There is no direct evidence to show who killed Jones, but a witness, Charlie Basch, told the authorities Tisdale's murderer was range detective Frank Canton. Canton split before Basch had the courage to tell his story and never stood trial.

In early 1892 the powerful members of the Wyoming Stock Growers Association started planning a foray into Johnson County designed to solve their problems with homesteaders and small cattlmen, whom they considered rustlers. They lined up fifty-two men—gunmen, association members, range detectives, and twenty-two Texans recruited with the promise of $5 per day plus expenses and a $50 bonus for every man they killed. Calling themselves the Regulators, the cattlemen easily pulled the governor and a pair of senators into line, invited a couple of members of the press along, and formulated a "dead list" of men to be eliminated in the spring campaign. They called it an invasion; others called it a war. No matter the name, it went down in history as a despicable act. It also proved a failure when the raiders themselves had to be rescued.

The campaign started April 5, 1892, when the early afternoon train from Denver rolled right on time into the Cheyenne station. A car holding the Texans and Maj. Frank Wolcott, a well-known Wyoming cattleman, soon coupled with a different train, "The Invasion Special," which had three stock cars filled with horses, a flatcar holding three new Studebaker wagons, and another car filled with baggage and supplies. Before long the Pullman full of Texans became more crowded, as cattlemen left the Cheyenne Club (see page 217) in twos and threes to join the party. They planned to ride the rails north, make a lightning march from Casper to Buffalo, seize the town, round up the "rustlers," and repeat the process wherever necessary before the populace realized what was happening.

That evening the train reached Casper, where the party mounted and rode out of town. After stopping to cut the telegraph wires leading to Buffalo and Sheridan, the invaders arrived at a ranch owned by J. N. and Robert Tisdale (no relation to John Tisdale, killed the previous fall). Had the Regulators stuck to their original plan, they might have had a different ending to their adventure, but while at the Tisdale ranch they learned some of the men on their dead list were at the KC Ranch. Although some urged caution and the need to stick to the original plan, the majority ruled otherwise, and the invaders headed toward the KC.

Early reports placed fourteen men at the KC, but when the Regulators arrived only four remained: Nate Champion, Nick Ray, Ben Jones, and Bill Walker. The cattlemen had no quarrel with Jones and Walker, whom they grabbed just after dawn as the men left the ranch house on errands, but they did target Champion and Ray. The two had rustled a few calves over the years; now they faced off with the invaders April 9, 1892, in the first engagement of the Johnson County War.

Johnson County Invaders—prisoners at Fort D. A. Russell, 1892, following their failed invasion. They include, in no particular order, A. B. Clark, E. W. Whitcomb, A. D. Adamson, C. S. Ford, W. H. Tabor, G. R. Tucker, A. R. Pourve, D. E. Booke, B. M. Morrison, W. A. Wilson, M. A. McNally, Bob Barlin, W. S. Davis, S. Sutherland, Alex Lowther, W. J. Clarke, J. A. Garrett, William Armstrong, Buck Garrett, F. H. Labertraux, J. Johnson, Alex Hamilton, F. M. Canton, W. C. Irvine, J. N. Tisdale, W. B. Wallace, F. De Billier, H. Teenmaker, W. E. Guthrie, F. G. S. Hesse, Phil DuFran, William Little, D. R. Tisdale, J. D. Mynett, M. Shonsey, Joe Elliott, C. A. Campbell, J. Borlings, L. H. Parker, S. S. Tucker, B. Wiley, J. M. Beuford, K. Rickard, Frank Walcott, B. Schultz. —Wyoming State Museum

Not long after breakfast, Ray left the house and was immediately shot. Loyal partner Champion dragged him back into the cabin and tended him as best he could while the Regulators fired volley after volley at the house. Ray died during that long day, and as Champion alone defended his life he penned his final thoughts in a small notebook: "Boys, I feel pretty lonesome just now. I wish there was someone here with me so we could watch all sides at once. They may fool around until I get a good shot before they leave."

But the invaders didn't leave. Champion clearly had no idea of the size of the force pinning him down in the cabin. In late afternoon he saw a buckboard pass the ranch but didn't know the man was a friend, Jack Flagg, and Flagg's stepson, Alonza Taylor. The invaders knew, however, and fired on the two as they passed. Jack Flagg's name headed the dead list, but he escaped the bullets. As the shadows lengthened, Champion wrote:

> Well, they have just got through shelling the house again like hail. I heard them splitting wood. I guess they are going to fire the house tonight. I think I will make a break when night comes, if alive.
>
> Shooting again. I think they will fire the house this time.
>
> It's not night yet. The house is all fired. Goodbye, boys, if I never see you again.

The invaders, unable to shoot Champion while he remained in the house, eventually pushed a burning hay-filled rack against the cabin, and when the building started to burn, Champion made his break. He got about fifty yards from the cabin before his bullet-battered body fell. Major Walcott retrieved the blood-stained notebook in which Champion wrote his final thoughts and gave it to Sam Clover, correspondent for the *Chicago Herald*. Within a week the *Herald* ran the full text of the notebook diary, and Champion's last words went out to the nation. It's never been clearly shown why Major Wolcott gave the notebook to Clover.

After killing Champion, the invaders raced toward Buffalo. They'd missed when they shot at Flagg and Taylor and knew the word of their presence had now spread.

The Scene in Buffalo

As expected, Flagg and Taylor reported the invasion to the people of Buffalo. Sheriff Red Angus swore in 100 deputies to ride with him to the KC Ranch, where they found Ray's charred body and Champion's bullet-riddled remains. Angus and his men then returned to town with the grim news. Buffalo townspeople became outraged. Robert Foote, one of the town's leading merchants, mounted his black horse and galloped up and down the streets. With his black cape and long white beard flying in the wind, Foote called the citizens to arms; then he opened his store and sold them guns, ammunition, and tobacco.

Warned by friends and neighbors, settlers from the outlying country converged on the little county seat and quickly organized the "Home Defenders," according to a WPA account. Churches and schoolhouses became barracks and places of refuge for wives and children, and guards stood at approaches to Buffalo.

The cattlemen never reached town. They stopped briefly at the TA Ranch, fourteen miles away, then resumed their journey. But when they heard that Buffalo townspeople were in an uproar, the Regulators prudently returned to the TA to fort up. Suddenly the invaders found themselves trapped like gophers in a hole, much the way Champion and Ray had been the previous day.

All day April 11, they remained pinned down in the TA Ranch buildings. The surrounding townsmen, under the direction of Eli Snider and Rap Brown, intercepted provisions intended for the invaders. A messenger managed to escape the siege and headed to the telegraph station at Gillette, about 100 miles east. From there he sent an urgent dispatch asking Gov. Amos W. Barber to order troops from Fort McKinney to rescue the besieged party. The request passed from the governor to Senators Francis E. Warren and Joseph M. Carey, themselves known supporters of the Wyoming Stock Growers Association—and ultimately to President Benjamin Harrison, who ordered Colonel Van Horn of Fort McKinney to ride to the scene of the insurrection and take the invaders into custody.

The Regulators gave themselves up to the military, but Van Horn refused to turn the cattlemen over to Johnson County because he feared mobs would lynch the entire bunch. Instead he removed the invaders to Cheyenne at the expense of Johnson County. As the weeks dragged by and the cost of keeping the prisoners became too great for Johnson County to handle, they were released on their own recognizance. A trial began in January 1893, and the court spent weeks trying to seat a jury. Finally, at the request of the defense and with the concurrence of the prosecution, the judge dismissed the charges because of the difficulties of the case and the expense involved.

Crazy Woman Battlefield

At a site on Crazy Woman Creek, east of I-25 midway between Kaycee and Buffalo, native Americans more than once attacked travelers on the Bozeman road. Two stories circulate about how Crazy Woman Creek got its name. One has it that a demented Indian woman once lived in a wickiup on the banks of the stream and was eventually buried there. Another is that a white trader's wife went insane after watching Indians kill and scalp her husband.

Local legend also says treasure lies hidden in the upper canyons of Crazy Woman Creek. In the fall of 1865, two prospectors stumbled into Fort Reno and told how they, with five companions, had found a fabulously rich gold lode. They told of building a small cabin and gleaning $7,000 worth of gold within a few days. Then Indians attacked, killing their companions. The two prospectors escaped with as much gold as they could stow in a baking-powder can. They showed the gold to Fort Reno's commander, but he didn't believe the story and arrested them instead. After their release, the two wintered at

Fort Laramie before heading out in the spring of 1866 with about ten men to find the lode. They weren't heard of again, and neither was the gold.

Buffalo

In 1855 Capt. H. E. Palmer, once of the 11th Kansas Volunteer Cavalry, arrived in Powder River country with four wagon loads of goods to trade. He had three half-breed interpreters and stopped on Clear Creek, near the present site of Buffalo. Palmer erected a sod hut, and for nearly a week the Indians ignored him. Then a small party of Cheyenne came in, and a pipe of peace passed among the group. But as the last one puffed, the chief grunted, and blankets fell from the Indians' shoulders. Arrows on taut bowstrings pointed at the interlopers. The Indians dismantled the house, returning the sod to its place on the prairie, while the chief explained that the land was virgin buffalo ground, which the white man should not break. He told Palmer and his associates to take their goods and leave the area immediately.

Undaunted, Palmer went north to the Tongue River, where he traded with the Arapaho until the first Sioux War, or Red Cloud's War, started. Then the Arapaho, allies of the Sioux, confiscated his goods. Once again Palmer got permission from the native Americans to leave.

Buffalo Becomes a Sheep Town

Cattlemen, nesters, miners, and freighters broke over the land in a wave when the Sioux's former territory opened. They settled Buffalo in 1879. Though steeped in the blood of Indians and military men, the surrounding country quickly became range to thousands of cattle and, eventually, sheep. By the 1980s it was one of Wyoming's greatest sheep-production areas, and it became popular among Basque herders and their families. A late-spring snowstorm here in 1984 killed thousands of head of sheep. Deep snow and cold temperatures took their toll on animals still trying to regrow wool already shorn for the coming summer. The dead sheep and some cattle piled in draws and coulees in scenes reminiscent of the Great Die-Up of 1886–87.

Low market prices made it impossible for most sheepmen to fully recover. They struggled to revive an industry attacked by nature on one hand and changes in traditional economic supports on the other. In the late 1980s, sheep producers said they needed about 65 cents per pound to break even but the market rate was only about 45 to 50 cents per pound. Then changes in governmental regulation limited their ability to kill predators, primarily coyotes, and in April 1993 a lawsuit by the Humane Society of the United States halted all but emergency control of predators. In October 1993 the sheepmen appealed to a federal judge to lift the ban imposed by the U.S. Bureau of Land Management in response to the April lawsuit.

Buffalo street scene, from the courthouse yard. —J. E. Stimson Collection/Wyoming State Museum

On top of everything else, Congress in 1994 approved a measure to eliminate wool subsidies, even though the funds came from a tariff on foreign wool and not from taxes on Americans. That, the range-sheep industry predicted, could be the final nail in its coffin.

US 16
Buffalo—Ten Sleep
65 miles

Fort McKinney

Just west of Buffalo, south of US 16 as it heads into the Bighorn Mountains over the Cloud Peak Skyway, stands the Wyoming Veteran's Home. Originally known as Fort McKinney, it served as an important military post after the second Sioux War of 1876–78. Its troops guarded communication lines, helped suppress the Crow during the "Sword Bearer" incident in 1887, and dealt with the Lakota during the Ghost Dance affair and the battle of Wounded Knee in 1890.

The army built Fort McKinney to stop Indians from leaving the reservations and returning to their traditional life on ancestral hunting grounds. Although often confused with an earlier military outpost with the same name located some sixty miles farther east, Fort McKinney had no real connection to that facility, also known as Cantonment Reno (see page 302).

The fort west of Buffalo was named for Lt. John A. McKinney, who died in the Dull Knife fight on Red Fork. Troops began occupying the post in July 1878. It sat at the base of the Bighorns in almost complete isolation. The nearest military posts were Fort Custer, 125 miles northwest, in Montana; Fort Fetterman, some 140 miles southeast; and Fort Washakie, about 150 miles southwest. Fort McKinney lay nearly 225 miles from the nearest railroad station, Rock Creek on the Union Pacific in southern Wyoming Territory, not far from Laramie.

In addition to keeping the Indians in check, the troops at Fort McKinney guarded communication lines, including the Rock Creek stage, which provided mail, passenger, and express service from Rock Creek to Terry's Landing on the Yellowstone River. They also built and maintained the first telegraph line into the Powder River country. From their post, the soldiers watched civilian sport hunters exterminate the buffalo herds that roamed in Powder River country, and they saw cattle move onto the range. They rode to the TA Ranch in April 1892 to arrest the cattlemen in the Johnson County Invasion, taking them into custody and almost certainly saving them from a vigilante lynch mob.

In 1903 the State of Wyoming obtained control of the facilities at Fort McKinney. It dismantled or removed many of the buildings through the years but kept the site in use as the Veteran's Home.

Black and Yellow Trail

A highway from Chicago to Yellowstone National Park emerged in 1912 when representatives of communities along the route joined to promote it. Officially the Chicago, Black Hills and Yellowstone Highway but better known as the Black and Yellow Trail, the route entered Wyoming on US 14, continued on US 14-16 from Gillette to Ucross, then followed US 16 to Buffalo and over the Bighorn Mountains to Cody via Ten Sleep, Worland, Basin, and Greybull.

Early on people were skeptical, arguing that automobiles couldn't cross the rugged Bighorn Mountains west of Buffalo. However, promoter Anson Higby proved otherwise. Higby, his daughter, and passenger "Brownie" Carland drove a Studebaker over the range from Basin to demonstrate the highway's feasibility. When completed, the Black and Yellow Trail crossed four states: Illinois, Wisconsin, South Dakota, and Wyoming.

Now there are two automobile routes across the Bighorns: the original Black and Yellow Trail—now called the Cloud Peak Skyway west of Buffalo—and the Bighorn Scenic Byway on US 14, connecting Ranchester with Lovell and Greybull.

Buffalo—Montana Line
58 miles

The interstate highway swings toward the Bighorns as it heads north out of Buffalo toward Sheridan and the Montana state line. About a dozen miles north of Buffalo, I-90 crosses the Bozeman Trail as that route moves up Piney Creek toward Fort Phil Kearny.

Fort Phil Kearny, 1866–68

As 1865 drew to a close, the northern Plains were bloody from the calculated attacks of the Sioux, making good on their promise to fight for every inch of the Powder River country. But gold seekers clamored for a quick route to Montana's gold country, and the military became determined to open the Bozeman Trail.

Maj. Gen. John Pope, commander of the Department of the Missouri, ordered two forts built north of Fort Connor. He made Col. H. B. Carrington commander of the mountain district, with orders to proceed from Fort Kearny, Nebraska, to garrison the new posts. When Carrington arrived at Fort Laramie in June 1866, he found Red Cloud in council with government envoys, who were trying to obtain tribal permission for the forts. Red Cloud refused and left the conference, vowing to fight for his land (see page 298).

Though warned by the Cheyenne that the Sioux meant business when they told the military not to venture north of the North Platte River, Carrington proceeded to build his headquarters on a high plateau between the forks of Big and Little Piney creeks. Named Fort Phil Kearny, the stockaded post had a strategic location and could be used "to defy thousands when I get ammunition," Carrington said in a July 31, 1866, letter to General Sherman.

Fort Phil Kearny was one point in a three-pronged system of forts along the Bozeman Trail. The first, Fort Connor, sat about seventy-five miles east of Fort Phil Kearny. Later named Fort Reno, that location saw limited action. Construction on the final outpost, Fort C. F. Smith, started August 12, 1866, ninety-one miles north of Fort Phil Kearny on the Little Bighorn River in Montana Territory.

Although he enjoyed a strategic location at Fort Phil Kearny, Carrington had to operate under less-than-ideal circumstances. His troops had old, muzzle-loading Springfield rifles that fell far short of the quality needed by infantry and were wholly unsuited for use by mounted men. Carrington often lobbied his superiors for better guns, more ammunition, and increased food and other supplies, but the response was never immediate and seldom positive. It seemed that higher authorities refused to acknowledge any serious problems on the road through Powder River country.

Fort Phil Kearny's location provided a decent view of the surrounding countryside, but it had disadvantages. Soldiers had to constantly haul wood from the pinery in the nearby Bighorn Mountains to the fort for construction as well as for heating and cooking fuel. That routine left an opening for the Lakota, who watched for weaknesses in the military's position.

Military lookouts stationed on Pilot Hill, just south of the fort, used a system of signals to indicate attacks on wood trains by the Indians. One such incident took place December 6, 1866, about two miles from the fort, when Red Cloud and his warriors charged. The wood train's escorting troops panicked, and it was all the officers could do to save them from annihilation.

Fetterman's Fight, 1866

A couple of weeks later, Lt. William J. Fetterman of the 18th Cavalry and eighty men found what a little confidence could do for the Indians. Often disparaging of the Indians' fighting ability, Fetterman had once boasted that with eighty men he "could ride through the whole Sioux nation." On December 21, he and his command rode from the fort to relieve a beleaguered wood train. None of the eighty-one rescuers returned alive.

As Fetterman and his troops left the confines of Fort Phil Kearny, Carrington told him not to pursue the Indians beyond Lodge Trail Ridge. Fetterman's command rode out of the fort and headed north on a line somewhat parallel to today's I-90 and US 87. As the command came in sight of the Lakota, Fetterman disobeyed Carrington's orders and crossed Lodge Trail Ridge. On a high hogback between the two present-day highways and about five miles from Fort Phil Kearny, the Lakota caught Fetterman's party in a cleverly designed trap. The troops at the fort heard the intense firing, and seventy-six men under Capt. Tenodore Ten Eyck hurried out. They found the bodies of Fetterman and his entire command halfway down the ridge. The wood train Fetterman was to assist reached the fort late that afternoon, unaware that there had been a major encounter.

None of the Fetterman party survived the battle, which is remembered as the Fetterman Massacre. It wasn't really a massacre but rather an engagement between two fighting forces. The superior side inflicted a stunning defeat upon its opponent. The site is marked now with a tall rock monument and a series

Dedication of the Fetterman Massacre Monument, July 4, 1908, by Col. H. B. Carrington. The two-track road in the foreground, marked by telegraph poles, is now Wyoming 196. I-90 crosses the ridge near the top of this photo. —Wyoming State Museum

of trails at the edge of US 87 and clearly visible from I-90, looking west about midway between Buffalo and Sheridan. Visitors can plan trips to historic sites in the area by first visiting Fort Phil Kearny State Historic Site, which has a detailed interpretation of the battles, including location maps.

When Carrington learned of the loss, he immediately reinforced Fort Phil Kearny, knowing if the Lakota pressed their victory they could overrun the fort. While Captain Ten Eyck rode to Fetterman's aid, Carrington armed the orderlies, the cooks, and the prisoners from the guardhouse. Carrington himself went out the next morning to recover some of the bodies. Before leaving he secretly instructed a soldier to blow up the munitions storehouse, with the women and children inside, if Indians stormed the fort.

In the fort's darkest hour, with the news of Fetterman's disastrous foray fresh in his mind and knowing that hundreds of hostile Indians roamed the rolling hills just outside the fort's gates, Portuguese civilian John Phillips stepped forward. Phillips and about sixty other miners under the leadership of Robert Bailey had prospected in the Pryor and Bighorn mountains west and north of Fort Phil Kearny during the summer and autumn of 1866. When snow began to fall in the Bighorns, forty-two of the miners, including Phillips and Bailey, moved to Fort Phil Kearny. Bailey soon started working as a post guide and mail carrier for $10 per day. Phillips didn't work for the government prior to December 21, 1866.

Legend has it that on that fateful day Phillips told Carrington he would take the news to Fort Laramie and ask for help if he could choose his own mount. The legend further says Phillips took the colonel's own thoroughbred, Grey Eagle, but that story is of doubtful veracity.

Under cover of darkness and a buffalo robe, with a sackful of oats for his horse and a few biscuits for himself, Phillips rode from Fort Phil Kearny into a blinding subzero snowstorm. He did not make the ride alone. Daniel Dixon, another citizen courier, also rode from Fort Phil Kearny that winter night. It's not clear if they left together or separately. The men stopped for up to ten hours at Fort Reno and likely made one camp on the Cheyenne River and another at Bridger's Ferry on the North Platte. Phillips and Dixon delivered their message from Carrington to the telegraph operator at Horseshoe Station, some 190 miles away, four days after they started. Phillips then carried another message on to Fort Laramie. It's not clear whether or not Dixon accompanied him on that last forty-mile stretch. Each man earned $300 for his work (see page 132).

Immediately after Phillips and Dixon delivered the messages, Lt. Col. Henry Wessels of Fort Reno got orders to take two companies of cavalry and four of infantry to Fort Phil Kearny. They arrived in early January. Carrington lost his command. General Sherman ordered retaliation upon the Indians, writing, "It is not necessary to find the very men who committed the acts, but destroy all of the same breed."

Maj. James W. Powell, standing, commanded troops during the Wagon Box Fight in August 1867 when Sioux under Crazy Horse attacked soldiers gathering wood near Story. John "Portugee" Phillips, seated, rode 236 miles from Fort Phil Kearny to Fort Laramie in December 1866 following a fight that involved Lt. William J. Fetterman with eighty men and Red Cloud, Crazy Horse, and their Lakota warriors. Fetterman's entire command died in the battle.
—Wyoming State Museum

The army quickly began formulating plans for a retaliatory campaign to begin about March 1, 1867. In a letter to Maj. Gen. Christopher C. Augur, Sherman requested authority to manage the Indians and said the government should consider all the Sioux near the Powder River and Yellowstone hostile and "punish them to the extent of utter extermination if possible."

But for the time being, the Sioux controlled Powder River country, and for all practical purposes the Bozeman road closed. Along the South Platte conditions were nearly as bad, with fighting at numerous locations, including at Brady's Island and Ash Hollow in Nebraska. The tribes also interfered with construction of the Union Pacific Railroad. Most of the Oregon-California Trail traffic shifted to the Overland Trail, which crossed farther south.

In July 1867 Congress created an Indian Peace Commission to call together the various chiefs and negotiate treaties to remove the causes of war, provide for safety along the Union Pacific Railroad line and in frontier settlements, and begin a plan to civilize the tribes.

Wagon Box Fight, 1867

The Lakota, in no mood for a peace commission, continued their attacks. Sioux forces under Crazy Horse and Red Cloud struck on a flat area northwest of Fort Phil Kearny, just below the pinery where wood companies gathered supplies.

After the Fetterman battle, the Lakota constantly harassed Fort Phil Kearny's wood and hay crews, which worked outside the stockade only under heavy guard. Near the pinery, a barricade made of the boxes from sixteen wooden wagons served as a temporary fortification for the men whenever Indians threatened. The makeshift rampart covered a flat sagebrush area about five miles northwest of the fort near Big Piney Creek.

On July 31, 1867, Civil War veteran Maj. James Powell took fifty-one troopers to the pinery to guard a wood crew. Finding the wood cutters divided into two camps about a mile apart, he separated his small force. Wood cutting continued without incident on August 1, although Lakota farther north had great success near Fort C. F. Smith in a battle known as the Hayfield Fight.

The situation changed on Piney Creek the morning of August 2, when the Sioux attacked the wood crews and the stock tenders, who were looking after the wood haulers' horses and mules. Some of the haulers escaped to Fort Phil Kearny, but Red Cloud and his warriors surrounded twenty-eight soldiers and four civilians in the wagon-box corral.

If the attack had gone as Red Cloud expected, it might have ended similarly to the Fetterman battle. Accustomed to a delay between rifle volleys, Red Cloud timed his assaults to catch the soldiers reloading. But Powell's men had new breech-loading Springfield rifles and about a thousand rounds of ammunition. The warriors rushed in when they thought the soldiers would be reloading, only to meet another hail of gunfire. Facing the unexpected firepower, Red Cloud's warriors dismounted and crept as close as possible to the barricade, then charged on foot, hoping to overwhelm the soldiers by sheer numbers. That tactic failed, too, but only because the Indians didn't press their numerical advantage.

The Indians charged recklessly and bravely around the battlefield, retrieving their fallen comrades even as the men in the wagon-box barricade shot at them. But the native Americans weren't the only brave ones that day. When the men in the corral became frantic with thirst, two of them crawled about 100 feet from the relative safety of the wagon boxes and retrieved two kettles full of cooking water.

In a last, desperate attempt to overrun the soldiers, the Indians massed together and swarmed on foot up a ravine toward the fortification. Once again the thirty-two men behind the wagon boxes held back the attack. Early that afternoon the Indians broke ranks and started away from the hillside site. Fortunately for the defenders, reinforcements were on the way.

Powell and his troops agreed the Lakota could have easily overrun them had they advanced steadily with their entire force, which was estimated to include at least 1,500 warriors. If the Indians had succeeded, many of the troopers were prepared to die by their own hand. About half of the soldiers pulled off their shoes, tied the laces together, and attached them to their rifles and their toes to "blow our heads off before we would be captured by Red Cloud's cut-throat Sioux Indians," Pvt. Sam Gibson said in an account of the battle. The wagon-box fight was not nearly the military disaster the Fetterman battle had been. Indians killed three soldiers in the attack on the corral and wounded two others. It's uncertain how many Lakota fell; estimates range from 50 to 60, with an additional 200 to 300 wounded.

There are two markers at the battle site, which is now owned by the Phil Kearny/Bozeman Trail Association. To reach it, follow a gravel road from Fort Phil Kearny that heads directly up the creek along the route of the wood caravans or go to Story on Wyoming 193 and then follow the "Wagon Box" signs.

Fort Phil Kearny was located about a dozen miles north of present-day Buffalo. Wyoming 193 gives access to the site, the Wagon Box and Fetterman battlegrounds, and the small towns of Banner and Story.

Red Cloud's Demands

Although a peace commission convened at Fort Laramie during the fall of 1867, Red Cloud didn't participate. All the army had to do to make peace was abandon the Bozeman road, Red Cloud said. Surprisingly, it appeared that the government might accept those terms. The army was taking a pounding on the Bozeman Trail and did not have a force adequate to keep that route open and simultaneously protect crews constructing the transcontinental railroad. Besides, the army reasoned, with the railroad in place, soldiers could break a new road to Montana from some other point west of Fort Laramie, making the Bozeman route unnecessary.

For these reasons, the military decided to abandon the three Bozeman Trail forts. Troops at Fort C. F. Smith marched away on July 29, 1868; at dawn the next day Red Cloud and his warriors swept down on the post and set it afire. Within days Forts Phil Kearny and Reno stood empty, and the Lakota torched them as well.

Red Cloud had held the Powder River country; he'd destroyed the hated forts and closed the Bozeman road. His warriors hunted during the late summer and early fall. Finally, on November 4, 1868, the chief went to Fort Laramie and "with a show of reluctance and tremulousness washed his hands with the dust of the floor" and put his mark on the peace treaty. It held eight years before the struggle erupted again.

Lake De Smet

Located east of I-90 a few miles south of Sheridan, Lake De Smet is a popular recreational area. Named for Father Pierre Jean De Smet, who is believed to be the first white man known to have seen it, the lake has spawned several legends. For example, locals say that a monster sometimes appeared amid the mist rising from Lake De Smet. One story goes that in 1938 a group of Sheridan sportsmen, equipped with life preservers, a shortwave radio set, a cow for bait, Izaak Walton's book on fishing, and a pitchfork, set out to capture this creature. The fishermen hooked the monster, but as they pulled it from the water it exploded; the debris included twelve horseshoes, the wheel of a road grader, Father De Smet's Bible, thirteen Indian scalps, a backless bathing suit, a piece of track from the old north-south railroad, and an outboard motor.

Now, if you believe *that* one, try this second legend. Crow Indians tell a story of Little Moon, who asked his love, Star Dust, to meet him at the edge of the lake. While waiting for her, he saw a lovely maiden's face in the dark waters. He prepared to join the beautiful girl in the lake when Star Dust touched his arm. Furious, he commanded her to leave him and returned his gaze to the lake, only to find the face gone. As the sun rose over the eastern hills the next morning, the Crows found Star Dust drowned on the shore. Her father tied Little Moon to a rock, leaving him to watch for the water maiden. The Crows say that when the wind moans over the lake, the warrior is calling.

Sheridan

According to her own account, it was on the future site of Sheridan that Martha Jane Canary became Calamity Jane. The story is told in the *Life and Adventures of Calamity Jane, by Herself*, which the frontierswoman published and peddled during her old age. There are many tales about how she earned her nickname; this is just one of them, but it makes a pretty good story. Let Martha Jane tell it:

It was during this campaign [Big Horn, 1872] that I was christened Calamity Jane. It was on Goose Creek, Wyoming, where the town of Sheridan is now located, Captain Egan was in command of the post. We were ordered out to quell an uprising of the Indians, and were out for several days, had numerous skirmishes during which six of the soldiers were killed and several severely wounded. When returning to the post we were ambushed about a mile and a half from our destination. When fired upon Captain Egan was shot. I was riding in advance and on hearing the firing turned in my saddle and saw the captain reeling in his saddle as though about to fall. I turned my horse and galloped back with all haste to his side and got there in time to catch him as he was falling. I lifted him onto my horse in front of me and succeeded in getting him safely to the post. Captain, on recovering, laughingly said, "I name you Calamity Jane, the heroine of the plains."

First Settlers in Sheridan

Trappers, like gold miners, seem to appear everywhere in Wyoming's history. Trapper Jim Mason probably erected the first building at what became Sheridan in 1878. In 1881 Harry Mandel converted the one-room Mason cabin into a store and post office, calling the tiny settlement Mandel.

In 1882 J. D. Loucks purchased the Mandel property, drew a plat of Sheridan on a piece of brown wrapping paper, prepared a petition for incorporation, got the signatures needed, and mailed it off with the $3 registration fee. Loucks staked the forty-acre town on May 10, 1882, and named it for his Civil War commander, Gen. Philip H. Sheridan. On March 6, 1883, the Wyoming Territorial Assembly approved Sheridan's incorporation, and Loucks became mayor. It is the lowest town in Wyoming, sitting only 3,745 feet above sea level.

Cattle ranchers helped build Sheridan in the 1880s, and it remains a stock-raising area, although coal mining is now an important part of the economy as well. The early-day cattle barons came to town surrounded by their legions of armed riders, and homesteaders traveled the range in armed groups. The homesteaders were branded rustlers by the big men in the Wyoming Stock Growers Association, and men from the two groups avoided each other in the streets. The early days of Sheridan's settlement became a period of war not only between the military and the Indians but also between homesteaders and cattlemen.

The Railroad Arrives

In 1892 the Chicago, Burlington & Quincy Railroad reached Sheridan, making development of coal seams in the area possible. That same year George Holdredge, the railroad's general manager, developed the idea for a lavish inn in Sheridan. As the rail line moved toward the town, Holdredge organized a company that hired architect Thomas R. Kimball of Omaha, Nebraska, to design the facility. Kimball used his impression of an old Scottish country inn in formulating the plans. When completed and opened in 1893, the 130-foot-long Sheridan Inn became the town's social center; decked out with electric lights and bathtubs, it marked a new era.

The story goes that William F. Cody led the grand march at the opening, where Sheridan Inn managers served champagne from iced tubs. From 1894 until 1896 Cody operated the inn, which served as the Sheridan headquarters for his Wild West Show. He added an elaborate set of barns and a livery stable for the Cody Transportation Company. At times Cody auditioned cowboys for his show by having them race and ride along the street and grounds as he sat watching from the wide veranda.

In the huge dining room, the cattle-raising aristocracy danced the schottische and the Virginia reel. Wealthy sportsmen drawn to the area for the hunting opportunities in the nearby Bighorn Mountains often stayed at the inn.

Eventually the Sheridan Inn closed and fell into disrepair. It was condemned in 1967, but local artist Neltje Kings rescued the historic building. She remodeled and restored the inn, preserving many features of the original oak and mahogany Buffalo Bill bar. A local group later obtained the building and in 1993 the Sheridan Inn celebrated its centennial while the restoration continued.

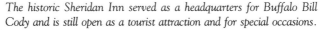

The historic Sheridan Inn served as a headquarters for Buffalo Bill Cody and is still open as a tourist attraction and for special occasions.

Big Horn

Nestled against the Bighorn Mountains a few miles south of Sheridan on Wyoming 335, the town of Big Horn gained renown as a retreat for wealthy cattlemen and English aristocrats. The Bozeman Trail ran through the town in the 1860s. In 1878, when O. P. Hanna moved into the Big Horn Valley, he found a log house on Little Goose Creek with stables large enough for twenty horses. The facility may have been a hideout for Jesse and Frank James and a loose confederation of outlaws and road agents led by Big Nose George Parrott.

The area is really more well-known for its citizenry at the other end of the social scale. Malcolm and William Moncrieffe arrived from Scotland during the Boer War to buy horses for the British army. They did well at that task, shipping about 20,000 horses to Africa. They used the proceeds to buy a parcel of land along Little Goose Creek and stock it with sheep. In 1923 William returned to England, but Malcolm remained in charge of the Moncrieffe Ranch, where he raised prize-winning Rambouillet and Corriedale breeding sheep. He sold the animals throughout the United States and several foreign countries.

With the ranch's ties to the nobility in England, it wasn't surprising that when Queen Elizabeth visited Wyoming in the 1980s, she stayed at the Moncrieffe-Wallop Ranch as the guest of U.S. Senator Malcolm Wallop, a descendant of the Moncrieffes with a blood tie to the British royalty. The queen toured throughout this area of Wyoming, including a visit to the King Saddlery in downtown Sheridan, where for nearly half a century Don King and his sons have been producing exquisite floral-patterned saddles and some of the top ropes made in the West. This town is well-known for its saddlemakers who carve "Sheridan Style" saddles for working cowboys on the range and for collectors as well. Sheridan Style is characterized by floral patterns with intricate stems and designs.

US 14
Ranchester—Burgess Junction
33 miles

Connor Battle, 1865

About fourteen miles north of Sheridan, the Tongue River swings around and through Ranchester. In late August 1865 a tragic battle of the Indian war in Wyoming took place nearby. Sentiment ran high that year against the native Americans, with many in the military holding the opinion that the only good Indian was a dead Indian. Maj. Gen. P. E. Connor surrounded Black Bear and Old David's Arapaho village the morning of August 29. About 700

Arapahoes, who had theretofore been passive in the Indian conflicts, came under fire by Connor's troops, who destroyed about 250 lodges, killing women and children. The battle had many similarities to the Sand Creek Massacre in Colorado the year before.

The battle site is now a state park. Picnic tables and children's play areas mark the spot where the Indians fell under Connor's attack.

US 14 heads west from Ranchester, leading into the Bighorn Mountains and providing a scenic route to the Big Horn Basin. The highway gives access to the Bighorn National Forest, the historic McShane Timber Company Tongue River Tie Flume, and, on the east side of the divide, the Medicine Wheel. Before heading up the mountain, however, the road crosses through prime ranching country and the town of Dayton.

Dayton

Because the Indians ruled the Powder River country for so long, white settlers feared them well into the 1880s. Often out of ignorance people spread news of attack when nothing of the sort had happened. In one such incident, on November 4, 1887, a rumor raced through the area that Indians had started burning Dayton. A party en route to Sheridan saw red flames against the sky and concluded it was the work of the Crows.

Ranch families fled to Sheridan, where barricades went up at some of the larger public buildings. They feared for Dayton residents and worried the attack would reach Sheridan. At dawn scouts went to Dayton and found there had been no attack by Indians. Instead, a drunk, ordered out of town, had sought refuge in a haystack. As the temperature dropped, the man, whose mind obviously remained sodden with liquor, started a fire in a straw stack to keep himself warm.

Even knowing that a drunk had precipitated the fire and the scare, residents stayed on edge. Several days later the *Sheridan Post* reported: "A number of our settlers have laid in a heavy supply of ammunition. Sackett bought 500 rounds. He has a large cellar under his new house, and thinks that with his force of work hands he can stand off quite a bunch [of Indians]."

Wyoming's First Dude Ranch

Western dude ranching started in South Dakota at the Custer Trail Ranch, owned by Howard Eaton. Joined by brothers Alden and Willis, Eaton came from Pittsburgh, Pennsylvania. Their friends visited the Custer Trail Ranch, returning time after time. Eventually the guests insisted on paying their way, leading Eaton to begin charging for the hospitality his ranch offered.

Eaton sold the South Dakota property and moved to northern Wyoming in 1904, where he established the Eaton Ranch on Wolf Creek, about ten miles from Dayton. The ranch is a miniature town, with a post office, store, telephone system, individual houses, and hotel.

That property is considered the first dude ranch in Wyoming, although some ranches in western parts of the state had guests staying with them at about the same time. Dude ranching grew from the desire of nonresidents, primarily Easterners, to visit western ranches, where they could ride horses, eat and sing around roaring campfires, and still have the comfort of a soft bed in a western cabin.

Dude ranching spread throughout Wyoming and the West. Some ranches survived the Depression and World War II to continue in business into the 1990s. Many have become exclusive western resorts featuring tennis courts, golf courses, and swimming pools in addition to gourmet-style meals. One thing hasn't changed: The guests still sleep in soft beds in western cabins.

Following the lead of dude ranches, many working ranches during the 1980s and 1990s started hosting paying guests as well. They allowed the customers to help with ranch chores such as trailing and branding cattle, fixing fences, and stacking hay. The city slickers paid for the privilege of doing work and provided an economic shot in the arm to ranchers facing tough times when livestock prices fell and costs rose.

Bighorn Scenic Byway

As it crosses the Bighorn Mountains, US 14 becomes the Bighorn Scenic Byway. It switchbacks up the east-facing mountains, giving a magnificent view of the towns of Dayton, Ranchester, and Sheridan and such points as Black Mountain and Steamboat Point. Crow Indians called one 1,800-foot limestone outcrop on the face of the mountain La-zee-ka for its resemblance to the tongue of a buffalo. Later residents called it the Tongue; thus, the stream that begins on the mountain and travels to the valley floor below became Tongue River.

The Tongue River Tie Flume operated high in the Bighorn Mountains from 1893 to 1913, providing a quick, efficient way to transport everything from railroad ties to groceries, fish, and people. The first tie floated downstream on September 20, 1893, when the *Sheridan Post* reported, "the tie, gaily and patriotically dressed in flags and ribbon rosettes of red, white and blue . . . sped swiftly away, gracefully winding around the curve into the canyon, bearing aloft the stars and stripes which proudly waved to and fro in the evening breeze."

Besides the ties, the flume transported other goods in rough vessels called flume boats that might have been the forerunner to some of Disney's Magic Kingdom rides. At times the boats flew out of the flume trough and landed on the canyon floor. Loose splinters stabbed passengers as the craft sped down the mountain raceway. On one five-mile descent the boats dropped about 2,700 feet in elevation in four minutes. Tie-flume worker Oscar A. Granum said of that portion of the ride in 1912:

After my first horror-stricken glimpse of what faced us, I have little or no recollection of what followed. . . . I recall that a stream of water was coming up through the boat and into my right nostril, but I seemed powerless to move my head to get away from it. That was the only distinct recollection I have of this entire wild ride.

A series of fires at the McShane Timber Camp, owned by J. H. McShane and F. J. McShane, and a decreased need for railroad ties eventually led to the decline of the tie industry in this region. The flume ceased operation in 1913, but remnants of the massive timber structure litter the forest floor.

View of the log work in the McShane Timber Camp tie flume, Bighorn National Forest. —State Historic Preservation Office

Beulah—Devils Tower

A loop road north of I-90 through Beulah, Aladdin, Alva, Hulett, and Devils Tower Junction tours the country explored by Lt. Col. George A. Custer in 1874 as he determined whether the military should build a base to enforce Indian ownership of the Black Hills and keep gold-hungry miners out. When Custer's expedition confirmed the presence of gold in the hills, however, establishment of a military site became a moot point. The miners intended to get into the hills, and nothing, not even the army, had much chance of stopping them.

Swinging up and over the Black Hills, Wyoming 24 rolls through fields of alfalfa and grain. There is little or no irrigation in this part of Wyoming, so the crops depend mostly upon winter snow for soil moisture and spring and summer rains for growth. This area has something else that's even more unusual for Wyoming: an oak forest. Nowhere else in the state do oak trees grow and thrive. From Beulah through Aladdin and Alva to Hulett, the oaks send their roots into the dark red soil.

This might be about the only place in the state that experiences a regular autumn, with red and orange leaves like those you see pictured in New England postcards. Here the oak leaves glow when the nights turn cool, the days become short, and the sap drops in the trees. In other areas of Wyoming, fall brings a splash of yellow and sometimes orange foliage on cottonwood and aspen trees.

Beulah

The 1875 gold rush to the Black Hills in the Lead and Deadwood, South Dakota, area temporarily spilled over to Wyoming's Sand Creek, and a settlement by that name quickly grew. It later became Beulah, possibly as a tribute to the hymn "Beulah Land" or perhaps to an early-day teacher, Beulah Sylvester. The gold didn't last long and the area soon became cattle range, giving the town a measure of stability most gold-mining boomtowns never see.

Aladdin

No doubt many a tale got its start or kept spinning on the "Liar's Bench" in front of the Aladdin General Store. Bill Robinson built the store in 1892 from lumber cut at the Pearson sawmill. At one time it served as the depot and freight office for the Burlington & Northern Railroad, and the general store

Liar's Bench and post office at the Aladdin General Store, August 1993.

still offers an upstairs filled with antiques, the post office, a pay phone, and the Liar's Bench.

Aladdin apparently took its name from the Arabian folktale and once boasted about twenty houses owned by the Aladdin Coal Mine Company, as well as a hotel, boardinghouse, saloon, and barber shop. The highway that connects Aladdin and Alva crosses the trail Custer and the U.S. 7th Cavalry took in 1874 as they explored the Black Hills region.

Hulett

The economy of Hulett depends on tourism, ranching, and timbering. In the 1980s local rancher John Dorrance, an heir to the Campbell Soup fortune, tried to bring exotic game animals into Wyoming. His ranch bordered Devils Tower National Monument, and Dorrance wanted to provide an additional tourist attraction as a way to support the local economy. Dorrance imported a variety of exotic species from Europe and Asia and built elaborate fences, only to land in the middle of a court fight when the Wyoming Game and Fish Department argued that introduction of the exotic deer and other animals could lead to disease in Wyoming's native game species.

The game department won the battle, and Dorrance removed the imported animals from his ranch. Ironically, cattle rancher Dorrance briefly raised one argument during the court fight to the effect that cattle breeds such as Hereford, Angus, and shorthorn and sheep breeds such as Columbia and Suffolk aren't indigenous to Wyoming and perhaps shouldn't have been allowed into the state, either.

Devils Tower

Rising from the green hills, Devils Tower climbs into view long before you get there, regardless of the direction from which you approach. This first national monument in the United States is the basis for many Indian legends. Trappers likely saw the strange formation, and scientists H. Newton and Walter P. Jenney studied it in 1875 in connection with their geological survey of the Black Hills. By 1890 ranchers had claimed land within site of the tower, but in 1892 the government withdrew the area around the tower's base from homestead acreage and created Devils Tower Reserve.

President Theodore Roosevelt designated a 1,194-acre tract around the tower the country's first national monument on September 24, 1906. Devils Tower, as it's known in modern times and by Euro-Americans, rises from the Belle Fourche River Valley, with a beard of pine trees and a jumble of huge granite boulders at its base. The cylindrical column inspires and impresses visitors. The grooved pieces of rock that make up the tower's edges look as if they could tumble down with great force, and the pile of boulders at the tower's base suggests that such erosion does take place, but geologists say no sections of the tower have crashed down during the twentieth century.

Devils Tower is one of three notable rock formations in this area of Wyoming. The other two, known as the Missouri Buttes, stand about four miles to the northwest. All three landmarks are of the same type of stone, which suggests they formed during the same period, perhaps 50 or 60 million years ago. Although scientists believe the tower today looks much the same as it did 10,000 years ago, they still debate exactly how it formed.

Several native American legends involve the tower. Many tribes frequented the area, including the Kiowa, Arapaho, Crow, Cheyenne, and Sioux. Indians still consider this a sacred site. The Kiowa call it Tso-aa, meaning "tree rock." They have a story that seven sisters and their brother played near the tree rock one day. Suddenly the boy began to change into a bear. The terrified sisters ran to the stump of a great tree, with the bear—who used to be their brother—chasing them. The seven girls climbed the stump, which rose into the air as the bear clawed its sides. The Kiowa legend, according to N. Scott Momaday in *The Way to Rainy Mountain*, says "the seven sisters were borne into the sky, and they became the stars of the Big Dipper."

The Crows called the rock tower Dabicha Asow (Bear's Lair) and have a similar story about how a bear chased some girls to the big rock and tried to catch them. The Arapaho and Cheyenne called the tower Bear's Tipi, and the Sioux named it Mato Tipila (Bear's Lodge).

Devils Tower is the first national monument. It rises above the hill country in northeastern Wyoming and is a unique geological marker in the state. Numerous native American legends involve Devils Tower, including several versions that say the huge columns were created when a bear raked his claws upon the stone.
—Shawn Moulton

Before the tower became a national monument, it drew visitors and climbers wanting to challenge its sheer face. William "Bill" Rogers and W. A. Ripley built an oak peg ladder up the side of the rock wall, and Rogers used it to climb the tower in the first recorded ascent, on July 4, 1893. Wearing a patriotic suit of red, white, and blue, Rogers carefully went up the vertical rock wall as about 2,000 people watched from below. He hoisted a flag on the summit and then descended the tower to the sound of fiddle and organ music. Other people at the celebration that day also reportedly climbed the tower

Devils Tower.
—Wyoming Division of Tourism

using Rogers' ladder. Two years later Rogers convinced his wife, Linnie, to scale the walls. In a navy blue boomer suit and wearing knee-high leather boots, she became the first woman to climb the tower, scaling its granite walls on July 4, 1895.

A number of famous artists and photographers captured Devils Tower on film and canvas, including photographer William Henry Jackson and artist Thomas Moran, but the filming of Steven Spielberg's motion picture *Close Encounters of the Third Kind* by Columbia/EMI Film Crews in mid-May 1976 brought the most attention to the tower. The blockbuster hit featured a story line about encounters with extraterrestrial beings.

Shortly after the movie's release, wrote Mary Alice Gunderson in *Devils Tower, Stories in Stone,* a middle-aged couple known as Herff and Bonnie led a couple dozen followers out of Los Angeles "looking for a spacecraft to take them to a new kingdom. . . . Cult members prefer to stay to themselves, searching out 'high strangeness' in remote locations with high rates of UFO sightings. Followers of Herff and Bonnie have been noted by observers, in the parking lot across from the visitor's center at the base of Devils Tower."

Wyoming 585 and US 85
Sundance—Newcastle
45 miles

Inyan Kara

Native Americans called the mountains of northwestern Wyoming and western South Dakota Paha Sapa (Black Hills) or Mess Sapa (Black Mountains). White people call them the Black Hills. They extend from the northeast corner of Wyoming into western South Dakota, although in the mid-nineteenth century the mountain range extending south—now known as the Laramie Range—was also considered part of the Black Hills.

Either level or rolling plains surround today's Black Hills, separating them from the main chain of the Rockies. They might have gotten their name because the pine and spruce trees predominant in the region make them look black from a distance. A number of other types of trees grow in the hills, including white elm, cedar, hackberry, ash, burr oak, box elder, aspen, white birch, cottonwood, and ironwood. The Black Hills harbor the only sizeable stands of native timber in the area that lies east to west between the Missouri River and the Rocky Mountains and north to south between Canada and the thirty-seventh parallel (roughly the southern borders of Kansas and Colorado).

In July 1874, a major military expedition led by Lt. Col. George A. Custer explored the Black Hills. On July 20 Professor A. B. Donaldson, a member of Custer's party, described the first evening in the hills:

The sunset was of unusual splendor. The lines of stratus [sic] and each fleecy rock in the west, were tinged with orange, red and golden hues; while in the east, the purple twilight bow extended its broad arch of beauty, modest in its fainter glory; towards the south, dark mountains of cumulus were edged with brightest silver, a gorgeous pathway fit for steps of deity. But these short-lived splendors fade away. . . . The stars come out, one by one, and troop by troop, till all the constellations burn, the "music of the spheres" begins and "all the hosts of heaven rejoice." The band plays, and thus with mingled earthly and heavenly music, terrestrial beauty and celestial glory, the first day ends and the first night is ushered in to the strangers among the Black Hills.

Custer's party camped on a branch of Inyan Kara Creek on July 22 and 23, 1874. While here, Custer climbed Inyan Kara Mountain and carved his name. Two soldiers died of unknown causes and they lie in graves on the hillside east of the highway. A geologist with Custer said Inyan Kara resembled "a lunar mountain, having a rim in the shape of a horseshoe, one and a half mile across with an elongated peak rising sharply from the center . . . towering 170 feet above the rim and resembling a formation of basaltic columns." The mountain lies west of today's US 85 between Four Corners and Moskee.

Upon leaving Inyan Kara, Custer's expedition camped on Spring Creek, which he called Floral Valley because of the profusion of wildflowers. In writing of the camp, one member of Custer's party said, "The entire expedition for the time revelled in the delights of the place, the soldiers festooning their hats and their horses' bridles with flowers while the expedition's band, seated on an elevated rock ledge played 'Garey Owen,' 'The Mocking Bird,' 'The Blue Danube,' snatches from 'Il Trovatore' and other popular tunes of the day."

Jenney Stockade

A year after Custer's trip to the Black Hills, a government expedition under the leadership of Walter P. Jenney, a geologist from the New York School of Mines, moved into northeast Wyoming. That land belonged to the Sioux by treaty, but as soon as the Custer expedition confirmed the existence of gold in the Black Hills, governmental leaders started manipulations to take the land. The Lakota under Red Cloud, Spotted Tail, and other chiefs tried to retain their ownership and to keep the miners out. As before, the government maneuvered and finessed until the Indians threw up their hands in disgust and took what they could get.

When Jenney's party organized at Fort Laramie in May 1875, the Sioux still had ownership rights to the Black Hills. With total disregard for that fact, Jenney traveled on the east side of the Rawhide Buttes to Old Woman Creek and the Cheyenne River along a route that became famous as the Cheyenne-Deadwood Stage Route.

Jenney's party reached the east fork of Beaver Creek, where in early June he started constructing a stockade. In his report to the government, Jenney

331

estimated that at least 800 whites were already in the Black Hills and that "the miners poured by the hundreds into the hills, accompanying me, and gave me great assistance in prospecting the country." It was not long before definite and well-traveled trails led past the lonely outpost and the Cheyenne-Deadwood route had become a major thoroughfare. The stockade became a road ranch for travelers.

After Jenney filed his reports, the government opened negotiations with the Sioux to purchase the Black Hills, or at least to obtain mineral rights. The Sioux had little bargaining power. Hunters for the railroad had decimated the buffalo and other animals upon which they depended for food and sustenance; government officials urged the Indians to sell the Black Hills because the tribes could not feed themselves without government annuities. The army couldn't keep the gold miners out of the country, and the Lakota could do so only by waging another war, negotiators said. The gold meant nothing to the tribes, the government men said, and the land could be returned to the Indians once mining operations ceased. Red Cloud and other Lakota chiefs saw how much gold miners were taking from their land and named their price: $70 million. The Indian Peace Commission offered $6 million, and the two sides walked away from the negotiations.

In the fall of 1876, after the Sioux victory at the Little Bighorn, both sides returned to discuss ownership and use of the Black Hills. Although the Indian chiefs held out for their people, the government eventually got its way, paying $4.5 million for all of northeastern Wyoming and the Black Hills of South Dakota.

Cattlemen Claim the Land

Soon after the Black Hills opened to settlement, cattlemen recognized the value of the land. They noted the wild buffalo and wheat grasses, the rolling hills and protective draws. By 1877 cattle had started spreading across the hills, and efforts to identify the actual line between Wyoming and South Dakota territories began. Legislators in Cheyenne thought Central City, Deadwood, and Lead City were in Wyoming and wanted a legal boundary to show that fact. But when Wyoming delegates went to Washington with a proposal to have the Black Hills annexed to their territory, Congress refused.

Coming of the Railroad

Before long the Chicago, Burlington & Quincy Railroad (CB&Q) had pushed across Nebraska, the corner of Dakota Territory, and into Wyoming Territory to tap newly discovered coal fields and to serve the cattle companies. One of the contractors working on CB&Q construction, Kilpatrick Brothers & Collins of Beatrice, Nebraska, did its work with horses and mules, shovels, and a small iron scraper with two handles known as a slip.

As the grade crawled slowly toward the Nebraska-Wyoming line, one town after another sprang up ahead of the workers. In northeastern Wyoming, one such settlement started with the small log cabin of Deloss Tubbs, from Custer, South Dakota, as its nucleus. Tubbs foresaw the need for a supply point somewhere along the Belle Fourche–Custer Trail and built the cabin on the west side of Salt Creek. He ordered enough lumber to build a store on the east bank of Salt Creek on a comparatively flat area covered with scrub sage and cactus. The level ground was the site's only redeeming quality; people couldn't drink the salt water and had to haul a supply in from Stockade Beaver, several miles away. Even so, a day or two after Tubbs built his store, A. F. R. Curran built a bar. He constructed the bar itself first, then put up the building around it.

Like other towns spawned by a railroad, the community mushroomed, and by July 1, 1889, it boasted three or four saloons, gambling and dance halls, two restaurants, a dry-goods store, a small drugstore, a milkman, a Chinese laundryman, and a roofed counter where meat was sold after being killed and dressed on the open range. The town had an official name, Field City, but the title soon became lost in the hurry and bustle of the busy community, and it became Tubb Town, for Deloss Tubbs. Wrote Shelly Ritthaler in *History of Weston County*:

> Tubb Town was a busy, bustling, raunchy place. But the locals didn't care. In later years, Tubb Town would come to be referred to as "Satan's Toadstool of Prairie Dog Flats." The reference was probably well deserved because with the presence of all that transient male population, it didn't take long for the "girls" to show up.
>
> In her recollections, May Nelson Dow said, "A band of thirty of forty sporting women lived around the saloons. There was Big Maude, Old Humpy, Jimmy the Tough and dozens of others. Jimmy the Tough was a pretty little thing, reckless and wild. One time, we saw her run from a saloon, half clad in a chemise, and leap onto the back of a bronc that belonged to some cowboy. She raced round for a while through the timber then rode back to the saloon."

More settled society soon arrived in Tubb Town; the community had a Sunday school and a minister, and residents planned and donated funds for a church. Then, just two months after the town's birth, word came that the railroad route had changed and would bypass Tubb Town. That was that. Businesses packed up and moved, and within two days of hearing the railroad wasn't coming, Tubb Town had become a ghost.

Coal on the Line

Kilpatrick Brothers & Collins not only built the railroad but also saw the potential for development of area coal deposits. Two homesteading families, the Fullers and the Valentines, held claims in the canyon seven miles north of Newcastle. One day a man located a streak of coal up the canyon, which he

The narrow valley left little room for Cambria to expand. —Wyoming State Museum

later showed to Mike Gladhough, a trapper-prospector. Gladhough couldn't seem to keep the news to himself and soon informed officials of the CB&Q. The railroad men convinced Gladhough to get a sample of the coal for testing. As soon as officials at Kilpatrick Brothers & Collins realized the grade of coal in the canyon seam, Ritthaler reported, they issued an order: "Get the coal, get it quick, and get it all."

The Valentines and the Fullers had no intention of selling their homestead claims—at least, not until the money offered by company representative Frank Mondell became too large to resist. Then they gladly took the cash for the land. Mondell set up mining operations during the fall of 1887. Originally the railroad men thought of building a line to Jenney Stockade, but later they moved the route closer to the coal deposits.

By October 1888, Cambria Coal Company had formed to oversee the mining operations, with large mines on either side of the canyon. It appeared the coal deposits had no end, so the company built a camp with company-owned homes, stores, a school, hotels, lodge halls, an opera house, and even a hospital. Unlike Tubb Town, Cambria Camp was "dry"—it had no gambling halls or saloons, although the Kilpatrick brothers allowed a beer wagon to come up from Newcastle.

The Antelope Mine operated toward the west; the Jumbo, toward the east. Between 1,250 and 1,500 men worked the mines during peak production, a period of about forty years. About 13 million tons of coal came from the rich veins, but then the coal played out and the company abandoned Cambria in 1928.

Newcastle

Though not the first community in Weston County, Newcastle survived the test of time and became the county seat. In 1889, J. H. Hemmingway, first superintendent of the Cambria Coal Company, named the town for Newcastle-on-Tyne, a coal-mining center in England. The September day Newcastle lots went on sale for $150 each is the day Tubb Town died.

Miners had started a syndicate oil business near Newcastle as early as 1880 when they found oil oozing from a spring near the town. The miners built a dam below the spring, then skimmed the oil and put it into barrels to haul to Deadwood, according to the *Lusk Free Lance*, October 6, 1932. Early settlers used a pie tin to skim the oil from the spring when axle grease grew scarce. The pie tin had small holes in it to separate the oil from the water. When combined with a little mica, the oil became a good lubricant.

Although some efforts to develop oil wells started in 1890, not until 1930 did the area have any good producing wells. The oil fields extended about forty miles southwest of Newcastle and efforts to develop natural gas and bentonite got started.

The Only Indian Scare

Weston County's one and only genuine "Indian scare" came at a time of unrest on the Pine Ridge Indian Reservation just weeks after the tragedy at Wounded Knee. According to the *Newcastle Journal* of January 2, 1891, "Reports from Beaver Creek say that sixty wagons of Indians camped within five miles of here tonight. Captain O'Connor and four soldiers arrived this morning from Pine Ridge agency for the purpose of inducing the friendly Indians to return to the agency. They will leave for Beaver Creek this morning, and will ship the Indians from here—if they will go."

Newcastle mayor John L. Baird asked Governor Amos W. Barber to send 500 guns and ammunition to Newcastle, and local leaders united in asking that troops be stationed in the area. The army replied that troops weren't necessary and that Young-Man-Afraid-of-His-Horses had a pass from his agent to hunt and visit the Crows. The army general in charge described Young-Man-Afraid as "the most peaceable of the Indians and most loyal to the government."

Meanwhile, a message from the Upton area indicated about 200 Indians camped on the Belle Fourche River, with another party of about 100 to 150 native Americans moving through the area. Residents reported another group of sixty wagons camped about five miles south of Upton, saying the Indians broke into a ranch building and took all the supplies stored there. In response, officials tried to obtain additional arms or troops for Newcastle. Fortunately, the situation quieted within a matter of days, and no real conflict occurred.

I-90
South Dakota Line—Buffalo
152 miles

Vore Buffalo Jump

At a site just inside the present Wyoming–South Dakota border on I-90, native Americans traditionally ran buffalo into a sinkhole to kill the animals for meat and clothing. Excavations at the site showed that native Americans butchered the carcasses, taking the meat, hides, and other useful body parts. In 1992 community development officials in Sundance prepared a plan to preserve the Vore buffalo jump, adding an interpretive center and excavation exhibits to provide information about how people in hunting and gathering cultures survived.

South of I-90, midway between the South Dakota–Wyoming state line and Sundance, is an exclusive club that started as a private retreat for Chicago millionaire Moe Annenberg in 1931. Known in the 1990s as Ranch A, the facility started as a cabin. But it was one heck of a cabin, costing about $900,000 in 1931.

Annenberg had Charles Molesworth design furniture for the cabin. That project—which involved 245 pieces of handcrafted furniture ranging from couches and chairs to beds, tables, and lights—established Molesworth as a western furniture designer. His rustic wood style became popular during the 1930s and had a resurgence in Cody half a century later. Ranch A eventually became the property of Wyoming governor Nels Smith, who hand-dug a well that seeped oil. It may be the only hand-dug well of its type in the world, and oilmen say the pure crude needed no refining.

Temple of the Sioux

Just as I-90 separates the Temple of the Sioux—Sundance Mountain— from the town of Sundance, this land witnessed a separation of cultures. The Sioux took this land from the Crows and claimed it as their own. When white men came, they waged a bloody war on the Powder River west of here to keep the Black Hills. But in spite of tremendous victories, the Sioux ultimately lost this ground. The government gave the native Americans reservations in South

Dakota and Nebraska and promised support for the tribes, but support always came too little and too late. The Indians almost forfeited their culture as well as their land as they assimilated into white society.

On the mountain southeast of Sundance, the Sioux held a summer rendezvous to hunt, gather berries, and perform their sacred Sun Dance—at least, they did until the white government forbade them from practicing that form of their religion. For the Sun Dance, a medicine man would gather the skin on a young man's back, cut a slit, and then thread a piece of rawhide through it. The young man then became fastened to a scaffold by the rawhide thong, letting his weight pull against the tether until it tore through his flesh. While he swayed against the thong, other Indians formed a circle and danced to lend courage.

The town of Sundance lies between the sacred Sundance Mountain on the south and the Bear Lodge Mountains to the north. The community traces its roots to a trading post for ranchers built by Albert Hoge in 1879. Harry Longabaugh spent time in jail here before riding as the Sundance Kid with Butch Cassidy in the Hole-in-the-Wall country, the Little Snake River Valley, Canada, and Bolivia.

In the 1950s Sundance became the site for a U.S. Air Force base and radar station, with discussion and planning under way for a nuclear power plant. In 1962 the PM-1 nuclear reactor went on line, but it remained in place only a few years before air force personnel abandoned the plant, removing much of the equipment. Officials ordered radioactive valves and other fittings buried on the site in cylindrical tanks filled to the top with concrete grout and covered with dirt.

Moorcroft

West of Sundance the bawl of beef echoes through the Moorcroft area, a pass-through point and shipping station for cattle coming to Wyoming and Montana on the Texas Trail. Texas cattle started moving into the northern Plains during the 1870s. Cattlemen trailed beef to the Wyoming range from areas north of Texas even after the disastrous winters in the late 1880s, and in 1894 thirty-two trail herds passed through Moorcroft.

While some of the cattle came on the Chicago, Burlington & Quincy Railroad and unloaded at Orin Junction, others detrained at Harrison, Nebraska, and trailed across eastern Wyoming. Each of the herds of 2,000 to 4,000 animals strung out two miles long and a half mile wide as the cattle moved across and grazed on the Wyoming grasslands. During the 1890s the Moorcroft CB&Q shipping yards became the busiest on the line.

Not all of the Texas cattle moved on up the trail to Montana or into the Powder River Basin lands nearer to the Bighorn Mountains. Several ranchers released their herds near Moorcroft; one, John Winterling, filed on land in

1881 and built his structures in the form of a V in case of Indian attack. He never needed the defense. Few Texas cattle came into Wyoming after 1884 because quarantine laws—passed over concern about Texas tick fever—went into effect that year. Cattle continued to move onto the range from Colorado and Nebraska as well as from western Oregon and Idaho.

Gillette

Wyoming's richest northern city, Gillette, started as a livestock center but really gained prominence as a mineral hub. Coal underlies much of the Powder River Basin, and the largest deposits are in the vicinity of Gillette. The city serves as county seat for Campbell County, organized in 1869 and named for John A. Campbell, first territorial governor of Wyoming. Gillette itself, like so many other Wyoming communities, takes its name from a railroad man, in this case Edward Gillette, an engineer for the CB&Q.

Gillette first gained recognition as the place of origin for the first air flight over Wyoming, the unassembled plane having arrived in a boxcar. Charles Lindbergh is said to have landed near here on one of his flights, and the story goes that he borrowed a horse from a local boy and rode it into town.

Gillette also became a large livestock-shipping area after the Burlington Railroad moved into the area. Powder River Basin cattle and sheep trailed to town for shipment on the rail line. At times up to 40,000 head of sheep and 12,000 cattle blatted and bawled in the yards at one time, waiting their turn to load onto stock cars for shipment to midwestern markets.

The country near Gillette offers a prime example of governmental do-gooders who don't know what the devil they are doing. The 1862 Homestead Act allowed men and women to claim up to 160 acres of land. Any man or woman who was twenty-one years old or the head of a family, a U.S. citizen or in the process of becoming one, and had never fought in a war against the United States could claim a homestead.

Up for grabs were hundreds of thousands of unappropriated public acres, primarily west of the Mississippi River. In order to gain title, an individual had to live on his or her claim for at least six months each year during a five-year period and make improvements, including construction of a twelve-by-twelve cabin. After five years of development, the land became the homesteader's property. For those not wanting to wait so long, title also could be obtained by paying $1.25 per acre under a process known as preemption. Propaganda from the government, railroads, and other businesses about the good life available on free land in the West—combined with a shortage of land elsewhere—resulted in a swarm of pioneers claiming homestead tracts. Settlers brought more new United States soil under cultivation between 1862 and 1890 than in the previous two and a half centuries combined.

Like the Homestead Act, the 1873 Timber Culture Act entitled a person to 160 acres. To "prove up" ownership on the land the homesteader had to plant and keep growing 40 acres of trees for eight years. That obligation was reduced to 10 acres of trees in 1878. Although many people eventually got title to their land under the Homestead Act of 1862, only about 10 percent of those who tried were successful under the Timber Culture Act. Of the 3,123 Timber Culture Act filings in Wyoming, just 333 led to final entry under the law, according to T. A. Larson in *History of Wyoming*.

The Desert Land Act of 1877 allowed settlers to purchase or claim up to 640 acres of land that needed irrigation before it could be cultivated. Settlers could occupy the land for three years by paying 25 cents an acre, or they could obtain title for an additional dollar an acre. Many paid the 25-cent fee and used the desert land to graze their cattle or sheep, never intending to make the improvements necessary to own the ground.

Congress wanted land in the hands of individuals with small, independent farms when it limited the size of a homestead claim to 160 acres. But the government sponsors of the Homestead Act either didn't know or, more likely, didn't care that such an amount of ground in the West wouldn't sustain anywhere near enough crops or livestock to support a family.

When it became clear that they couldn't make it on their land, many homesteaders simply walked away from their toil and hardship. Others managed to sell. Government authorities purchased 35,452 acres near Spring Creek, northeast of Gillette, from forty-eight owners in order to provide larger blocks of land. Acreage in the purchase plan included small dryland farms, abandoned homesteads, and tracts of range located at strategic points for water development. Besides the privately owned land, the government obtained eleven forfeited homesteads amounting to 5,828 acres. The land acquisition cost $111,000. The U.S. Soil Conservation Service reported on effects of the program:

> The average size of operating units in the area was increased from 1,700 acres to 4,760 acres. Each operator in the area now has the use of enough land for a successful stock ranch. . . . Considerable work has been done on the land to improve its usefulness for grazing. Water facilities, including stock reservoirs and spring developments, have been the outstanding improvements made. Fence lines were altered to facilitate the management of the range. After tearing down purchased farm buildings that were no longer of any use, the salvaged material was utilized in the construction of a small recreation center and community hall, filling a long-felt need. . . . To provide for proper conservation and management of the range, the Spring Creek Cooperative Livestock Association, consisting of the 22 stockmen remaining in the area, was formed in November 1936.

Gillette's Minerals

By far most of Gillette's history is tied to minerals. Indians and trappers told of coal deposits burning in this area in the 1800s, and by 1941 at least thirty fires smoldered in area coal seams, perhaps started by lightning, campers, or spontaneous combustion.

The earliest mining activity in Wyoming occurred along the Union Pacific line, with underground and open-pit coal mines operating in the Hanna Basin and the Rock Springs area by the 1870s. During the resurgence in coal development a century later, Union Pacific ventures once again led the pace.

Emphasis on environmental preservation mushroomed during the 1960s, climaxing on Earth Day, April 22, 1970. The 1967 Federal Air Quality Act mandated increased reliance on low-sulphur coal. This type of coal, found primarily in the West, burns cleaner than other varieties. The subsequent 1970 Clean Air Act, which required coal-fired generating plants to assist in the effort to improve air quality, gave western coal a final boost. One way for these plants to avoid installing expensive scrubbers to keep their smokestacks from spewing ash, sulfur oxide, and nitrogen oxide into the air was to burn low-sulfur western coal.

Wyoming's coal industry reaped the benefits. Hanna Basin mines promoted their low-sulfur product, which had the added advantage of a high British Thermal Unit (BTU) rating. Production became fast and furious, as the southern Wyoming mines led the state in output and broke previous records. At the same time, companies leased an increasing amount of land in the Powder River Basin, as projects outlined years earlier reappeared on the planning tables of major firms.

When it became apparent that Powder River coal companies could mine less expensively than southern Wyoming operators because the coal wasn't as deep under the ground, another boom started. The Thunder Basin mine opened in 1978 and produced more than 6 million tons of coal the next year. That figure jumped to 10.5 million tons in 1980 and to 34.2 million tons in 1993, the largest amount produced by any mine in Wyoming. By comparison, in 1910 the entire state produced 7 million tons of coal.

During the 1970s and early 1980s, keen competition existed between the Hanna Basin and Powder River mines as they vied for coal contracts from midwestern utilities. The key to success became soil depth. In the Hanna Basin the coal lay buried under tons and tons of dirt, which—in open-pit mining—had to be moved before coal could be dug. Powder River coal lay much closer to the surface, so mining it was much easier and cheaper. The less expensive coal ended up getting the contracts. Production declines at Hanna dovetailed with increases in the Powder River Basin. However, in 1993 companies in both basins continued digging coal, and Wyoming led the nation with 209.9 million tons of coal produced. Of that total, 192 million tons, or 92 percent, came from the Powder River Basin. The southern mines combined for about 14 million tons. The reason for the huge difference lay not in supply but in cost. Powder River coal sold for $3 to $4 per ton for spot contracts, whereas the southern Wyoming coal sold for $25 to $30 per ton on long-term contracts.

Gillette, feeling both the positive and negative effects of the Powder River coal boom, quickly attained a reputation as a rough-and-tumble place, with occasional reports of out-of-control miners, including one who drove a bull-dozer through the middle of town. The community worked on its image and built a huge livestock pavilion and arena facility—Cam-Plex—where it could host activities ranging from concerts, craft fairs, and horse shows to the National High School Rodeo Association finals.

US 14/16
Gillette—Buffalo or Sheridan
91 or 102 miles

Heading north from Gillette, US 14/16 provides access to the small towns of Recluse, Spotted Horse, Arvada, Leiter, Clearmont, and Ucross. The trip takes you over rolling hills of dryland wheat, native grasses, and sagebrush. Some of Campbell County's largest coal mines lie north of Gillette.

Spotted Horse is a one-stop bar and restaurant. It is said to be named for an Indian chief. The Astorians camped near here in 1811 as they headed to the mouth of the Columbia River. That party also camped near the future site of Buffalo before continuing west.

Arvada is south of US 14/16 on Wyoming 341. It was originally named Suggs and features natural gas flowing from an artesian well. The story goes that local residents lit the water on fire and drank "burning water." US 14/16 forks at Ucross, known as an artist's retreat. US 16 continues to Buffalo and US 14 proceeds to Sheridan.

Wyoming 59
Gillette—Douglas
112 miles

The great mineral fields of the Powder River Basin underlie this highway, which passes through Thunder Basin National Grassland. The road rolls over grass-covered hills between the faint trace of the Bozeman road to the west and the Texas Trail to the east. At Reno Junction the road intersects Wyoming 387, which provides access to the town of Wright, the historic sites of Fort Reno, Cantonment Reno, and Fort McKinney, and farther west, to Kaycee.

Wright

Wyoming's most recent company town started at Reno Junction. Huge companies led by Amax Coal started stripping the land between Gillette and Reno Junction in the late 1970s, spawning one of the great economic booms in Wyoming. Hundreds of miners moved in, home construction escalated, and Campbell County coped with the growth the best it could.

Keeping pace with the demand for such necessities as housing, schools, and sewer and water services left officials gasping, but the huge, steady stream of income from increased sales taxes and mineral royalty revenues helped ease the pain. Housing was one of the first problems in all coal mining regions. Mineral companies used the same solution that had worked for the Union Pacific more than a century earlier: the company town. The UP built towns at Carbon, Hanna, Rock Springs, and Evanston; they included company housing and, usually, a company store.

During the energy boom of the 1970s, mineral producers once again attempted to help employees. Energy Development Corporation built company housing in Hanna; Pacific Power & Light did the same in Rock Springs. Wright, at Reno Junction, south of Gillette, was built by Atlantic Richfield. An August 11, 1975, agreement between a newly organized community development group and the corporation's Black Thunder Mine required the mine to help defray the cost of the town through a surcharge of 43 cents per ton of coal levied on their customers, according to Robert Righter, in *The Making of a Town: Wright, Wyoming*.

In July 1976 Atlantic Richfield settled a lawsuit over environmental concerns raised by the Sierra Club. Mining could then begin, so the company provided its first housing at Reno Junction: the 108-unit Cottonwood Mobile Home Park. Even as construction started, plans for a better development were in the works. That blueprint called for 1,881 housing units, including mobile homes, multifamily and single-family homes, parks, schools, commercial development, and light industry. The total cost: $14 million.

Atlantic Richfield carried through on its promises and plans. The company built the town, the miners moved into the homes, and by 1990 the well-established community had a population of 1,236.

Battle of Lightning Creek, 1903

Wyoming's final battle between Indians and whites took place October 30, 1903, in a remote area of Converse County when a party of twenty-five Sioux returning from Montana and lawmen from Newcastle locked horns. Lightning Creek is located midway between the town of Bill and Lance Creek, east of Wyoming 59.

Circumstances surrounding the fight remain shrouded in the cloak of years and uncertainty. The incident involved Eagle Feather, known to the white men as Charlie Smith; He Dog, who had a reputation as a troublemaker on the Sioux reservation; and a number of other men. As the Indians returned to their reservation homes, lawmen accused them of breaking newly enacted game laws when they camped along the old Indian trail leading from Powder River to Pine Ridge.

Some Sioux said the men left the reservation to hunt when they didn't receive the government annuities to which they were entitled. Others said they weren't hunting but *were* off the reservation, which in itself violated the treaty agreement.

Urged by Newcastle residents to enforce the game laws, Sheriff W. H. "Billy" Miller organized, deputized, and armed a posse of between five and twenty men to go with him to the Indian camp, located southwest of Newcastle. Just what went wrong when the posse met the Indians—or who fired the first shot— isn't clear, but in the fight that followed Sheriff Miller, Jackie Mills of the T7 Ranch, and Deputy Falsenburg died. The lawmen wounded or killed several Lakota, and the remaining Indians fled due east. Lee Mathews took charge of the posse and selected a group of men to pursue the native Americans. Near Hat Creek Station the Indians surrendered. Authorities took the case to trial in Douglas but lacked proof of who shot whom and how the incident became a shootout in the first place. The Indians won acquittal and returned to their reservation.

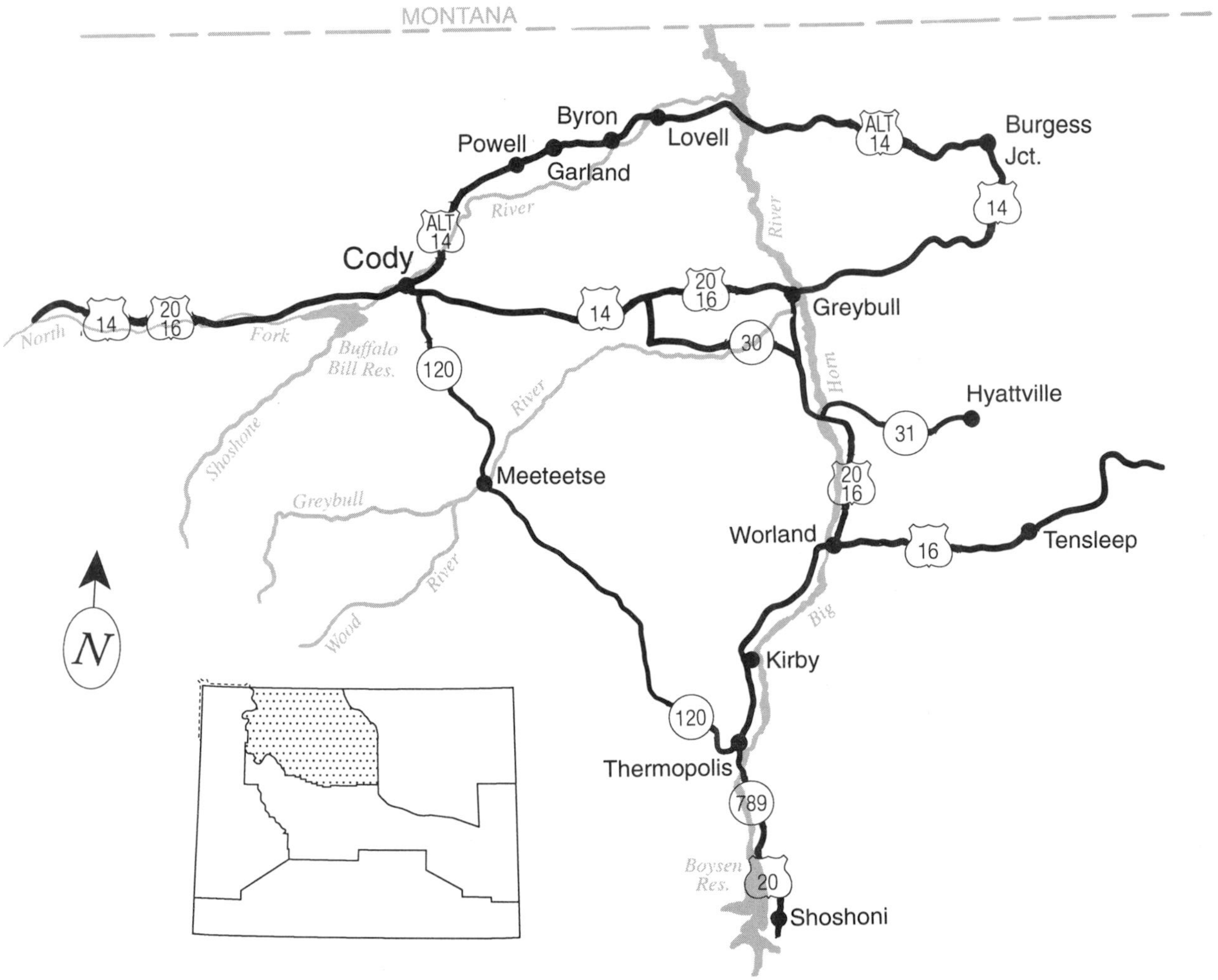

MONTANA
Powell
Byron
Garland
Lovell
Burgess
Jct.
Cody
Greybull
Hyattville
Meeteetse
Worland
Tensleep
Kirby
Thermopolis
Shoshoni
North
Fork
Buffalo
Bill Res.
Shoshone
Greybull
River
Wood
River
River
River
Horn
Big
Boysen
Res.
ALT 14
14
20 16
30
31
120
16
789
20
N

Part 5

Bighorn Country

John Colter is the first white man known to have visited the Big Horn Basin, but there is no evidence that he saw the Wind River Canyon or the hot springs at Thermopolis. The first official government exploration came with Lt. H. E. Maynadier of the Raynolds-Maynadier expedition of 1859–60.

Maynadier had trouble getting through Wind River Canyon and eventually crossed the mountains to the east with empty wagons. He hauled goods over the mountains on horseback and later abandoned his wagons. Maynadier's lousy luck continued when he lost his mules and instruments in the Stinking Water River, now known as the Shoshone.

Old mountain man Jim Bridger led the first extensive caravans into the Big Horn Basin in 1864 at the same time John M. Bozeman and John Jacobs were pioneering their trail up the east side of the Bighorns. Bridger knew the Sioux would fight to keep the Powder River lands, and he told Bozeman and Jacobs— and anyone else who would listen—not to use the route up the sunrise face of the Bighorns.

Familiar with nearly every section of Wyoming, Bridger knew the Big Horn Basin well, and he offered to guide a train of miners through this country. He forged his trail west from Fort Caspar and crossed a swale in the mountains, thereafter known as Bridger's Saddle. His crossing point lay less than ten miles from where Maynadier's wagons had stalled just a few years earlier. The route he took is now a dirt road that connects Lost Cabin with Thermopolis. Bridger then moved north and west to the Bighorn River near the present town of Lucerne, just north of Thermopolis. The trail followed the river north to a point just west of Manderson, where it turned west to a location south of Burlington. From there it moved almost due north, leaving Wyoming at a site near the present town of Frannie.

The Bridger Trail had a big advantage over Bozeman's route—less threat from Indians—but it had the distinct disadvantage of crossing a desert, the

Big Horn Basin badlands, with scarce water supplies and summer temperatures of well over 100 degrees.

For his part, Maynadier reported gold in the basin, but no one took him seriously until about 1870. At that time the Sioux peace continued tenuously. Shoshone chief Washakie resisted early efforts to force his people onto a reservation much smaller than their ancestral lands, and federal soldiers just south of the Big Horn Basin at Fort Brown and Fort Stambaugh refused to let whites enter the Big Horn Basin.

Gold seekers loathed delay, and even more they loathed being denied any opportunity to find a rich claim. From their perspective, the government's keeping them from the basin meant the gold lode must be *really* rich. They formed the Big Horn Mining Association and petitioned officials in Cheyenne for admittance to the basin.

As the grass turned green in 1870, a 1,200-member prospecting expedition started north from Cheyenne. The army permitted the group to proceed only after it promised not to go beyond the Sweetwater gold district. They agreed but didn't keep the promise. On July 19, 1870, the miners camped eight miles from Greybull River, where they feasted on buffalo and wild fruit. A cavalry troop struck out after them from Fort Brown, but it found the company in total disarray. The soldiers left the miners in the basin. Eventually the Big Horn Mining Association left the basin anyway, without any gold.

In 1879 Charles Carter trailed the first cattle from Oregon to the Big Horn Basin, and by 1883 the area had cattle on range controlled by English, Scottish, and German investors.

The Arapaho called the Big Horn Basin "Ethity Yugala." It had abundant grass for large herds of buffalo and antelope as well as Indian ponies. The Arapaho believed the spring of the great medicine man Tel-Ya-Ki-Y at present-day Thermopolis gave new life and cured ills. One Arapaho reportedly said: "It is the *Ijis*, the heaven of the Red Man. My heart cries out for it. The hearts of my people are not happy when away from the Ethity Yugala."

US 20/Wyoming 789
Shoshoni—Worland
60 miles

Wind River Canyon

The Wind River separates the Burlington Northern Railroad from US 20 as all three slice through the ancient rocks of Wind River Canyon between Shoshoni and Thermopolis. A strong wind almost always blows down the canyon, which is sheltered by high walls. According to a Shoshone legend, a young chief once walked at the head of the canyon with his sweetheart. The wind plucked an eagle feather from the girl's hair, and it floated down the canyon to settle on the earth about where Thermopolis is located. The Shoshone man and woman followed the feather to a place where steam hissed from the ground. They believed that the Great Spirit had led them to the site, so they weren't afraid as they bathed in the hot springs. They later told their people of the good qualities of the water.

At the northern end of the Wind River Canyon, where steep rock walls give way to red hills, the river changes. At a location called the Wedding of the Waters, the Wind becomes the Bighorn River. The Shoshones once claimed this land, as did the Crows. When the government established reservations, this section went to Chief Washakie and his Shoshones. The chief and his people believed this to be a sacred place, and they came here to bathe in Thermopolis's hot springs.

Smoking Water

The Shoshones called the mineral springs Bah-gue-wana, or "smoking water." They believed strongly in the springs' curative capabilities and guarded them jealously from the whites. In the early 1890s, German physician Dr. Julius Schuelke visited the hot springs and took water samples to analyze. Shortly thereafter the government began its campaign to regain that section of land for use by white Americans.

In 1896 the government negotiated a joint treaty with the Shoshone and Arapaho, who by then shared the Wind River Reservation. The accord gave a tract of land ten miles square to the federal government in the area of Big Spring. The Indians received $60,000. Washakie agreed to cede his tribe's Bah-gue-wana only on the condition that a portion of the waters be kept free and open to the use of all people forever and that a campground be reserved for the Indians. As he signed the treaty, Washakie is reported to have said, "I have given you the spring. My heart feels good."

For once the government fulfilled its promise. It gave a square-mile parcel of land, including the hot springs, to the State of Wyoming, which developed a state park and bath house and maintained them for the free use of all. Every year in early August the Indians return to Thermopolis, where they reenact in pageantry the "Gift of the Waters." In 1994 Wyoming state park officials proposed charging a fee for admission to the park, but lawmakers rejected it.

Thermopolis

In contrast to Wyoming's railroad communities, which often grew almost at the whim of nature and were scattered as if by the wind itself, Thermopolis had an organized beginning. Andersonville, located on Owl Creek, dwindled, as did Torrey and Smithville, so Thad Slane and Ed Anderson created a new community, which they carefully platted and designed near the mineral hot springs. Originally called Old Town Thermopolis, Anderson shortened the name to Thermopolis after an analysis of the water revealed its beneficial qualities.

The hot springs and the state park gave the town a reason to exist, and it has been a recreational and healing center ever since because of the mineral waters and the healing powers some feel they possess. Local chamber of commerce leaders made some of the first claims regarding the water. A 1910 chamber publication reported that "any person wishing to better his worldly condition, or searching for health and recreation, should not fail to visit Thermopolis. Nowhere on earth are climatic conditions more favorable for the cure of consumption than here."

In 1950 the *Northern Wyoming Daily News* reported, "The blue-green water, used in treatment of rheumatism and infantile paralysis, bubbles and boils from an unknown depth at the foot of Monument Hill and flows into large enclosed pools."

The town's development was aided by the region's numerous mineral deposits, including pockets of copper, oil, coal, sulphur, and magnesium. Construction of the Boysen Dam at the south end of the Wind River Canyon by the U.S. Bureau of Reclamation and the arrival of the railroad through town put Thermopolis permanently on the map.

All manner of famous and infamous people spent time at Thermopolis's hot springs, including Teddy Roosevelt and outlaw Butch Cassidy. In 1895, the *Wind River Mountaineer* reported on the war with Cassidy's Hole-in-the-Wall Gang:

> The little city presented a lively appearance. . . . Scores of men with six shooters strapped to their sides and not a few carrying Winchesters, were seen hurrying in and out or leaning lazily against some convenient building or hitching rack; some wore a sleepy expression, others were drowning their cares and sorrows in the bowl, while all had a set look of determination stamped upon the face and each was watching the other slyly out of the corner of his eye. Judge Joe Magill, with knee leggings and .45 colts and full cartridge belt, had the air of a commanding general.

Kirby

Texas cowboy Kris Kirby became the first settler on the Bridger Trail when he claimed land on the Bighorn River in 1878. Kirby eventually left his name on the town and the creek. In the 1880s, the Casper–Thermopolis stage and freight road followed a route from Lucerne to Kirby Creek and the vicinity of the Black Mountain oil field. The outlaws from the Hole-in-the-Wall often rendezvoused at Kirby Creek.

Worland

From its founding by a tree-seedling salesman, Worland has always depended on the land, and it continues to be a leading crop production center in Wyoming. Boasting one of the state's longest growing seasons and the warmest temperatures in the summer—albeit often the coldest in the winter—Worland has a deep and varied agricultural background.

C. H. Worland, better known as Dad Worland, sold seedlings for the Start Nursery Company of Missouri when he saw the possibilities of the land at the mouth of Fifteen Mile Creek. In 1900 he gave up his buggy full of plants and claimed a homestead. Then he obtained a supply of whiskey and opened the Hole-in-the-Wall as a stop on the stage route midway between Basin and Thermopolis.

As an agricultural salesman, Worland recognized the importance of deep, rich soil. He also recognized that without water it had little production value. However, the Bighorn River ran through the area, and in 1903 the Lincoln Land Company started efforts to develop a canal and irrigation system. Two years later Worland persuaded engineers of the Hanover Canals to select a location near his homestead for a townsite.

The Hanover Canal is one of many now serving the Big Horn Basin and the area near Worland's homestead. Men dug other ditches as early as 1888 on both banks of the Bighorn River. By 1906 the new town had located on the east side of the river; that same year the Burlington & Northern Railroad completed its line from Billings, Montana, to Worland.

On November 10, 1907, fire swept through Worland, destroying half of the city. —Wyoming State Museum

Agriculture Takes Over

Worland wasn't alone in recognizing the area's potential as an agricultural center. University of Wyoming professor B. C. Buffum took samples of emmer wheat to Worland. He farmed some land himself and shared the seeds with others. By 1909 Buffum had built a cereal factory, making a product called Emmer Food. Although popular with the residents, the factory operated only a few years. Buffum closed it because of either failing health or failing finances, or perhaps a combination of the two.

Closure of the factory left farmers in search of a new cash crop. Eventually they turned to alfalfa. Some residents call the era from 1912 to 1917 the Alfalfa Period. During that time, men of the community organized the Alfalfa Club and sponsored a Washakie Days celebration that included a carry-in picnic of tremendous proportions, a baseball game, and other activities.

By 1916 work had started on a sugar beet factory, but World War I delayed its opening until 1918. Since that time sugar beets have been the primary cash crop in the region. The Wyoming Sugar Company became Holly Sugar Company in the 1920s and is the oldest sugar-processing mill in Wyoming; other sugar plants operate in the Big Horn Basin and in southeastern Wyoming. Today sugar remains one of the few products grown and processed within Wyoming. Growers export most other agricultural products in raw form for final processing out of state.

A beet field shows good production near Worland. —Wyoming State Museum

Beet workers in the field near Worland. —Wyoming State Museum

As sugar beets became the biggest crop raised in the Big Horn Basin, the rural population grew, with many Mexican, Russian-German, and Japanese workers and residents. By the 1980s farmers had expanded to other crops, including beans, and a number of feedlot operations located near Worland as well.

Wheat and barley production occur throughout Wyoming, and large amounts grow in the Big Horn Basin. Its climate is uniquely suited to such crops, with more moisture than southern areas of the state and a longer growing season. By the 1990s, barley producers under contract to Coors and Anheuser-Busch raised crops for the beer those companies brew in different localities.

But Worland isn't all beets and beans, barley and beer. It has a bottling plant (Pepsi), a boys' school (for those juveniles in the criminal justice system), and bronze monuments to early pioneers.

Ten Sleep

It took Jim Bridger and his mountain companions ten sleeps to get to the western base of the Bighorn Mountains traveling on foot or horseback from Fort Laramie, Fort Yellowstone, or the Indian agency at Stillwater, Montana. That's how the community there now got the name Ten Sleep. But at one time the mountain men called the area Sackett Fort for a Colonel Sackett, who mapped the area (not one of Louis L'Amour's fictional Sacketts).

More War on the Range

During Wyoming's range feud of the late 1800s, cattlemen near Ten Sleep, as other places, opposed sheep grazing for two reasons: Cattle already overstocked the land, and, the cowmen believed, sheep ruined the range.

In 1903 masked riders shot several herders and camp tenders, then slaughtered their sheep or scattered them to die. During the next six years, more herders lost their lives. Whistling, shouting raiders dynamited herds or "rimrocked" them by driving them over cliffs. They burned camps and turned vicious dogs lose on the sheep. The sheepmen were a gritty bunch, though, and they prospered in spite of the attacks. In 1908 fall lamb shipments from the Big Horn Basin totaled about $2 million, and wool growers announced plans to expand the industry.

Cattlemen eventually realized they might make a profit by raising sheep themselves, and some began to import the animals. One of the first to do so in the Big Horn Basin was Joe Emge. In 1909 he and Joe Allemand brought in 5,000 sheep. They had barely turned the animals loose on the range, however, when seven armed and masked men attacked. The raiders surrounded Allemand and his tenders on Spring Creek, killed the owners and herd, then cremated two of the men's bodies in the wagons. Authorities heard of the nighttime raid the morning of April 3.

The National Wool Growers' Association immediately appropriated $20,000 for prosecution of the "Ten Sleep Raiders." Officials launched a grand jury investigation that almost perpetuated the violence. Jurors and sheriff's officers received threats, and one witness committed suicide, leaving a note that incriminated several prominent cattle ranchers. Early in May authorities arrested seven men, and two of them agreed to testify against their cohorts. The situation in the area turned tense as the sheepmen and cattlemen squared off. Newspapers took sides, as did nearly everyone in the area. Men who formerly felt no need to protect themselves strapped on guns. Key witnesses got tickets out of town until the trial started because prosecutors feared for their safety. Military troops were called to the area to help keep the peace.

When convictions of the five raiders became certain, influential friends intervened and cut a deal. Those arraigned pleaded guilty to lesser charges and received prison sentences ranging from three years to life. One of the guilty parties, George Saban, escaped from prison and deserted his family. He may have died in Argentina in the 1930s. The others served part or all of their sentences.

The incident at Ten Sleep finally brought the situation to a head: Sheepmen and cattlemen would have to share the range; the cattlemen no longer had control. The battle that had brewed and often boiled over in Wyoming since 1882 finally settled to a simmer. Along the way, though, some fifteen men and one boy lost their lives, as did an uncertain number of sheep. Though minor conflicts arose after 1909, an increasing number of stockmen diversified and started raising both cattle and sheep. By the 1990s, when the agricultural industry found itself under attack from environmentalists and some politicians, the sheepmen and the cattlemen worked cooperatively. They knew they had to if they hoped to survive the newest "war on the West."

Wyoming 31

Hyattville—Manderson

22 miles

Paintings from a Different Era

At the junction of Medicine Lodge and Paintrock creeks is Hyattville, a small town surrounded by ranches. This area has served as a gathering center for people for at least 8,000 years. About five miles northeast of Hyattville on Medicine Lodge Creek early people left behind a legacy of ancient petroglyphs (rock carvings) and pictographs (rock paintings).

A 1971 archaeological investigation revealed details about a campsite at the confluence of the dry and running forks of Medicine Lodge Creek. Located at the base of a sandstone bluff, the campsite today has chokecherry, cottonwood, and willow trees and an abundance of game. It also is a state archaeological site administered by Wyoming's recreation department.

Historically, native people used it as a temporary campsite. Evidence they left behind includes glass trade beads, pottery fragments, projectile points, and food, including grass, seeds, wild fruit, and roots. Site use dates back 8,300 years. Archaeological research further indicates that the people using the area probably only lived until their early or mid-thirties. They prepared much of

Ten Sleep Canyon Indian war lodge. —State Historic Preservation Office

their food by grinding it with sandstone *metates* that left sandy grit in the food. Years of eating such a coarse diet eventually wore down their teeth. Wyoming state archaeologist George Frison explained the short lives of the campsite's inhabitants this way:

> If you look at prehistoric burials in this part of the country you find a person thirty to thirty-five years old had no teeth—they were worn down so badly. You get a lot of sand when you grind food on sandstone slabs. Life expectancy was probably no more than thirty-five years—once their teeth were gone, they didn't have much chance to live.

Crow and Shoshone Indians frequented this area in more recent periods, and evidence of their occupation lingers in stick-built war lodges and perhaps spiritual sites found at various locations high in the Bighorns.

The town of Hyattville originally went by the name Paintrock for the Medicine Lodge Creek petroglyphs, but in 1886 Sam Hyatt of Buffalo became the first postmaster, and the place soon wore his name. Once a month cowboys carried the mail from Fort Washakie, 175 miles away, over the Owl Creek Mountains, which stand across the basin to the west.

A Rabble-Rouser Finally Settles

Asa Mercer jumped into the national spotlight in the mid-1800s when he went to New York and recruited women to sail to Washington state with him to become brides for the men there. Among the women was his own bride. Mercer later helped establish the University of Washington and served as its first president before leaving that area and landing in Cheyenne, where he ran the *North Western Live Stock Journal* and reported on the dealings of the powerful cattlemen.

Early in that endeavor, Mercer supported the cattlemen and the Wyoming Stock Growers Association, but in 1894 he published *Banditti of the Plains*. That story about the Johnson County Invasion of two years earlier landed Mercer in a heap of trouble because it didn't defend the cattlemen. His newspaper office went up in flames, and the copies of his book disappeared or also were reduced to ashes. Mercer himself fled Cheyenne, likely just a step ahead of a lynch mob. He found a place to settle near Hyattville.

Mercer's family still lives in the Hyattville area, and some of his grandchildren and great-grandchildren participated in Wyoming's centennial by driving a wagon along the Bridger Trail from Fort Caspar to Cody. The family kept a scrapbook of the events. Shelley Mercer Foard wrote while riding in the family wagon to Cody on July 2, 1990:

> We of the Mercer wagon have fixed this scrapbook to donate to the Art and Memorabilia Auction. We decided we aren't real good at art, but memorabilia we can do.
>
> Our goal was to have everyone sign this book. We'd just stroll around camp in the evenings and get every signature in camp. What we didn't know is how busy we'd be in the evenings. First, after we circled the wagons, it was time to fix a picket that would hold our 6 or 8 horses. Then put up 2 or 3 tents, the lean-to on our wagon (that belongs to Spike Jensen), catch the water truck to fill up the water jugs, set up cooking and eating equipment, water and feed horses, and every other night we did most of this twice because the wind blew everything down and scared the horses and a layer of dust covered everything!
>
> We learned: how to wash our hair at the water truck when we fetched water, pay attention when we parked so we wouldn't be on top of an ant hill, and that the best way to eat in windy dusty camps is with a can opener and a spoon! Any spare moments were usually spent sitting and drinking all the water we could hold!
>
> So this book was sometimes on its own to be passed around for signatures and comments. The dirt between the pages is right off the trail between Emblem and Cody.

US 16/20/Wyoming 789
Worland—Greybull
39 miles

Throughout Wyoming communities argued and fought for county seat status as the state's original five counties got divided into twenty-three. More than one disagreement arose in the Big Horn Basin, but the best documented fight pitted Basin against Otto in 1896, when Big Horn County was formed. At that time the county encompassed a much larger area than it does now.

The fight for the seat quickly drew in the newspapers and their editors. On the one side stood Otto, named for Otto Franc, the first big rancher in the Big Horn Basin. The favored contender, it was represented by the *Otto Courier* and its editor, Tom Dagget, a journalist from New York. The underdog, Basin, had the *Basin City Herald*, formerly published in Hyattville as the *Paintrock Record*. Joe Magill, an Embar cowboy and journalist, edited the paper and thus became the voice of the town's position.

Basin won, but only because a spoiler entered the fight: At the last minute Cody joined the race for county seat. That split the vote among people on the western side of Big Horn County and gave Basin its victory. Charges flew that Cody entered the fray at the instigation of Basin, which knew it could win if it divided the opposition. Ironically, Big Horn County later split to form Park County, and Cody got to be a county seat anyway.

US 14/16/20
Greybull—Cody
52 miles

Greybull gets its name from an albino buffalo bull. Since 1909 the town has relied on farming and energy development—primarily oil and gas production—for its stability.

The earliest men to occupy this region came thousands of years ago. They camped at sites like Medicine Lodge Creek and may have engaged in spiritual vision quests throughout the Bighorns. At a site on Bear Creek Ranch near Greybull stand the remains of a small stone effigy, often called a medicine wheel. The Bear Creek Medicine Wheel is one of many such sites in this area. There also are stone arrows, wheels, and cairns. Most of these features are so-called tipi rings, circles of stones that appear individually or in groups and often in conjunction with fire hearths.

The Bear Creek Ranch site, like others, may have been used by Plains Indians and their ancestors for vision quests. During such spiritual journeys native Americans sought inspiration, guidance, courage, healing, or other forms of personal power. Most individuals prepared for a vision quest by undergoing a purification ritual in a sweat lodge; after this, they sought a high, isolated spot.

The purpose of medicine wheels is not clear, and many theories exist to explain them. They could be memorials, vision quest sites, navigational figures, master symbols of myth or cosmology, celestial alignments, or animal effigies. The Bear Creek Medicine Wheel is small, only about seven feet in diameter with seven spokes. Several other stone figures mark the site, including those in the shape of figure eights and double squares.

Mormons Arrive

Like the Star Valley in western Wyoming, the Big Horn Basin can thank members of the Church of Jesus Christ of Latter-day Saints for its early settlement.

In 1892 David P. Woodruff, the son of the Mormon Church president in Utah, established a home on Wood River, and before long other Mormons followed him to the region. They located on the Greybull River and started a town they called Burlington.

It can never be said that the Mormon people who moved to the Big Horn Basin lacked fortitude and foresight. The country they chose is high desert, complete with sandy soil, sagebrush, and scorpions. Perhaps drawing from their experiences in the Great Salt Lake Valley, the new inhabitants diverted water from the rivers and made the land productive, raising a variety of crops.

The process began with an ambitious irrigation scheme in 1893. The Mormons designed a ditch system to cover 15,000 acres of the long, elevated flat near today's Burlington and Emblem with water from the Greybull River. Although working with limited funds and manual labor, the Mormons kept digging despite a drought in 1894 that left many families without food. The bench canal itself took years to complete, and workers didn't consider it done until 1907. That year hundreds of families arrived in the basin, lured by the possibilities created by the irrigation system. Besides Mormons, a number of German immigrants settled on the benchland near Emblem, and the area became known as Germania Bench until World War I. After that conflict it became the Emblem Bench.

Burgess Junction—Cody

The Medicine Wheel

High atop Medicine Mountain is the largest and best-known medicine wheel in Wyoming. A site of spiritual significance for native Americans, the structure, known simply as the Medicine Wheel, is about seventy-five feet in diameter and has twenty-eight spokes. Native Americans don't always speak of spiritual matters to outsiders, which might be part of the reason why the Medicine Wheel is shrouded is mystery.

The origin of the wheel, made of limestone slabs and boulders, is not clear. Present-day Indians have no known legends or traditions to explain its background, but the pattern and orientation imply that the builders were sun worshipers.

George B. Grinnell, an expert on the Cheyenne culture, pointed out similarities between the Medicine Wheel and the Cheyenne medicine lodge, and other experts on native American culture also suggest the wheel resembles the Northern Cheyenne Sun Dance lodge. A buffalo skull found facing east in 1902 suggests a connection with the Sun Dance, but the wheel could be merely a marker for important ceremonies.

The Medicine Wheel, showing the wall erected in the 1930s to protect the wheel. —Elsa Spear Edwards/Wyoming State Museum

Various other theories suggest that the Crow, Arapaho, Shoshone, or Sheepeater tribes may be responsible for the wheel's placement; some even hint it came from French or Russian explorers. Some researchers maintain that the Medicine Wheel is related to the worship of the Aztecs; others believe it dates back to an even earlier period.

A piece of in-place wood recovered from the walls of the west cairn provided a tree-ring date of A.D. 1760. The hub consists of a circular stone mound about three feet high from which the spokes radiate, possibly representing the days of the lunar month. Around the edge of the wheel, at different distances from the center, are six "medicine tipis" to symbolize the planets. In the 1930s the tipi on the east side was higher than the others and nearly square, and its openings were on the north side, whereas all the other openings faced the hub. The tipis may have been shelters for the chiefs or medicine men during worship, and once there were large excavations under them. Now they appear only as small rock mounds.

Worn travois trails to the site scar the Bighorns, evidence that the Medicine Wheel attracted native Americans for generations. Sitting high on Medicine Mountain, the wheel lies unprotected from harsh winds. A few pines cling to the west face of the mountain, their branches deformed from the nasty climate. This is a sacred place to native Americans, an altar from which they offer prayer bundles. For the site's protection, only limited vehicle access is allowed, primarily to the elderly and people with disabilities. Besides the Medicine Wheel itself, a number of other features mark the area, including small circles or tipi rings and stone arrows.

Other well-known medicine wheels in the area include one at Fort C. F. Smith, Montana, thirty-five miles to the north; one west of Barnum, ninety miles southeast; and a small wheel near Glendo in southeastern Wyoming. Stone markers shaped like arrows point to the Medicine Wheel from near Meeteetse and from Steamboat Mountain in southwest Wyoming near Rock Springs.

In 1935 the U.S. Forest Service built a three-foot-high rock wall around the wheel to keep livestock away, and in 1957 the Department of the Interior set aside about eighty acres at the site to protect and preserve the wheel's archaeological value. Later officials constructed a chain-link fence with barbed wire around the top to protect the site.

In February 1993, American Indian leaders identified forty-four sacred sites they say are endangered by tourism, development, and vandalism. One of those sites is the Medicine Wheel, which thousands of people visit annually. In the summer of 1993, the Forest Service implemented restrictions on the number of tourists and vehicles allowed to visit the site. It also hired native American interpreters to explain the wheel's significance and to help visitors understand that it is a spiritual place, an outdoor church of sorts requiring proper respect. The Indians, the Forest Service, and local residents are continuing

In addition to the Medicine Wheel, other stone circles and markers depicting arrows, crosses, and boxes lie upon Medicine Mountain.

work to allow use and visitation at the Medicine Wheel without harming its spiritual value for the tribes.

The site is sacred to the Arapaho, Shoshone, Sioux, Cheyenne, Crow, and Blackfeet tribes. However, its survival is threatened by logging and recreational development, according to a report from the Associated Press. A number of other Wyoming sites are similarly endangered. They include Carter Mountain, southwest of Cody, sacred to the Shoshone and threatened by oil and gas exploration; both the north and south forks of Owl Creek, west of Thermopolis, sacred to Shoshone and Arapaho and threatened by road construction and oil and gas exploration; Devils Tower, sacred to Sioux and Cheyenne and endangered by tourism and rock climbing; and various petroglyph sites, which are threatened by vandalism and tourism.

From atop Medicine Mountain, Alternate US 14 descends to the Bighorn River Canyon and eventually Lovell. The steep, winding road offers a spectacular view across the entire Big Horn Basin. Bighorn Canyon National Recreation Area encompasses the river canyon from Yellowtail Dam in Montana to near Lovell.

The Mason-Lovell Ranch

The highway crosses the Bighorn River at the site of the ML Ranch, started by Henry Clay Lovell and Anthony L. Mason in 1882. Mason had the money for the enterprise, and Lovell had the know-how. Lovell trailed two large herds of cattle into the Big Horn Basin in 1880, turning them loose a few miles above the mouth of Nowood Creek near Ten Sleep. By 1882 Lovell had brought another 12,000 head of cattle from Oregon and turned them loose on Shell Creek, farther north than his original range.

Lovell realized he needed a headquarters near the railroad, which then ran through southern Montana, so in 1883 he established a cow camp on Willow Creek east of Lovell. At roundup time, the cowboys herded the cattle across the Crow Indian Reservation in southern Montana to Custer Junction. They let the herd of about 1,000 animals go at a leisurely pace across the reservation in order to keep them in top condition for market. As the cowboys moved north, their trip had little excitement until a group of tribal members objected to the herd's crossing their land. They demanded a lump-jawed cow as

Steve Sikes. —Dan Abernathy

361

Jess Cline. —Dan Abernathy

toll. Lovell agreed and ordered the animal cut from the herd. As the cowboys pushed their herd onward, the young Indian men killed and butchered the old cow.

The Mason-Lovell Ranch had as many as 30,000 head of cattle prior to the Great Die-Up of 1886–87. After that time it operated on a more modest scale. The ranch was one of the first to push cattle to the Bighorn Mountains for summer grazing and also one of the leaders in using high-quality, blooded breeding stock in that region of the state.

A Child's Namesake

Many places in Wyoming take their names from unusual incidents or people who made their mark on an area. Examples include Lovell, named for Henry Clay Lovell; Powell, named for John Wesley Powell; and Cody, named for

Buffalo Bill Cody. But the small town of Frannie took its name from a six-year-old child, Frannie Morris. Her father obtained permission to open a post office near the Wyoming-Montana state line and named it for his daughter.

Local legend says Frannie Morris once rode with the Buffalo Bill Wild West Show, which is the town's only real claim to fame. When Jim Bridger pioneered a trail through the Big Horn Basin to Montana in 1864, the route left the present boundaries of Wyoming at a site near Frannie.

Big Horn Colonization Company

In 1900, Abraham O. Woodruff led members of the Church of Jesus Christ of Latter-day Saints to the Big Horn Basin as part of the church's colonization program. Woodruff's colonists gathered at Ham's Fork Station near Kemmerer in southwestern Wyoming, then started the journey to the Big Horn Basin.

The colonists had about 200 head of cattle. In order to move to the basin as quickly as possible, Woodruff decided to have the people go on ahead and leave a few men in charge of the cattle herd, which they could trail to the basin at a more leisurely pace.

Moving the animals proved quite a task. At one point the party's horses mixed with a herd of wild horses, and considerable time and effort passed before the men had their mounts back. The group also had to contend with a supply wagon that got stuck while fording the Big Sandy River, cattle that got mired in bog, and stampedes. As the herd crossed South Pass, some of those helping decided they wanted to go on ahead. That left only Captain H. K. North and cook Henry Hergett to move the cattle. Captain North said, "We were out in a strange country many miles from our destination and without help." In the language of Hergett, "Ve cannot drive de cattle and de vagons, too, but I told Mr. Woodruff that I vould stay vid you, and I vill. Never mind, ve have plenty of provisions and if ve can't do no better I vill herd the cattle and you can do the cooking."

North eventually hired additional help in Lander, and the trail drive resumed. After crossing one dry stretch, the cattle caught the smell of water on Indian farms in the Wind River Basin and raced into irrigation ditches. That brought out the Indian police, but North eased the tension by inviting the Indians to join the Mormons for dinner. After the meal the Mormons and the Indians joined forces in getting the cattle out of the ditches and on their way.

It took two months, but the cattle herd finally made it to the "Colony Camp" near the site of present-day Lovell. Woodruff's party, known as the Big Horn Colonization Company, settled along the Shoshone River and immediately started building a canal to get water from the river for the arid benchlands. Every man in the company could claim land, and the colony soon had a commissary to provide supplies. The people of the camp had an austere life. They lived in tents and had no doctor, railroad, hospital, or mail service. The animals had little feed, only sparse grass and some salt sage. When the Mormons arrived there was no water on the entire flat where the towns of Powell and Garland now sit. That land is today a major crop production center for Wyoming.

In *History of the Big Horn Basin*, Charles A. Welch, a member of the colonization company, wrote, "To show how few people there were, it is only necessary to state that where the town of Lovell now stands there were but two houses and the school district that took in the country from near Kane to . . . near Cody, a distance of fifty miles, contained only four children, and in order to conduct a school they borrowed four children from Montana."

The Sidon Canal

The first of the Mormons in Woodruff's company arrived from Ham's Fork in late May 1900. They pitched their tents and, on May 28, knelt upon the dry soil for Woodruff's dedication of a canal and the land it would water. Following the prayer, Woodruff held the plow, and construction manager Byron Sessions drove the team to begin breaking ground. The camp quickly organized into work crews, with some men involved in canal construction and others herding horses. Everyone, regardless of the type of work he did, got the same pay for a day's labor: canal stock.

Sessions even enlisted boys in the canal construction effort. In one case he had the youngsters digging sand from around a large rock that stood in the way of the canal route. As the boys worked, Sessions started to worry about their safety. Fearing the boulder would fall upon them, Sessions went to the huge rock and knelt in prayer, asking the Lord for the wisdom to prevent an accident.

That day the boys scooped sand from around the rock until mid-morning, when Sessions called them from the area. Welch wrote, "The last teams had scarcely moved to safety before the rock began to move; the crevice opened to the bottom of the rock while one half fell to one side, the other half fell the other way leaving a channel for the canal between the two pieces. Since that event occurred, it has been styled Prayer Rock."

It took the Mormons four years to build the Sidon Canal, at a cost of $100,000, or about $10 per acre for the water. The viaduct was sixteen feet wide at the bottom and twenty-four feet wide at the top. Today it still provides water to the large, predominantly Mormon agricultural fields near Byron and Cowley.

At the same time they built the Sidon Canal, Mormons prepared a grade for the Burlington & Northern Railroad as it entered the Big Horn Basin south of Pryor Gap, and they later constructed sections of the highway to Cody. The Big Horn Colonization Company settled three communities: Lovell, Byron, and Cowley. The area soon had small intensively cultivated farms and diversified crops.

Construction on the Hanover Canal, south of Worland. —Wyoming State Museum

After the Mormons completed the Sidon Canal, they turned to raising crops, including sugar beets. In 1906 the Great Western Sugar Factory opened and the Chicago, Burlington & Quincy Railroad arrived. Other industries followed, including a brick and tile factory, a glass factory, and eventually a gypsum plant. As the Wyoming State Penitentiary in Rawlins became overcrowded in 1990, legislative committees and the Wyoming Board of Charities and Reform started looking at an expansion plan. Several communities bid for the location of a new minimum-security prison, and in 1991 the state agreed to build it in Lovell. But as of 1995 the prison remained unfunded and unbuilt, though prison crowding hadn't eased in Rawlins.

Byron

Not long after the town of Byron—named for Sidon Canal construction manager Byron Sessions—settled in 1900, a farmer observed gas escaping from a fence-post hole. When lit, the gas continued burning for several years. In 1906 developers drilled a test hole and struck oil sands at a depth of 700 feet. The first well flowed without pumping, but the heavy head of gas made control difficult. Subsequent wells produced gas for use in Byron, Cowley, Powell, and Lovell.

A Legacy for John Wesley Powell

In 1894 the federal government approved the Carey Desert Land Act, and in 1902 the Newlands Act received approval. The latter provided for development of reclamation projects throughout the West to turn the arid region into a productive "oasis." The 1902 act led to establishment of the U.S. Bureau of Reclamation and development of huge water projects of the kind perhaps envisioned by John Wesley Powell as he explored the Colorado River a quarter of a century earlier.

The first reclamation project launched in Wyoming under the Newlands Act continued a dream of Col. William F. Cody. The Shoshone Reclamation Project developed water rights originally held by Cody and his partners, George Beck and Horace Alger. It stored water from the Shoshone River drainage behind the Buffalo Bill Dam in Buffalo Bill Reservoir just west of Cody, providing irrigation for an area extending to Powell and Garland.

The first town in the region, established as headquarters for the Shoshone Reclamation Project, went by the name Camp Coulter. Eventually Powell, named for John Wesley Powell, replaced Camp Coulter.

The high upland area just northwest of Powell, known as Polecat Bench, marks the northern boundary of the irrigated area. In this vicinity early settlers and explorers found fossilized remains of crocodiles, turtles, and doglike animals believed to be 60 million years old.

Northwest College

In 1946 Northwest Community College opened in Powell, the second such institution in Wyoming. Casper had opened a college earlier. History professor John Hinckley wrote of Northwest Community College's birth:

> Donald Streeter came to Park County with the Civilian Conservation Corps and stayed to become Powell's most indefatigable promoter. Northwest Community College was his biggest and most successful dream. Stimulated by the GI bill—and collateral state and federal commitments to "do right" by our boys and girls from the Services—schools and colleges were sprouting up all over the country at the end of WW II. That Casper had early seized the opportunity to bootleg a two-year post-high school program through the state legislature suggested to Streeter a chance for one for Powell.

Today Wyoming has seven community colleges, located in Casper, Powell, Rock Springs, Torrington, Sheridan, Riverton, and Cheyenne, as well as the University of Wyoming. All of the facilities offer outreach programs to towns within their region, making it increasingly possible for Wyoming's residents to earn degrees without moving to one of the eight college or university towns.

The Camp at Heart Mountain

Most of the settlement of the Big Horn Basin followed from the Homestead Act and reclamation projects, as people moved in to develop the land and raise crops. However, one group of residents came not because of opportunity in the basin but because the winds of war blew them there.

After the Japanese bombed Pearl Harbor in 1941, anti-Japanese sentiment ran at fever pitch. By early 1942, the United States rounded up all Japanese living on the West Coast and shipped them to isolated camps, some in the nation's interior. This action gave birth to the third largest city in Wyoming in 1942—the Heart Mountain Relocation Center—on a barren, windswept, sagebrush- and buffalo-grass-covered plateau in the lee of Heart Mountain.

One of ten relocation centers nationwide, Heart Mountain covered more than 4,600 acres. From 1942 until 1945, about 14,000 Japanese-Americans passed through the Heart Mountain Relocation Center, which reached a peak population of 11,000. The people who lived here during those war years were among the 110,000 Japanese-Americans evacuated from the Pacific Coast after the attack on Pearl Harbor. Their movement came as the result of war hysteria, racial prejudice, and perceived military necessity. People feared the Japanese would attack the West Coast and that Americans of Japanese ancestry would turn on the United States in the attack. At least two-thirds of the people of Japanese descent living in Washington, Oregon, and California were

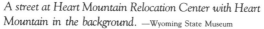

A street at Heart Mountain Relocation Center with Heart Mountain in the background. —Wyoming State Museum

Nisei, or second-generation Americans—and, legally, American citizens. The remainder were Issei, born in Japan and banned from citizenship by U.S. law.

Heart Mountain represents a dark period in Wyoming's history. Though it was called a relocation center, in reality it was a concentration camp surrounded by barbed-wire fences and nine guard towers. The people housed inside could not leave; they endured Wyoming's bitter cold and blistering sun in a "city made of acres and acres of celotex." The hastily constructed frame buildings had poured-concrete floors and gable roofs and lacked ornamentation and permanence. The hospital and administration buildings had asphalt shingles and asbestos siding, and the barracks had inexpensive tar-paper exteriors and celotex insulation.

Initially, the U.S. government tried to quiet the fears of West Coast citizens that Japanese-Americans would turn on their fellow citizens. Lt. Gen. John L. DeWitt, commander of the Western Defense Command, said, "An American citizen, after all, is an American citizen and while they all may not be loyal, I think we can weed the disloyal out of the loyal and lock them up if necessary."

Others in power disagreed, including Secretary of War Henry Stimson, who demanded an evacuation of Japanese-Americans from "critical areas." In February 1942 President Franklin D. Roosevelt signed Executive Order No. 9066 authorizing the relocation. Japanese-Americans had to register at Wartime Civil Control Administration stations, and they got a week or less to dispose of their homes, businesses, possessions, and even their pets. The evacuees to Heart Mountain and other relocation centers could take with them bedding, linens, toilet articles, clothing, and kitchen items, but only as much as they could physically carry.

The sentiment against the Japanese on the West Coast spread to Wyoming. In February 1942 the Union Pacific Railroad fired seventy-five employees, all of Japanese descent, after an alleged sabotage attempt on the rail line between Cheyenne and Laramie. Governor Nels Smith announced that Wyoming would accept evacuees at Heart Mountain only if they remained under federal control and maintenance. He further demanded that they "should be kept in concentration camps—not reception centers, should be worked under guard, and should be removed at the end of the emergency."

Heart Mountain's disadvantages as a camp site included cold winters and a short growing season, but the advantages tipped the scale. They included a good water supply, federal land, transportation facilities on US 14 and the Chicago, Burlington & Quincy Railroad, existing power lines, public works, and no serious objections from nearby residents. Construction started June 8, 1942, with speed of completion the greatest consideration. On August 10, 1942, the camp opened at a cost of $5 million.

It looked exactly like what it was: a prison camp. Writing in "Heart Mountain: The History of an American Concentration Camp," Douglas Newlon said, "The prevailing impression was of mechanical orderliness, blackness, and

The remaining buildings at Heart Mountain Relocation Center in Park County are becoming dilapidated and the bricks and mortar in the chimney on this building, which was once a hospital, are cracked and beginning to crumble.

bleakness. . . . Most settlements . . . look as if they belonged. This one looks stuck here; it doesn't fit the landscape; it is so obviously created by decree."

Each apartment had an army cot, a mattress, and a blanket for every person. There was a single, unshaded light in the rooms, no running water, community baths, and common dining facilities. Although the buildings had coal-burning stoves, a shortage of fuel left them less than adequate in warding off the cold, and the Nisei and Issei had inadequate and improper clothing for the climate.

Despite the harsh conditions, Heart Mountain detainees eventually turned the place into a community and a home. They had a hospital with seven physicians and four dentists, and beds for about a hundred patients. They operated three general stores, a newspaper, barber shops, a beauty shop, a radio repair shop, and a telegram service. School took place in classrooms with no blackboards, no curtains, and no decoration, but the children learned their lessons, and a high school opened in 1943. In 1945 Heart Mountain schools received the highest possible rating from the University of Wyoming Committee on Secondary Schools. The evacuees received a monthly stipend of $8, and adults employed within the camp earned wages ranging from 7 cents an hour, or $12 a month, for unskilled workers to 11 cents an hour, or $19 per month, for professionals such as doctors.

In addition to turning the concentration camp into a community, the Japanese-Americans turned the barren landscape into a productive farmland. They completed an irrigation system of ditches and canals and raised twenty-seven varieties of fruits and vegetables. In 1945 Heart Mountain's hog and poultry centers had an output of 6 million pounds, including 30,000 pounds of poultry meat, half a million pounds of pork, and 95,000 dozen eggs.

Some regional newspapers, including the powerful *Denver Post*, condemned the camp and its operation, saying that authorities hoarded food, wasted coal and lumber, and allowed inmates to trade food for liquor. However, the *Lovell Chronicle* was a strong defender of the camp administration. Lovell's Mormon population worked hard for friendly relations, as did the Park County American Legion. Not all local residents welcomed or accepted the Japanese-Americans, but opposition wasn't overwhelming, likely because of efforts by the detainees themselves. Many worked in Big Horn Basin sugar beet fields, providing necessary agricultural labor; some made a substantial and well-publicized contribution to fire-fighting efforts in Yellowstone National Park in the fall of 1943; and more than 900 men went to fight alongside their fellow Americans in the European theater during World War II.

But not all Japanese-Americans were willing to risk their lives for a country that had labeled them traitors and stripped them of their rights. The camp's "Fair Play Committee" urged young Nisei men to refuse induction into the armed services as long as the U.S. government treated them like aliens—and kept them in relocation camps—rather than like citizens. Sixty-three Heart Mountain resisters were tried, convicted, and sent to federal prisons for three-year terms for refusing to respond to the draft. Some might say they simply exchanged one prison for another.

In January 1945 U.S. officials finally lifted the ban on Japanese-American settlement on the West Coast, and the relocation camps closed. There is little at Heart Mountain today to remind Americans of that dark period during World War II. Only a few buildings remain, along with foundations for others. The red-brick chimney of the hospital stands tall, but it is crumbling and cracking from within, symbolic, perhaps, of the way democratic values crumbled and cracked during World War II, when the United States locked its own citizens behind barbed wire and housed them in tar-paper shacks.

Thermopolis—Cody
84 miles

In 1871, J. D. Woodruff built a house in the Owl Creek Valley. The humble abode formed the nucleus of the Embar Ranch, which eventually ran 50,000 head of cattle. At one time turkey raising was an important part of the valley economy, with growers herding up to 3,000 birds in the foothills, where they fattened on grasshoppers and seeds.

Jay Lin Torrey came to Wyoming in 1890. Born in Pittsfield, Illinois, in 1852, Torrey attended the University of Missouri at Columbia and Washington University in St. Louis. While attending law school, Torrey delivered newspapers for the *St. Louis Globe-Democrat*. After completing his studies in bankruptcy law, Torrey came to Wyoming and became involved in ranching and politics. He served in the Wyoming House of Representatives in 1895 and operated the Embar Cattle Company with George Pennoyer from 1895 to 1901. Torrey gained his greatest prominence during the Spanish-American War by organizing the 2nd U.S. Volunteer Cavalry into a fighting force known as Torrey's Rocky Mountain Riders. During that period he attained the military rank of colonel.

Colonel Torrey originated the idea of forming frontiersmen, who were good marksmen and top horsemen, into combat units. Fighting forces of this type that saw action in the Spanish-American War included Roosevelt's Rough Riders and Griggsby's Cowboys.

Torrey bought horses for his Rocky Mountain Riders at Cheyenne, Laramie, Rawlins, Evanston, Sheridan, and Casper. He even obtained some from Blackfoot, Idaho, and Denver, Colorado. The mounts were those "found most serviceable in the Western Country as saddle horses," the *Globe-Democrat* reported on May 5, 1898. Each horse needed to stand about fifteen hands high, weigh 1,000 pounds, and be bay, chestnut, black, brown, or roan in color.

As the dozen troops of eighty-one men each prepared to leave St. Louis, one newspaper reported: "All the men are experts in handling horses and the use of rifles and pistols. They are nearly all large men and sunburnt until they look as swarthy as an Indian." The troops hailed from Wyoming, Utah, Colorado, Nevada, and Idaho. For weapons they had Krag-Jorgensen carbines and Colt .45s; the officers carried .38-caliber double-action Colts. However, the Rocky Mountain Riders saw little action, largely because their troop train wrecked at Tupelo, Mississippi; they never reached Cuba. After the conflict, Torrey returned to the Embar Cattle Company. He also operated the Anchor Cattle Company and the Owl Creek Cattle Company from 1899 to 1901. Jay Torrey died in 1920.

Butch Cassidy Meets the Count

German Count Otto Franc Von Lichtenstein left behind a banana business in New York in 1878 to claim land and build a cabin on the Greybull River. The next fall the count, who in Wyoming went by Otto Franc, trailed a herd of cattle to the Big Horn Basin from Montana. To avoid Indian conflicts, he brought the animals through Idaho, over South Pass, and then across the Owl Creek Mountains to the Greybull River.

Franc's ranch had a good location and looked like a meadow full of buffalo wallows. In fact, when Franc had continuing difficulties with bison, which knocked down the buck fence around his home, he shot some of them. In 1882 Franc opened the first U.S. post office in the Big Horn Basin at his ranch.

The ranch initially went by his name but soon became known as the Pitchfork, for his brand. Like other early-day cattle barons in Wyoming, Franc locked horns with rustlers. He had little trouble with legitimate homesteaders, however, and particularly extended a welcoming hand to the Mormons who settled along the Greybull River near Burlington and Germania (later Emblem).

The one thing Franc didn't countenance was livestock rustling, and he left his mark on more than one outlaw, the most famous of them being Butch Cassidy himself. Butch and his buddies in the Hole-in-the-Wall Gang roamed throughout the Big Horn Basin, hanging around Thermopolis and Ten Sleep and riding over the Owl Creek Mountains to Dubois, where Cassidy had a ranch of sorts. A large ring of horse thieves, including Teton Jackson, ranged from Buffalo to Jackson Hole and on into Idaho. In 1892, Cassidy and partner Al Hainer camped at the foot of the Owl Creek Mountains, where they met a young man named Nutcher who had three fine-looking horses. Cassidy bought the horses but paid little attention to details—such as accurate paperwork.

At that time Franc served as justice of the peace and he swore out warrants against Hainer and Cassidy for the theft of one of the horses. The two were arrested, but both were acquitted at a trial in Lander. Not long afterward Franc registered a second complaint for horse stealing against the pair. Hainer went free on that charge, but Cassidy was convicted, in part because Nutcher couldn't be found to testify on his behalf. Arriving at the state prison on July 15, 1894, Cassidy unexpectedly found Nutcher, also serving time for horse theft. Cassidy spent two years behind bars in Laramie—it was the only prison he ever spent time in—and often said later that Otto Franc drove him to a life of crime.

Franc continued to build his cattle ranch and became one of the early leaders in conservation efforts. When other area ranchers fought establishment of the Yellowstone Reserve, which became the Shoshone National Forest at the turn of the century, Franc lent his support. He died of a shooting in 1903, and it is still not clear whether it was an accident or suicide. Franc had taken his shotgun to go duck hunting; sometime later friends found the cattle baron's body beside a fence, with the shotgun leaning on the wire.

Arland

In 1880, Victor Arland and John Corbett started a trading post on Cotton-wood Creek. It spawned the first true community in this section of Wyoming. In a March 1, 1882, letter, Arland wrote:

> Now we are running a little store to supply the needs of the hunters and trappers of this region and of the Indians, Crows and Shoshones, who are hunting in this vicinity. The winter hunt was not outstanding this year because of the mildness of the temperature. The game has not yet come down from the mountains. We have had almost no snow up to now.
>
> The buffalo hunters on the Yellowstone haven't done much this winter. We still have a few in the neighborhood. Elk, deer, mountain sheep, and antelope are in large numbers, without counting the bears, which are fairly numerous and of respectable size.

Arland and Corbett moved their trading post to Cottonwood Creek in 1883 because there was a bridge across the Stinking Water (Shoshone) River there and because the main trail from Camp Brown to Billings passed nearby, along the track of today's Wyoming 120.

The trading post on Cottonwood Creek was four miles north of Cody, but then the traders moved their business to Meeteetse Creek. Of the new location, Arland wrote on June 17, 1884:

> Our place on the Meeteetse is very well situated for our business, being directly in the center of the cattle raisers of this area. . . . There are at the present time about 30,000 head of cattle between Stinking Water and Greybull [rivers]. In a radius of 20 miles of here, there are about 15 cattle ranches.
>
> We have a coach from Fort Washakie twice a week, we hope that the coach will come directly from Billings to Fort Washakie the first of July, passing right by our place.

Arland's business thrived because of the cattle ranches, and he often remarked in his letters, now preserved at the Buffalo Bill Historical Center in Cody, about the nature of the men who worked the country in those early days. On December 5, 1884, he wrote: "The cowboys are singular characters, very violent and without their equals in their spirit of independence; but they know how to appreciate a man of courage and energy. In the towns of the Far West they are getting a most deplorable reputation through their audacity and lack of restraint."

By 1886 there was a post office at the site, and a town soon grew up around it, complete with a hotel, saloon, dance hall, brothel, livery barn, corrals, and bunkhouse. What the community had in the way of amenities it lacked in law and order; many violent incidents were reported. Stories of bar brawls and shootings during the early days abound.

By the end of 1896, Arland had withered to ghost-town status, and the following year people moved several of the abandoned buildings to Meeteetse, which rapidly became the center of activity for the Greybull River country.

Meeteetse

William McNally, blacksmith and Civil War veteran, claimed a homestead on August 28, 1893, at the spot where Meeteetse now stands. He paid $6 in fees; two years later he sold his land to Anna W. Thomas for $2,500. The following year residents established Meeteetse. It was a cow town, strongly influenced by Otto Franc's Pitchfork Ranch and other ranches up the Wood River. Since 1980 the town has been more heavily influenced by oil and mineral development, although the ranchers remain.

The Phelps Family Arrives

After the death of Otto Franc in 1903, the Pitchfork Ranch was sold to Louis Graham Phelps, a wealthy cattleman who once owned land in Wyoming, Montana, New Jersey, Illinois, Minnesota, and Missouri. Phelps and his descendents have operated the ranch ever since, purchasing other holdings to expand the ranch to some 250,000 acres.

Phelps and his wife, Annice, had two children: a son, Eugene, and a daughter, Frances. As the ownership of the ranch has passed from generation to generation, it's gone in the female line, from mother to daughter; by 1995 L. G. and Annice's great-granddaughters worked the land with their husbands and children.

The Pitchfork enjoyed its first period of national acclaim during the 1930s. Eugene Phelps attended Michigan Institute of Technology, where he became friends with Charles Belden. Belden and Frances Phelps met as a result, and in 1922 they tied the knot. Although Belden worked the Pitchfork with his wife and brother-in-law for many years, he really wasn't a rancher. His true skills lay in the area of electronics and photography, and that is what drew attention to the Pitchfork.

Belden used photographs to portray the vanishing way of life on a big western cattle ranch. He captured cowboys eating, playing poker in the bunkhouse, chasing cows in the mountains, riding through blizzards, and working cattle. His photos appeared in a variety of national publications. Some of Belden's photos are classics. "Chowin' Down" depicts Charlie Collins with his tin plate on his lap and a knife and fork clutched in each hand. Then there is "The Long Trail," which shows an "S" curve of Hereford cattle and a lone cowboy trailing through the snow.

Eugene Phelps died in a car accident in 1944, and Frances and Charles Belden separated, though they never divorced. Frances Belden and Eugene's widow, Helen, split the Pitchfork holdings. Frances remained on the Pitchfork, where she reared daughters Annice and Margot. In later years she hired the husband of her granddaughter, Frances Abarr (who goes by the nickname Lili), to manage the ranch.

When Jack and Lili Turnell and their three daughters, Tracy, Cindy, and Tammy, returned to the Pitchfork in 1972, they found the place a fraction of the size it was in L. G. Phelps's heyday. After Eugene's death in 1945, the ranch became divided into separate holdings, but in 1979 Jack Turnell bought for his wife's family operation the Bar TL Ranch, once part of the Pitchfork. That restored the ranch to near the size it had been in 1945, when the original division took place. Only one piece of property remains out of the fold.

Less than a month after Turnell bought the Bar TL back under Pitchfork management, the ranch celebrated its centennial. "The Belden families at the Pitchfork Ranch can hardly believe that, on the 100th anniversary of the Ranch, a goodly portion has been put back together," Turnell wrote in *Brand of a Legend*. At a time when most ranches split, the Pitchfork grew.

Last Wild Home of the Ferrets

In 1981 a rare discovery took place on the Pitchfork, once again drawing the ranch into the national spotlight. Researchers found black-footed ferrets, the only known wild colony of the mammals anywhere in the world.

Wildlife researchers removed all of the ferrets because an outbreak of canine distemper threatened to kill them. They were taken to Sybille Research Station between Laramie and Wheatland, where the Wyoming Game and Fish Department started a captive breeding program. In 1992 the first captive-raised ferrets were released into the wild near Shirley Basin. Plans call for continued release in Wyoming, South Dakota, and Montana.

On a prominent hogback between Spring and Rush Creeks, west of Meeteetse, is a great arrow built of rocks. Fifty-eight feet long and five feet across at the head, the arrow points toward the Medicine Wheel in the Bighorn Mountains.

Irrigation projects for the Big Horn Basin extended to the Oregon Basin, which lies midway between Meeteetse and Cody. Developers spent millions of dollars on the Wiley Canal, advertised the availability of land, and then found the canal wouldn't deliver the water as promised. Hundreds of people came for the land auction of Oregon Basin property, but most of them left disgusted with the way Wyoming had promoted the Wiley water project. Today the land still isn't watered, but it does have productive oil and gas wells.

Cody

William F. Cody, better known as Buffalo Bill, lent his name to this community, which provides access to the east gate of Yellowstone National Park. But Bill Cody had no role in founding the town.

John Colter, after leaving the Lewis and Clark expedition, trekked through here in the fall of 1807, following the river he called the Stinking Water (now known as the Shoshone). He spied bubbling cauldrons and steaming water at this place, which is the original "Colter's Hell" (a term now often applied to Yellowstone as a whole). The site is near the De Maris Springs, down along the Shoshone in the canyon at the western edge of Cody. Today it is almost, but not quite, an inactive geyser district.

Colter followed the south fork of the Stinking Water, noted landmarks such as Castle Rock, some fifteen miles upstream, and eventually crossed the mountains into Jackson Hole. He left oral descriptions of his travels, but embellishment makes it difficult to get an accurate picture of what Colter saw.

In the fall of 1830, Joe Meek visited the site of Colter's Hell after a fight between his fur brigade and Blackfeet Indians. Meek wandered alone for a time in Yellowstone and eventually reached the two forks of the Stinking Water. His story is recounted by historian Ned Frost this way:

> [Meek] came upon the waters of the Stinking Fork, a branch of the Bighorn, which derives its unfortunate appellation from the fact that it flows through a volcanic tract . . . [T]he men unanimously pronounced it the "back door to that country which divines preach about." As this volcanic district had previously been seen by one of Lewis and Clark's men named Colter, while on a solitary hunt, and by him also denominated "hell," there must certainly have been something very suggestive in its appearance.

By the late 1870s, cattlemen ran their herds throughout the Big Horn Basin, and in 1885 Charles De Maris homesteaded along the Shoshone. The De Maris Springs, also called Needle Plunge, are named for him. Tipi rings sit nearby; legend tells that it was a neutral ground where the various Indian tribes laid aside their weapons to bathe and drink from the spring.

The first attempt at development in the Cody area came in 1894, when George T. Beck of Sheridan sent a survey party into the Big Horn Basin to see what, if any, possibilities existed. Specifically, Beck liked the idea of turning the region into a garden spot by providing irrigation water from the Shoshone River. The survey party included state engineer Elwood Mead and Horton Boal, son-in-law of William F. Cody.

Their report to Beck made development seem possible and perhaps even probable. Back in Sheridan, Beck enlisted banker Horace C. Alger as treasurer of his firm, the Shoshone Land and Irrigation Company.

Bill Cody had interests in Sheridan, too; his daughter lived nearby, and he managed the Sheridan Inn. When Cody heard of Alger and Beck's plans for the Big Horn Basin, he became the third partner. Alger and Beck no doubt realized Cody's name and reputation could help them attract investors and settlers. Cody knew the basin country well. He guided Yale archaeologist O. C. Marsh—who recognized the significance of Como Bluff in southern Wyoming—through part of the region in 1871 on a fossil hunt. He also guided foreign hunters through the area.

In the fall of 1895, Alger, Beck, and Cody platted the first townsite, and a post office opened under the name Richland near De Maris Springs. When Beck insisted that the town be moved downriver from the springs to the present site, some, particularly Buffalo Bill, thought the town should go by the name Cody.

According to the Wyoming Writers' Program guide, George Beck later said: "Horace [Alger] and I had a talk, and we concluded that as Cody *was* probably the best advertised man in the world, we might organize a company and make him president." After some debate they used Cody's name. "This did no harm to us, and it highly pleased the colonel," Beck said.

Alger, Beck, and Cody's company dug a canal to divert water from the Shoshone, and homesteaders began to move in, both because of the availability of water for irrigation and because of the settlement's famous namesake. Within a year the railroad—using Mormon labor—built a branch from Frannie. The town of Cody tried unsuccessfully to become the seat of Big Horn County in a three-way battle with Otto and Basin; not until creation of Park County in 1909 did Cody win that status.

The association with Bill Cody brought immediate attention to the region when the town first began, and it continues to attract an international audience.

The Legend of Buffalo Bill

Without doubt, William F. Cody is one of the best-recognized characters in Western history and certainly one of Wyoming's leading legends. His ability to grab headlines and attention compares with that of Annie Oakley, Wild Bill Hickok, Calamity Jane, and Billy the Kid; his exploits stand alongside those of Portugee Phillips, Tom Horn, and Jim Bridger in Wyoming. He is a man and a myth.

Cody spent his early life in Kansas and started for the California goldfields in 1857 with his father, who died en route. He found work with the great freighting firm of Russell, Majors, and Waddell, herding cattle to Salt Lake City and riding for the Pony Express between Red Buttes and Sweetwater Station. In 1868, at age twenty-two, Cody became a scout for the U.S. Army's 5th Cavalry, and earned the Congressional Medal of Honor for valor in 1872. He served as a frontier scout for northern armies during the Plains Indian Wars, working for and with such men as George Armstrong Custer.

Cody acquired his nickname after the Civil War, when he reportedly killed 4,280 bison in eighteen months as part of a contract with the Kansas Pacific Railroad. He earned his reputation as an Indian fighter in a hand-to-hand battle with Sioux chief Yellow Hair (sometimes called Yellow Hand), personally avenging the death of Custer and his men at Little Bighorn. Although the fight with Yellow Hair may not have occurred as it has been portrayed by dime novels, it is undisputably part of the Buffalo Bill legend.

Birth of the Wild West Show

In 1882, Buffalo Bill planned the "Old Glory Blow Out" in North Platte, Nebraska. In the show he would demonstrate his buffalo-hunting methods, using steers and blank ammunition. He even knew where he might borrow a

small herd of privately owned buffalo. Cody also wanted to hold contests for roping, shooting, riding, and bronco-breaking, and he persuaded businessmen to offer prizes. He sent out 5,000 handbills to promote the event.

Cody hoped for 100 cowboys; 1,000 showed up to participate. The unprecedented and unexpected success gave Cody an idea: He announced his intention of organizing a cowboy exhibit called the Wild West Show. Buffalo Bill had been pursuing a theatrical career, and he continued to do so during the winter of 1882–83, but he also signed talent and sought properties for the Wild West Show.

In the first rehearsal of the show, at Columbus, Nebraska, a runaway Deadwood Stagecoach drawn by a team of half-broke mules nearly caused a disaster. Maj. Frank North, who organized the Pawnee Scouts in Nebraska, suggested they needed more illusion and less realism—some worn-out horses and old Indians with little ambition.

Buffalo Bill's show took to the road for a tour of the United States in 1884 after the showman cut a deal with James A. Bailey of Barnum and Bailey Circus to provide transportation. It was an instant success. In 1889, Buffalo

Bill took his show to Europe for the first time. The Shah of Persia, Nasr-ul-Deen, attended, and Queen Isabella of Spain rode in the Deadwood Stagecoach. The 1891 tour went through Germany, and the 1892 season opened in London.

Wyoming Cowboys Join the Show

Buffalo Bill recruited crack cowboy riders from throughout Wyoming for his show. He auditioned them in front of the Sheridan Inn and saw them in action at Cheyenne Frontier Days after that festival started in 1897. Harry Webb became one of Buffalo Bill's riders by tangling with an out-of-control horse in the streets of Cody.

Webb spent his early days in Colorado, then headed toward Wyoming, where he worked in the Lander area and learned to ride under the guidance of top Indian horsemen. He moved on up to the Big Horn Basin and landed a job for Jay Torrey and George Pennoyer of the Embar Ranch on Owl Creek.

One day in 1909 Webb met Buffalo Bill in Cody. The story reported in the *Denver Post* goes this way:

> After loading a train with cattle one day in 1909 just outside Cody, Wyoming, a ranch hand declared that the last one to town would have to buy drinks, so the group lit out for the saloon. Webb was riding a skittery

"The Scout" is a symbol of Cody, Wyoming, and portrays Buffalo Bill himself.

horse that once was bitten by a rattlesnake. When the group reached the center of town, Webb's horse pulled up in front of some bailing wire that had been thrown into the street from the livery stable. The horse's feet tangled in the wire, and being nervous from having been bitten by a rattlesnake not long before, he bucked across the street, up the sidewalk, and right through a drugstore window.

The whole town came running down the street to see what had happened, while the druggist applied medicine to Webb's neck and head. Among the crowd of onlookers was Buffalo Bill.

"Not a bad ride, young gobbler, for as long as it lasted," Cody is remembered to have said. He then handed Webb a business card and told him to write Johnny Baker in New York for a contract to join the Buffalo Bill Wild West Show.

Webb and his best friend, George "Gaspipe" Mullison, wrote for the contract, which had some fifty clauses under which riders could be dismissed without pay. The cowboys weren't to get drunk, ogle girls, use bad language, or refuse to ride any horse assigned to them. Webb and Gaspipe liked the pay, though—$60 a month, as compared with $40 a month at the Embar—and both joined Cody's entourage. Webb and the other cowboys in the Buffalo Bill show often convinced Colonel Cody to give them complimentary tickets, which they passed on to people, mostly girls, they met while performing. Webb rode for Buffalo Bill two years, traveling more than 42,000 miles and visiting thirty-one states. Webb strongly admired Cody and served as the showman's valet for a time.

The Irma

Cody built the lavish Irma Hotel, named for his youngest daughter, in downtown Cody. He owned the TE Ranch on the South Fork of the Shoshone and the Pahaska Teepee hunting lodge on the North Fork. It's said one of his favorite places in the region was Cedar Mountain, which rises south of the Shoshone just west of the town. Indians called the site Spirit Mountain because they saw steam coming from underground caverns and believed it to be of supernatural origin. Later excavations and caving gave the site the name Frost Caves. Cody knew it as Spirit Mountain, and that is where he wanted to be buried.

Buffalo Bill made a farewell speech in Madison Square Garden in 1910, by which time his show had grossed a million dollars. Even so, he extended his series of farewell exhibitions through 1910 and 1911. As profits slid, Buffalo Bill and Pawnee Bill joined forces and offered the "Two Bills Show." But by then they were no match for their competition. After much legal maneuvering the shows sold at auction in September 1913.

Upon his death June 10, 1917, at age seventy-one, Buffalo Bill didn't return to Spirit Mountain west of Cody. Rather, he is entombed on Lookout Mountain west of Golden, Colorado.

The Irma Hotel in 1912, Cody. —Wyoming State Museum

The Story of Caroline

Few men matched the exploits of Buffalo Bill, but a woman came mighty close.

Caroline Lockhart spent her childhood in Elk Rock, Illinois, as the daughter of a rancher. She started a career as an actress but later switched to journalism, becoming Boston's first woman newspaper reporter. Before long she rivaled her famous contemporary, Nellie Bly, of the *New York World*. Lockhart went to almost any length, and a few depths, to get her stories. She walked on the bottom of Boston Harbor in a deep-sea diving rig, jumped from a fourth-floor window to test Boston's first fire nets, and entered the cage of a lion that had just killed its trainer.

When the Osage Indians suddenly became rich from oil development, the tribe banned reporters from the reservation. Lockhart, undeterred, took a job as a cook for Osage chief Bacon Rind. The story she later wrote scooped the rest of the nation's newspapers.

Lockhart probably came to Cody because of the inspiration of Buffalo Bill, whom she interviewed during one of his trips to the East. In Cody she wrote several novels, including *The Lady Doc, Me Smith, Man from Bitter Roots*, and *The Dude Wrangler*. Lockhart bought the *Cody Enterprise* in 1919 and became

381

its editor and columnist. She used the paper to comment on local activities and espouse her personal causes for women's and Indian rights and conservation.

Considered a "wet" during the years of Prohibition, Lockhart raised the ire of many in Cody who were "dry" during that period. She caused further consternation with her novels, which often offered thinly disguised portrayals of real-life people. One less-than-satisfied reader, Park County prosecuting attorney Ernest Goppert, filed a $30,000 libel lawsuit against her in July 1923. The *Northern Wyoming Daily News* in Worland called the case "a fancy piece of soiled linen brought over to this county to iron out." The paper noted that the case was in some ways an extension of "a fight between the wet and dry forces in Park County." After a three-day trial in Worland in April 1926, the jury ruled in Lockhart's favor and ordered Goppert to pay $305 in legal costs.

Lockhart sold the paper in 1924 to purchase and operate a cattle ranch. Her penchant for riding through Cody on her favorite horse, wearing a split skirt, boots, spurs, and a Stetson hat earned her the disdain of local women. The fact that she "entertained" their husbands in her home and opposed Prohibition didn't endear her to the Cody women, either.

A Fire Claims Two

One of the great tragedies in the Wyoming newspaper business took place in Cody in May 1974 when an arsonist set fire to the alley behind the *Cody Enterprise*. The blaze spread to the newspaper building, but firemen thought they had it out. During the noon hour on May 20, the fire reignited. *Enterprise* columnist Sarah Fritjofson said, "When I saw the black column of smoke, I realized it had to be the *Enterprise*. I spent the rest of the day watching the fire trucks. It was raining, and I was crying and so was everyone else."

Their tears were for the destruction of the newspaper building and the deaths of two men. Young reporter Eric Olson and photographer Dewey Vanderhoff were in the basement darkroom when the fire broke out. Vanderhoff knew the building layout well and negotiated the narrow stairs from the basement, then made his way through the maze-like composing room to an exit. Olson hadn't worked long for the *Enterprise*, and Vanderhoff couldn't get him up the stairs and out of the building.

Three volunteer firemen, including one who formerly worked at the paper and knew the floor plan, tried to save Olson. Roped together, they entered the building immediately after Vanderhoff's escape. They didn't reach the basement before the roof collapsed. Only two of the rescuers emerged; Olson and the other fireman, Bob Moore, died in the inferno.

The fire burned nearly a quarter of a city block. Even so, the *Enterprise* came out on time two days later, thanks to help from neighboring publishers in Greybull, Powell, Jackson, Riverton, and Lander, as well as Billings and Red Lodge, Montana. The town fire station is named for Moore. Vanderhoff—

who severely cut his left hand when he pushed it through a glass exit door—still works as a photographer in Cody, although not at the *Enterprise*.

The Carey Act

When President Grover Cleveland signed the Carey Desert Land Act into law in 1894, he changed the course of Wyoming's destiny. The purpose of the act, named for Senator Joseph M. Carey of Wyoming, was to encourage reclamation and settlement of public land for private uses. It provided money for development of irrigation projects. Wyoming became the first state to implement provisions of the Carey Act when it undertook the project initially organized by Horace Alger, George Beck, and Bill Cody as the Shoshone Land and Irrigation Company in 1895.

The 1902 Shoshone Reclamation Project, built under provisions of that year's Newlands Act, expanded the 1895 development and led to construction of Buffalo Bill Dam across the Shoshone River. That project, completed in 1910, not only led the way in reclamation efforts in Wyoming and the West but also became one of the most successful projects. Buffalo Bill Dam provided irrigation water, flood protection, and electricity for 110,000 acres in the Big Horn Basin and created tremendous benefits for Cody, with thousands of acres reclaimed—or put into production—between 1910 and 1930. In 1987 the U.S. Bureau of Reclamation expanded the project, raising the dam to impound even more water and ensure agricultural production.

Although agriculture created the basis for Cody's existence, other industries contributed to its growth. The Elk Basin Oil Field north of town, discovered in 1915, once was the most productive field in the nation. Additional development in Oregon Basin, south of Cody, furthered the energy industry, and oil companies established headquarters in Cody. With Yellowstone National Park at its back door, Cody quickly became a tourist center. The popularity of dude ranching and the scenic beauty on both the North and South forks of the Shoshone added to that appeal.

But the community gets its international allure from Buffalo Bill Cody's legacy: the Buffalo Bill Historical Center. That world-class facility started as the Buffalo Bill Museum and later expanded to include four major museums.

The Buffalo Bill Historical Center

The Buffalo Bill Memorial Association organized just three weeks after Cody's death "to perpetuate the memory of our late lamented fellow townsman." The first step in that process was the commissioning of a monument to Cody—the man and the myth. Sculpted by Gertrude Vanderbilt Whitney in 1924, "The Scout" stands on forty acres of land overlooking the Shoshone River. It depicts the man on his horse with his arm raised, rifle in hand. The horse represents the colonel's favorite, Smoky, who was taken to Mrs. Whitney's New York studio and photographed in fast and slow motion to assure faithfulness to the original.

Other groups, including the Buffalo Bill Museum Association (now defunct) and the Cody Family Association, joined forces to develop the museum complex. With the backing of wealthy Easterners, the Buffalo Bill Historical Center made a quantum leap from a log cabin with a $4,800 annual budget and 25-cent admission in 1930 to the present 237,000-square-foot facility operating under a multimillion dollar budget. In 1992, on the occasion of the museum's Diamond Jubilee, director Peter Hassrick said the facility's quality and size are the result of "people who thought bigger than they were."

Four museums make the Buffalo Bill Historical Center the largest western heritage center in the nation. The Buffalo Bill Museum presents the memorabilia and mementos of the famous scout, buffalo hunter, and showman. Opened in 1927, it has since moved to larger quarters but continues its emphasis on the life and times of Buffalo Bill Cody.

The Whitney Gallery of Western Art houses one of the world's finest collections of western art and sculpture by important nineteenth- and twentieth-century American artists ranging from Charles R. Russell and Frederick Remington to Edgar S. Paxson and contemporary figures such as James Bama and Harry Jackson. A grant by Cornelius Vanderbilt Whitney from the Gertrude Vanderbilt Whitney Trust gave the museum its start. The Whitney Gallery opened in the spring of 1959, and a huge window at the north end of the building gives an uncluttered view of "The Scout."

The Plains Indian Museum developed from Buffalo Bill's personal collection of artifacts, many of which were presented to him by the native Americans appearing in his Wild West Show. The institution opened in 1927 in the original Buffalo Bill Museum building. It now has its own wing in the museum complex, which opened in 1979. Indians themselves participated in the planning for the expanded facility, with representatives of the Northern Cheyenne, Blackfeet, Shoshone, Arapaho, Sioux, Crow, Cherokee, and Gros Ventre tribes involved in the Plains Indian Advisory Committee.

The Winchester Arms Collection is an incomparable assemblage of arms made by the Winchester Repeating Arms Company and its predecessors. The collection first moved to the Buffalo Bill Historical Center in 1975 and expanded into the Winchester Arms Museum in 1981. A decade later the museum evolved again when a new wing was dedicated as the Cody Firearms Museum.

Two Roads Lead to the West

Two highways run west out of Cody. Wyoming 291 follows the South Fork of the Shoshone through ranching country, passing Castle Rock, the TE Ranch of Bill Cody, and Carter Mountain, named for Charles Carter, who brought the first cattle into the Big Horn Basin. This road dead-ends about thirty miles out of town and provides access to the Thorofare Wilderness country and the Shoshone National Forest. The other road is US 14/16/20.

Cattle line through the Shoshone Canyon tunnel just west of Cody. —Adrian Clary, Wyoming State Museum

US 14/16/20
Cody—Yellowstone National Park
52 miles

The main branch leading west is US 14/16/20, which passes Colter's Hell and follows the North Fork of the Shoshone to Yellowstone National Park. President Teddy Roosevelt called the Wapiti Valley between Cody and Yellowstone "the most scenic fifty-two miles in the U.S." *Wapiti* is an Indian word for elk, an animal commonly seen in this region, along with deer and grizzly bear.

The First Forest

The Shoshone National Forest was the first such tract in the nation, created from the Yellowstone Park Preserve. The Wapiti ranger station, about twenty-five miles west of Cody, is the oldest in the United States, built in 1903. The Shoshone National Forest borders Yellowstone National Park and the Bridger-Teton National Forest, which also came out of the Yellowstone Park Preserve. The park, forest, and adjacent wilderness areas provide a huge section of land in which people can get away from civilization and spent time in remote high country.

Mummy Joe Cave

One site of archaeological significance lies near the east entrance to Yellowstone National Park adjacent to US 14/16/20. In a rocky cave shelter in 1962, archaeologists found evidence of early man in the mummified remains of a Paleo-Indian, known locally as Mummy Joe. His burial spot, Mummy Cave, had deposits radiocarbon-dated to 7280 B.C., making it one of the oldest such sites known in Wyoming. The cave included fire hearths and artifacts ranging from projectile points to chipped-stone knives and scrapers. The site yielded a complete prehistoric occupation sequence. Evidence also gave researchers a clear look at the early animal population in northwestern Wyoming in prehistoric times.

Prehistoric people occupied Mummy Cave almost continually from 7280 B.C. to A.D. 1580. The archaeological excavation of the site shows a constantly recurring pattern of use through the various time periods, and it gives detail about animal migration and placement. For example, the cave yielded no bison remains until the Late Prehistoric strata, dated at A.D. 720 to 1580. Earlier remains included fragments and evidence of birds, horses, cottontails, marmots, and mountain sheep.

The occupied portion of the cave extended about seventy-five feet from north to south and was about forty feet deep. Site excavation took place in 1962 under the auspices of the Buffalo Bill Historical Center, and many of the items excavated, including Mummy Joe, went on display at the Cody facility. Adhering to the wishes of native Americans, the museum no longer keeps Mummy Joe on exhibit, but his remains are still within the collections at the historical center. The cave entrance is now filled with earth, and the site is not open.

Pahaska's Teepee

Buffalo Bill Cody had the Indian name Pahaska, or Long Hair. He built a hunting lodge at the entrance to Yellowstone National Park near the turn of the century. Known as Pahaska Teepee, it served as a base for hunting excursions along the North Fork of the Shoshone. Now it is the trailhead for pack trips into the North Absaroka Wilderness and horseback or snowmobile excursions into Yellowstone National Park.

Absaroka, Land of the Crows

The Crows called this land Absaroka (pronounced *ab-sork-a*). They liked to hunt here and believed that no other place was quite as good. In *The Adventures of Captain Bonneville*, Washington Irving gives one Crow chief's view of this land: "When the summer heats scorch the prairies, you can draw up under the mountains, where the air is sweet and cool, the grass fresh, and the bright streams come tumbling out of the snow-banks."

To the Crows, there is no country like Absaroka. To Cowboy State natives, there is no place like Wyoming with its Rocky Mountains, barren deserts, glacier-capped peaks, and clear streams. As a Jackson Hole schoolgirl once wrote, "God Bless Wyoming and keep her wild."

Bibliography

Alcorn, Gay Day. *Tough Country*. Saratoga, WY: Legacy Press, 1984.

Allen, Marion V. *Early Jackson Hole*. Redding, CA: Press Room Printing, 1981.

Augspurger, Marie M. *Yellowstone National Park*. Middletown, OH: The Naegele-Auer Printing Company, 1948.

Beebe, Ruth. *Reminiscing Along the Sweetwater*. Boulder, CO: Johnson Books, 1973.

Betts, Robert B. "A Man Called Beaver Dick." *Teton, The Magazine of Jackson Hole* (1977).

_____. *Along the Ramparts of the Tetons: The Saga of Jackson Hole, Wyoming*. Niwot: University Press of Colorado, 1978.

Black, Rosa Vida Bischoff. *Lovell: Our Pioneer Heritage*. Salt Lake City: Olympus, 1984.

Blevins, Winfred. *Give Your Heart to the Hawks: A Tribute to the Mountain Men*. New York: Avon, 1973.

_____. *Roadside History of Yellowstone Park*. Missoula: Mountain Press Publishing Company, 1989.

Bonney, Orrin H., and Lorraine G. Bonney. *The Grand Controversy*. New York: AAC Press, 1992.

Bradley, Glenn Danford. *The Story of the Pony Express*. Edited by Waddell F. Smith. San Francisco: Hesperia House, 1960.

Brown, Joseph E. *The Mormon Trek West*. Garden City, NY: Doubleday & Company, 1980.

Brown, Mark H. *The Plainsmen of the Yellowstone: A History of the Yellowstone Basin*. Lincoln: University of Nebraska Press, 1961.

Bryans, Bill. *Deer Creek: Frontiers Crossroad in Pre-Territorial Wyoming*. Glenrock, WY: Glenrock Historical Commission, 1990.

Burroughs, John. *Old Yellowstone Days*. Edited by Paul Schullery. Boulder: Colorado Associated University Press, 1979.

Butruille, Susan G. *Women's Voices from the Oregon Trail*. Boise: Tamarack Books, 1993.

Call, Lee R., ed. *Star Valley and its Communities*. Afton, WY: Star Valley Independent, 1970.

Carlisle, Bill. *Bill Carlisle, Lone Bandit*. Pasadena, CA: Trail's End Publishing Company, 1946.

Carlson, Chip. *Tom Horn: "Killing Men Is My Specialty. . . ."* Cheyenne: Beartooth Corral, 1991.

Chamblin, Thomas S., ed. *The Historical Encyclopedia of Wyoming*. Vols. 1 and 2. Cheyenne: Wyoming Historical Institute, 1954.

Chittenden, Hiram Martin. *The Yellowstone National Park*. 3rd rev. ed. St. Paul: J. E. Haynes, 1927.

Davis, John W. *A Vast Amount of Trouble: A History of the Spring Creek Raid*. Niwot: University Press of Colorado, 1993.

DeArment, R. K. "Teton Jackson." *True West* (March 1993).

Dillon, Richard. *Meriwether Lewis*. Santa Cruz, CA: Western Tanager Press, 1988.

Drago, Harry Sinclair. *The Great Range Wars: Violence on the Grasslands*. Lincoln: University of Nebraska Press, Bison Books, 1985.

Ellison, R. S. *Fort Bridger: A Brief History*. Cheyenne: Wyoming State Archives, Museums and Historical Department, 1981.

Eversman, Sharon, and Mary Carr. *Yellowstone Ecology: A Road Guide*. Missoula: Mountain Press Publishing Company, 1992.

Frison, George C. *Prehistoric Hunters of the High Plains*. New York: Academic Press, 1978.

Fritz, William J. *Roadside Geology of the Yellowstone Country*. Missoula: Mountain Press Publishing Company, 1985.

Grinnell, George Bird. *The Cheyenne Indians: History and Society*. Vol. 1. Reprint. Lincoln: University of Nebraska Press, Bison Books, 1972.

_____. *The Cheyenne Indians: War, Ceremonies, and Religion*. Vol. 2. Reprint. Lincoln: University of Nebraska Press, Bison Books, 1972.

Griswold, Wesley. *A Work of Giants*. New York: McGraw-Hill, 1962.

Gunderson, Mary Alice. *Devils Tower: Stories in Stone*. Glendo, WY: High Plains Press, 1988.

Hafen, Leroy, and Ann W. Hafen. *Handcarts to Zion: The Story of a Unique Western Migration, 1856–1860*. Glendale, CA: Arthur H. Clark Company, 1960.

Haines, Aubrey L. *Yellowstone National Park: Its Exploration and Establishment.* Washington, D.C.: U.S. Department of Interior, National Park Service, 1974.

_____. *Historic Sites Along the Oregon Trail.* St. Louis: Patrice Press, 1981.

Hall, Charles "Pat." *Documents of Wyoming Heritage.* Cheyenne: Wyoming Bicentennial Commission, 1976.

Hayden, Elizabeth Wied. *From Trapper to Tourist.* Jackson: Grand Teton Natural History Association, 1992.

Hebard, Grace Raymond, and E. A. Brininstool. *The Bozeman Trail.* Cleveland: Arthur H. Clark, 1922.

Hendrickson, Gordon Olaf, ed. *Peopling the High Plains: Wyoming's European Heritage.* Cheyenne: Wyoming State Archives and Historical Department, 1977.

History of the Union Pacific Coal Mines. Omaha: The Colonial Press, 1940.

Homsher, Lola M. *The History of Albany County, Wyoming, to 1880.* Lusk, WY: Lusk Herald, 1965.

Hufsmith, George W. *The Wyoming Lynching of Cattle Kate, 1889.* Glendo, WY: High Plains Press, 1993.

Huseas, Marion McMillan. *Sweetwater Gold: Wyoming's Gold Rush 1867–1871.* Cheyenne: Corral of Westerners International, 1991.

Irving, Washington. *The Adventures of Captain Bonneville.* New York: The Co-Operative Publication Society, n.d.

Jackson, John C. *Shadow on the Tetons: David E. Jackson and the Claiming of the American West.* Missoula: Mountain Press Publishing Company, 1993.

Johnson, Dorothy M. *The Bloody Bozeman: The Perilous Trail to Montana's Gold.* Reprint. Missoula: Mountain Press Publishing Company, 1983.

Jording, Mike. *A Few Interested Residents: Wyoming Historical Markers and Monuments.* Helena, MT: SkyHouse, 1992.

Judge, Frances. "Not Mean, but Menor." *Empire Magazine, Denver Post* (December 2, 1951).

Langeson, David R., and Darwin R. Spearing. *Roadside Geology of Wyoming.* Rev. 2nd ed. Missoula: Mountain Press Publishing Company, 1991.

Larson, T.A. *History of Wyoming.* Lincoln: University of Nebraska Press, 1965. 2nd rev. ed., 1978.

_____. *Wyoming: A History.* New York: W. W. Norton & Company, 1984.

Lindsay, Charles. *The Big Horn Basin.* Lincoln: University of Nebraska Press, 1932.

Mattes, Merrill. "Jackson Hole, Crossroads of the Western Fur Trade, 1807–1829." *Pacific Northwest Quarterly* (April 1946).

Mead, Jean. *Casper Country: Wyoming's Heartland*. Boulder, CO: Pruett Publishing, 1987.

Mockler, Alfred J. *History of Natrona County, Wyoming, 1888–1922*. Chicago: R. R. Donnelley & Sons, 1923.

Momaday, N. Scott. *The Way to Rainy Mountain*. Albuquerque: University of New Mexico Press, 1976.

Moulton, Candy Vyvey. *Legacy of the Tetons: Homesteading in Jackson Hole*. Boise: Tamarack Books, 1994.

Moulton, Candy Vyvey, and Flossie Moulton. *Steamboat: Legendary Bucking Horse*. Glendo, WY: High Plains Press, 1992.

Murray, Robert A. *The Army on the Powder River*. Bellevue, NE: Old Army Press, 1969.

Newlon, Douglas. "Heart Mountain: The History of an American Concentration Camp." Masters thesis, University of Wyoming, 1970.

Nielsen, Cynthia. *Origins: A Guide to the Place Names of Grand Teton National Park and the Surrounding Area*. Jackson: Grand Teton Natural History Association, 1988.

Olson, James. C. *Red Cloud and the Sioux Problem*. Lincoln: University of Nebraska Press, 1965.

Peterson, Gwen. *Yellowstone Pioneers: The Story of the Hamilton Stores and Yellowstone National Park*. San Diego: Oak Tree Publications, 1985.

Pinkerton, Joan Trego. *Knights of the Broadax: The Story of the Wyoming Tie Hack*. Caldwell, ID: Caxton, 1981.

Platte County Extension Homemakers Council. *Wyoming Platte County Heritage*. Marceline, MO: Walsworth Publishing, 1981.

Platts, Doris B. *Cunningham Ranch Incident*. Wilson, WY: N.p., 1992.

Righter, Robert. *The Making of a Town: Wright, Wyoming*. Boulder, CO: Roberts Rinehart, 1985.

Ritthaler, Shelly, ed. *History of Weston County*. Dallas: Weston County Heritage Group and Curtis Media, 1988.

Roberts, Philip J., David L. Roberts, and Steven L. Roberts. *Wyoming Almanac*. Laramie: Skyline West Press. 1989.

Rosenberg, Robert G. *Wyoming's Last Frontier: Sublette County, Wyoming*. Glendo, WY: High Plains Press, 1990.

Sandoval, Judith Hancock. *Historic Ranches of Wyoming*. Casper: Nicolaysen Art Museum, 1986.

Schlissel, Lillian. *Women's Diaries of the Westward Migration*. New York: Schocken Books, 1982.

Settle, Raymond, and Mary Settle. *Saddles and Spurs: The Pony Express Saga*. Harrison, PA: Stackpole Company, 1955.

Smith, Helena Huntington. *The War on Powder River: The History of an Insurrection*. Lincoln: University of Nebraska Press, Bison Books, 1966.

Spring, Agnes Wright. "An Indian Fight in Jackson Hole." *Old West* (Spring 1967).

_____. *The Cheyenne and Black Hills Stage and Express Routes*. Lincoln: University of Nebraska Press, 1948.

Spring, Agnes Wright, and Dee Linford. *Wyoming: A Guide to Its History, Highways, and People*. New York: Oxford University Press, 1941.

Stewart, Elinore Pruitt. *Letters of a Woman Homesteader*. Lincoln: University of Nebraska Press, Bison Books, 1989.

Stone, Elizabeth Arnold. *Uinta County: Its Place in History*. Laramie: The Laramie Printing Company, 1924.

Sublette County Artist Guild. *More Tales of the Seeds-Ke-Dee: Historical Lore of Wyoming's Green River Valley*. Marceline, MO: Walsworth Publishing, 1976.

Trenholm, Virginia Cole. *The Arapahoes, Our People*. Norman: University of Oklahoma Press, 1970.

Trenholm, Virginia Cole, and Maurine Carley. *The Shoshonis: Sentinels of the Rockies*. Norman: University of Oklahoma Press, 1964.

Trevathan, Mary Ann. *More Than Meets the Eye: Wyoming Along Interstate 80*. Glendo, WY: High Plains Press, 1993.

Turnell, Jack. *Brand of a Legend*. Basin, WY: Wolverine Gallery, 1978.

Urbanek, Mae. *Wyoming Place Names*. Missoula: Mountain Press Publishing Company, 1988.

Wallace, Eunice Ewer. *They Made Wyoming Their Own*. Boise: Joslyn and Rentschler Lithoprinters, 1971.

_____. *Wyoming's Own*. Boise: Joslyn and Rentschler Lithoprinters, 1976.

Welch, Charles A. *History of the Big Horn Basin*. Salt Lake City: Deseret News Press, 1940.

Wilson, Charles Alma, and Elijah Nicholas. *The White Indian Boy and Its Sequel: The Return of the White Indian*. Rapid City, SD: Fenske Printing, 1985.

Wister, Fanny Kemble. *Owen Wister Out West: His Journals and Letters*. Chicago: University of Chicago Press, 1958.

Wister, Owen. *The Virginian.* New York: Macmillan Company, 1902.

Writers' Program, Works Progress Administration, State of Wyoming. American Guide Series. *Wyoming: A Guide to Its History, Highways, and People.* New York: Oxford University Press, 1941.

Wyoming Press Association. *Wyoming Newspapers: A Centennial History.* Cheyenne: Pioneer Printing, 1990.

Wyoming Recreation Commission. *Wyoming: A Guide to Historic Sites.* Basin, WY: Big Horn Book Company, 1976.

Zwinger, Ann. *Run, River, Run.* New York: Harper and Row, 1975.

Newspapers

Big Piney Examiner	*Laramie Daily Boomerang*
Billings Gazette	*Laramie Daily Sentinel*
Buffalo Bulletin	*Medicine Bow Post*
Casper Star-Tribune	*Newcastle Journal*
Cheyenne Sun Leader	*Northern Wyoming Daily News*
Cheyenne Daily Leader	*Rawlins Daily Times*
Chicago Herald	*Riverton Review*
Cody Enterprise	*Saratoga Sun*
Denver Post	*Sheridan Post*
Dillon Doublejack	*Star Valley Independent*
Grand Encampment Herald	*St. Louis Globe-Democrat*
Jackson Hole Guide	*Wind River Mountaineer*
Jackson's Hole Courier	*Wyoming Tribune*

The biographical and subject files of many of Wyoming's towns, counties, and events yielded a rich bank of information used in this book. The facilities used during the research phase for this volume include the Wyoming State Museum, Cheyenne; American Heritage Center/University of Wyoming, Laramie; Old West Museum, Cheyenne; Saratoga Historical and Cultural Center; Grand Encampment Museum; Teton County Historical Center, Jackson; Buffalo Bill Historical Center/McCraken Research Library, Cody; Jim Gatchell Museum, Buffalo; and Lusk Stagecoach Museum.

About the Author

Candy Moulton, a third-generation Wyoming native, grew up on a ranch near Encampment, in the south-central portion of the state.

After receiving degrees in journalism from Northwest Community College, in Powell, and the University of Wyoming, in Laramie, she worked five years as an editor for the *Saratoga Sun*. Moulton continues to write for several newspapers in the state, including the Casper *Star-Tribune*, Rawlins *Daily Times*, and *Wyoming Livestock Roundup*. Her articles and photographs have also appeared in *Time*, the *Denver Post*, the *Chicago Tribune*, the *Arizona Daily Star*, *True West*, *Western Horseman*, *American Cowboy*, *Adventure West*, *Southwest Art*, and *Tours and Resorts Magazine*. In addition, she is active in several writers' associations, including Wyoming Writers, Inc., Women Writing the West, and Western Writers of America.

Roadside History of Wyoming is Moulton's third book, following *Steamboat: Legendary Bucking Horse* (1992, with Flossie Moulton) and *Legacy of the Tetons: Homesteading in Jackson Hole* (1994).

Moulton and her husband, Steve, built a log home at the foot of the Sierra Madres just south of Encampment. They live there with their two children, Shawn and Erin Marie.

Index

241; sacred sites, 360; treaties with, 120; tribal lands, 12, 151, 293

Cheyenne-Deadwood Stage, 13, 119, 102, 136, 138–44, 150, 331, 332, **139**

Chicago & Northwestern Railroad, 176, 203

Chicago, Black Hills and Yellowstone Highway, 311

Chicago, Burlington & Quincy Railroad, 319, 332; 333, 337, 365, 368

Chicago Daily Mail, 267

Chicago Times-Herald, 267

Chief Joseph, 110–11, 199

Chinatown, Rock Springs, 280; Evanston, 290

Chinese: in mines, 14, 290; labor riot, 277–80; celebrate new year, 280–81; violence in western states, 280; joss house, 290; **279, 280**

Chisholm, Jesse, 135

Chislett, John, 190

Chittenden, Hiram M., 101, 117, 183

Chittenden Bridge, 103

Chivington, John, 169

Christian, Will, 261–62

Chugwater, 135, 150

Chug Water Ranch, 150

Chug Water Hotel, 151

Church, Harrison, 25

Church of Jesus Christ of Latter-day Saints, 59, 289, 357, 363. *See also* Mormon, Latter-day Saints

Civil War, 130–31

Civilian Conservation Corps, 236, 270

claim jumping, 204–5, 294

Clark, Badger, 136

Clark, Hugh, 153

Clay, John, 305

Clean Air Act, 340

Clean Water Act, 39

Clearmont, 341

Cleveland, Grover, 383

Cloud Peak Skyway, 312

Clover, Sam, 307

coal production, 276–77, 289–91, 339–40

Cobb, Charlie, 164

Coble, John, 155; 157

Cody, 336, 362, 375–84

Cody Enterprise, 381–82

Cody Family Association, 384

Cody Firearms Museum, 384

Cody Transportation Company, 320

Cody, William F. "Buffalo Bill," 16, 363, 375–81; Pony Express rider, 134, 188–89; owns Sheridan Inn, 320; promotes water project, 366; TE Ranch, 384;

Pahaska Teepee, 386–87; **188, 378**

Coe and Carter Company, 21, 63, 206

Cokeville, 21, 25

Cole, Forney, 84

Collett, Syl, 21

Collins, Charlie, 374

Collins, Caspar, 170–73, 174, 178

Collins, William O., 249, 363

Colorado River, 1, 32, 38–39

Colter, John, 11, 19, 64, 65, 95, 345, 375–76

Colter's Hell, 375, 376

Columbia Exposition, 285

Columbia River, 1

Columbus, Nebraska, 378

Company towns, 242–43, 253, 342

Comanches, 2

Como Bluff, 257–58, **257**

Condict, Jonathan Dickinson, 238

Condict, Winthrop, 238

Conner, Bob, 182

Connor Battle, 321

Connor, P. E., 200, 321, 322

Conquering Bear, 122

Continental Divide, 195, 234

Converse County, 12

Coolidge, Calvin, 71

Cooper, Robert, 66

Coors, 351

Copperton, 268, 270

Cora, 30

Corbett, John, 373

Corn Creek Project, 177

Cottonwood (Smoot), 60

Cottonwood Mobile Home Park, 342

Cowan, Emma, 111–12

Cowan, George, 111–12

Cowan, Ida, 111

"Cowboy's Prayer," 136

Cowley, 364, 365

Crabtree, Henry, 71

Crabtree Hotel, 71

Crabtree, Rose, 71–73, **72**

Craighead, Frank, 106, 107

Craighead, John, 106, 107

Crawford, Will, 69

Crazy Horse, 3, 144, 155, 197, 199, 315, 301

Crazy Woman Battlefield, 308

Crazy Woman Creek, 14

Creighton Telegraph, 13, 119, 131, 191, 196, 235

Creighton, William, 131

Crook County, 14

Crook, George, 3, 66, 180, 197, 300–1

Crosby, Harry, 164